Leviathan

shi: ———— t
I'm breaking wild.
your mother sucks candy in the
gay.   Bronx.

FONTANA PHILOSOPHY CLASSICS

GENERAL EDITOR: *G. J. Warnock,*
Magdalen College, Oxford.

LEVIATHAN
Thomas Hobbes. *Edited by John Plamenatz*

AN ESSAY CONCERNING HUMAN UNDERSTANDING
John Locke. *Edited by A. D. Woozley*

THE PRINCIPLES OF HUMAN KNOWLEDGE
and
THREE DIALOGUES BETWEEN HYLAS AND PHILONOUS
George Berkeley. *Edited by G. J. Warnock*

A TREATISE OF HUMAN NATURE
David Hume. *Book I edited by D. G. C. Macnabb*
Books II & III edited by P. S. Árdal

HUME ON RELIGION
Selected and edited by Richard Wollheim

UTILITARIANISM
Selections from the writings of Jeremy Bentham,
John Stuart Mill, and John Austin
Selected and edited by Mary Warnock

This series is being continued under the general editorship
of A. M. Quinton, New College, Oxford

Leviathan

THOMAS HOBBES

Edited and abridged with an introduction by
JOHN PLAMENATZ
Chichele Professor of Social and Political Theory
at the University of Oxford

COLLINS / FONTANA

Leviathan was first published in 1651
First issued in Fontana 1962
Sixth Impression September 1972

© *in the Editor's Introduction and Abridgement*
William Collins Sons & Co. Ltd.

Printed in Great Britain
Collins Clear-Type Press
London and Glasgow

CONTENTS

EDITOR'S NOTE

This edition omits the whole of Part Four of *Leviathan* and a large part of Part Three; it excludes whatever, in the editor's opinion, adds little or nothing to Hobbes's philosophy of man and government.

INTRODUCTION

by John Plamenatz

1. *Hobbes's Life*

HOBBES lived as quietly as he could contrive to do in a troubled age, and might never have turned his mind to politics had political events not forced themselves upon his notice.

He was born in April 1588, the son of the Vicar of Wesport near Malmesbury, in which town he went to school until an uncle sent him, when he was fourteen years old, to Magdalen Hall at Oxford. He stayed there five years till he took his degree, and in 1608 left Oxford to become tutor to the son of William Cavendish, Earl of Devonshire. With his pupil he visited France and Italy, and on his return devoted himself to classical scholarship. In the Cavendish circle he came to know Francis Bacon, who confirmed him in his dislike for the scholastic and Aristotelian philosophy taught at the two universities. In 1628 Hobbes published his translation of Thucydides, whom he described as the most political of historians and the most averse to democracy. That same year a Parliament hostile to the king was elected, and the Petition of Right was passed.

Hobbes paid his second visit to the Continent in 1629, as companion to the son of Sir Gervase Clinton, and it was then that he discovered and 'fell in love' with geometry, and came to believe that true knowledge in every sphere is to be gained by the method of the geometer. In 1634, again with a young Cavendish, he went abroad for the third time and did not return to England till 1637. It was on this visit that he was converted to 'materialism', the doctrine that all operations of the mind can be explained in terms of bodily motions, and became the close friend of Gassendi, the most prominent of French exponents of this doctrine. Hobbes, on this visit abroad and the one before it, acquired his general philosophy, his conceptions of knowledge and of nature. Sometime before 1637 he completed his first work on philosophy, the *Little*

Treatise, in which he tried to explain sense-experience in terms of bodily motion.

His first political treatise, the *Elements of Law*, was not completed till 1640; it circulated in manuscript form and was not published until ten years later in two separate parts. But Hobbes believed that Parliament, which had just met, might take offence at his treatise, and so fled to France and remained there till the end of 1651. It was while he was in France that his two most famous works, *De Cive* (a first edition in 1642, and a second in 1647) and *Leviathan* (1651), appeared. In 1646 Hobbes had been appointed tutor in mathematics to the future Charles II, but *Leviathan*, which was published in England, was badly received at the English court in exile. For that reason, and for others, Hobbes decided to return home after a stay abroad of more than ten years.

From the time he went down from Oxford in 1608 until his flight to France, Hobbes had lived, as tutor and friend, mostly with the Cavendish family, but when he returned to England in 1651 he settled in London. There he made friends with Harvey, discoverer of the circulation of the blood, with the poet Cowley, and with Selden, the jurist. He was by now famous, and Harrington, the author of *Oceana*, though he disliked his political philosophy, acknowledged him as the greatest thinker of his age. In 1655 Hobbes published *De Corpore*, a treatise on body or matter which he had been working on for years, in 1656 his *Questions Concerning Liberty, Necessity and Chance*, in which he defended his determinism against Bishop Bramhall, and in 1657 his *De Homine*, dealing with optics and human nature. During this period Hobbes was more concerned with the physical sciences and with psychology than with society and government.

At the Restoration he feared the resentment of the Royalists, but the generous and tolerant Charles II, of all English kings the most at home with men of intellect, dealt kindly with him. He received a pension of £100 a year and was well received at Court. If he was never elected to the Royal Society, which he aspired to join, it was not owing to any reluctance on the part of its Royal Patron; it was because he had incurred the hostility of various professors by his attacks on the universities and his failure to respect competence greater than his own. He was a very clever man who thought he understood more than he in fact did, a fault which Oxford seldom overlooks except in men who have grown old in Oxford.

In 1666 Hobbes produced a *Dialogue between a Philosopher and a Student of the Common Laws of England*, and in 1668 completed *Behemoth*, an account of events in England from 1640 to 1660; but these two works were not published until after his death, the first in 1681 and the second the year after. The first is an attack on those who refused to look upon the laws, as Hobbes did, as mere commands of the sovereign, and the second is recent history served up to drive home the lessons expounded in *De Cive* and *Leviathan*. Though both works are interesting to the student of Hobbes' political philosophy, neither adds anything much to what he had said before. At the age of eighty-four Hobbes wrote his autobiography in Latin verse, and two years later produced translations of the Iliad and the Odyssey. He was indefatigable, and was in better health and spirits in middle and old age than he had been in his youth. In 1675 he left London for the country, to live once more with the Cavendishes. He died on 4th December, 1679, in his ninety-second year.

Though Hobbes saw himself as much more than a political philosopher, it is as a political philosopher that he is remembered. His first treatise on politics circulated in manuscript in 1640, when he was already fifty-two and by the time he had completed *Leviathan*, at the age of sixty-three, he had said all that he had to say that was important about society and government. If England had remained domestically at peace, he might never have written his two master works, *De Cive* and *Leviathan*, and might have devoted his mind entirely to other branches of philosophy and to classical scholarship.

As a protégé and friend of the Cavendishes, as a tutor and pensioner of Charles II, Hobbes might have been expected to be an ardent Royalist. But he was not. The Royalists did not claim for the king what Hobbes claimed for the sovereign, nor did their opponents claim it for Parliament. The parties to the civil war quarrelled about how power was by tradition distributed among the possessors of it, whereas Hobbes argued that the whole of it ought to be in the hands of only one man or body of men. It was in the seventeenth century that the English laid the foundations of the political system which, more than any other, has served as a model to the world, and it was then also that the masterpiece of English political literature was produced. In the masterpiece there is to be found no hint of the model.

2. *His Political Philosophy Considered Generally*

IF not by universal consent, at least in the opinion of close students of political theory, Hobbes is the greatest of English political philosophers, and the most exciting. To read *Leviathan* is exhilarating. For so large a treatise it is wonderfully concise; it is also well constructed. It is all of a piece, and every part of it contributes to the whole. It is powerful and quick, robust, colourful and witty. Its author comes resolutely to extreme conclusions, and lacks the moderation of Locke and other writers who have seemed more typically English.

And yet Hobbes possesses, in high degree, intellectual virtues as conspicuous in the English as in any people. He looks carefully at the words he uses, he aims at economy of explanation, he dismisses questions as improper on the ground that they rest on confusions of thought. He is the enemy of 'insignificant speech', and is never more pleased than when he can show up an abuse of words. He is a deflater; he delights in bringing down elaborate structures with a sharp knock at their foundations. He is the heir of Occam and the ancestor of Hume. He belongs to an English tradition established in the century after Aquinas in Paris and in Oxford, a centre of philosophy and therefore a home of causes which are never lost and never won.

Among the political masterpieces of the modern age, only Hegel's *Philosophy of Right* has the breadth, the conciseness, and the firmness of design of *Leviathan*. From the writings of Machiavelli, it is possible to extract a coherent philosophy of man and society, and a larger and more subtle one than might be gathered from some of his admirers, who seem bent on taking as narrow a view of him as his detractors have done.

But that philosophy was never put together by him. Of his two important political works, one, *The Prince*, is a short essay on a limited theme, and the other, *The Discourses*, though rich in content, is a commentary on another book. Bodin's *Republic*, original and suggestive though it is, is remarkably ill-planned; and as much can be said of Montesquieu's *Spirit of the Laws*, for all its brilliance. Burke never attempted a systematic treatise. Locke, Hume, Rousseau, Bentham, Kant, Marx and Mill never put into any one work on politics nearly as much as Hobbes contrived to do; they wrote what may fairly be called, when compared with *Leviathan*, fragments on government. Some of them, no doubt, produced many fragments: as, for example, Rousseau, none of whose essays and discourses is an enlarged version of another as *Leviathan* is of *De Cive*.

Nevertheless, among the great books on politics of the modern age, *Leviathan* and *The Philosophy of Right* are in a class apart. They are systematic treatises; and ordinarily, at least in politics, such treatises are the works of academic persons who, vigorous, lucid, elegant, scrupulous and even imaginative though they sometimes are, are men of order rather than inspiration, consolidators rather than pioneers. And pioneers, because they make their way through unmapped territory, often do not know what direction they are moving in; and their movement is less orderly than the progress of those who come after them along well-trodden paths. Hobbes and Hegel are remarkable among the great innovators in political theory for having unusually clear ideas about what they wanted to do. Their masterpieces are well matured and elaborate; they are tightly packed, though not with facts but ideas and arguments.

Hegel requires an heroic effort of his readers; he requires that they become familiar with the peculiar concepts which he uses. He claims for these concepts that they alone are adequate to a full understanding of the world, and that only by using them can he transcend the limitations and contradictions implicit in ordinary or scientific language, in ideas which may be good enough for everyday use or to give the sort of explanations at which the natural sciences aim but are incapable of conveying the essence of reality. Hobbes makes much more modest demands on his readers; though he requires their close attention, he aims at simplicity and clarity. We get into difficulties, as we follow his argument, not because he requires us to learn to use unfamiliar and elusive ideas, but because his ideas are too few and his definitions too simple for the tasks he has set himself. The concepts needed to explain what men do when they reason and make choices, or how they feel and behave towards one another and themselves, or how their social and political institutions function, are more numerous and more complex than those offered to us by Hobbes. His explanations do not go to the hilt; they fall short of the truth and leave too much out of account.

If now, three centuries after the appearance of *De Cive* and *Leviathan*, we take notice of what Hobbes neglected, some of his explanations cannot but seem simple-minded or superficial to us. Yet to accuse him of simple-mindedness and superficiality would be absurd and ungrateful. Absurd, because, by the standards of his day, he was an extraordinarily subtle and close reasoner; and ungrateful, because many of the distinctions and refinements used to demolish such arguments as his were made by critics who felt a pressing need to reply to him. Much of English (and not only English) political theory has been, in one way or another, a response to Hobbes.

For Hobbes, by his method and style, invites us to think clearly about society and government by repeatedly drawing our attention to the concepts we use when we discuss them. Power, authority, freedom, law, right, obligation, sovereignty, covenant and representation: these are among the terms he uses in what were, in his day, new or unusual ways, and his purpose in so using them is to dispel confusion and to provide his readers with definite and simple ideas. He does not always use these terms in the senses he defines, and is sometimes unaware that he has passed from one sense to another. His definitions are not always clear, his arguments not always cogent; he is sometimes illogical and not merely inadequate. Nevertheless, he is a challenger to argument, a sharpener of wits; and the close attention he demands makes the reader look closely at what he seeks to explain and the language used to explain it.

Part of the fascination of Hobbes is that, though he makes large demands on us, we can always come to grips with him. He does not, as Rousseau and Burke, Hegel and Marx, so often do, elude us. With him a reckoning is nearly always possible; we can nearly always – as with Hume and the Utilitarians – make up our minds just where he is inadequate, confused or inconsequent. We can, if we take the trouble, discover where he stands; or we can discover it within fairly narrow limits. The range of possible interpretations is not wide. We can even at times convict him of 'insignificant speech' without the uncomfortable feeling that he is a Rousseau making obscurely some important point which we have failed to take.

But Hobbes is more than a clear thinker; or, perhaps I should say, more than a political theorist who puts himself to unusual trouble in the hope of being clear. He is also the maker of a new type of theory. More resolutely than anyone before him, he tries to imagine what men might be like if there were no social relations between them, and then seeks to explain some of these relations (those involved in governing and being governed) as effects of the passions and expectations of such men. His is the method neither of Aristotle nor of the mediaeval thinkers. He does not speak of man's *potentialities* and their being made *actual* in society and the state; he does not take the capacities which distinguish man from other animals and seek to show how they are developed in him by communal and political life; he does not want to justify society and government by explaining how they help man to become what he ought to be. Nor, for all that he speaks so often of God, does he explain society and government as remedies for sin or as means to the attainment of divine purposes for man. Man, as Hobbes sees him, is neither a political animal in the Aristotelian sense nor a creature marked from birth by sin and to be saved only by the grace of God.

Hobbes' method is, at bottom, the same as that of Hume and the Utilitarians. He seeks first to determine the strongest and most recurrent of men's appetites and passions, he then considers their situation and their needs as creatures who cannot avoid contact with one another and who have to compete for the wherewithal to satisfy their appetites, and finally seeks to explain the rules they observe and their institutions as arising from their appetites and passions, their situation and their needs. No doubt, not all men have the same appetites and passions, nor do they have them in the same degree, and their situations and needs would vary even if they did not live in stable communities; but the user of this method supposes that there are appetites and passions which they all share, and needs common to them which they would have even if there were no enduring social relations between them.

This method has been much criticized. It has been objected to it that we know man only in society, that his desires and passions, as we know them, are the desires and passions of a social being. As Hobbes himself admits 'all men, because they are born in infancy, are born unapt for society', and are 'made fit for society not by nature but by education.'* While they are still untouched by social influences, they are helpless babes incapable of keeping themselves alive for a day, no matter how strong in them the appetites on whose satisfaction life depends. They acquire the capacity to fend for themselves in the process of education, in the process of adapting themselves to a social environment; and they acquire not only these capacities but also many of the passions said to be natural to them, passions inconceivable except among creatures socially related to one another.

Certainly, it is an odd undertaking to determine what adult men able to keep themselves alive might be like untouched by society, in an imagined state of nature, and then to explain social rules and institutions as devices to meet their needs. Rousseau was among the first to object that Hobbes had attributed to man in the state of nature passions which he could only have acquired by living in society.

But it is not so odd an undertaking to look for passions and needs which are common to men in all societies and to try to show how certain rules and institutions serve to enable

* Hobbes's *English Works*. Vol. ii, p. 2, note.

creatures having these passions and needs to live at peace together. There is an obvious sense in which human passions and needs are prior to rules and institutions, a sense which all social and political theorists have admitted. Rules and institutions serve to control behaviour which springs from the passions, and serve also to satisfy needs. If men were not rational as well as passionate creatures, truly social relations, which involve the observance of rules, could not arise among them. But these social relations in their turn affect men's passions and needs. So that, although we can say that human beings, when they are mere infants, have passions and needs before they know anything of rules and institutions, and also that rules and institutions arise to control passions and to meet needs, we cannot, when we contemplate any society of men, conclude that their rules and institutions are mere effects of their actual passions and needs. We can seek to show, as for example Rousseau tried to do, in *Emile*, how the infant 'born unapt for society' is 'made fit for society . . . by education'; how, in the process of learning to live with others it becomes a willing observer of rules and acquires passions and needs it would not otherwise have. Or we can, as Montesquieu did in the *Spirit of the Laws*, establish correlations between passions and needs, on the one hand, and rules and institutions, on the other, without inquiring into how they come to be what they are. Or we can show how, over a period of time, men's situations and needs have changed and their rules and institutions along with them. All these are useful undertakings. But to seek to explain social rules and institutions as devices to meet the needs of adults born 'unapt for society' and not made fit for it by education is surely absurd.

Put like that, it does look absurd. But we need not treat the state of nature as the condition of man before he becomes a social being; we can treat it as the condition into which he would lapse if the social order disintegrated. And if we do so treat it, we treat it as Hobbes often did. We can treat the passions which he ascribes to men in the state of nature, not as passions which men would have had if they had never lived in society, but as destructive passions which are strong in them in all societies, and which (unlike most of their other passions, except fear) would remain strong even if the social order disintegrated. We can consider these passions, though they too are products of social life, apart from its other products; we can consider the passions apart from the rules. And we can show how men having such passions must also have the rules if they are to live peacefully together; they must have the rules and be provided with sufficient motives for keeping them. And though these are not the only passions, they are always strong, and are not weakened but made stronger by anarchy; whereas the other passions, the gentle passions, though they too are products of social life, are apt to grow weak where there is anarchy. It is the destructive passions, and not the gentle ones, which need to be kept in check by law and government; and where there is anarchy, the passion which will make men submit once again to law and government will not be a passion weakened by anarchy but a passion which anarchy makes strong. And that passion, as Hobbes says, is fear.

It has been objected against Hobbes that he tries to derive prescriptive statements from statements of fact, that he reaches conclusions about how men ought to behave from descriptions of what they are and how they are situated. This is a fault supposed to be common to him and the Utilitarians.

The objection, if brought against Hobbes, is wide of the mark. He does not claim to infer the laws of nature from descriptive statements about either men or God; nor does he treat them as 'self-evident truths'. He treats them as *imperatives* and does so both when he speaks of them as maxims of prudence and as commands of God. As 'maxims of prudence' or 'dictates of reason' (that is to say, considered not as commands of God but as rules which men would want to see generally observed even in a world without God), they are but 'conclusions' which men reach about 'what conduceth to the conservation and defence of themselves'. They are not 'truths' to be derived logically from statements which describe men, their passions and intentions, but rules which, when they are generally observed, do conduce to the conservation of the creatures observing them. If men, having the passions they do have, are to avoid the dangers which these passions create for them, they must be able to reach conclusions about what makes for their conservation; they must use their reason. Thus the laws of nature are 'dictates of reason', not as imperatives which follow logically from statements of fact, but as rules which only creatures capable of reasoning could think of or could want to see observed. Men do seek to preserve themselves, and they are aware that other men do so too; they can take stock of the condition in which they find themselves and can conceive of another which they greatly prefer to it. They can also conceive of ways to remove themselves out of the first condition into the second; they can conceive of rules of conduct which, if they were generally observed, would put them into the preferred condition.

In all this, there is no inferring of rules of conduct from descriptive statements; there is merely an ingenious attempt to show how creatures situated in what Hobbes calls 'the state of nature', having the passions and needs which he ascribes to them in that state, come to conceive of certain rules of conduct and to desire their general observance. Hobbes, at least in this part of his argument, is no more guilty of deriving an *ought* from an *is* than Hume itself, who warns us against this proceeding. His method is altogether different from that of the philosophers who begin by asserting that God made man and has certain intentions for him, or that man has certain capacities peculiar to his kind, and then conclude that therefore he ought to do some things and refrain from others.

Nor is Hobbes guilty of deriving prescriptive from descriptive statements when he treats the laws of nature as commands of God. To say that they are commands of God is, of course, to make a descriptive statement about them. Such statements can be made about rules of conduct just as much as about anything else, and to make them is not to be guilty of the improper inference that Hume condemns.

No doubt, Hobbes's account of rules and their social functions is seriously defective, and so too, as we shall see later, is his account of obligation; but as much could be said of the accounts of these matters which Hume gives. Hobbes distinguishes between descriptive and prescriptive statements, and makes no show of deducing the second kind from the first, as many much later writers (Montesquieu, Rousseau and Burke prominent among them) do. Even Bentham, the avowed disciple of Hume, sometimes does what Hume forbids. He sometimes speaks as if the greatest happiness principle were a truth which followed logically from all men's desiring pleasure and being averse to pain, though at other times he merely puts it forward as the rule which all men everywhere are disposed to accept and to prefer to any rule which conflicts with it when they can compare the consequences of conforming to the two rules. On the occasions when Bentham speaks of his greatest happiness principle in this second way, he speaks of it much as Hobbes does of the rules which he calls *maxims of prudence* and *dictates of reason*.

It is to be held against Hobbes, as it is against the Utilitarians, that he did not see how deeply men's passions, needs and ambitions are affected by the claims which, as creatures made fit for society by education, they learn to make and to allow, by the moral and legal relations in which they stand to others; but it is not to be held against him that he failed to make a distinction which is now so much insisted upon by some writers on ethics or committed a 'fallacy' which they now so deliberately avoid. On the contrary, he was among the first to make the distinction, and he avoided the 'fallacy' more successfully than several of the Utilitarian admirers of Hume. He practised what Hume preached before Hume preached it. He did not point to the supposed fallacy and may not even have been conscious of it; his state may have been one of mere innocence, when the sin which is not committed is also not conceived.

The theorist who explains in this way how rules arise from what is enduring in the nature and situation of man (a derivation which does not involve deducing rules from statements of fact) need not confine himself, as Hume mostly did, to this task of explanation; he can also be critical, and not only of institutions but also of rules. He can put forward some rules as taking precedence over others; he can treat them as basic rules. He can argue that, given what is enduring in man's nature and situation, there are certain rules which are basic in the sense that they are preferred to any rule which conflicts with them by anyone who sees the consequences of not so preferring them. We have seen that Bentham believed the greatest happiness principle to be basic in this sense. And although he made other claims for it in the endeavour to establish its special status, he need not have done so. He could have claimed no more for it than this, and still have used it to challenge, not only institutions and positive laws, but also rules which those who favour them put forward as moral. All rules, he might have said (and he sometimes came close to saying it), arise because men, the better to achieve their purposes, feel the need to control each other's and their own behaviour, and there are no rules to be preferred on the ground that they have some 'higher' function than this; but there is one rule which is the master rule because, given men's purposes and their situation, it is the one which they in fact prefer to all others when they see their situation clearly.

Hobbes's laws of nature, as maxims of prudence, as conclusions about what conduces to men's conservation, are basic in this same sense. And Hobbes, like Bentham, uses his basic rules for a critical purpose, although not for the same purpose as Bentham. Bentham uses his basic rule to criticize the laws and established institutions; his purpose is above all to advise rulers what they should do for the good of their subjects, and he puts forward his rule as the measure of that good. Hobbes is not concerned to reform particular laws and institutions but to argue that, if men are to have full security, if it is to be made as safe as it can be for them to observe the basic rules whose general observance is peace, they must live in communities where all authority belongs to one person or assembly of persons. First he establishes what rules all men must observe if any man is to have the security which every man desires, and then argues that, if the motives which cause men to observe the rules are to be as strong and general as they can be, certain conditions must hold. He therefore condemns all communities in which these conditions do not hold, in which authority is not concentrated as it must be if men are to get as much security as they can have in this world.

Hobbes's purpose is to show how authority ought to be

distributed in the state; and this is a quite proper undertaking for someone who holds (as Hobbes does, except when he says that the laws of nature are commands of God) that all rules are man-made, being merely human solutions to human problems, and that their obligatoriness consists in how men feel about them or respond to them or use them to control behaviour.

And though Hobbes does call the laws of nature commands of God, he also makes it clear that God requires nothing of men which they would not require of each other if there were no God. Atheists, no less than other men, can discover that the laws of nature are rules which it is every man's interest should be generally observed, and have as powerful a motive for creating the conditions in which it is most likely that they will be observed. As we shall see later, in the opinion of Hobbes, the function of rules, the senses in which men are obliged to observe them, and their motives for observing them remain the same whether or not there is a God who intervenes in human affairs.

I have said that Hobbes, compared with most other great political theorists, has unusually clear ideas about what he is doing. That is not to say that his own estimate of his enterprise is correct or that he is never confused. His defects are not always inadequacies, failures to take into account all that needs to be so taken. He is sometimes mistaken about what he is doing.

Hobbes, it has often been observed, was fascinated by geometry, and his account of what is involved in all reasoning applies more nearly to mathematics than to either the natural or the social sciences. 'Reason . . . is nothing but reckoning, that is adding and subtracting, of the consequences of general names agreed upon for the *marking* and *signifying* of our thoughts; I say *marking* them when we reckon by ourselves, and *signifying*, when we demonstrate or approve our reckonings to other men.'* Reason is here restricted to the making of inferences from definitions. It may be that Hobbes's account is defective even if applied to only this kind of reasoning, but this plainly is the kind he has in mind and to which he wants

* *Leviathan.* Fontana Edition. Ch. v, p. 82.

to reduce all other kinds. Science, which is the product of reason, is (we are told) 'the knowledge of consequences', and this knowledge is also called knowledge of the 'dependence of one fact upon another.'* It would seem, then, that Hobbes is claiming that, by a purely deductive method like that of the geometer, we can arrive at knowledge of causal connexions; for it is clear from the context that by 'the dependence of one fact upon another' he means a causal connexion. It would seem that he has failed to distinguish logical relations between propositions from causal connexions between events, and has not understood how the knowledge reached merely by the making of definitions and inferences differs from the kind which involves the making and testing of hypotheses.

Clearly, if Hobbes had been invited to give an account of his method, he would not have given one which would satisfy the twentieth century logician, who has learnt to make distinctions not yet made or not widely understood at the time that *Leviathan* was written. But we must take care not to accuse Hobbes unjustly. If he had been asked what method he was using in *Leviathan*, he would have described a method something like that of the geometer; and that, we may think, is not the method suited to his purpose. No doubt, it is not suited to his purpose; but then it is also not the method that Hobbes used, even though he thought it was. It is therefore pointless to accuse him of treating politics as if it were a kind of geometry.

The method of Hobbes is the method neither of the geometer nor of the natural scientist, though it is in some important ways more like geometry than it is like the natural sciences. It is a method still used by the social theorist, though its nature and limitations are now better understood than they were in the seventeenth century. Certain assumptions are made about the desires and preferences of men and about the situation in which they find themselves, and then either (or both) of two kinds of conclusions are drawn: conclusions about how they are likely to behave, and conclusions about how they would be well advised to behave. Economists often use this method and find it useful; they construct what they

* *Leviathan*. Ch. v, p. 85.

call theoretical models. The value of the method (if it is to be more than just an intellectual exercise) depends upon the assumptions made about men's desires and preferences and their situation. If these assumptions are realistic, if they select for consideration what is important in the real world, they do enlarge our understanding of how men behave and enlighten us as to what they should do in their own interests. The *model* is ordinarily much simpler than the reality; but then it is precisely because reality is so complicated that it is useful to construct a variety of simple models to help us understand it. If we do not forget that the model is not an image of reality but only a device for the better understanding of it, we need not be misled by it. The student of society can seldom make experiments in the manner of the natural scientist, and this other method is indispensable to him. Hobbes's political theory is one of the earliest and most impressive examples of this method.

Hobbes did not properly understand the method he used; he did not see how it differs from the method of the geometer, who makes no assumptions about the real world. No doubt, some of the virtues of the geometer are needed by whoever uses the method of Hobbes: he must know how to put his assumptions clearly and how to draw valid conclusions from them. But, precisely because these assumptions refer to realities – to desires, passions, preferences, acts of will, rules of conduct, modes of behaviour, etc. – it is much more difficult for him to put them clearly than for the geometer to construct clear definitions. The geometer uses such terms as *line*, *triangle* and *circle* in only one sense, and defines his terms adequately provided he defines them clearly; they have the meanings which he ascribes to them, and he has no difficulty in consistently using them in the senses he has defined. But the terms embodied in the assumptions of the social or political theorist are often used in several senses which it is not easy to distinguish from one another. Therefore the theorist, in the course of his argument, may interpret his own assumptions in a number of different ways, without being aware that he has done so, and so may arrive at conclusions which do not follow from *any* consistent interpretation of them.

He can, of course, define his terms. But a definition, even when it is clear, may be inadequate for either of two reasons. It may not define any of the senses in which the term is currently used, though the maker of the definition intends that it should. In that case, he will probably soon revert to using the term in a current sense which he has failed to define and his definition will be merely a source of confusion. Or he may intend to give to the term a new meaning, hoping thereby to provide himself with a tool better suited to explain what he wants to explain, and yet the meaning, though clearly defined, may not be suited to his purpose. In this case, too, he will probably not use the term in the sense defined, and the definition, for all its clarity, will be an impediment and not a help.

The making of assumptions is different from the defining of terms; and this Hobbes did not see, for he put forward his assumptions about men, their passions, desires and preferences, as if they were so many definitions. Nor did he see why it is so much more difficult for the political theorist to make his assumptions clear than for the geometer to produce impeccable definitions. And lastly, because he did not understand what is involved in the making of assumptions, it never occurred to him that assumptions different from his own, though not less realistic, could be made and different conclusions drawn from them. He was under the illusion that he was applying the method of the geometer to politics, and his theory is the worse because he was under it. If he had understood the method he did use, he would have been aware of its difficulties and limitations. Nevertheless, it can be claimed for him that he did use a method appropriate to his subject, and that he used it as no one before him had done.

Hobbes believed that he got his ideas about man from introspection, that he read mankind in himself. Here too he was mistaken. He put together his image of man by selecting those human qualities which best served his purpose, which was to explain how the need for security arises and how it is to be met. Besides, introspection does not produce self-knowledge in the way that Hobbes thought it did. We learn about ourselves by observing others as well as ourselves; and we cannot learn much until we have acquired a language. But the language we acquire is a public language, and in learning to use it we learn to think about the world (which includes ourselves) as others think about it. No doubt, to understand what we hear about the passions and desires of men we have to recognize them in ourselves; but what we take notice of depends largely on what we hear said, and on the need to understand current opinions. We are as likely to read what we hear of mankind into ourselves as to read mankind in ourselves. If Hobbes's portrait of man is a caricature, it is as much a caricature of Hobbes as of other men.

Nothing is more puzzling about Hobbes's philosophy than the rôle it ascribes to God. I do not have in mind here what Hobbes says about religion and its place in the commonwealth, for that part of his theory, whatever its defects, is not less clear than the others. He speaks of religion much as Machiavelli did before him and Montesquieu was to do after him; he speaks of it as a powerful influence on behaviour. And, since he recognizes its power, he wants it controlled by the sovereign in the interests of peace. We may find this position unsatisfactory but there is nothing about it to puzzle us.

What is puzzling is the rôle attributed to God as a maker of law and a creator of obligation. In both *De Cive* and *Leviathan* Hobbes sometimes treats the laws of nature as mere maxims of prudence and at other times as commands of God. Sometimes he speaks as if men were not obliged to obey these laws until there is a human sovereign strong enough to enforce obedience to them, and at other times as if the obligation to obey human rulers derived from a prior obligation to obey God's commands, and especially the third of them, that men perform their covenants.

It is, I think, possible to show that, given the senses in which Hobbes uses the word *obligation*, there is no need to derive the obligation to obey the civil law, the commands of the human sovereign, from a prior obligation to obey the law of God; and also that, given the passions and motives for action ascribed to men by Hobbes, there is no need to postulate any fear of God or desire to please him to explain how men come to submit to human rulers. God is useless to

Hobbes's argument, an 'unnecessary hypothesis'. Why, then, is he brought into it? Because Hobbes mistakenly believed in the need for the hypothesis? Or because he felt that a political philosophy which failed to take large account of God would not go down well with his readers? It is idle to speculate.

Today, the author of a political theory making no reference to God would not be suspected of atheism. In the seventeenth century it was different. Nevertheless, though Hobbes does not provide us with a political theory free of theology, there is nothing essential missing when the theology is taken out. Whatever is wanting in the theory, considered apart from the rôle it attributes to God, is not made good by taking that rôle into account.

3. The Argument for Absolute Government from the Need for Security

HOBBES, it is said (and no doubt said truly), was a materialist. He sometimes spoke as if our passions and our thoughts were motions in the brain or in other parts of the body, at other times as if they were how these motions *appear* to us, and at still other times as if these motions were merely their causes. Fortunately, since our concern is with his political theory, we do not have to decide which of these positions he came closest to holding or whether and how often he moved from one to another. Nor need we decide whether, when he spoke of passions and thoughts as effects of bodily motions, he believed them to be effects which were not in their turn causes. For we know that when he spoke of them without speaking of their physical causes, he spoke as if they were themselves causes. He could have started with an account of our passions and mental operations, without a word about their physical causes, and constructed precisely the same political philosophy.

It may be that, if he had not had the shifting and obscure opinions he did have about bodily motions and their connexions with our passions and mental operations, he would have described those passions and operations differently; but still we need not consider his views about the connexions in order to understand the descriptions. Certainly, the descriptions are sometimes obscure and more often deficient; but they are not made clearer or more complete by anything that Hobbes says about their physical causes. He knew much less about what he took to be the causes than about what he took to be the effects. He knew nothing of motions in the brain and very little about them in other parts of the body, but he did know a good deal about human desires and passions and the operations of the human mind. Not as much, no doubt, as he thought he knew, but much, much more than he knew about their supposed physical causes.

We lose nothing and do Hobbes the political philosopher no injustice if we neglect his materialism, and take up his argument at the point where he describes the passions and the operations of the mind. Men, like other animals, have desires (appetites) and aversions. They can desire incompatible things or can alternate between desire for and aversion from something, and so can have a quick succession of desires or of desires and aversions. This train of desires and aversions and of thoughts about the consequences of action (or abstention therefrom) Hobbes calls *deliberation*, and he calls *will* the last appetite in deliberating. He means, presumably, that it is the appetite (or aversion) which, whether or not it leads to action, puts an end to deliberation. From this it follows that an action or abstention, to be voluntary, must be deliberate. But, though this is what follows from Hobbes's definition of *will*, it does not give us the sense in which he ordinarily speaks of voluntary action. By a voluntary act he usually means any action (or failure to act) caused by a desire or aversion, whether or not there has been deliberation. And the object of every voluntary act, we are told, is some advantage to the doer of it.

Though other animals besides man can deliberate and will, only man can use words to mark his thoughts or to communicate them to others. Only he can have an extensive knowledge of 'consequences' and the 'dependence of one fact upon another'. His ability to foresee the effects of actions, his own and others, is enormously greater than that of other animals; and so too is his ability to imagine ways of getting what he has an appetite for and avoiding what he is averse to. He can also foresee that he will have desires in the future, and can desire now the means of providing for his future desires. In other words, he can desire power; for a man's power, Hobbes tells us, is 'his present means to obtain some future apparent good'. And a *good*, in this context, is only an object of desire, for what men desire they call *good* and what they are averse to *evil*.

Other animals besides man compete for what satisfies their present appetites, whenever there is not enough of it to satisfy them all; but, having little foresight, they do not compete for the present means of satisfying future appetites; they do not compete for power. Whereas men compete for power, not only to provide for their future appetites, but also for different reasons: because they want to be superior to others or because they delight in the possession of power. It is true that superiority adds to a man's means to satisfy his future appetites because it makes men defer to his wishes rather than to other people's. But this is not the only reason, nor the strongest, why men desire superiority; they desire it above all for its own sake. So, too, they desire the three forms of power (*command* or the ability to get obedience, *wealth* and *reputation*) not only as 'present means' to future goods but also as marks of superiority.

There are three principal causes of quarrels among men: *competition* for the means of satisfying their appetites, *diffidence* or mistrust which moves them to attack others for fear of being attacked by them, and *glory* which makes them attack for the sake of reputation. Hobbes defines *glory* as the joy a man takes in the contemplation of his own power. But, presumably, when Hobbes says that glory is a cause of quarrels, he does not mean that this joy of itself makes a man aggressive; he means rather that a man is moved to aggression by the desire to preserve or increase his power, and especially his reputation (which he calls a form of power). And the implication is that the man whom glory makes aggressive is concerned for power or reputation as a mark of superiority or for the joy he can take in the contemplation of it, and not as a means to other things. When a man believes that he has greater power than he in fact has, and takes joy in the illusion of power, he suffers from what Hobbes calls *vain-glory* or pride. So pride is a kind of glory; and is a most dangerous kind, for it moves men to act in ways which offend one another. When a man makes a just estimate of his power, he is unlikely to require of others more than they are willing to concede, for his power consists largely in their willingness to do what he requires. But if he over-values his own power or under-values theirs, he is very likely to require more than they are willing to concede, and therefore to quarrel with them. How deeply Hobbes believed that men suffer from pride is evident from the name he gives to the commonwealth and uses as the title of his most famous book, a name taken, as he himself tells his readers, from the last verses of the forty-first chapter of *Job*, where *Leviathan* is called *King of the Proud*.

These then are the passions to which men are liable, given their appetites, their need to compete with one another for the means of satisfying them, and the capacities peculiar to them which not only make them provident but also lovers of power for its own sake and for the sake of superiority. Where there is neither law nor government, these passions make men one another's enemies and move them to the behaviour which Hobbes calls *the war of all against all*. While this condition lasts, there is neither right nor wrong, neither justice nor injustice; for where there is no common power over men, no one to command them, able to compel their obedience, there is no law; and where there is no law there is no injustice and no wrong, for *unjust* and *wrong* mean only *contrary to law*. 'The desires, and other passions of men, are in themselves no sin. No more are the actions, that proceed from those passions, till they [that is, men] know a Law that forbids them: which till laws be made they cannot know.'

Fortunately, the war of all against all increases a passion which runs counter to the passions which produce that war; it magnifies fear and above all the fear of death; and fear is the most urgent of the passions which incline men to peace. Since men can reason and can acquire knowledge of consequences, they can discover the means to peace; they can imagine rules whose general observance would give them peace. And because they desire the end, which is peace, they desire the means to that end; they desire that the rules should be generally observed. Hobbes calls these rules 'convenient articles of peace, upon which men may be drawn to agreement'; but, though he also calls them 'laws of nature', he says that they are not laws 'properly so called', because 'law properly is the word of him that by right hath command over others.' In the state of nature, presumably, no man has this right; and Hobbes, when he first explains what the laws of nature are, does not say that anyone not a man has it.

Well-grounded objections can and have been made to Hobbes's account of this or that passion, to his calling *will* the last appetite in deliberating, and above all to his doctrine that the object of every voluntary action is some advantage to the doer of it. From the time of Bishop Butler onward these objections have been made either directly against Hobbes or against someone else whose views were the same as his. It has been argued that the making of a decision is not sufficiently described as being moved to action or inhibited therefrom by the last desire or aversion in a succession of desires, aversions and thoughts, of the kind which Hobbes calls deliberation. It has also been argued that to say that someone's desire is satisfied is merely to say that its object has been attained or that the attainment of it has given him pleasure, and that the object, which is not to be confused with the pleasure that comes of attaining it, may be someone else's advantage and not the advantage of the person having the desire. No one would deny that Hobbes, the psychologist, often takes too simple a view of what he seeks to explain.

Nevertheless, if we take it as a whole, without looking too closely at the details, Hobbes's account of the passions and of how men come to conceive of rules of conduct and to desire that they be generally observed is clear and consistent. And we must remember that Hobbes does not pretend that there really was, some time in the past, a state of nature, a war of all against all; he allows that the state he describes is imaginary, and describes it only to bring home to his readers what the human condition would be like if men, being what they are, were not under law and government.

Our first real difficulty is to decide in what sense, if any, the laws of nature are supposed by Hobbes to be binding on men in the state of nature. For he sometimes speaks as if men were not obliged to obey these laws until there is a sovereign strong enough to compel obedience to them, and sometimes as if it were only because these laws are binding even where there is no sovereign that men can put themselves under an obligation to obey a sovereign. He also says that in the state of nature 'the laws of nature oblige *in foro interno*; that is to say, they bind to a desire they should take place: but *in foro externo*; that is, to the putting them in act, not always;'* and he says it in a place where he treats these laws as mere conclusions of reason and not as commands of God. All this is puzzling.

In the hope of solving the puzzle, let us begin by noticing that Hobbes uses the word *obligation* in two senses, which I shall call, to mark the difference between them, the *weaker* and the *stronger* sense. Hobbes does not himself explain how they differ, and in some parts of his argument even takes it for granted that only obligation in what I have called the stronger sense is obligation properly so called. He does so whenever he speaks as if there were no obligation when what he really means is that there is no obligation in the stronger sense. Where there is obligation in the weaker sense there need be no one who commands and has power to compel obedience; but where there is obligation in the stronger sense, there must be someone. Obligation in both senses can be either *in foro interno* or *in foro externo*.

If a man is to be obliged in the weaker sense it is enough that something should be to his advantage and that he should be capable of seeing that it is. If the something is an action which he can do, he is obliged *in foro externo*; but if it is a form of behaviour which is not to his advantage until it is generally practised, he is obliged only *in foro interno*, 'to a desire it should take place'. Thus, in order that there should be obligation *in foro interno*, there must be rules of conduct which it is in men's interest should be generally observed. And though Hobbes does not speak of obligation *in foro externo* as if it were necessarily obligation to act in accordance with a rule, he is so predominantly concerned with the

* *Leviathan.* Ch. xv, p. 166.

observance of rules that we can neglect the cases in which he is not.*

Where men are convinced that the general observance of certain rules is or would be to their advantage, and they therefore desire that observance, it is reasonable for them to observe the rules themselves or to do whatever they can do safely to make it more likely that they will be generally observed. Even when the rules are not generally observed, it is reasonable for men to observe them when they can do so without risk to themselves, if by so doing they make their general observance more likely. It is reasonable for them to do whatever is likely to increase their security, and their security is greatest when rules which are to their advantage are generally observed. Therefore, if, in the hope of security, they agree with one another to choose some person, whom they undertake to obey, to interpret these rules, it is reasonable for them to do what they have undertaken, provided they can do so safely. If any one makes an agreement in the hope of gaining by it, it is unreasonable of him not to keep it, if he can keep it without danger to himself, for otherwise he frustrates his own purpose. Therefore he *ought* to keep it; and in this sense of *ought* it makes sense to say that he ought to keep it even where there is no one powerful enough to enforce agreements. It may be that, except where there is someone powerful enough to do this, it is very seldom safe for a man to do what he has undertaken. Nevertheless, when he can do so safely, he ought, in this sense of ought, to do it. Thus, even in this weaker sense of obligation a man can be obliged *in foro externo* as well as *in foro interno*.

Hobbes does not explain this sense of obligation clearly nor distinguish it from the other, and he sometimes passes from one sense to the other in ways that can only bewilder his readers; and yet it is clear that he uses both senses. He even comes near to explaining the weaker sense; for example,

* Actually, it is when he speaks of obligation in the stronger sense that Hobbes sometimes speaks as if it were not obligation to observe a rule. Someone powerful enough to compel obedience to his commands may issue a particular command to one or more persons on only one occasion. In that case he does not make a rule for their guidance, and yet Hobbes would say that they were obliged to obey him.

when he speaks of a man's not doing what he has undertaken, he likens his conduct to what 'in the disputations of scholars is called absurdity.'* Just as it is an *absurdity* for a man to contradict himself, so it is an *injustice* for him voluntarily to undo what he has voluntarily done, which is what he does when he frustrates his own purpose. And, clearly, *injustice* cannot here mean what is contrary to law 'properly so called'. Hobbes even says of a man that 'he ought, and it is his duty, not to make void that voluntary act of his own.'†

If there is to be obligation in the stronger sense there must be someone powerful enough to compel obedience to his commands; and though such commands may be particular, Hobbes is concerned with them only where they are general, when they lay down rules of conduct. He is concerned with them when they are laws. And, as we have seen, Hobbes defines law, 'properly so called', as 'the word of him that by right hath command over others'. In both *De Cive* and *Leviathan* he sometimes speaks as if the laws of nature were not laws 'properly so called', and therefore not obligatory in this stronger sense, until there is a human sovereign to interpret them and to compel obedience to them; but he also says that they are commands of God, which implies that they are obligatory in the stronger sense even where there is no human sovereign. As God's commands they are obligatory in this sense not only *in foro interno* but also *in foro externo*. True, they oblige *in foro externo* only to the extent that it is safe to obey them; but this is true of all laws, no matter whose commands they are. The only difference between the state of nature and the civil state is that, whereas in the first it is very seldom safe to observe the laws, in the second it is so nearly always.

It has been argued that Hobbes believed that men could not by covenant lay themselves under an obligation to obey a human ruler unless they were already obliged under God's law to keep their covenants. Now, since, according to Hobbes, the obligation to obey human rulers is always created by covenant, express or tacit, this amounts to saying that the

* *Leviathan.* Ch. xiv, p. 147.
† Ibid. Ch. xiv, p. 147.

obligation to obey these rulers, which is clearly an obligation in the stronger sense, presupposes an obligation in the same sense to obey God. There are passages in both *Leviathan* and *De Cive* which could be cited in support of this argument, and others which could be cited against it. Hobbes sometimes inclined to the belief here attributed to him and at other times not, and it is pointless either to affirm or to deny that it was his *real* opinion; it was presumably his opinion when he expressed or implied it and not when he said what is incompatible with it, and the evidence is that he did both.

In any case, the opinion, whether or not Hobbes held it, is false. If obligation is understood as he understood it, there is no need to derive the obligation to obey human rulers from any prior obligation to God. For men to be obliged, in the stronger sense of obligation, to obey a sovereign, all that is needed is that there should be a sovereign: that there should be some man or body of men powerful enough to compel obedience to his or their commands, and that those to whom the commands are addressed should recognize this to be so. And in order that there should be a sovereign, all that is needed is that those subject to him should have sufficient motives for so behaving that he has the power to compel obedience. Thus, to show how there can be a sovereign whose subjects are obliged to obey him, in the stronger sense of obligation, all that we have to do is to show how men can have adequate motives for so behaving that there is a sovereign. We do not have to show that they are also obliged, in the stronger sense, to obey God; nor indeed that they have any other kind of prior obligation.

No doubt, creatures capable of so behaving that a sovereign can arise among them are also capable of reaching conclusions about what is to their enduring advantage; and if they can reach such conclusions they can be obliged in what I have called Hobbes's weaker sense of obligation. They can conceive of rules which they desire should be generally observed because it is to their advantage that they should be, and they are therefore obliged, in the weaker sense, to observe them when they can do so safely. But the obligation, in the stronger sense, to obey the sovereign does not derive from this obligation in the weaker sense; it merely arises in a situation in which only creatures capable of obligation in the weaker sense could find themselves. Those capacities in men which make it possible for them to be obliged in the one sense also make it possible for them to be obliged in the other. This we can admit, and yet deny that there is any need to derive obligation in the second sense from obligation in the first.

The obligation to obey God, as Hobbes conceives of it, does not differ in kind from what the obligation to obey a human sovereign would be in a world without God. In both cases we have obligation in the stronger sense. Hobbes makes it abundantly clear that man's obligation to obey God arises only from God's power. 'The right of nature, whereby God reigneth over men, and punisheth those that break his laws, is to be derived, not from his creating them, as if he required obedience as of gratitude for his benefits; but from his *irresistible power*.'* True, Hobbes here speaks of *irresistible* power, which, in at least one sense of *irresistible*, is greater power than any man can have. But then he is speaking of the state of nature, where *ex hypothesi* no man is powerful enough to compel other men's obedience, and the only person (God) with the power to do so, if he chose to exercise it, happens to have irresistible power. But Hobbes says nothing to explain why power should be *irresistible*, in the sense in which only God's power can be so, if men are to be obliged to obey the possessor of it. There can be obligation, in the stronger sense, wherever there is someone who issues commands and is powerful enough to compel obedience to them.

Certainly, when Hobbes says that God's power is irresistible, he does not mean that God's commands are always obeyed. In the state of nature, where no man but only God has power to compel obedience, the laws of nature (which are God's commands) are so little obeyed that it is ordinarily unsafe for a man to obey them, and he is therefore not obliged to do so.† For no man, says Hobbes, is obliged to do what

---

* *Leviathan*. Ch. XXXI, pp. 311-2.

† Only God has *irresistible* power in the sense that he can always, if he chooses, compel anyone to obey him. But a man's power can be *irresistible* in another sense, at least if we accept Hobbes's assumptions about human

tends to his own destruction, and his obeying the laws will ordinarily tend to it, unless other men also obey them; and this in the state of nature they do not do. God has chosen to punish and reward men, not in this world but in the next, and has so made them that fear of distant punishment and hope of distant reward are not strong passions with them. He has chosen not to provide them with sufficient motives for obeying his laws, and so has not made it safe for them to do so unless they are under human government. God's power is irresistible in the sense that he can achieve whatever he wants to achieve. If he chooses to be obeyed, he will be obeyed; for he can, if he chooses, ensure that those to whom he addresses his commands understand them and have sufficient motives for obedience. But he has chosen not to provide men with sufficient motives for obeying his commands in the state of nature, and therefore, while that state lasts, their obligation to obey is severely limited; for the purpose of these commands is the safety of the creatures to whom they are addressed, creatures so endowed and situated that they are not safe unless the commands are generally obeyed, and therefore are not obliged (except rarely) to obey them until there is a human ruler to provide the motives which God has not chosen to provide.

Hobbes says nothing about obligation in the stronger sense from which it follows that it can exist only where there is irresistible power; nothing which entails that, unless men were obliged in this sense to obey someone whose power is *irresistible*, they could not be obliged in the same sense to obey anyone having lesser power. At the most, he says that men in the state of nature are obliged to keep the laws of nature as far as they can do so safely, and points to this obligation (which he takes in the weaker sense more often than in the stronger) to explain how *by covenant* they can make it their duty to obey a human sovereign. In all this

---

nature. Man, Hobbes tells us, necessarily acts for his own advantage, as he sees it; if, therefore, one man commands another and threatens to punish him in a case of disobedience, and the other thinks it to his advantage to obey, he cannot help but obey. Whoever has been success-fully compelled has yielded to *irresistible* power.

there is nothing to suggest any connexion between obligation in the stronger sense and irresistible or divine power.

The two senses of obligation are closely connected; indeed, the stronger sense can be treated as a case of the weaker. And both senses, for Hobbes, imply causal necessity. When Hobbes says that a man is obliged, even in the weaker sense, to do something, he implies that, if he saw his advantage clearly, he would necessarily do it. For man, so Hobbes tells us, always acts from hope of advantage (or fear of hurt) to himself. If there is something which it is to his advantage to do, and he sees that it is so, he necessarily does it. Thus, if there is a rule which it is to his advantage to obey, and he sees that it is, he cannot help but obey it. If he does not obey it, it is because he has momentarily lost sight of his advantage. Blinded by passion he has mistaken his lesser good for his greater. Or, if he sees that it would be to his advantage to obey a rule provided he had reasonable assurance that others were doing so too, he cannot but desire to have this assurance. Thus, when Hobbes says of the laws of nature, even when he speaks of them as mere maxims of prudence, that they oblige *in foro interno*, 'to a desire they should take place', he is not only saying that the desire is reasonable; he is also implying that men necessarily have it whenever they see clearly that the laws are to their advantage.

Obligation *in foro externo* in the stronger sense differs from obligation in the weaker sense only because it is a duty to obey commands. Wherever there is this duty, we can always say (as we can of obligation in the weaker sense), that men are obliged to do only what is for their own advantage, only what they could not help but do if they saw that advantage clearly. And the difference, where the obligation is *in foro interno*, is similar; the desire which men, if they see their advantage clearly, cannot help but have is that rules which are also commands should be generally obeyed.

If we are to explain how men can by covenant set up a human sovereign whom they are obliged to obey, in Hobbes's sense of obligation, we need not concern ourselves with their obligations before they set him up. We have only to explain how they could come to make such a covenant and keep it, for, clearly, unless they do keep it, the man they choose for sovereign will not be able to do what the makers of the covenant expect of him: which is to address general commands to them all and compel obedience from the reluctant. Unfortunately, Hobbes did not see that this is all that requires explanation; and he therefore thought it incumbent upon him to show how men, already obliged by the law of nature to keep their covenants, could by covenant lay a duty upon themselves to obey the man chosen for sovereign. He did not see that the obligation to obey this man arises only from the situation created by setting him up as sovereign. No doubt, unless the makers of the covenant do what they undertake, they have not set up a sovereign, and so have not created a situation in which they are obliged to obey a human ruler. But the obligation to obey this ruler is created by what they do to enable him to issue general commands and compel obedience to them. Even if they were not obliged to do this, they would, by doing it, create the situation in which it became their duty to obey the man whom they had thus made powerful. There is no objection to Hobbes's saying that men have obligations even in the state of nature; the objection is only to his sometimes speaking as if their duty to obey a human ruler powerful enough to compel obedience *implied* some sort of prior obligation.

Hobbes admits that men, no matter what their obligations in the state of nature, are obliged to obey the sovereign they set up only if it is safe for them to do so, only if he can compel the reluctant to obey and can protect the willing. Though they set up a sovereign by covenant, every man agreeing with every other to obey some person (or body) who is to declare the law to them all, the covenant is not binding unless the person chosen to be sovereign is powerful enough to enforce it. And yet, unless the makers of the covenant keep it, there is no one powerful enough to enforce it. It would seem then that the covenant must be kept before there can arise the power which alone makes it safe, and therefore reasonable and obligatory, for the covenanters to keep it.

This has seemed to many the crucial weakness of the theory. Hobbes tries to surmount it by distinguishing between two kinds of covenant: the kind in which the parties 'presently perform' (that is to say, do simultaneously) what they undertake, no one having to trust anyone to keep his part of the bargain later; and the kind in which the parties do not do simultaneously what they undertake but some or all of them have to trust the others to do it in the future. Covenants of the second kind, because they require mutual trust, are (so Hobbes tells us) unreasonable in the state of nature where there is no power strong enough to compel men to do what they have undertaken. Thus the covenant setting up the sovereign must be of the first kind; the parties to it must all 'presently perform' what they undertake. Hobbes presents them to us as all at the same time laying down their natural right – the right to do whatever they judge necessary for their conservation – in favour of the man or body chosen to be sovereign.

But this is absurd. This laying down of right is merely a simultaneous making of promises and not a keeping of them. The parties to the covenant, when they lay down their natural right, do no more than promise to obey the sovereign; and they do not keep the covenant unless they do in the future what they now promise to do. The laying down of right is not the keeping of the covenant but only the making of it; and the covenant is one which involves mutual trust. And therefore, if Hobbes is right about covenants involving mutual trust, this covenant, in the mere state of nature, is unreasonable. It is an idle covenant, an exchange of promises which leaves the situation unaltered.

But is Hobbes right? Why should not the parties to the covenant have sufficient motives for keeping it quite apart from fear of the sovereign's punishments? Because – so Hobbes would have us believe – men are apt to be unreasonable, to be swayed by passion and so to lose sight of their enduring good. If those blinded by passion are not compelled to keep the covenant, then it is no longer reasonable for those who are not blinded to keep it; for it is to their advantage to keep it only if it is generally kept.

This may be true, but does not prove that covenants involving mutual trust are unreasonable until there is a power to enforce them. For, true though it may be that any man, under the sway of passion, is liable to break the covenant unless fear prevents his doing so, it is also true that every man wants all other men to keep it. It is to every man's advantage that other men should obey the sovereign, and this is an advantage to which passion is not likely to blind him. There-fore, if a man breaks the covenant, if he disobeys the sovereign, he will find other men eager that the sovereign should punish him. The sovereign will therefore find it easy to enlist support against the breaker of the covenant; he will be able to get power because men will have a powerful motive for obeying him when he calls upon them for help against the law-breaker, the disturber of the peace. But this motive will not be fear of punishment; for, unless men were moved by it, the sovereign would never have the power to punish and to make himself feared. Thus, though the covenant which institutes a sovereign is not one in which the parties presently perform what they undertake (which is future obedience to the sovereign), it does create a situation in which each party can reasonably expect the other parties to keep it, even though the sovereign acquires the power to enforce it only because most of them keep it from some other motive than fear of his power. Of course, if the sovereign does not do what is expected of him, if he does not coerce the recalcitrant, if he does not make laws and lay down punishments, the covenant becomes a dead letter. But that does not make it any the less true that the covenant involves mutual trust and can establish no coercive power unless those who make it do in the future what they undertake in the present.

Once the sovereign's power is effective, his subjects are obliged to obey him. The sovereign's right of command, his authority as distinct from his power, could be derived simply from this obligation. Wherever there is effective power, no matter how established, there is obligation in what I have called Hobbes's stronger sense; and authority could be treated as the mere correlate of this kind of obligation. This, for someone constructing such a theory as Hobbes's, would be the simplest and the soundest course. Yet Hobbes does not take it, or does not take it consistently. Sometimes he speaks as if the sovereign, when he is instituted, acquires no right which he did not already have in the state of nature; and this is to imply that, in that state, everyone has a right of command though no one is obliged to obey, which is surely odd. Sometimes, too, he speaks as if authority were bestowed upon the possessor of it by those over whom it is exercised, as if it arose from consent or, as he more often puts it, from covenant express or tacit. He does this, for example, when he says that from the 'institution of the commonwealth are derived all the rights and the faculties of him, or them, on whom the sovereign power is conferred by the consent of the people assembled,'* and also in those passages (which are not few) where he says or implies that subjects are the 'authors' of their sovereign's public acts and he is their 'representative'. Hobbes does not treat the covenant merely as an agreement which, if those that make it keep it, enables someone to issue commands and to compel obedience, so that a situation arises in which obedience becomes obligatory and the commander acquires authority; he sometimes treats it as an actual bestowal of authority on the possessor of it. With Hobbes, as with Locke, there are puzzles about what he understands by consent. And there are also puzzles about his use of the term *natural right*. I shall consider these last puzzles first and then turn to the others.

Hobbes says that, in the state of nature, men have a right to all things. If we take him literally, this can mean only that they have no obligations; for it is only if right is taken to mean absence of obligation, that all men can have a right to all things. For, clearly, in the sense of right in which one man's right entails another man's obligation, there cannot be a universal right to all things. Yet Hobbes also says that, even in the state of nature, men are obliged to observe the laws of nature when they can safely do so, which they sometimes can — for we are not told that they are *never* obliged *in foro externo* but only *not always*. Thus it would appear that Hobbes both denies and asserts that men have obligations in the state of nature.

This apparent contradiction has moved at least one writer to

* *Leviathan.* Ch. XVIII, p. 178.

suggest that Hobbes, by the right to all things, does not mean the complete absence of obligation, but merely that in the state of nature it is left to every man to decide for himself what he ought to do.* He is the sole judge of what the laws of nature require of him. This is so whether these laws are no more than maxims of prudence or whether they are also commands of God. For God does not choose to interpret his commands to men but leaves it to every man to interpret them for himself so long as there is no acknowledged public interpreter of them, no human sovereign. In the state of nature a man may do whatever he honestly believes is necessary to his safety, for the laws of nature are binding only while it is safe to observe them, and whether or not it is so is something which, in the absence of a sovereign, every man must decide for himself.

If we accept this suggestion (which assumes that Hobbes does not really mean what he quite often says), we get rid of an apparent contradiction, but we make it no easier to explain how it is that the man who becomes sovereign acquires no right which he did not have before. If, in the state of nature, his right to all things consisted in his being sole judge of what the laws of nature required of him, that right clearly did not include the right to interpret those laws to other men, which is a right attributed to the sovereign by Hobbes. What is for Hobbes the essential right of sovereignty, the right to declare to others what the law is, what their obligations are, is clearly not included in the natural right to all things, whether that right is understood as complete absence of obligation or as every man's right to decide what his obligations are.

However we interpret the natural right to all things, it is clear that whoever becomes sovereign acquires a right he did not have before. He acquires the right which is the correlate of the obligations which his subjects have acquired. He also acquires an obligation he did not have before, which is to make and enforce laws for his subjects' security. This is so whether we take *obligation* in the weaker or the stronger of the two senses in which Hobbes uses the word. Even if the

* Professor H. Warrender in *The Political Philosophy of Hobbes*, see especially Chapters III and IV.

laws of nature are not divine commands, it is to the sovereign's advantage to rule effectively; and it is so even in the unlikely event of his desiring no more than security and not superiority as well. It is not only subjects but rulers who benefit from stable government. Therefore, in the weaker sense of *ought*, the sovereign ought to do what he can to ensure that government is stable, which he can do best by seeing to it that civil laws conform to the laws of nature and are impartially administered. Though Hobbes often seems to lose sight of the fact, the setting up of effective government takes the sovereign out of the state of nature just as much as his subjects, and his obligations *in foro externo* are greatly enlarged, since he too can now do safely many things which it would not be safe for him to do were he still in that state. And if the laws of nature are divine commands, then this enlarged obligation is obligation in the stronger sense.

Hobbes ought not to have said that the sovereign is not bound by his own laws; he ought to have said only that he is not accountable to any man for what he does as his subjects are to him. Until the sovereign changes the law, he ought to obey it where it applies to him, even though he is not accountable to his courts as his subjects are. Because the sovereign cannot be his own subject and is subject to no other man, it does not in the least follow that he has only the rights and obligations he would have in the state of nature. To be subject to no man where effective government is established is not to remain in the state of nature.

Given his assumptions about human nature and the senses he gives to the term *obligation*, Hobbes's theory would have been simpler and more consistent if he had not attempted to derive the obligation to obey the sovereign from a prior duty to keep covenants; if he had been content to say that wherever there is effective power, there is a duty of obedience to the possessor of it. He could then have used the covenant, not to show how the duty of obedience derives from a prior duty, but to explain men's motives for so behaving that effective power arises among them. He could have used it to bring home to his readers the needs that government serves by showing what might induce men without a government to set one up and what they would have to do to make its power effective. But, if he had done that, he could hardly have spoken, as he did, of the sovereign's being his subjects' representative, or have insisted that subjects are only obliged to obey their rulers by virtue of a covenant, express or tacit. He used the covenant as a device to explain, not only what interests and motives in men inspire the behaviour which makes government possible, but also to argue that whoever owes obedience owes it only because he has agreed to obey.

The idea of a covenant was used in his day to explain the duties and rights of rulers and their subjects, and Hobbes wanted to use it for the same purpose. Others used it to show that the authority of rulers is limited, and that subjects have the right to resist them when they exceed their authority. They have only as much authority as their subjects bestow upon them by covenant, express or tacit. This argument implies that there can be effective power where there is no authority; that there can be rulers who govern without the consent of their subjects. Hobbes wanted to show that there cannot be; and in the attempt to prove his point made odd use of such terms as *covenant*, *consent* and *liberty*.

To make his point Hobbes undertakes to show that the duty to obey a conqueror derives as much from consent as the duty to obey the man who has been chosen by his subjects to rule over them. The conqueror could kill or otherwise damage the conquered, and if he refrains from doing so he does so on the tacit condition that they obey him. And they, by ceasing to resist him, by submitting to him, tacitly accept this condition; they consent to their subjection. There is a covenant here, so Hobbes would have us believe, just as much as when a sovereign is set up by agreement between his subjects: the only difference between the two cases being that, in the first, the covenant is tacit and the sovereign is a party to it, whereas in the second the covenant is express and the sovereign is not a party but a beneficiary only. The effects of the two covenants are the same, though the first is a submission to someone who is already powerful and the second gives power to someone who does not already have it.

It might be objected that, while submission to the conqueror is forced, the agreement which sets up a sovereign is free. Hobbes is ready with an answer. The submission is as much an act of will as the agreement; the man who submits chooses or wills to do so as much as the man who makes an express agreement. He is not used by the conqueror as a workman uses a tool; his action proceeds from a desire which arises in him when he contemplates his situation just as much as the action of the man who takes part in setting up a sovereign. The situations and motives of the two men may be different, but each does what in the circumstances he desires to do. According to Hobbes, we do not deprive a man of freedom by providing him with a sufficient motive for doing what we require of him, any more when we threaten than when we bribe him; we deprive him of it only when we prevent his doing what desire or aversion moves him to do. To act from desire or aversion is for Hobbes to act willingly, to choose to act. When we ask, Is an action free? our question makes sense only if it means, Does it proceed from desire or aversion? which for Hobbes is the same as to ask, Is it an act of will? But to ask of an act of will, Is it free? is an improper question. So Hobbes concludes that submission, since it is no less an act of will, and therefore free, than the covenant instituting a sovereign, is just as much an action which lays upon the doer of it an obligation to obey. And he fires a parting shot at his opponents: if it is said that those who submit to a conqueror do it from fear, it is equally true that those who set up a sovereign by express covenant do it from fear; the difference being that the first do it from fear of the conqueror, and the others from fear of one another.

Hobbes speaks as if this difference were irrelevant; but it is highly relevant. If two men who have good reason to fear one another make an agreement intended to remove the cause of their fear, they are held to be bound by their agreement. But if one man induces another by threats, express or implied, to make a promise, the promise is held to be void. Though in both cases the promises are inspired by fear and are acts of will (not merely in the sense defined by Hobbes but also in a more usual sense), the two cases are unlike in the one respect which is relevant here. In the first case, neither man is 'in the power' of the other, while in the second one of them is. For it is only when a man has cause to fear another who has no cause to fear him, that he is said to be in that other's power. And if, being in another's power, he makes a promise, it is beside the point to say that he is bound by it because his making it is an act of will. And it is equally beside the point to say that it is a free act. No doubt, in Hobbes's sense of freedom, it is free; but then those who say it is not free are not using the word *freedom* in Hobbes's sense. They are using it in another sense which happens to be the relevant one here.

Hobbes does not deny that covenants made under duress are everywhere held to be void; he merely insists that they are so only because sovereigns do not enforce them. If a sovereign chose to enforce them and had the power to do so, the parties to them would be obliged to keep them. No doubt they would be, in Hobbes's stronger sense of obligation. But that is nothing to the purpose; for, in that sense of obligation, they would not be obliged to keep covenants not made under duress if the sovereign did not choose to enforce them. According to Hobbes, men are obliged to keep their covenants either because it is reasonable that they should, the keeping of them (when they can be kept safely) being in general to their advantage, or because they are commanded to keep them by someone powerful enough to compel obedience. In the first case they are obliged in the weaker sense, and in the second in the stronger. But covenants made under duress differ in an important respect from those not so made. Ordinarily, it is to the advantage of those who make them under duress to keep them only while it is dangerous to break them, whereas it is to the advantage of the parties to covenants not made under duress to keep them as long as they can safely do so. The rule about covenants which, if it is generally observed, makes for peace and is to every man's enduring advantage is not *that men perform their covenants no matter how made*; it is *that they perform their covenants not made under duress*. This is the proper formulation of the third law of nature, if the purpose of that law is what Hobbes says it is – the conservation of the creatures required to observe it.

Besides, it is an abuse of language to call mere submission to force a tacit promise to obey. We submit to the powerful when we obey them, and to obey is not to promise obedience. No doubt, there may be occasions when the convention is that an act of obedience is to be taken for a promise to obey, so that anyone who understands the convention and does the act is held to have made the promise. In that case the obedience is symbolic; it expresses an intention intelligible to the initiated; it is a statement, though not in ordinary language; and is therefore more than a mere act of obedience. Though even then, if it is made under duress, it is ordinarily held not to be binding.

Though Hobbes's philosophy would have been logically sounder if he had not argued that the obligation of subjects to obey their rulers is established by covenant, express or tacit, it would also have been less persuasive. His arguments were suited to the public to whom they were addressed. This is not to suggest that he rigged his arguments to achieve his purpose, that he did not find them convincing himself but used them in the hope of convincing others. No doubt, Hobbes took as seriously as any those parts of his philosophy which in our eyes spoil its consistency or obscure its originality, and yet to us, who no longer use the idea of covenant or contract to explain either the uses of law and government or the rights and duties of rulers and subjects, what is perhaps most impressive is the attempt made to explain how rules and obligations arise from the desires and preferences of men and from what they do in the hope of satisfying them. The sociologist today might agree with Hobbes 'that all men are born unapt for society' and are made fit for it 'not by nature but by education'; that is to say, by learning painfully to adjust their claims on others to the claims others make on them. It is the discipline of society which makes them law-abiding; they learn to be just, not by apprehending eternal truths by the light of reason, but by learning to live together.

Where the philosophy of Hobbes is most conspicuously deficient is in its failure to take proper account of moral obligation. If the laws of nature are mere maxims of prudence, then to say that men are obliged to observe them is only to say that it is reasonable that they should. Or, following other suggestions of Hobbes, it is to say that men would necessarily observe them if they saw clearly what was to their advantage, or that they fear the evil consequences of not observing them. And their obligation to obey laws 'properly so called', rules which they are commanded to observe on pain of punishment, is really no more than obligation in the weaker sense under the special conditions which make it obligation in the stronger sense. Where there is command and punishment, it is reasonable to observe rules not only because to observe them (where it can be done safely) is in general to a man's advantage, but because he is liable to punishment if he breaks them, and fear of the evil consequences of not observing them now includes fear of punishment. In all this there is nothing about properly moral obligation. It is true that Hobbes, speaking of the laws of nature as commands of God, sometimes calls them moral laws; but he thinks of them as differing from civil laws only because the lawgiver is divine and not human. He says nothing to suggest that, as laws of God, they are obligatory in a sense in which civil laws would not be in a Godless world.

In the next century the need to distinguish moral rules from 'laws properly so called' was felt more strongly. Neither Hume nor Bentham spoke of moral rules as if they were commands, divine or otherwise. They thought of them as rules which men come to adopt because experience teaches them that it is their enduring interest that such rules be generally observed; and to that extent they thought of them much as Hobbes thought of the laws of nature when he called them maxims of prudence. But, for both Hume and Bentham, what makes a rule moral is the way men react to the observance and the breach of it; they approve of the observance and disapprove of the breach. For Bentham, to be morally obliged to do something is to be liable to suffer disapproval for not doing it; and for the more subtle Hume, it is to feel uneasy at the thought of not doing it, a feeling not to be confused with fear of evil consequences. For Rousseau, the mark of a moral rule is that the man who breaks it condemns himself for doing so. Rousseau believed (to judge by what he said of the education of Emile) that a child becomes moral as experience teaches it to impose upon itself rules which make it a good neighbour to others. Whatever the defects of these views, they do at least make it possible to distinguish between moral rules and 'laws properly so called'. But we can also treat them as attempts to elaborate Hobbes's thesis that 'men are made fit for society by education'; for by 'education' Hobbes meant the learning which comes with social intercourse generally and not only at school.

4. *The Proper Extent of Authority*

THE makers of the covenant lay down their natural right in favour of the man or assembly chosen to rule over them. In the state of nature, each of them interprets the laws of nature for himself; but, as soon as there is a sovereign, it is for him (or them) alone to interpret those laws. This is the sense in which, for Hobbes, the law of nature and the civil law 'contain one another'. Subjects are committed by covenant, express or tacit, to accept the sovereign as sole interpreter of natural law, and are therefore bound to treat all his laws as if they were in keeping with that law. This does not mean that they are bound to believe that every civil law conforms with the law of nature, for that would be an absurd requirement. Men's 'interior cogitations' are not 'subject to command'. Besides, Hobbes appeals to men's reason, and does not ask them to believe what is against reason. When he says that 'natural law' and 'civil law' contain one another, he is not denying that men may have good grounds for believing that a civil law is contrary to the law of nature; he is saying that they ought always to do what they promised, which was to accept the sovereign's interpretation of natural law as alone valid. They must never use the law of nature as an excuse for not obeying the civil law. For them to make such use of it is unreasonable because it frustrates their purpose in instituting a sovereign or submitting to one. That purpose was to achieve peace, and the condition of peace is that there shall be only one interpreter, maker and enforcer of law. Thus, though the sovereign is obliged to observe the law of nature, the subject has no recourse to that law against the sovereign. Where his private judgment goes against the judgment of the sovereign, he must behave as if the sovereign were right and not he. It is reasonable for him to do this, no matter how strong his conviction that he is right and the sovereign is wrong.

The sovereign must have all the authority he needs to carry out his office, which is to maintain peace; and must therefore have a monopoly of it, for if anyone else has any, he may use it against the sovereign and so disturb the peace. Hobbes admits that rulers do not always have all the authority they need; for he says that 'a man to obtain a kingdom is sometimes content with less power than to the peace and defence of the commonwealth is necessarily required.'* But limitations extorted from a ruler or consented to by him because he does not foresee their dangerous consequences are not binding on him. Nothing, no matter how long established, binds him if it curtails the full reach of power needed to keep the peace. There must be no sharing of supreme authority among several, and no appeal to old customs or fundmanetal laws of the commonwealth against the sovereign. Of course, the sovereign must act through subordinates, who therefore have some authority; but they have it only as his agents. They have only the authority he chooses to give them for as long as he chooses that they shall have it.

Since all authority belongs to the sovereign, there can be no spiritual authority, no church, independent of him. State and church are but one community, and a community is made one by having one sovereign, one man or assembly by whom or in whose name or by whose permission all authority is exercised inside it. Hobbes notices that only among Christians is a distinction made between church and state, and says 'a church . . . is the same thing with a civil commonwealth, consisting of Christian men; and is called a *civil state*, for that the subjects of it are *men*, and a *church*, for that the subjects thereof are Christians. Temporal and spiritual government are but two words brought into the world to make men see double, and mistake their lawful sovereign.'†

* *Leviathan*. Ch. xxix, p. 285. † *Leviathan*. Ch. xxxix, p. 330.

Though men's 'interior cogitations' are not 'subject to command', their beliefs are affected by what is taught and said around them, and their actions proceed from their beliefs as well as their desires. Therefore the sovereign, if he is to maintain the peace, must have authority to forbid the teaching and publishing of dangerous beliefs and to require the teaching of beliefs conducive to order, and it is for him alone or those authorized by him to decide what those beliefs are. No subject has a right, for conscience sake, to publish beliefs proscribed by the sovereign, for a man's conscience is his private judgment, and he is bound by the covenant not to set his judgment above that of the sovereign. Though he cannot at the bidding of the sovereign cease to believe what he believes, he can and ought to refrain from publishing his beliefs and seeking to convert others to them.

Property is the creature of law, which is the command of the sovereign. Therefore subjects have no rights of property which the sovereign, as the sole legislator and enforcer of law, may not touch. Subjects are obliged to pay such taxes as the sovereign demands of them, for he cannot exercise his office without expense, and he must decide what expense is necessary and how it is to be met.

Thus Hobbes demolishes in turn all the arguments put forward to limit the sovereign's authority: that there is a spiritual power independent of him, that there are fundamental laws regulating the use of power by which he is bound, that his subjects have a right to disobey him for conscience sake, and that they have rights of property which he cannot touch except with their express consent. No one before him ever made so elaborate and uncompromising a case for absolute government. When Henry VIII broke with Rome, there were lawyers ready to argue that he was the supreme head of church and state, but they rested their case largely on tradition or what they took to be such; they did not argue that all authority in the kingdom belonged properly to one person to be exercised by him and his agents or with his permission. Hobbes claimed for the sovereign, for one man or one assembly, an authority which the royalists did not claim for Charles I nor the parliamentarians for parliament.

Even Bodin, who argued that in every commonwealth the sole right to make and enforce law belongs to one man or body to be exercised in person or through delegates, and who claimed this right in France for the king, denied that the king of France could take from his subjects any part of their property without their consent; and by their consent he meant nothing less than the vote of the Estates. And Bodin, like the other royalists in France, writing in a Catholic country, could not say that in every Christian commonwealth church and state are, or ought to be, one.

Hobbes allows a right of resistance in only one case. Where the sovereign seeks to kill, wound or imprison a subject, the subject is not obliged to suffer meekly; he has the right to resist. The subject submitted to the sovereign (or took part in instituting a sovereign if there was not one already) to get security, and it is therefore against reason that he should not resist when the sovereign seeks to deprive him of it. Moreover, men are so made that they always act for their own advantage. Therefore, when resistance is clearly to his advantage, a man will resist, whether or not he has undertaken not to. He is not obliged to do what he cannot do and he cannot refrain from resistance where a grave evil threatens him unless he believes that resistance is hopeless. The right of resistance is thus confined by Hobbes to the right of self-defence. No man may resist the sovereign to defend other men or for the sake of a law higher than the sovereign's. Obedience is obligatory except where, on psychological grounds, it is impossible, and there must be no disobedience for conscience sake, in defence of a principle. And this right of self-defence in no way abridges the right of the sovereign to kill, wound or imprison a subject who has deserved punishment, nor the obligation of other subjects to assist the sovereign in carrying out his sentence. It is not a right dangerous to peace, for the man who exercises it stands alone against the sovereign. The man who threatens the peace is not the one who resists for dear life's sake or who by his crimes puts himself in a position where a desperate course is the least unsafe open to him; it is the man who challenges the sovereign on principle and has a cause which he expects other men to join.

Writing when he did, Hobbes could not (and perhaps did not wish to) deny that there is a law of God higher than human law. He had therefore to reconcile this doctrine, that there is a divine law higher than the human, with his account of sovereignty. The content of God's law is either discovered by reflection on what is needed to secure peace among men, the assumption being that God desires their peace, or else God makes it known to particular men to whom he speaks in person. God's law is either discovered by reason or else is given in revelation. As discovered by reason it is the law of nature; and we have seen already how Hobbes, without denying that divine law is higher than human, contrives to argue that subjects may not appeal to the law of nature to justify disobedience to the sovereign. The reflection on what is needed to secure peace which brings men to know the law of nature also teaches them that they cannot have peace unless they agree on a single interpreter of that law, unless they behave on the assumption that the law is whatever he says it is. Since they owe it to God to obey his law, they also owe it to him to keep the agreement which makes it possible for them to obey it. They obey God when they obey the sovereign. If the sovereign misinterprets God's law, he is responsible to God alone for his act; for, if he were responsible to his subjects, they would have retained their right to interpret God's law, a right which they had to abandon in order to fulfil that law, in order to get peace.

What of God's law made known by revelation? Only those to whom God has actually spoken can know that he has done so. Others can but take them on trust. But those who claim that God has spoken to them contradict and accuse one another. Therefore some of their claims must be false; some of them must be false prophets. We, to whom God has not spoken, cannot know for certain which are the true prophets. If each of us decides for himself, it is unlikely that we shall come to the same decisions. We are therefore unlikely to agree about what is the revealed law of God. And if we disagree, the disagreement may be dangerous to peace. Just as our safety requires that there shall be only one authorized interpreter of the law of nature, so it requires that there shall be only one person to decide what is the revealed law of God; and this person must be the same as the authorized interpreter of the law of nature. He must be the sovereign.

Here again Hobbes takes care not to suggest that subjects are obliged to believe what the sovereign tells them to. Their beliefs are out of his immediate reach, and he can affect them only by deciding what may or may not be taught or published. Just as a subject may have good grounds for believing that civil law is contrary to the law of nature, so he may have good grounds for believing that a prophet declared to be false (or true) by the sovereign is not what the sovereign declares him to be. In that case, he must keep his belief to himself; for this he can do, even though he cannot divest himself of the belief at the sovereign's bidding.

But what of the man to whom God has spoken? If God has commanded him to do what the sovereign forbids, must he obey God or the sovereign? Clearly, he must obey God, and in so doing must disobey the sovereign; and Hobbes does not deny that he must. He is one of the elect of a God whose power is incomparably greater than the sovereign's; if he were to obey the sovereign rather than God, he would incur a greater evil in order to avert a lesser one, which is unreasonable. Indeed, according to Hobbes, it is something which a man cannot do if he sees clearly what he is doing. But this right of disobedience, confined as Hobbes confines it, is even less dangerous to the peace than the right of self-defence. For those to whom God has spoken are few in number, and the others do not know who they are. What is dangerous is that those to whom God has not spoken (who are the vast majority) should prefer the word of men whom they take to be true prophets to the word of him who by right has command over them. Such men say they put God above their sovereign, but in fact they put above him other men whose claim to speak in God's name must always be doubtful.*

* If we take Hobbes literally, it would seem to follow that the very existence of God – or at least of a God worth taking account of – is doubtful to all but a few. Reason without revelation, says Hobbes, assures us only that there is a 'first mover' or 'first cause' and tells us nothing of its attributes. But if we know nothing about this cause except that it is the first, why should we take greater account of it than of the

This is an extreme but clear position put with great force. Yet Hobbes, in the course of his argument, sometimes retreats from this position. And it is only to be expected that he should. He is addressing a Christian public, and therefore (whatever his private beliefs) cannot put Christianity on a level with other revealed religions. Moreover, he appeals to the Scriptures to support his arguments, and though he strikes hard at those who use them to set limits on sovereign power, he also makes concessions without being aware that he does so. The third and fourth parts of *Leviathan*, which are almost half the book, are largely taken up with ingenious attempts to use the Scriptures to confute those who, in Hobbes's opinion, have misused them.

For example, the Bible had long been used, and was still used in Hobbes's day, to claim for the church an authority independent of the state; to claim for it something more than a right to teach. Christians, it was said, owe obedience to the church as well as to the state. This Hobbes wanted to deny, and he was not content to use the general arguments we have already considered. He also, and at great length, appealed to the Scriptures. He denied that Christ had ever claimed for himself or had granted to the apostles a right of command in this world. Those teaching in the name of the Christ who said *My Kingdom is not of this World*, have no authority from him to deny that the right of command belongs only to the sovereign. But Hobbes, in the course of his elaborate attempt to prove that Christ never gave to the apostles and their successors any right of command, admits that he gave them authority to teach. And, since he is appealing to Scripture to support the

---

hundred and first? Hobbes says of this first cause that it is 'what men mean by the name of God', but he is mistaken; for by God they mean someone they stand in awe of, someone to rouse their fears and hopes. If reason cannot assure them that there is such a God, then their belief in him, if it is not sheer fantasy, must be grounded in revelation. Thus only the few to whom God has spoken can know that he exists; others can only believe that he does. But this, though it follows from what Hobbes says about reason and revelation as sources of knowledge, is not a conclusion he actually reaches. Ordinarily, he takes it for granted that reason assures men that there is an Omnipotent and Omniscient Being concerned for their welfare. For example, he nowhere suggests that men owe to revelation their belief that the laws of nature are commands of God.

claims he makes for the sovereign, he refrains from reminding the reader that the appeal is valid only because the sovereign has ruled that Scripture is the word of God. He tacitly concedes that men to whom God has not spoken may have authority from God alone to teach his word.

If the sovereign forbids them to teach, what ought they to do? Hobbes should say that they ought to obey the sovereign, unless Christ has actually spoken to them, which very few who teach in his name claim that he has done; but he does not say this. He admits that 'some have received a calling to preach and profess the Kingdom of Christ openly'; and though he begins by suggesting that they are only 'those that conversed with him, and saw him after he was risen', the only true martyrs who bear witness to what they have seen and not to what others have reported, he later speaks of martyrs of the 'second degree' who have 'a warrant to preach Christ come in the flesh.'* These martyrs get their authority from Christ indirectly, and are sent, so Hobbes says, 'to the conversion of infidels', but he does not, at this point of the argument, suggest that the authority they get from Christ does not suffice unless it is confirmed by the sovereign, presumably himself an infidel. How could he, writing for a public who believed that there were truths necessary to salvation and that the mission of the church was to teach them?

Hobbes does not claim infallibility for the sovereign; his argument does not imply that, where sovereign and subject differ, the sovereign must be right. He admits that a subject cannot get rid of his beliefs merely because the sovereign has condemned them. If, then, one or other of his beliefs requires him to do what the sovereign forbids, why should he not do it? Hobbes's answer, briefly, is this: Because by such action he threatens the peace, which is his greatest good in the world. If the subject believes in God, he has better reasons for believing that God requires him to keep the peace than that he requires him to act on a belief which the sovereign, the keeper of the peace, has condemned; he has better reasons for believing this unless God has actually spoken to him and

* *Leviathan.* Ch. XLII, pp. 344 and 346.

required him to act on the condemned belief. Any man to whom God has not spoken has better grounds for believing that the laws of nature (which can only be safely obeyed where there is a sovereign to enforce them) are commands of God than that any 'revealed truth' which requires him to disobey his sovereign is what those who teach it say it is: the authentic word of God.

The flaw in this argument is that, if (as Hobbes says) unaided reason can assure men of no more than that there is a 'first mover' or 'cause' of all things, it does not assure them that there is a God who requires them to observe the laws of nature. This assurance must come to them from the other source of knowledge about God, from revelation, which also assures them that God requires other, more specific, things of them. Thus, they have no better reason for believing that God requires them to observe the laws of nature than that he requires these other specific things, things which (since God requires them) are presumably in keeping with the laws of nature. Subjects who then obey God's specific commands disobey, not the laws of nature, but the sovereign who forbids what God commands. Their being bound to accept the sovereign as the only interpreter of the laws of nature makes no difference here. For the disobedient subject will not justify his disobedience on the ground that what the sovereign requires of him is contrary to the law of nature; he will justify it on the ground that it is contrary to the specific commands of God.

Despite Hobbes's bold attempt to prove the contrary, his political philosophy is incompatible with any kind of faith in God except a kind which is rarely found. It is possible to believe in a God who, having some of the properties usually attributed to him, lacks others; a God who is omnipotent (or at least incomparably more powerful than his creatures) but also quite indifferent to them. Some of the deists of the eighteenth century believed in such a God. Again, it is possible to believe that God requires no more of man than that he should keep the peace. If God is indifferent to man or requires so little of him, then Hobbes's philosophy is compatible with faith in God. But then few men have believed in such a God,

and faith would not be what it has been, and still is to those
that have it, if there were no more to it than that.

No part of Hobbes's philosophy has been more strongly
attacked than the doctrine that every man always acts from
hope of advantage to himself. Yet Hume, who rejected the
doctrine on general grounds, thought it an assumption
sufficient to explain man's political behaviour. Enlightened
self-interest suffices, he thought, to explain how men come
to have governments and why they obey them. Yet Hume
was not a believer in absolute government. It is worth noticing
that, without troubling to contest the doctrine of universal
egoism, we can dispute Hobbes's argument that rational
creatures for whom peace is the highest good ought in their
own interest to be under absolute government, and also his
tacit assumption that to rational egoists peace is the highest
good.

Why, we may ask, should the subject have a right to resist
the sovereign only when the sovereign seeks to kill, wound
or imprison him? Why should he not have this right whenever, taking the long view, he has reasonable grounds for
believing that he has less to lose by resisting than by not
doing so? If the sovereign is attacking others and not him,
may he not have good grounds for believing that he will be
attacked later? And may it not be less dangerous for him to
resist the sovereign now than it would be to do so later?
Even if we allow no more to complete egoists than a right of
self-defence, we must not interpret that right as narrowly
as Hobbes does. For, if we do, we either contradict ourselves
or make a false statement about the facts. We either forbid
men to do what, taking the long view, is to their advantage,
which is absurd, given that they are complete egoists and
cannot be obliged to refrain from doing it; or we assert that
it is never to their advantage, taking the long view, to resist
except when they are themselves attacked, which is not true.

Hobbes sets before his readers a false dilemma: he speaks
as if there were no alternative to the sort of polity he recommends except the total anarchy of the war of all against all.
But, even if it were true (and it is not obviously so), that
sovereignty, as he defines it, reduces the risk of anarchy more

than it can be reduced any other way, it still would not follow
that men ought to prefer it to a system where authority is
divided or subjects are inclined to resist their rulers when
they find them oppressive. It does not follow even if anarchy
is held to be worse than the worst government. The risk of
anarchy where authority is divided and subjects are jealous
of their 'rights' may be much smaller than the risk of oppression where authority all belongs to one man or body of men;
and it may be reasonable to take the smaller risk, even
though anarchy is worse than oppression. Just as it may be
reasonable for a man to risk death to avoid enslavement,
even though death seems to him the greater of the two
evils.

Hobbes had only to reflect on the condition of England
during the civil war to see that resistance does not lead to
complete anarchy. Men do not cease to be law-abiding merely
because they take up arms against their rulers. War, even
civil war, is a social activity; the opposing armies, if they are
to be formidable to one another, must be disciplined, and
there must be order in the territories they control if the armies
are to get their supplies and remain formidable. All rules are
not broken when authority is defied. The war of all against all
is an extreme condition which is never reached, except by
small numbers of men for short periods of time; for it is
intolerable to creatures whose need of one another is so strong
that they dare not be aggressors except in company. No doubt,
if men accustomed to society (and virtually all men are so)
were thrown into a condition where no man could trust any
other and no collaboration was possible, that condition would
be worse than the worst of oppressive governments. But the
chances of their being thrown into it if they resist their rulers
are small indeed.

If men are as Hobbes describes them, it is difficult to see
why the fear of death should be so powerful a motive with
them or peace worth preserving at so great a price. For men,
Hobbes tells us, are full of pride. They desire to be important
in the eyes of other men and their own. That being so, fear
of disgrace or insignificance must often be stronger in them
than fear of death or wounds or imprisonment. It is then more

their interest to preserve their reputations (or even their self-respect) than their lives or their health or their freedom of movement. It may be that men come to desire power as a means to other things, and learn to care for reputation and superiority as they compete for power; it may be that the passions which overcome the fear of death in them arise as effects of what they do to provide for natural appetites which must be satisfied if they are to keep alive and healthy. But, once they have these passions, no matter how they come by them, they have needs which it is just as reasonable to strive to satisfy as the appetites necessary to life and health. At least Hobbes must think so, for he asks no more of men than that they should consult their interests; that they should make up their minds what is really precious to them and how it is to be obtained. If then, in order to obtain it, they demand more of their rulers than the maintenance of order, why should they not do so? If the security they look for is not mere safety as Hobbes conceives of it but the opportunity to live worthily (whatever their standards of worth may be), and if their deepest anxieties are not about providing for their future appetites but about their 'place in the world', then they may have good reason to disturb the peace at great risk to themselves in the hope of getting what they want. In the Kingdom of the Proud, safety cannot be enough.

Hobbes stimulates more than he persuades. The most disputatious of political philosophers, he continually invites us to argument. By his very manner, he puts us on our guard against him. But he also raises, sharply and vividly, issues of enduring interest, philosophical and practical.

LEVIATHAN
OR
THE MATTER, FORM AND POWER
OF A
COMMONWEALTH
ECCLESIASTICAL & CIVIL

THE INTRODUCTION

NATURE, the art whereby God hath made and governs the world, is by the *art* of man, as in many other things, so in this also imitated, that it can make an artificial animal. For seeing life is but a motion of limbs, the beginning whereof is in some principal part within; why may we not say, that all *automata* (engines that move themselves by springs and wheels as doth a watch) have an artificial life? For what is the *heart*, but a *spring*; and the *nerves*, but so many *strings*; and the *joints*, but so many *wheels*, giving motion to the whole body, such as was intended by the artificer? *Art* goes yet further, imitating that rational and most excellent work of nature, *man*. For by art is created that great LEVIATHAN called a COMMONWEALTH, or STATE, in Latin CIVITAS, which is but an artificial man; though of greater stature and strength than the natural, for whose protection and defence it was intended; and in which the *sovereignty* is an artificial *soul*, as giving life and motion to the whole body; the *magistrates*, and other *officers* of judicature and execution, artificial *joints*; *reward* and *punishment*, by which fastened to the seat of the sovereignty every joint and member is moved to perform his duty, are the *nerves*, that do the same in the body natural; the *wealth* and *riches* of all the particular members, are the *strength*; *salus populi*, the *people's safety*, its *business*; *counsellors*, by whom all things needful for it to know are suggested unto it, are the *memory*; *equity*, and *laws*, an artificial *reason* and *will*; *concord, health*; *sedition, sickness*; and *civil war, death*. Lastly, the *pacts* and *covenants*, by which the parts of this body politic were at first made, set together, and united, resemble that *fiat*, or the *let us make man*, pronounced by God in the creation.

To describe the nature of this artificial man, I will consider.

First, the *matter* thereof, and the *artificer*; both which is *man*.

Secondly, *how*, and by what *covenants* it is made; what are the *rights* and just *power* or *authority* of a *sovereign*; and what it is that *preserveth* or *dissolveth* it.

Thirdly, what is a *Christian commonwealth*.

Lastly, what is the *kingdom of darkness*.

Concerning the first, there is a saying much usurped of late, that *wisdom* is acquired, not by reading of *books*, but of *men*.

Consequently whereunto, those persons, that for the most part can give no other proof of being wise, take great delight to show what they think they have read in men, by uncharitable censures of one another behind their backs. But there is another saying not of late understood, by which they might learn truly to read one another, if they would take the pains; that is, *nosce teipsum, read thyself*: which was not meant, as it is now used, to countenance, either the barbarous state of men in power, towards their inferiors; or to encourage men of low degree, to a saucy behaviour towards their betters; but to teach us, that for the similitude of the thoughts and passions of one man, to the thoughts and passions of another, whosoever looketh into himself, and considereth what he doth, when he does *think, opine, reason, hope, fear,* &c. and upon what grounds; he shall thereby read and know, what are the thoughts and passions of all other men upon the like occasions. I say the similitude of *passions*, which are the same in all men, *desire, fear, hope,* &c.; not the similitude of the *objects* of the passions, which are the things *desired, feared, hoped,* &c.: for these the constitution individual, and particular education, do so vary, and they are so easy to be kept from our knowledge, that the characters of man's heart, blotted and confounded as they are with dissembling, lying, counterfeiting, and erroneous doctrines, are legible only to him that searcheth hearts. And though by men's actions we do discover their design sometimes; yet to do it without comparing them with our own, and distinguishing all circumstances, by which the case may come to be altered, is to decypher without a key, and be for the most part deceived, by too much trust, or by too much diffidence; as he that reads, is himself a good or evil man.

But let one man read another by his actions never so perfectly, it serves him only with his acquaintance, which are but few. He that is to govern a whole nation, must read in himself, not this or that particular man; but mankind: which though it be hard to do, harder than to learn any language or science; yet when I shall have set down my own reading orderly, and perspicuously, the pains left another, will be only to consider, if he also find not the same in himself. For this kind of doctrine admitteth no other demonstration.

Part One

OF MAN

CHAPTER I

Of Sense

CONCERNING the thoughts of man, I will consider them first singly, and afterwards in train, or dependence upon one another. Singly, they are every one a *representation* or *appearance*, of some quality, or other accident of a body without us, which is commonly called an *object*. Which object worketh on the eyes, ears, and other parts of a man's body; and by diversity of working, produceth diversity of appearances.

The original of them all, is that which we call SENSE, for there is no conception in a man's mind, which hath not at first, totally, or by parts, been begotten upon the organs of sense. The rest are derived from that original.

To know the natural cause of sense, is not very necessary to the business now in hand; and I have elsewhere written of the same at large. Nevertheless, to fill each part of my present method, I will briefly deliver the same in this place.

The cause of sense, is the external body, or object, which presseth the organ proper to each sense, either immediately, as in the taste and touch; or mediately, as in seeing, hearing, and smelling; which pressure, by the mediation of the nerves, and other strings and membranes of the body, continued inwards to the brain and heart, causeth there a resistance, or counter-pressure, or endeavour of the heart to deliver itself, which endeavour, because *outward*, seemeth to be some matter without. And this *seeming*, or *fancy*, is that which men call *sense*; and consisteth, as to the eye, in a *light*, or *colour figured*; to the ear, in a *sound*; to the nostril, in an *odour*; to the tongue and palate, in a *savour*; and to the rest of the body, in *heat*, *cold*, *hardness*, *softness*, and such other qualities as we discern by *feeling.* All which qualities, called *sensible,* are in the object, that causeth them, but so many several motions of the matter, by which it presseth our organs diversely. Neither in us that are pressed, are they any thing else, but divers motions; for motion produceth nothing but motion. But their appearance to us is fancy, the same waking, that dreaming. And as pressing, rubbing, or striking the eye, makes us fancy a light; and pressing the ear, produceth a din; so do the bodies also we see, or hear, produce the same by their strong, though unobserved action. For if those colours and sounds were in the bodies, or objects that cause them, they could not be severed from them, as by glasses, and in echoes by reflection, we see they are; where we know the thing we see is in one place, the appearance in another. And though at some certain distance, the real and very object seem invested with the fancy it begets in us; yet still the object is one thing, the image or fancy is another. So that sense, in all cases, is nothing else but original fancy, caused, as I have said, by the pressure, that is, by the motion, of external things upon our eyes, ears, and other organs thereunto ordained.

But the philosophy-schools, through all the universities of Christendom, grounded upon certain texts of Aristotle, teach another doctrine, and say, for the cause of *vision,* that the thing seen, sendeth forth on every side a *visible species,* in English, a *visible show, apparition,* or *aspect,* or *a being seen*; the receiving whereof into the eye, is *seeing.* And for the cause of *hearing,* that the thing heard, sendeth forth an *audible species,* that is an *audible aspect,* or *audible being seen*; which entering at the ear, maketh *hearing.* Nay, for the cause of *understanding* also, they say the thing understood, sendeth forth an *intelligible species,* that is, an *intelligible being seen*; which, coming into the understanding, makes us understand. I say not this, as disproving the use of universities; but because I am to speak hereafter of their office in a commonwealth, I must let you see on all occasions by the way, what things would be amended in them; amongst which the frequency of insignificant speech is one.

CHAPTER II

Of Imagination

THAT when a thing lies still, unless somewhat else stir it, it will lie still for ever, is a truth that no man doubts of. But that when a thing is in motion, it will eternally be in motion, unless somewhat else stay it, though the reason be the same, namely, that nothing can change itself, is not so easily assented to. For men measure, not only other men, but all other things, by themselves; and because they find themselves subject after motion to pain, and lassitude, think every thing else grows weary of motion, and seeks repose of its own accord; little considering, whether it be not some other motion, wherein that desire of rest they find in themselves, consisteth. From hence it is, that the schools say, heavy bodies fall downwards, out of an appetite to rest, and to conserve their nature in that place which is most proper for them; ascribing appetite, and knowledge of what is good for their conservation, which is more than man has, to things inanimate, absurdly.

When a body is once in motion, it moveth, unless something else hinder it, eternally; and whatsoever hindreth it, cannot in an instant, but in time, and by degrees, quite extinguish it; and as we see in the water, though the wind cease, the waves give not over rolling for a long time after: so also it happeneth in that motion, which is made in the internal parts of a man, then, when he sees, dreams, &c. For after the object is removed, or the eye shut, we still retain an image of the thing seen, though more obscure than when we see it. And this is it, the Latins call *imagination*, from the image made in seeing; and apply the same, though improperly, to all the other senses. But the Greeks call it *fancy*; which signifies *appearance*, and is as proper to one sense, as to another. IMAGINATION therefore is nothing but *decaying sense*; and is found in men, and many other living creatures, as well sleeping, as waking.

The decay of sense in men waking, is not the decay of the

original imagination.

motion made in sense; but an obscuring of it, in such manner as the light of the sun obscureth the light of the stars; which stars do no less exercise their virtue, by which they are visible, in the day than in the night. But because amongst many strokes, which our eyes, ears, and other organs receive from external bodies, the predominant only is sensible; therefore, the light of the sun being predominant, we are not affected with the action of the stars. And any object being removed from our eyes, though the impression it made in us remain, yet other objects more present succeeding, and working on us, the imagination of the past is obscured, and made weak, as the voice of a man is in the noise of the day. From whence it followeth, that the longer the time is, after the sight or sense of any object, the weaker is the imagination. For the continual change of man's body destroys in time the parts which in sense were moved: so that distance of time, and of place, hath one and the same effect in us. For as at a great distance of place, that which we look at appears dim, and without distinction of the smaller parts; and as voices grow weak, and inarticulate; so also, after great distance of time, our imagination of the past is weak; and we lose, for example, of cities we have seen, many particular streets, and of actions, many particular circumstances. This *decaying sense*, when we would express the thing itself, I mean *fancy* itself, we call *imagination*, as I said before: but when we would express the decay, and signify that the sense is fading, old, and past, it is called *memory*. So that imagination and memory are but one thing, which for divers considerations hath divers names.

Much memory, or memory of many things, is called *experience*. Again, imagination being only of those things which have been formerly perceived by sense, either all at once, or by parts at several times; the former, which is the imagining the whole object as it was presented to the sense, is *simple* imagination, as when one imagineth a man, or horse, which he hath seen before. The other is *compounded*; as when, from the sight of a man at one time, and of a horse at another, we conceive in our mind a Centaur. So when a man compoundeth the image of his own person with the image of the actions of another man, as when a man imagines himself a Hercules or an Alexander, which happeneth often to them that are much taken with reading of romances, it is a compound imagination, and properly but a fiction of the mind. There be also other imaginations that rise in men, though waking, from the great impression made in sense: as from gazing upon the sun, the impression leaves an image of the sun before our eyes a long time after; and from being long and vehemently attent upon geometrical figures, a man shall in the dark, though awake, have the images of lines and angles before his eyes; which kind of fancy hath no particular name, as being a thing that doth not commonly fall into men's discourse.

The imaginations of them that sleep are those we call *dreams*. And these also, as all other imaginations, have been before, either totally or by parcels, in the sense. And because in sense, the brain and nerves, which are the necessary organs of sense, are so benumbed in sleep, as not easily to be moved by the action of external objects, there can happen in sleep no imagination, and therefore no dream, but what proceeds from the agitation of the inward parts of man's body; which inward parts, for the connexion they have with the brain, and other organs, when they be distempered, do keep the same in motion; whereby the imaginations there formerly made, appear as if a man were waking; saving that the organs of sense being now benumbed, so as there is no new object, which can master and obscure them with a more vigorous impression, a dream must needs be more clear, in this silence of sense, than our waking thoughts. And hence it cometh to pass, that it is a hard matter, and by many thought impossible, to distinguish exactly between sense and dreaming. For my part, when I consider that in dreams I do not often nor constantly think of the same persons, places, objects, and actions, that I do waking; nor remember so long a train of coherent thoughts, dreaming, as at other times; and because waking I often observe the absurdity of dreams, but never dream of the absurdities of my waking thoughts; I am well satisfied, that being awake, I know I dream not, though when I dream I think myself awake.

And seeing dreams are caused by the distemper of some of the inward parts of the body, divers distempers must needs cause different dreams. And hence it is that lying cold breedeth dreams of fear, and raiseth the thought and image of some fearful object, the motion from the brain to the inner parts and from the inner parts to the brain being reciprocal; and that as anger causeth heat in some parts of the body when we are awake, so when we sleep the overheating of the same parts causeth anger, and raiseth up in the brain the imagination of an enemy. In the same manner, as natural kindness, when we are awake, causeth desire, and desire makes heat in certain other parts of the body; so also too much heat in those parts, while we sleep, raiseth in the brain an imagination of some kindness shown. In sum, our dreams are the reverse of our waking imaginations; the motion when we are awake beginning at one end, and when we dream at another.

The most difficult discerning of a man's dream, from his waking thoughts, is then, when by some accident we observe not that we have slept: which is easy to happen to a man full of fearful thoughts, and whose conscience is much troubled; and that sleepeth, without the circumstances of going to bed or putting off his clothes, as one that noddeth in a chair. For he that taketh pains, and industriously lays himself to sleep, in case any uncouth and exorbitant fancy come unto him, cannot easily think it other than a dream. We read of Marcus Brutus, (one that had his life given him by Julius Caesar, and was also his favourite, and notwithstanding murdered him), how at Philippi, the night before he gave battle to Augustus Caesar, he saw a fearful apparition, which is commonly related by historians as a vision; but considering the circumstances, one may easily judge to have been but a short dream. For sitting in his tent, pensive and troubled with the horror of his rash act, it was not hard for him, slumbering in the cold, to dream of that which most affrighted him; which fear, as by degrees it made him wake, so also it must needs make the apparition by degrees to vanish; and having no assurance that he slept, he could have no cause to think it a dream, or any thing but a vision. And this is no very rare accident; for even they that be perfectly awake, if they be timorous and superstitious, possessed with fearful tales, and alone in the dark, are subject to the like fancies, and believe they see spirits and dead men's ghosts walking in churchyards; whereas it is either their fancy only, or else the knavery of such persons as make use of such superstitious fear, to pass disguised in the night, to places they would not be known to haunt.

From this ignorance of how to distinguish dreams, and other strong fancies, from vision and sense, did arise the greatest part of the religion of the Gentiles in time past, that worshipped satyrs, fawns, nymphs, and the like; and now-a-days the opinion that rude people have of fairies, ghosts, and goblins, and of the power of witches. For as for witches, I think not that their witchcraft is any real power; but yet that they are justly punished, for the false belief they have that they can do such mischief, joined with their purpose to do it if they can; their trade being nearer to a new religion than to a craft or science. And for fairies, and walking ghosts, the opinion of them has, I think, been on purpose either taught or not confuted, to keep in credit the use of exorcism, of crosses, of holy water, and other such inventions of ghostly men. Nevertheless, there is no doubt, but God can make unnatural apparitions; but that he does it so often, as men need to fear such things, more than they fear the stay or change of the course of nature, which he also can stay, and change, is no point of Christian faith. But evil men under pretext that God can do any thing, are so bold as to say any thing when it serves their turn, though they think it untrue; it is the part of a wise man, to believe them no farther, than right season makes that which they say, appear credible. If this superstitious fear of spirits were taken away, and with it, prognostics from dreams, false prophecies, and many other things depending thereon, by which crafty ambitious persons abuse the simple people, men would be much more fitted than they are for civil obedience.

And this ought to be the work of the schools: but they rather nourish such doctrine. For, not knowing what imagination or the senses are, what they receive, they teach: some saying, that imaginations rise of themselves, and have no cause; others, that they rise most commonly from the will;

and that good thoughts are blown (inspired) into a man by God, and evil thoughts by the Devil; or that good thoughts are poured (infused) into a man by God, and evil ones by the Devil. Some say the senses receive the species of things, and deliver them to the common sense; and the common sense delivers them over to the fancy, and the fancy to the memory, and the memory to the judgment, like handing of things from one to another, with many words making nothing understood.

The imagination that is raised in man, or any other creature indued with the faculty of imagining, by words, or other voluntary signs, is that we generally call *understanding*; and is common to man and beast. For a dog by custom will understand the call, or the rating of his master; and so will many other beasts. That understanding which is peculiar to man, is the understanding not only his will, but his conceptions and thoughts, by the sequel and contexture of the names of things into affirmations, negations, and other forms of speech; and of this kind of understanding I shall speak hereafter.

CHAPTER III

Of the Consequence or Train of Imaginations

By *Consequence*, or TRAIN of thoughts, I understand that succession of one thought to another, which is called, to distinguish it from discourse in words, *mental discourse*.

When a man thinketh on any thing whatsoever, his next thought after, is not altogether so casual as it seems to be. Not every thought to every thought succeeds indifferently. But as we have no imagination, whereof we have not formerly had sense, in whole, or in parts; so we have no transition from one imagination to another, whereof we never had the like before in our senses. The reason whereof is this. All fancies are motions within us, relics of those made in the sense: and those motions that immediately succeeded one another in the sense, continue also together after sense: insomuch as the former coming again to take place, and be predominant, the latter followeth, by coherence of the matter moved, in such manner, as water upon a plane table is drawn which way any one part of it is guided by the finger. But because in sense, to one and the same thing perceived, sometimes one thing, sometimes another succeedeth, it comes to pass in time, that in the imagining of any thing, there is no certainty what we shall imagine next; only this is certain, it shall be something that succeeded the same before, at one time or another.

This train of thoughts, or mental discourse, is of two sorts. The first is *unguided, without design,* and inconstant; wherein there is no passionate thought, to govern and direct those that follow, to itself, as the end and scope of some desire, or other passion: in which case the thoughts are said to wander, and seem impertinent one to another, as in a dream. Such are commonly the thoughts of men, that are not only without company, but also without care of any thing; though even then their thoughts are as busy as at other times, but without harmony; as the sound which a lute out of tune would yield to any man; or in tune, to one that could not play. And yet in this wild ranging of the mind, a man may oft-times perceive the way of it, and the dependance of one thought upon another. For in a discourse of our present civil war, what could seem more impertinent, than to ask, as one did, what was the value of a Roman penny? Yet the coherence to me was manifest enough. For the thought of the war, introduced the thought of the delivering up the king to his enemies; the thought of that, brought in the thought of the delivering up of Christ; and that again the thought of the thirty pence, which was the price of that treason; and thence easily followed that malicious question, and all this in a moment of time; for thought is quick.

The second is more constant; as being *regulated* by some desire, and design. For the impression made by such things as we desire, or fear, is strong, and permanent, or, if it cease for a time, of quick return: so strong it is sometimes, as to hinder and break our sleep. From desire, ariseth the thought of some means we have seen produce the like of that which we aim at; and from the thought of that, the thought of means to that mean; and so continually, till we come to some beginning within our own power. And because the end, by the greatness of the impression, comes often to mind, in case our thoughts begin to wander, they are quickly again reduced into the way: which observed by one of the seven wise men, made him give men this precept, which is now worn out, *Respice finem*; that is to say, in all your actions, look often upon what you would have, as the thing that directs all your thoughts in the way to attain it.

The train of regulated thoughts is of two kinds; one, when of an effect imagined we seek the causes, or means that produce it: and this is common to man and beast. The other is, when imagining any thing whatsoever, we seek all the possible effects, that can by it be produced; that is to say, we imagine what we can do with it, when we have it. Of which I have not at any time seen any sign, but in man only; for this is a curiosity hardly incident to the nature of any living creature that has no other passion but sensual, such as are hunger, thirst, lust, and anger. In sum, the discourse of the mind, when it is governed by design, is nothing but *seeking*, or the faculty of invention, which the Latins called *sagacitas*, and *solertia*; a hunting out of the causes, of some effect, present or past; or of the effects, of some present or past cause. Sometimes a man seeks what he hath lost; and from that place, and time, wherein he misses it, his mind runs back, from place to place, and time to time, to find where, and when he had it; that is to say, to find some certain, and limited time and place, in which to begin a method of seeking. Again, from thence, his thoughts run over the same places and times, to find what action, or other occasion might make him lose it. This we call *remembrance*, or calling to mind: the Latins call it *reminiscentia*, as it were a *re-conning* of our former actions.

Sometimes a man knows a place determinate, within the compass whereof he is to seek; and then his thoughts run over all the parts thereof, in the same manner as one would sweep a room, to find a jewel; or as a spaniel ranges the field, till he find a scent; or as a man should run over the alphabet, to start a rhyme.

Sometimes a man desires to know the event of an action; and then he thinketh of some like action past, and the events thereof one after another; supposing like events will follow like actions. As he that foresees what will become of a criminal, re-cons what he has seen follow on the like crime before; having this order of thoughts, the crime, the officer, the prison, the judge, and the gallows. Which kind of thoughts, is called *foresight*, and *prudence*, or *providence*; and sometimes *wisdom*; though such conjecture, through the difficulty of observing all circumstances, be very fallacious. But this is certain; by how much one man has more experience of things past, than another, by so much also he is more prudent, and his expectations the seldomer fail him. The *present* only has a being in nature; things *past* have a being in the memory only, but things *to come* have no being at all; the *future* being but a fiction of the mind, applying the sequels of actions past, to the actions that are present; which with most certainty is done by him that has most experience, but not with certainty enough. And though it be called prudence, when the event answereth our expectation; yet in its own nature, it is but presumption. For the foresight of things to come, which is providence, belongs only to him by whose will they are to come. From him only, and supernaturally, proceeds prophecy. The best prophet naturally is the best guesser; and the best guesser, he that is most versed and studied in the matters he guesses at: for he hath most *signs* to guess by.

A *sign* is the evident antecedent of the consequent; and contrarily, the consequent of the antecedent, when the like consequences have been observed, before: and the oftener they have been observed, the less uncertain is the sign. And therefore he that has most experience in any kind of business, has most signs, whereby to guess at the future time; and consequently is the most prudent: and so much more prudent than he that is new in that kind of business, as not to be equalled by any advantage of natural and extemporary wit: though perhaps many young men think the contrary.

Nevertheless it is not prudence that distinguisheth man from beast. There be beasts, that at a year old observe more, and pursue that which is for their good, more prudently, than a child can do at ten.

As prudence is a *presumption* of the *future*, contracted from the *experience* of time *past*: so there is a presumption of things past taken from other things, not future, but past also. For he that hath seen by what courses and degrees a flourishing state hath first come into civil war, and then to ruin; upon the sight of the ruins of any other state, will guess, the like war, and the like courses have been there also. But this conjecture, has the same uncertainty almost with the conjecture of the future; both being grounded only upon experience.

There is no other act of man's mind, that I can remember, naturally planted in him, so as to need no other thing, to the exercise of it, but to be born a man, and live with the use of his five senses. Those other faculties, of which I shall speak by and by, and which seem proper to man only, are acquired and increased by study and industry; and of most men learned by instruction, and discipline; and proceed all from the invention of words, and speech. For besides sense, and thoughts, and the train of thoughts, the mind of man has no other motion; though by the help of speech, and method, the same faculties may be improved to such a height, as to distinguish men from all other living creatures.

Whatsoever we imagine is *finite*. Therefore there is no idea, or conception of any thing we call *infinite*. No man can have in his mind an image of infinite magnitude; nor conceive infinite swiftness, infinite time, or infinite force, or infinite power. When we say any thing is infinite, we signify only, that we are not able to conceive the ends, and bounds of the things named; having no conception of the thing, but of our own inability. And therefore the name of God is used, not to make us conceive him, for he is incomprehensible; and his greatness, and power are unconceivable; but that we may honour him. Also because, whatsoever, as I said before, we conceive, has been perceived first by sense, either all at once, or by parts; a man can have no thought, representing any thing, not subject to sense. No man therefore can conceive any thing, but he must conceive it in some place; and indued with some determinate magnitude; and which may be divided into parts; nor that any thing is all in this place, and all in another place at the same time; nor that two, or more things can be in one, and the same place at once: for none of these things ever have, nor can be incident to sense; but are absurd speeches, taken upon credit, without any signification at all from deceived philosophers, and deceived, or deceiving schoolmen.

CHAPTER IV

Of Speech

THE invention of *printing*, though ingenious, compared with the invention of *letters*, is no great matter. But who was the first that found the use of letters, is not known. He that first brought them into Greece, men say was Cadmus, the son of Agenor, king of Phoenicia. A profitable invention for continuing the memory of time past, and the conjunction of mankind, dispersed into so many, and distant regions of the earth; and withal difficult, as proceeding from a watchful observation of the divers motions of the tongue, palate, lips, and other organs of speech; whereby to make as many differences of characters, to remember them. But the most noble and profitable invention of all other, was that of SPEECH, consisting of *names* or *appellations*, and their connexion; whereby men register their thoughts; recall them when they are past; and also declare them one to another for mutual utility and conversation; without which, there had been amongst men, neither commonwealth, nor society, nor contract, nor peace, no more than amongst lions, bears, and wolves. The first author of *speech* was God himself, that instructed Adam how to name such creatures as he presented to his sight; for the Scripture goeth no further in this matter. But this was sufficient to direct him to add more names, as the experience and use of the creatures should give him occasion; and to join them in such manner by degrees, as to make himself understood; and so by succession of time, so much language might be gotten, as he had found use for; though not so copious, as an orator or philosopher has need of: for I do not find any thing in the Scripture, out of which, directly or by consequence, can be gathered, that Adam was taught the names of all figures, numbers, measures, colours, sounds, fancies, relations; much less the names of words and speech, as *general*, *special*, *affirmative*, *negative*, *interrogative*, *optative*, *infinitive*, all which are useful; and least of all, of *entity*, *intentionality*, *quiddity*, and other insignificant words of the school.

But all this language gotten, and augmented by Adam and his posterity, was again lost at the Tower of Babel, when, by the hand of God, every man was stricken, for his rebellion, with an oblivion of his former language. And being hereby forced to disperse themselves into several parts of the world, it must needs be, that the diversity of tongues that now is, proceeded by degrees from them, in such manner, as need, the mother of all inventions, taught them; and in tract of time grew everywhere more copious.

The general use of speech, is to transfer our mental discourse, into verbal; or the train of our thoughts, into a train of words; and that for two commodities, whereof one is the registering of the consequences of our thoughts; which being apt to slip out of our memory, and put us to a new labour, may again be recalled, by such words as they were marked by. So that the first use of names is to serve for *marks*, or *notes* of remembrance. Another is, when many use the same words, to signify, by their connexion and order, one to another, what they conceive, or think of each matter; and also what they desire, fear, or have any other passion for. And for this use they are called *signs*. Special uses of speech are these; first, to register, what by cogitation, we find to be the cause of any thing, present or past; and what we find things present or past may produce, or effect; which in sum, is acquiring of arts. Secondly, to show to others that knowledge which we have attained, which is, to counsel and teach one another. Thirdly, to make known to others our wills and purposes, that we may have the mutual help of one another. Fourthly, to please and delight ourselves and others, by playing with our words, for pleasure or ornament, innocently.

To these uses, there are also four correspondent abuses. First, when men register their thoughts wrong, by the inconstancy of the signification of their words; by which they register for their conception, that which they never conceived, and so deceive themselves. Secondly, when they use words metaphorically; that is, in other sense than that they are ordained for; and thereby deceive others. Thirdly, by words, when they declare that to be their will, which is not. Fourthly, when they use them to grieve one another; for seeing nature hath armed living creatures, some with teeth, some with horns, and some with hands, to grieve an enemy, it is but an abuse of speech, to grieve him with the tongue, unless it be one whom we are obliged to govern; and then it is not to grieve, but to correct and amend.

The manner how speech serveth to the remembrance of the consequence of causes and effects, consisteth in the imposing of *names*, and the *connexion* of them.

Of names, some are *proper*, and singular to one only thing, as *Peter, John, this man, this tree*; and some are *common* to many things, *man, horse, tree*; every of which, though but one name, is nevertheless the name of divers particular things; in respect of all which together, it is called an *universal*; there being nothing in the world universal but names; for the things named are every one of them individual and singular.

One universal name is imposed on many things, for their similitude in some quality, or other accident; and whereas a proper name bringeth to mind one thing only, universals recall any one of those many.

And of names universal, some are of more, and some of less extent; the larger comprehending the less large; and some again of equal extent, comprehending each other reciprocally. As for example: the name *body* is of larger signification than the word *man*, and comprehendeth it; and the names *man* and *rational*, are of equal extent, comprehending mutually one another. But here we must take notice, that by a name is not always understood, as in grammar, one only word; but sometimes, by circumlocution, many words together. For all these words, *he that in his actions observeth the laws of his country*, make but one name, equivalent to this one word, *just*.

By this imposition of names, some of larger, some of stricter signification, we turn the reckoning of the consequences of things imagined in the mind, into a reckoning of the consequences of appellations. For example: a man that hath no use of speech at all, such as is born and remains perfectly deaf and dumb, if he set before his eyes a triangle, and by it two right angles, such as are the corners of a square figure, he may, by meditation, compare and find, that the three angles of that triangle, are equal to those two right angles that stand by it. But if another triangle be shown him, different in shape from the former, he cannot know, without a new labour, whether the three angles of that also be equal to the same. But he that hath the use of words, when he observes, that such equality was consequent, not to the length of the sides, nor to any other particular thing in his triangle; but only to this, that the sides were straight, and the angles three; and that that was all, for which he named it a triangle; will boldly conclude universally, that such equality of angles is in all triangles whatsoever; and register his invention in these general terms, *every triangle hath its three angles equal to two right angles*. And thus the consequence found in one particular, comes to be registered and remembered, as a universal rule, and discharges our mental reckoning, of time and place, and delivers us from all labour of the mind, saving the first, and makes that which was found true *here*, and *now*, to be true in *all times* and *places*.

But the use of words in registering our thoughts is in nothing so evident as in numbering. A natural fool that could never learn by heart the order of numeral words, as *one*, *two*, and *three*, may observe every stroke of the clock, and nod to it, or say *one*, *one*, *one*, but can never know what hour it strikes. And it seems, there was a time when those names of number were not in use; and men were fain to apply their fingers of one or both hands, to those things they desired to keep account of; and that thence it proceeded, that now our numeral words are but ten, in any nation, and in some but five; and then they begin again. And he that can tell ten, if he recite them out of order, will lose himself, and not know when he has done. Much less will he be able to add, and subtract, and perform all other operations of arithmetic. So that without words there is no possibility of reckoning of numbers; much less of magnitudes, of swiftness, of force, and other things, the reckonings whereof are necessary to the being, or well-being of mankind.

When two names are joined together into a consequence, or affirmation, as thus, *a man is a living creature*; or thus, *if he be a man, he is a living creature*; if the latter name, *living creature*, signify all that the former name *man* signifieth, then the affirmation, or consequence, is *true*; otherwise *false*. For *true* and *false* are attributes of speech, not of things. And where speech is not, there is neither *truth* nor *falsehood*; *error* there may be, as when we expect that which shall not be, or suspect what has not been; but in neither case can a man be charged with untruth.

Seeing then that truth consisteth in the right ordering of names in our affirmations, a man that seeketh precise truth had need to remember what every name he uses stands for, and to place it accordingly, or else he will find himself entangled in words, as a bird in lime twigs, the more he struggles the more belimed. And therefore in geometry, which is the only science that it hath pleased God hitherto to bestow on mankind, men begin at settling the significations of their words; which settling of significations they call *definitions*, and place them in the beginning of their reckoning.

By this it appears how necessary it is for any man that aspires to true knowledge, to examine the definitions of former authors; and either to correct them, where they are negligently set down, or to make them himself. For the errors of definitions multiply themselves according as the reckoning proceeds, and lead men into absurdities, which at last they see, but cannot avoid, without reckoning anew from the beginning, in which lies the foundation of their errors. From whence it happens, that they which trust to books do as they that cast up many little sums into a greater, without considering whether those little sums were rightly cast up or not; and at last finding the error visible, and not mistrusting their first grounds, know not which way to clear themselves, but spend time in fluttering over their books; as birds that entering by the chimney, and finding themselves enclosed in a chamber, flutter at the false light of a glass window, for want of wit to

consider which way they came in. So that in the right definition of names lies the first use of speech; which is the acquisition of science: and in wrong, or no definitions, lies the first
abuse; from which proceed all false and senseless tenets;
which make those men that take their instruction from the
authority of books, and not from their own meditation, to be
as much below the condition of ignorant men, as men endued
with true science are above it. For between true science and
erroneous doctrines, ignorance is in the middle. Natural
sense and imagination are not subject to absurdity. Nature
itself cannot err; and as men abound in copiousness of language, so they become more wise, or more mad than ordinary.
Nor is it possible without letters for any man to become
either excellently wise, or, unless his memory be hurt by
disease or ill constitution of organs, excellently foolish. For
words are wise men's counters, they do but reckon by them;
but they are the money of fools, that value them by the
authority of an Aristotle, a Cicero, or a Thomas, or any other
doctor whatsoever, if but a man.

Subject to names, is whatsoever can enter into or be considered in an account, and be added one to another to make a
sum, or subtracted one from another and leave a remainder.
The Latins called accounts of money *rationes*, and accounting
ratiocinatio; and that which we in bills or books of account
call *items*, they call *nomina*, that is *names*; and thence it seems
to proceed, that they extended the word *ratio* to the faculty of
reckoning in all other things. The Greeks have but one word,
λόγος, for both *speech* and *reason*; not that they thought there
was no speech without reason, but no reasoning without
speech: and the act of reasoning they called *syllogism*, which
signifieth summing up of the consequences of one saying to
another. And because the same thing may enter into account
for divers accidents, their names are, to show that diversity,
diversely wrested and diversified. This diversity of names may
be reduced to four general heads.

First, a thing may enter into account for *matter* or *body*; as
living, sensible, rational, hot, cold, moved, quiet; withall which
names the word *matter*, or *body*, is understood; all such being
names of matter.

Secondly, it may enter into account, or be considered, for some accident or quality which we conceive to be in it; as for *being moved*, for *being so long*, for *being hot*, *&c.*; and then, of the name of the thing itself, by a little change or wresting, we make a name for that accident, which we consider; and for *living* put into the account *life*; for *moved*, *motion*; for *hot*, *heat*; for *long*, *length*, and the like: and all such names are the names of the accidents and properties by which one matter and body is distinguished from another. These are called *names abstract*, because severed, not from matter, but from the account of matter.

Thirdly, we bring into account the properties of our own bodies, whereby we make such distinction; as when anything is seen by us, we reckon not the thing itself, but the sight, the colour, the idea of it in the fancy: and when anything is heard, we reckon it not, but the hearing or sound only, which is our fancy or conception of it by the ear; and such are names of fancies.

Fourthly, we bring into account, consider, and give names, to *names* themselves, and to *speeches*: for *general*, *universal*, *special*, *equivocal*, are names of names. And *affirmation*, *interrogation*, *commandment*, *narration*, *syllogism*, *sermon*, *oration*, and many other such, are names of speeches. And this is all the variety of names *positive*; which are put to mark somewhat which is in nature, or may be feigned by the mind of man as bodies that are, or may be conceived to be; or of bodies, the properties that are, or may be feigned to be; or words and speech.

There be also other names, called *negative*, which are notes to signify that a word is not the name of the thing in question; as these words, *nothing, no man, infinite, indocible, three want four*, and the like; which are nevertheless of use in reckoning, or in correcting of reckoning, and call to mind our past cogitations, though they be not names of any thing, because they make us refuse to admit of names not rightly used.

All other names are but insignificant sounds; and those of two sorts. One when they are new, and yet their meaning not explained by definition; whereof there have been abundance coined by schoolmen, and puzzled philosophers.

Another, when men make a name of two names, whose significations are contradictory and inconsistent; as this name, an *incorporeal body*, or, which is all one, an *incorporeal substance*, and a great number more. For whensoever any affirmation is false, the two names of which it is composed, put together and made one, signify nothing at all. For example, if it be a false affirmation to say *a quadrangle is round*, the word *round quadrangle* signifies nothing, but is a mere sound. So likewise, if it be false to say that virtue can be poured, or blown up and down, the words *inpoured virtue*, *inblown virtue*, are as absurd and insignificant as a *round quadrangle*. And therefore you shall hardly meet with a senseless and insignificant word, that is not made up of some Latin or Greek names. A Frenchman seldom hears our Saviour called by the name of *parole*, but by the name of *verbe* often; yet *verbe* and *parole* differ no more, but that one is Latin, the other French.

When a man, upon the hearing of any speech, hath those thoughts which the words of that speech and their connexion were ordained and constituted to signify, then he is said to understand it; *understanding* being nothing else but conception caused by speech. And therefore if speech be peculiar to man, as for aught I know it is, then is understanding peculiar to him also. And therefore of absurd and false affirmations, in case they be universal, there can be no understanding; though many think they understand then, when they do but repeat the words softly, or con them in their mind.

What kinds of speeches signify the appetites, aversions, and passions of man's mind; and of their use and abuse, I shall speak when I have spoken of the passions.

The names of such things as affect us, that is, which please and displease us, because all men be not alike affected with the same thing, nor the same man at all times, are in the common discourses of men of *inconstant* signification. For seeing all names are imposed to signify our conceptions, and all our affections are but conceptions, when we conceive the same things differently, we can hardly avoid different naming of them. For though the nature of that we conceive, be the same; yet the diversity of our reception of it, in respect of different constitutions of body, and prejudices of opinion, gives every thing a tincture of our different passions. And therefore in reasoning a man must take heed of words; which besides the signification of what we imagine of their nature, have a signification also of the nature, disposition, and interest of the speaker; such as are the names of virtues and vices; for one man calleth *wisdom,* what another calleth *fear*; add one *cruelty,* what another *justice*; one *prodigality,* what another *magnanimity*; and one *gravity,* what another *stupidity,* &c. And therefore such names can never be true grounds of any ratiocination. No more can metaphors, and tropes of speech; but these are less dangerous, because they profess their inconstancy; which the other do not.

CHAPTER V

Of Reason and Science

WHEN a man *reasoneth,* he does nothing else but conceive a sum total, from *addition* of parcels; or conceive a remainder, from *subtraction* of one sum from another; which, if it be done by words, is conceiving of the consequence of the names of all the parts, to the name of the whole; or from the names of the whole and one part, to the name of the other part. And though in some things, as in numbers, besides adding and subtracting, men name other operations, as *multilpying* and *dividing,* yet they are the same; for multiplication, is but adding together of things equal; and division, but subtracting of one thing, as often as we can. These operations are not incident to numbers only, but to all manner of things that can be added together, and taken one out of another. For as arithmeticians teach to add and subtract in *numbers*; so the geometricians teach the same in *lines, figures,* solid and superficial, *angles, proportions, times,* degrees of *swiftness, force, power,* and the like; the logicians teach the same in *consequences of words*; adding together two *names* to make an *affirmation,* and two *affirmations* to make a *syllogism*; and *many syllogisms* to make a *demonstration*; and from the *sum,* or *conclusion* of a *syllogism,* they subtract one *proposition* to find the other. Writers of politics add together *pactions* to find men's *duties*; and lawyers, *laws* and *facts*, to find what is *right* and *wrong* in the actions of private men. In sum, in what matter soever there is place for *addition* and *subtraction*, there also is place for *reason*; and where these have no place, there *reason* has nothing at all to do.

Out of all which we may define, that is to say determine, what that is, which is meant by this word *reason*, when we reckon it amongst the faculties of the mind. For REASON, in this sense, is nothing but *reckoning*, that is adding and subtracting, of the consequences of general names agreed upon for the *marking* and *signifying* of our thoughts; I say *marking* them when we reckon by ourselves, and *signifying*, when we demonstrate or approve our reckonings to other men.

And, as in arithmetic, unpractised men must, and professors themselves may often, err, and cast up false; so also in any other subject of reasoning, the ablest, most attentive, and most practised men may deceive themselves, and infer false conclusions; not but that reason itself is always right reason, as well as arithmetic is a certain and infallible art: but no one man's reason, nor the reason of any one number of men, makes the certainty; no more than an account is therefore well cast up, because a great many men have unanimously approved it. And therefore, as when there is a controversy in an account, the parties must by their own accord, set up, for right reason, the reason of some arbitrator, or judge, to whose sentence they will both stand, or their controversy must either come to blows, or be undecided, for want of a right reason constituted by nature; so is it also in all debates of what kind soever. And when men that think themselves wiser than all others, clamour and demand right reason for judge, yet seek no more, but that things should be determined, by no other men's reason but their own, it is as intolerable in the society of men, as it is in play after trump is turned, to use for trump on every occasion, that suite whereof they have most in their hand. For they do nothing else, that will have every of their passions, as it comes to bear sway in them, to be taken for right reason, and that in their own controversies: bewraying their want of right reason, by the claim they lay to it.

The use and end of reason, is not the finding of the sum and truth of one, or a few consequences, remote from the first definitions, and settled significations of names, but to begin at these, and proceed from one consequence to another. For there can be no certainty of the last conclusion, without a certainty of all those affirmations and negations, on which it was grounded and inferred. As when a master of a family, in taking an account, casteth up the sums of all the bills of expense into one sum, and not regarding how each bill is summed up, by those that give them in account; nor what it is he pays for; he advantages himself no more, than if he allowed the account in gross, trusting to every of the accountants' skill and honesty: so also in reasoning of all other things, he that takes up conclusions on the trust of authors, and doth not fetch them from the first items in every reckoning, which are the significations of names settled by definitions, loses his labour; and does not know anything, but only believeth.

When a man reckons without the use of words, which may be done in particular things, as when upon the sight of any one thing, we conjecture what was likely to have preceded, or is likely to follow upon it; if that which he thought likely to follow, follows not, or that which he thought likely to have preceded it, hath not preceded it, this is called *error*; to which even the most prudent men are subject. But when we reason in words of general signification, and fall upon a general inference which is false, though it be commonly called *error*, it is indeed an *absurdity*, or senseless speech. For error is but a deception, in presuming that somewhat is past, or to come; of which, though it were not past, or not to come, yet there was no impossibility discoverable. But when we make a general assertion, unless it be a true one, the possibility of it is inconceivable. And words whereby we conceive nothing but the sound, are those we call *absurd*, *insignificant*, and *non-sense*. And therefore if a man should talk to me of a *round quadrangle*; or, *accidents of bread in cheese*; or, *immaterial substances*; or of *a free subject*; *a free will*; or any *free*, but free from being hindered by opposition, I should not say he were in an error, but that his words were without meaning, that is to say, absurd.

I have said before, in the second chapter, that a man did excel all other animals in this faculty, that when he conceived any thing whatsoever, he was apt to inquire the consequences of it, and what effects he could do with it. And now I add this other degree of the same excellence, that he can by words reduce the consequences he finds to general rules, called *theorems*, or *aphorisms*; that is, he can reason, or reckon, not only in number, but in all other things, whereof one may be added unto, or subtracted from another.

But this privilege is allayed by another; and that is, by the privilege of absurdity; to which no living creature is subject, but man only. And of men, those are of all most subject to it, that profess philosophy. For it is most true that Cicero saith of them somewhere; that there can be nothing so absurd, but may be found in the books of philosophers. And the reason is manifest. For there is not one of them that begins his ratiocination from the definitions, or explications of the names they are to use; which is a method that hath been used only in geometry; whose conclusions have thereby been made indisputable.

I. The first cause of absurd conclusions I ascribe to the want of method; in that they begin not their ratiocination from definitions; that is, from settled significations of their words; as if they could cast account, without knowing the value of the numeral words, *one*, *two* and *three*.

And whereas all bodies enter into account upon divers considerations, which I have mentioned in the precedent chapter; these considerations being diversely named, divers absurdities proceed from the confusion and unfit connexion of their names into assertions. And therefore,

II. The second cause of absurd assertions, I ascribe to the giving of names of *bodies* to *accidents*; or of *accidents* to *bodies*; as they do, that say, *faith is infused*, or *inspired*; when nothing can be *poured*, or *breathed* into anything, but body; and that, *extension* is *body*; that *phantasms* are *spirits*, &c.

III. The third I ascribe to the giving of the names of the *accidents* of *bodies without us*, to the *accidents* of our *own bodies* as they do that say, the *colour is in the body*; *the sound is in the air*, &c.

IV. The fourth, to the giving of the names of *bodies* to *names*, or *speeches*; as they do that say, that *there be things universal*; that *a living creature is genus*, or *a general thing*, &c.

V. The fifth, to the giving of the names of *accidents* to *names* and *speeches*; as they do that say, *the nature of a thing is its definition*; *a man's command is his will*; and the like.

VI. The sixth, to the use of metaphors, tropes, and other rhetorical figures, instead of words proper. For though it be lawful to say, for example, in common speech, *the way goeth, or leadeth hither, or thither*; *the proverb says this or that*, whereas ways cannot go, nor proverbs speak; yet in reckoning, and seeking of truth, such speeches are not to be admitted.

VII. The seventh, to names that signify nothing; but are taken up, and learned by rote from the schools, as *hypostatical*, *transubstantiate*, *consubstantiate*, *eternal-now*, and the like canting of schoolmen.

To him that can avoid these things it is not easy to fall into any absurdity, unless it be by the length of an account; wherein he may perhaps forget what went before. For all men by nature reason alike, and well, when they have good principles. For who is so stupid, as both to mistake in geometry, and also to persist in it, when another detects his error to him?

By this it appears that reason is not, as sense and memory, born with us; nor gotten by experience only, as prudence is; but attained by industry; first in apt imposing of names; and secondly by getting a good and orderly method in proceeding from the elements, which are names, to assertions made by connexion of one of them to another; and so to syllogisms, which are the connexions of one assertion to another, till we come to a knowledge of all the consequences of names appertaining to the subject in hand; and that is it, men call SCIENCE. And whereas sense and memory are but knowledge of fact, which is a thing past and irrevocable. *Science* is the knowledge of consequences, and dependance of one fact upon another: by which, out of that we can presently do, we know how to do something else when we will, or the like another time; because when we see how any thing comes about, upon what causes, and by what manner; when the like causes come into our power, we see how to make it produce the like effects.

Children therefore are not endued with reason at all, till they have attained the use of speech; but are called reasonable creatures, for the possibility apparent of having the use of reason in time to come. And the most part of men, though they have the use of reasoning a little way, as in numbering to some degree; yet it serves them to little use in common life; in which they govern themselves, some better, some worse, according to their differences of experience, quickness of memory, and inclinations to several ends; but specially according to good or evil fortune, and the errors of one another. For as for *science*, or certain rules of their actions, they are so far from it, that they know not what it is. Geometry they have thought conjuring: but for other sciences, they who have not been taught the beginnings and some progress in them, that they may see how they be acquired and generated, are in this point like children, that having no thought of generation, are made believe by the women that their brothers and sisters are not born, but found in the garden.

But yet they that have no *science*, are in better, and nobler condition, with their natural prudence; than men, that by mis-reasoning, or by trusting them that reason wrong, fall upon false and absurd general rules. For ignorance of causes, and of rules, does not set men so far out of their way, as relying on false rules, and taking for causes of what they aspire to, those that are not so, but rather causes of the contrary.

To conclude, the light of human minds is perspicuous words, but by exact definitions first snuffed, and purged from ambiguity; *reason* is the *pace*; increase of *science*, the *way*; and the benefit of mankind, the *end*. And, on the contrary, meta-phors, and senseless and ambiguous words, are like *ignes fatui*; and reasoning upon them is wandering amongst innumerable absurdities; and their end, contention and sedition, or contempt.

As much experience, is *prudence*; so is much science *sapience*. For though we usually have one name of wisdom for them both, yet the Latins did always distinguish between *prudentia* and *sapientia*; ascribing the former to experience, the latter to science. But to make their difference appear more clearly, let us suppose one man endued with an excellent natural use and dexterity in handling his arms; and another to have added to that dexterity, an acquired science, of where he can offend, or be offended by his adversary, in every possible posture or guard: the ability of the former, would be to the ability of the latter, as prudence to sapience; both useful; but the latter infallible. But they that trusting only to the authority of books, follow the blind blindly, are like him that trusting to the false rules of a master of fence, ventures presumptuously upon an adversary, that either kills or disgraces him.

The signs of science are some, certain and infallible; some, uncertain. Certain, when he that pretendeth the science of any thing, can teach the same; that is to say, demonstrate the truth thereof perspicuously to another; uncertain, when only some particular events answer to his pretence, and upon many occasions prove so as he says they must. Signs of prudence are all uncertain; because to observe by experience, and remember all circumstances, that may alter the success, is impossible. But in any business, whereof a man has not infallible science to proceed by; to forsake his own natural judgment, and be guided by general sentences read in authors, and subject to many exceptions, is a sign of folly, and generally scorned by the name of pedantry. And even of those men themselves, that in councils of the commonwealth love to show their reading of politics and history, very few do it in their domestic affairs, where their particular interest is concerned; having prudence enough for their private affairs: but in public they study more the reputation of their own wit, than the success of another's business.

CHAPTER VI

Of the Interior Beginnings of Voluntary Motions; Commonly Called the Passions; and the Speeches by which they are Expressed

THERE be in animals, two sorts of *motions* peculiar to them: one called *vital*; begun in generation, and continued without interruption through their whole life; such as are the *course* of the *blood*, the *pulse*, the *breathing*, the *concoction*, *nutrition*, *excretion*, &c. to which motions there needs no help of imagination: the other is *animal motion*, otherwise called *voluntary motion*; as to *go*, to *speak*, to *move* any of our limbs, in such manner as is first fancied in our minds. That sense is motion in the organs and interior parts of man's body, caused by the action of the things we see, hear, &c.; and that fancy is but the relics of the same motion, remaining after sense, has been already said in the first and second chapters. And because *going, speaking,* and the like voluntary motions, depend always upon a precedent thought of *whither*, *which way*, and *what*; it is evident, that the imagination is the first internal beginning of all voluntary motion. And although unstudied men do not conceive any motion at all to be there, where the thing moved is invisible; or the space it is moved in is, for the shortness of it, insensible; yet that doth not hinder, but that such motions are. For let a space be never so little, that which is moved over a greater space, whereof that little one is part, must first be moved over that. These small beginnings of motion, within the body of man, before they appear in walking, speaking, striking, and other visible actions, are commonly called ENDEAVOUR.

This endeavour, when it is toward something which causes it, is called APPETITE, or DESIRE; the latter, being the general name; and the other oftentimes restrained to signify the desire of food, namely *hunger* and *thirst*. And when the endeavour is fromward something, it is generally called AVERSION. These

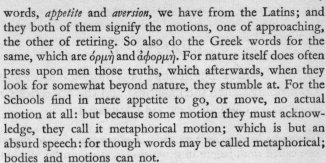

words, *appetite* and *aversion*, we have from the Latins; and they both of them signify the motions, one of approaching, the other of retiring. So also do the Greek words for the same, which are ὁρμὴ and ἀφορμὴ. For nature itself does often press upon men those truths, which afterwards, when they look for somewhat beyond nature, they stumble at. For the Schools find in mere appetite to go, or move, no actual motion at all: but because some motion they must acknowledge, they call it metaphorical motion; which is but an absurd speech: for though words may be called metaphorical; bodies and motions can not.

That which men desire, they are also said to LOVE: and to HATE those things for which they have aversion. So that desire and love are the same thing; save that by desire, we always signify the absence of the object; by love, most commonly the presence of the same. So also by aversion, we signify the absence; and by hate, the presence of the object.

Of appetites and aversions, some are born with men; as appetite of food, appetite of excretion, and exoneration, which may also and more properly be called aversions, from somewhat they feel in their bodies; and some other appetites, not many. The rest, which are appetites of particular things, proceed from experience, and trial of their effects upon themselves or other men. For of things we know not at all, or believe not to be, we can have no further desire, than to taste and try. But aversion we have for things, not only which we know have hurt us, but also that we do not know whether they will hurt us, or not.

Those things which we neither desire, nor hate, we are said to *contemn*; CONTEMPT being nothing else but an immobility, or contumacy of the heart, in resisting the action of certain things; and proceeding from that the heart is already moved otherwise, by other more potent objects; or from want of experience of them.

And because the constitution of a man's body is in continual mutation, it is impossible that all the same things should always cause in him the same appetites, and aversions: much less can all men consent, in the desire of almost any one and the same object.

But whatsoever is the object of any man's appetite or desire, that is it which he for his part calleth *good*: and the object of his hate and aversion, *evil*; and of his contempt, *vile* and *inconsiderable*. For these words of good, evil, and contemptible, are ever used with relation to the person that useth them: there being nothing simply and absolutely so; nor any common rule of good and evil, to be taken from the nature of the objects themselves; but from the person of the man, where there is no commonwealth; or, in a commonwealth, from the person that representeth it; or from an arbitrator or judge, whom men disagreeing shall by consent set up, and make his sentence the rule thereof.

The Latin tongue has two words, whose significations approach to those of good and evil; but are not precisely the same; and those are *pulchrum* and *turpe*. Whereof the former signifies that, which by some apparent signs promiseth good; and the latter, that which promiseth evil. But in our tongue we have not so general names to express them by. But for *pulchrum* we say in some things, *fair*; in others, *beautiful*, or *handsome*, or *gallant*, or *honourable*, or *comely*, or *amiable*; and for *turpe*, *foul*, *deformed*, *ugly*, *base*, *nauseous*, and the like, as the subject shall require; all which words, in their proper places, signify nothing else but the *mien*, or countenance, that promiseth good and evil. So that of good there be three kinds; good in the promise, that is *pulchrum*; good in effect, as the end desired, which is called *jucundum*, *delightful*; and good as the means, which is called *utile*, *profitable*; and as many of evil: for *evil* in promise, is that they call *turpe*; evil in effect, and end, is *molestum*, *unpleasant*, *troublesome*; and evil in the means, *inutile*, *unprofitable*, *hurtful*.

As, in sense, that which is really within us, is, as I have said before, only motion, caused by the action of external objects, but in appearance; to the sight, light and colour; to the ear, sound; to the nostril, odour, &c.: so, when the action of the same object is continued from the eyes, ears, and other organs to the heart, the real effect there is nothing but motion, or endeavour; which consisteth in appetite, or aversion, to or from the object moving. But the apparence, or sense of that motion, is that we either call *delight*, or *trouble of mind*.

This motion, which is called appetite, and for the apparence of it *delight*, and *pleasure*, seemeth to be a corroboration of vital motion, and a help thereunto; and therefore such things as caused delight, were not improperly called *jucunda, à juvando*, from helping or fortifying; and the contrary, *molesta, offensive*, from hindering, and troubling the motion vital.

Pleasure therefore, or *delight*, is the apparence, or sense of good; and *molestation*, or *displeasure*, the apparence, or sense of evil. And consequently all appetite, desire, and love, is accompanied with some delight more or less; and all hatred and aversion, with more or less displeasure and offence.

Of pleasures or delights, some arise from the sense of an object present; and those may be called *pleasure of sense*; the word *sensual*, as it is used by those only that condemn them, having no place till there be laws. Of this kind are all onerations and exonerations of the body; as also all that is pleasant, in the *sight*, *hearing*, *smell*, *taste*, or *touch*. Others arise from the expectation, that proceeds from foresight of the end, or consequence of things; whether those things in the sense please or displease. And these are *pleasures of the mind* of him that draweth those consequences, and are generally called JOY. In the like manner, displeasures are some in the sense, and called PAIN; others in the expectation of consequences, and are called GRIEF.

These simple passions called *appetite, desire, love, aversion, hate, joy*, and *grief*, have their names for divers considerations diversified. As first, when they one succeed another, they are diversely called from the opinion men have of the likelihood of attaining what they desire. Secondly, from the object loved or hated. Thirdly, from the consideration of many of them together. Fourthly, from the alteration or succession itself.

For *appetite*, with an opinion of attaining, is called HOPE.

The same, without such opinion, DESPAIR.

Aversion, with opinion of HURT from the object, FEAR.

The same, with hope of avoiding that hurt by resistance, COURAGE.

Sudden *courage*, ANGER.

Constant *hope*, CONFIDENCE of ourselves.

Constant *despair*, DIFFIDENCE of ourselves.

Anger for great hurt done to another, when we conceive the same to be done by injury, INDIGNATION.

Desire of good to another, BENEVOLENCE, GOOD WILL, CHARITY. If to man generally, GOOD NATURE.

Desire of riches, COVETOUSNESS; a name used always in signification of blame; because men contending for them, are displeased with one another attaining them; though the desire in itself, be to be blamed, or allowed, according to the means by which these riches are sought.

Desire of office, or precedence, AMBITION: a name used also in the worse sense, for the reason before mentioned.

Desire of things that conduce but a little to our ends, and fear of things that are but of little hindrance, PUSILLANIMITY.

Contempt of little helps and hindrances, MAGNANIMITY.

Magnanimity, in danger of death or wounds, VALOUR, FORTITUDE.

Magnanimity in the use of riches, LIBERALITY.

Pusillanimity in the same, WRETCHEDNESS, MISERABLENESS, or PARSIMONY; as it is liked or disliked.

Love of persons for society, KINDNESS.

Love of persons for pleasing the sense only, NATURAL LUST.

Love of the same, acquired from rumination, that is, imagination of pleasure past, LUXURY.

Love of one singularly, with desire to be singularly beloved, THE PASSION OF LOVE. The same, with fear that the love is not mutual, JEALOUSY.

Desire, by doing hurt to another, to make him condemn some fact of his own, REVENGEFULNESS.

Desire to know why, and how, CURIOSITY; such as is in no living creature but *man*: so that man is distinguished, not only by his reason, but also by this singular passion from other *animals*; in whom the appetite of food, and other pleasures of sense, by predominance, take away the care of knowing causes; which is a lust of the mind, that by a perseverance of delight in the continual and indefatigable generation of knowledge, exceedeth the short vehemence of any carnal pleasure.

Fear of power invisible, feigned by the mind, or imagined from tales publicly allowed, RELIGION; not allowed, SUPER-

STITION. And when the power imagined, is truly such as we imagine, TRUE RELIGION.

Fear, without the apprehension of why, or what, PANIC TERROR, called so from the fables, that make Pan the author of them; whereas, in truth, there is always in him that so feareth, first, some apprehension of the cause, though the rest run away by example, every one supposing his fellow to know why. And therefore this passion happens to none but in a throng, or multitude of people.

Joy, from apprehension of novelty, ADMIRATION; proper to man, because it excites the appetite of knowing the cause.

Joy, arising from imagination of a man's own power and ability; is that exultation of the mind which is called GLORY-ING: which if grounded upon the experience of his own former actions, is the same with *confidence*: but if grounded on the flattery of others; or only supposed by himself, for delight in the consequences of it, is called VAINGLORY: which name is properly given; because a well grounded *confidence* begetteth attempt; whereas the supposing of power does not, and is therefore rightly called *vain*.

Grief, from opinion of want of power is called DEJECTION of mind.

The *vain-glory* which consisteth in the feigning or supposing of abilities in ourselves, which we know are not, is most incident to young men, and nourished by the histories, or fictions of gallant persons; and is corrected oftentimes by age, and employment.

Sudden glory is the passion which maketh those *grimaces* called LAUGHTER; and is caused either by some sudden act of their own, that pleaseth them; or by the apprehension of some deformed thing in another, by comparison whereof they suddenly applaud themselves. And it is incident most to them, that are conscious of the fewest abilities in themselves; who are forced to keep themselves in their own favour, by observing the imperfections of other men. And therefore much laughter at the defects of others, is a sign of pusillanimity. For of great minds, one of the proper works is, to help and free others from scorn; and compare themselves only with the most able.

T—L.—D

On the contrary, *sudden dejection*, is the passion that causeth WEEPING; and is caused by such accidents, as suddenly take away some vehement hope, or some prop of their power: and they are most subject to it, that rely principally on helps external, such as are women, and children. Therefore some weep for the loss of friends; others for their unkindness; others for the sudden stop made to their thoughts of revenge, by reconciliation. But in all cases, both laughter, and weeping, are sudden motions; custom taking them both away. For no man laughs at old jests; or weeps for an old calamity.

Grief, for the discovery of some defect of ability, is SHAME, or the passion that discovereth itself in BLUSHING; and consisteth in the apprehension of some thing dishonourable; and in young men, is a sign of the love of good reputation, and commendable: in old men it is a sign of the same; but because it comes too late, not commendable.

The *contempt* of good reputation is called IMPUDENCE.

Grief, for the calamity of another, is PITY; and ariseth from the imagination that the like calamity may befall himself; and therefore is called also COMPASSION, and in the phrase of this present time a FELLOW-FEELING: and therefore for calamity arriving from great wickedness, the best men have the least pity; and for the same calamity, those hate pity, that think themselves least obnoxious to the same.

Contempt, or little sense of the calamity of others, is that which men call CRUELTY; proceeding from security of their own fortune. For, that any man should take pleasure in other men's great harms; without other end of his own, I do not conceive it possible.

Grief, for the success of a competitor in wealth, honour, or other good, if it be joined with endeavour to enforce our own abilities to equal or exceed him, is called EMULATION: but joined with endeavour to supplant or hinder a competitor, ENVY.

When in the mind of man, appetites, and aversions, hopes, and fears, concerning one and the same thing, arise alternately; and divers good and evil consequences of the doing, or omitting the thing propounded, come successively into our thoughts; so that sometimes we have an appetite to it; sometimes an aversion from it; sometimes hope to be able to do it; sometimes despair, or fear to attempt it; the whole sum of desires, aversions, hopes and fears continued till the thing be either done, or thought impossible, is that we call DELIBERATION.

Therefore of things past, there is no *deliberation*; because manifestly impossible to be changed: nor of things known to be impossible, or thought so; because men know, or think such deliberation vain. But of things impossible, which we think possible, we may deliberate; not knowing it is in vain. And it is called *deliberation*; because it is a putting an end to the *liberty* we had of doing, or omitting, according to our own appetite, or aversion.

This alternate succession of appetites, aversions, hopes and fears, is no less in other living creatures than in man: and therefore beasts also deliberate.

Every *deliberation* is then said to *end*, when that whereof they deliberate, is either done, or thought impossible; because till then we retain the liberty of doing, or omitting; according to our appetite, or aversion.

In *deliberation*, the last appetite, or aversion, immediately adhering to the action, or to the omission thereof, is that we call the WILL; the act, not the faculty, of *willing*. And beasts that have *deliberation*, must necessarily also have *will*. The definition of the *will*, given commonly by the Schools, that it is a *rational appetite*, is not good. For if it were, then could there be no voluntary act against reason. For a *voluntary act* is that, which proceedeth from the *will*, and no other. But if instead of a rational appetite, we shall say an appetite resulting from a precedent deliberation, then the definition is the same that I have given here. *Will* therefore *is the last appetite in deliberating*. And though we say in common discourse, a man had a will once to do a thing, that nevertheless he forebore to do; yet that is properly but an inclination, which makes no action voluntary; because the action depends not of it, but of the last inclination, or appetite. For if the intervenient appetites, make any action voluntary; then by the same reason all intervenient aversions, should make the same action involuntary; and so one and the same action, should be both voluntary and involuntary.

By this it is manifest, that not only actions that have their beginning from covetousness, ambition, lust, or other appetites to the thing propounded; but also those that have their beginning from aversion, or fear of those consequences that follow the omission, are *voluntary actions*.

The forms of speech by which the passions are expressed, are partly the same, and partly different from those, by which we express our thoughts. And first, generally all passions may be expressed *indicatively*; as *I love, I fear, I joy, I deliberate, I will, I command*: but some of them have particular expressions by themselves, which nevertheless are not affirmations, unless it be when they serve to make other inferences, besides that of the passion they proceed from. Deliberation is expressed *subjunctively*; which is a speech proper to signify suppositions, with their consequences: as, *if this be done, then this will follow*; and differs not from the language of reasoning, save that reasoning is in general words; but deliberation for the most part is of particulars. The language of desire, and aversion, is *imperative*; as *do this, forbear that*; which when the party is obliged to do, or forbear, is *command*; otherwise *prayer*; or else *counsel*. The language of vain-glory, of indignation, pity and revengefulness, *optative*; but of the desire to know, there is a peculiar expression, called *interrogative*; as, *what is it, when shall it, how is it done*, and *why so?* other language of the passions I find none: for cursing, swearing, reviling, and the like, do not signify as speech; but as the actions of a tongue accustomed.

These forms of speech, I say, are expressions, or voluntary significations of our passions: but certain signs they be not; because they may be used arbitrarily, whether they that use them, have such passions or not. The best signs of passions present, are either in the countenance, motions of the body, actions, and ends, or aims, which we otherwise know the man to have.

And because in deliberation, the appetites, and aversions, are raised by foresight of the good and evil consequences, and sequels of the action whereof we deliberate; the good or evil effect thereof dependeth on the foresight of a long chain of consequences of which very seldom any man is able to see to the end. But for so far as a man seeth, if the good in those consequences be greater than the evil, the whole chain is that which writers call *apparent*, or *seeming good*. And contrarily, when the evil exceedeth the good, the whole is *apparent*, or *seeming evil*: so that he who hath by experience, or reason, the greatest and surest prospect of consequences, deliberates best himself; and is able when he will, to give the best counsel unto others.

Continual success in obtaining those things which a man from time to time desireth, that is to say, continual prospering, is that men call FELICITY; I mean the felicity of this life. For there is no such thing as perpetual tranquillity of mind, while we live here; because life itself is but motion, and can never be without desire, nor without fear, no more than without sense. What kind of felicity God hath ordained to them that devoutly honour Him, a man shall no sooner know, than enjoy; being joys, that now are as incomprehensible, as the word of schoolmen *beatifical vision* is unintelligible.

The form of speech whereby men signify their opinion of the goodness of any thing, is PRAISE. That whereby they signify the power and greatness of any thing, is MAGNIFYING. And that whereby they signify the opinion they have of a man's felicity, is by the Greeks called μακαρισμός, for which we have no name in our tongue. And thus much is sufficient for the present purpose, to have been said of the PASSIONS.

CHAPTER VII

Of the Ends, or Resolutions of Discourse

OF all *discourse*, governed by desire of knowledge, there is at last an *end*, either by attaining, or by giving over. And in the chain of discourse, wheresoever it be interrupted, there is an end for that time.

If the discourse be merely mental, it consisteth of thoughts that the thing will be, and will not be; or that it has been, and has not been, alternately. So that wheresoever you break off the chain of a man's discourse, you leave him in a presumption of *it will be*, or, *it will not be*; or, *it has been*, or, *has not been*. All which is *opinion*. And that which is alternate appetite, in deliberating concerning good and evil; the same is alternate opinion, in the enquiry of the truth of *past*, and *future*. And as the last appetite in deliberation, is called the *will*; so the last opinion in search of the truth of past, and future, is called the JUDGMENT, or *resolute* and *final sentence* of him that *discourseth*. And as the whole chain of appetites alternate, in the question of good, or bad, is called *deliberation*; so the whole chain of opinions alternate, in the question of true, or false, is called DOUBT.

No discourse whatsoever, can end in absolute knowledge of fact, past, or to come. For, as for the knowledge of fact, it is originally, sense; and ever after, memory. And for the knowledge of consequence, which I have said before is called science, it is not absolute, but conditional. No man can know by discourse, that this, or that, is, has been, or will be; which is to know absolutely: but only, that if this be, that is; if this has been, that has been; if this shall be, that shall be: which is to know conditionally; and that not the consequence of one thing to another; but of one name of a thing, to another name of the same thing.

And therefore, when the discourse is put into speech, and begins with the definition of words, and proceeds by connexion of the same into general affirmations, and of these again into syllogisms; the end or last sum is called the conclusion; and the thought of the mind by it signified, is that conditional knowledge, or knowledge of the consequence of words, which is commonly called SCIENCE. But if the first ground of such discourse, be not definitions; or if the definitions be not rightly joined together into syllogisms, then the end or conclusion, is again OPINION, namely of the truth of somewhat said, though sometimes in absurd and senseless words, without possibility of being understood. When two, or more men, know of one and the same fact, they are said to be CONSCIOUS of it one to another; which is as much as to know it together. And because such are fittest witnesses of the facts of one another, or of a third; it was, and ever will be reputed a very evil act, for any man to speak against his *conscience*: or to corrupt or force another so to do: insomuch that the plea of conscience, has been always hearkened unto very diligently in all times. Afterwards, men made use of the same word metaphorically, for the knowledge of their own secret facts, and secret thoughts; and therefore it is rhetorically said, that the conscience is a thousand witnesses. And last of all, men, vehemently in love with their own new opinions, though never so absurd, and obstinately bent to maintain them, gave those their opinions also that reverenced name of conscience, as if they would have it seem unlawful, to change or speak against them; and so pretend to know they are true, when they know at most, but that they think so.

When a man's discourse beginneth not at definitions, it beginneth either at some other contemplation of his own, and then it is still called opinion; or it beginneth at some saying of another, of whose ability to know the truth, and of whose honesty in not deceiving, he doubteth not; and then the discourse is not so much concerning the thing, as the person; and the resolution is called BELIEF, and FAITH: *faith, in* the man; *belief*, both *of* the man, and *of* the truth of what he says. So that in belief are two opinions; one of the saying of the man; the other of his virtue. To *have faith in*, or *trust to*, or *believe a man*, signify the same thing; namely, an opinion of the veracity of the man: but to *believe what is said*, signifieth only an opinion of the truth of the saying. But we are to observe that this phrase, *I believe in*; as also the Latin, *credo in*; and the Greek, πιζένω εἰς, are never used but in the writings of divines. Instead of them, in other writings are put, *I believe him*; *I trust him*; *I have faith in him*; *I rely on him*; and in Latin, *credo illi*: *fido illi*: and in Greek, πιζένω αὐτω: and that this singularity of the ecclesiastic use of the word hath raised many disputes about the right object of the Christian faith.

But by *believing in*, as it is in the creed, is meant, not trust in the person; but confession and acknowledgment of the doctrine. For not only Christians, but all manner of men do so believe in God, as to hold all for truth they hear him say, whether they understand it, or not; which is all the faith and trust can possibly be had in any person whatsoever: but they do not all believe the doctrine of the creed.

From whence we may infer, that when we believe any saying whatsoever it be, to be true, from arguments taken, not from the thing itself, or from the principles of natural reason, but from the authority, and good opinion we have, of him that hath said it; then is the speaker, or person we believe in, or trust in, and whose word we take, the object of our faith; and the honour done in believing, is done to him only. And consequently, when we believe that the Scriptures are the word of God, having no immediate revelation from God himself, our belief, faith, and trust is in the church; whose word we take, and acquiesce therein. And they that believe that which a prophet relates unto them in the name of God, take the word of the prophet, do honour to him, and in him trust, and believe, touching the truth of what he relateth, whether he be a true, or a false prophet. And so it is also with all other history. For if I should not believe all that is written by historians, of the glorious acts of *Alexander*, or *Caesar*; I do not think the ghost of *Alexander*, or *Caesar*, had any just cause to be offended; or any body else, but the historian. If *Livy* say the Gods made once a cow speak, and we believe it not; we distrust not God therein, but *Livy*. So that it is evident, that whatsoever we believe, upon no other reason, than what is drawn from authority of men only, and their writings; whether they be sent from God or not, is faith in men only.

CHAPTER VIII

Of the Virtues Commonly Called Intellectual; and their Contrary Defects

VIRTUE generally, in all sorts of subjects, is somewhat that is valued for eminence; and consisteth in comparison. For if all things were equal in all men, nothing would be prized. And by *virtues intellectual*, are always understood such abilities of the mind, as men praise, value, and desire should be in themselves; and go commonly under the name of a *good wit*; though the same word *wit*, be used also, to distinguish one certain ability from the rest.

These *virtues* are of two sorts; *natural*, and *acquired*. By natural, I mean not, that which a man hath from his birth: for that is nothing else but sense; wherein men differ so little one from another, and from brute beasts, as it is not to be reckoned amongst virtues. But I mean, that *wit*, which is gotten by use only, and experience; without method, culture, or instruction. This NATURAL WIT, consisteth principally in two things; *celerity of imagining*, that is, swift succession of one thought to another; and *steady direction* to some approved end. On the contrary a slow imagination, maketh that defect, or fault of the mind, which is commonly called DULLNESS, *stupidity*, and sometimes by other names that signify slowness of motion, or difficulty to be moved.

And this difference of quickness, is caused by the difference of men's passions; that love and dislike, some one thing, some another: and therefore some men's thoughts run one way, some another; and are held to, and observe differently the things that pass through their imagination. And whereas in this succession of men's thoughts, there is nothing to observe in the things they think on, but either in what they be *like one another*, or in what they be *unlike*, or *what they serve for*, or *how they serve to such a purpose*; those that observe their similitudes, in case they be such as are but rarely observed by others, are said to have a *good wit*; by which, in this occasion, is meant a *good fancy*. But they that observe their differences, and dissimilitudes; which is called *distinguishing*, and *discerning*, and *judging* between thing and thing; in case, such discerning be not easy, are said to have a *good judgment*: and particularly in matter of conversation and business; wherein, times, places, and persons are to be discerned, this virtue is called DISCRETION. The former, that is, fancy, without the help of judgment, is not commended as a virtue: but the latter which is judgment, and discretion, is commended for itself, without the help of fancy. Besides the discretion of times, places, and persons, necessary to a good fancy, there is required also an often application of his thoughts to their end; that is to say, to some use to be made of them. This done; he that hath this virtue, will be easily fitted with similitudes, that will please, not only by illustrations of his discourse, and adorning it with new and apt metaphors; but also, by the rarity of their invention. But without steadiness, and direction to some end, a great fancy is one kind of madness; such as they have, that entering into any discourse are snatched from their purpose, by every thing that comes in their thought, into so many, and so long digressions, and parentheses, that they utterly lose themselves: which kind of folly, I know no particular name for: but the cause of it is, sometimes want of experience; whereby that seemeth to a man new and rare, which doth not so to others: sometimes pusillanimity; by which that seems great to him, which other men think a trifle: and whatsoever is new, or great, and therefore thought fit to be told, withdraws a man by degrees from the intended way of his discourse.

In a good poem, whether it be *epic*, or *dramatic*; as also in *sonnets*, *epigrams*, and other pieces, both judgment and fancy are required: but the fancy must be more eminent; because they please for the extravagancy; but ought not to displease by indiscretion.

In a good history, the judgment must be eminent; because the goodness consisteth, in the method, in the truth, and in the choice of the actions that are most profitable to be known. Fancy has no place, but only in adorning the style.

In orations of praise, and in invectives, the fancy is predominant; because the design is not truth, but to honour or dishonour; which is done by noble, or by vile comparisons. The judgment does but suggest what circumstances make an action laudable, or culpable.

In hortatives, and pleadings, as truth, or disguise serveth best to the design in hand; so is the judgment, or the fancy most required.

In demonstration, in counsel, and all rigorous search of truth, judgment does all, except sometimes the understanding have need to be opened by some apt similitude; and then there is so much use of fancy. But for metaphors, they are in this case utterly excluded. For seeing they openly profess deceit; to admit them into counsel, or reasoning, were manifest folly.

And in any discourse whatsoever, if the defect of discretion be apparent, how extravagant soever the fancy be, the whole discourse will be taken for a sign of want of wit; and so will it never when the discretion is manifest, though the fancy be never so ordinary.

The secret thoughts of a man run over all things, holy, profane, clean, obscene, grave, and light, without shame, or blame; which verbal discourse cannot do, farther than the judgment shall approve of the time, place, and persons. An anatomist, or a physician may speak, or write his judgment of unclean things; because it is not to please, but profit: but for another man to write his extravagant, and pleasant fancies of the same, is as if a man, from being tumbled into the dirt, should come and present himself before good company. And it is the want of discretion that makes the difference. Again, in professed remissness of mind, and familiar company, a man may play with the sounds, and equivocal significations of words; and that many times with encounters of extraordinary fancy: but in a sermon, or in public, or before persons unknown, or whom we ought to reverence; there is no gingling of words that will not be accounted folly: and the difference is only in the want of discretion. So that where wit is wanting, it is not fancy that is wanting, but discretion. Judgment therefore without fancy is wit, but fancy without judgment, not.

When the thoughts of a man, that has a design in hand, running over a multitude of things, observes how they conduce to that design; or what design they may conduce unto; if his observations be such as are not easy, or usual, this wit of his is called PRUDENCE; and depends on much experience, and memory of the like things, and their consequences heretofore. In which there is not so much difference of men; as there is in their fancies and judgment; because the experience of men equal in age, is not much unequal, as to the quantity; but lies in different occasions; every one having his private designs. To govern well a family, and a kingdom, are not different degrees of prudence; but different sorts of business; no more than to draw a picture in little, or as great, or greater than the life, are different degrees of art. A plain husbandman is more prudent in affairs of his own house, than a privy-councillor in the affairs of another man.

To prudence, if you add the use of unjust, or dishonest means, such as usually are prompted to men by fear, or want; you have that crooked wisdom, which is called CRAFT; which is a sign of pusillanimity. For magnanimity is contempt of unjust, or dishonest helps. And that which the Latins call *versutia*, translated into English, *shifting*, and is a putting off of a present danger or incommodity, by engaging into a greater, as when a man robs one to pay another, is but a shorter-sighted craft, called *versutia*, from *versuar*, which signifies taking money at usury for the present payment of interest.

As for *acquired wit*, I mean acquired by method and instruction, there is none but reason; which is grounded on the right use of speech, and produceth the sciences. But of reason and science I have already spoken, in the fifth and sixth chapters.

The causes of this difference of wits, are in the passions; and the difference of passions proceedeth, partly from the different constitution of the body, and partly from different education. For if the difference proceeded from the temper of the brain, and the organs of sense, either exterior or interior, there would be no less difference of men in their sight, hearing, or other senses, than in their fancies and discretions. It proceeds therefore from the passions; which are different, not only from the difference of mens' complexions; but also from their difference of customs, and education.

The passions that most of all cause the difference of wit, are principally, the more or less desire of power, of riches, of knowledge, and of honour. All which may be reduced to the first, that is, desire of power. For riches, knowledge, and honour, are but several sorts of power.

And therefore, a man who has no great passion for any of these things; but is, as men term it, indifferent; though he may be so far a good man, as to be free from giving offence; yet he cannot possibly have either a great fancy, or much judgment. For the thoughts are to the desires, as scouts, and spies, to range abroad, and find the way to the things desired: all steadiness of the mind's motion, and all quickness of the same, proceeding from thence: for as to have no desire, is to be dead: so to have weak passions, is dullness; and to have passions indifferently for everything, GIDDINESS, and *distraction*; and to have stronger and more vehement passions for anything, than is ordinarily seen in others, is that which men call MADNESS.

Whereof there be almost as many kinds, as of the passions themselves. Sometimes the extraordinary and extravagant passion, proceedeth from the evil constitution of the organs of the body, or harm done them; and sometimes the hurt, and indisposition of the organs, is caused by the vehemence, or long continuance of the passion. But in both cases the madness is of one and the same nature.

The passion, whose violence, or continuance, maketh madness, is either great *vain-glory*; which is commonly called *pride*, and *self-conceit*; or great *dejection* of mind.

Pride, subjecteth a man to anger, the excess whereof, is the madness called RAGE and FURY. And thus it comes to pass that excessive desire of revenge, when it becomes habitual, hurteth the organs, and becomes rage: that excessive love, with jealousy, becomes also rage: excessive opinion of a man's own self, for divine inspiration, for wisdom, learning, form and the like, becomes distraction and giddiness: the same, joined with envy, rage: vehement opinion of the truth of anything, contradicted by others, rage.

Dejection subjects a man to causeless fears; which is a madness, commonly called MELANCHOLY; apparent also in divers manners; as in haunting of solitudes and graves; in superstitious behaviour; and in fearing, some one, some another particular thing. In sum, all passions that produce strange and unusual behaviour, are called by the general name of madness. But of the several kinds of madness, he that would take the pains, might enrol a legion. And if the excesses be madness, there is no doubt but the passions themselves, when they tend to evil, are degrees of the same.

For example, though the effect of folly, in them that are possessed of an opinion of being inspired, be not visible always in one man, by any very extravagant action, that proceedeth from such passion; yet, when many of them conspire together, the rage of the whole multitude is visible enough. For what argument of madness can there be greater, than to clamour, strike, and throw stones at our best friends? Yet this is somewhat less than such a multitude will do. For they will clamour, fight against, and destroy those, by whom all their lifetime before, they have been protected, and secured from injury. And if this be madness in the multitude, it is the same in every particular man. For as in the midst of the sea, though a man perceive no sound of that part of the water next him, yet he is well assured, that part contributes as much to the roaring of the sea, as any other part of the same quantity; so also, though we perceive no great unquietness in one or two men, yet we may be well assured, that their singular passions, are parts of the seditious roaring of a troubled nation. And if there were nothing else that bewrayed their madness; yet that very arrogating such inspiration to themselves, is argument enough. If some man in Bedlam should entertain you with sober discourse; and you desire in taking leave, to know what he were, that you might another time requite his civility; and he should tell you, he were God the Father; I think you need expect no extravagant action for argument of his madness.

This opinion of inspiration, called commonly, private spirit, begins very often, from some lucky finding of an error generally held by others; and not knowing, or not remembering, by what conduct of reason, they came to so singular a truth, (as they think it, though it be many times an untruth they light on) they presently admire themselves, as being in the special grace of God Almighty, who hath revealed the same to them supernaturally, by his Spirit.

Again, that madness is nothing else, but too much appearing passion, may be gathered out of the effects of wine, which are the same with those of the evil disposition of the organs. For the variety of behaviour in men that have drunk too much, is the same with that of madmen: some of them raging, others loving, others laughing, all extravagantly, but according to their several domineering passions: for the effect of the wine, does but remove dissimulation, and take from them the sight of the deformity of their passions. For, I believe, the most sober men, when they walk alone without care and employ-

ment of the mind, would be unwilling the vanity and extrava-
gance of their thoughts at that time should be publicly seen;
which is a confession, that passions unguided, are for the
most part mere madness.

The opinions of the world, both in ancient and later ages,
concerning the cause of madness, have been two. Some
deriving them from the passions; some, from demons, or
spirits, either good or bad, which they thought might enter
into a man, possess him, and move his organs in such strange
and uncouth manner, as madmen use to do. The former sort
therefore, called such men, madmen: but the latter, called
them sometimes *demoniacs*, that is, possessed with spirits;
sometimes *enurgumeni*, that is, agitated or moved with spirits;
and now in Italy they are called, not only *pazzi*, madmen; but
also *spiritati*, men possessed.

There was once a great conflux of people in Abdera, a city
of the Greeks, at the acting of the tragedy of *Andromeda*,
upon an extreme hot day; whereupon, a great many of the
spectators falling into fevers, had this accident from the heat,
and from the tragedy together, that they did nothing but
pronounce iambics, with the names of Perseus and Andromeda; which, together with the fever, was cured by the
coming on of winter; and this madness was thought to
proceed from the passion imprinted by the tragedy. Likewise
there reigned a fit of madness in another Grecian city, which
seized only the young maidens; and caused many of them to
hang themselves. This was by most then thought an act of
the Devil. But one that suspected, that contempt of life in
them, might proceed from some passion of the mind, and
supposing that they did not contemn also their honour, gave
counsel to the magistrates, to strip such as so hanged themselves, and let them hang out naked. This, the story says,
cured that madness. But on the other side, the same Grecians,
did often ascribe madness to the operation of Eumenides, or
Furies; and sometimes of Ceres, Phoebus, and other gods;
so much did men attribute to phantasms, as to think them
aereal living bodies; and generally to call them spirits. And
as the Romans in this, held the same opinion with the Greeks,
so also did the Jews; for they called madmen prophets, or,

according as they thought the spirits good or bad, demoniacs:
and some of them called both prophets and demoniacs, madmen; and some called the same man both demoniac, and madman. But for the Gentiles it is no wonder, because diseases
and health, vices and virtues, and many natural accidents,
were with them termed, and worshipped as demons. So that
a man was to understand by demon, as well, sometimes an
ague, as a devil. But for the Jews to have such opinion, is
somewhat strange. For neither Moses nor Abraham pretended
to prophecy by possession of a spirit; but from the voice of
God; or by a vision or dream: nor is there anything in his law,
moral or ceremonial, by which they were taught, there was
any such enthusiasm, or any possession. When God is said,
(*Numb.* xi, 25) to take from the spirit that was in Moses, and
give to the seventy elders, the Spirit of God (taking it for the
substance of God) is not divided. The Scriptures, by the
Spirit of God in man, mean a man's spirit, inclined to godliness. And where it is said, (*Exod.* xxiii, 8) '*whom I have filled
with the spirit of wisdom to make garments for Aaron,*' is not meant
a spirit put into them, that can make garments, but the
wisdom of their own spirits in that kind of work. In the like
sense, the spirit of man, when it produceth unclean actions, is
ordinarily called an unclean spirit, and so other spirits, though
not always, yet as often as the virtue or vice so styled, is
extraordinary, and eminent. Neither did the other prophets of
the old Testament pretend enthusiasm; or, that God spake in
them; but to them, by voice, vision, or dream; and the
burthen of the Lord was not possession, but command. How
then could the Jews fall into this opinion of possession?
I can imagine no reason, but that which is common to all men;
namely, the want of curiosity to search natural causes: and
their placing felicity in the acquisition of the gross pleasures
of the senses, and the things that most immediately conduce
thereto. For they that see any strange, and unusual ability, or
defect, in a man's mind; unless they see withal, from what
cause it may probably proceed, can hardly think it natural;
and if not natural, they must needs think it supernatural; and
then what can it be, but that either God or the Devil is in him?
And hence it came to pass, when our Saviour (*Mark* iii, 21)

was compassed about with the multitude, those of the house doubted he was mad, and went out to hold him: but the Scribes said he had Beelzebub, and that was it, by which he cast out devils; as if the greater madman had awed the lesser: and that (*John* x, 20) some said, *he hath a devil, and is mad*; whereas others holding him for a prophet, said, *these are not the words of one that hath a devil*. So in the old Testament he that came to anoint Jehu, (2 *Kings* ix, 11) was a prophet; but some of the company asked Jehu, *what came that madman for?* So that in sum, it is manifest, that whosoever behaved himself in extraordinary manner, was thought by the Jews to be possessed either with a good, or evil spirit; except by the Sadducees, who erred so far on the other hand, as not to believe there were at all any spirits, which is very near to direct atheism; and thereby perhaps the more provoked others, to term such men demoniacs, rather than madmen.

But why then does our Saviour proceed in the curing of them, as if they were possessed; and not as if they were mad? To which I can give no other kind of answer, but that which is given to those that urge the Scripture in like manner against the opinion of the motion of the earth. The Scripture was written to shew unto men the kingdom of God, and to prepare their minds to become his obedient subjects; leaving the world, and the philosophy thereof, to the disputation of men, for the exercising of their natural reason. Whether the earth's, or sun's motion make the day, and night; or whether the exorbitant actions of men, proceed from passion, or from the devil, so we worship him not, it is all one, as to our obedience, and subjection to God Almighty; which is the thing for which the Scripture was written. As for that our Saviour speaketh to the disease, as to a person; it is the usual phrase of all that cure by words only, as Christ did, and enchanters pretend to do, whether they speak to a devil or not. For is not Christ also said (*Matt.* viii, 26) to have rebuked the winds? Is not he said also (*Luke* iv, 39) to rebuke a fever? Yet this does not argue that a fever is a devil. And whereas many of the devils are said to confess Christ; it is not necessary to interpret those places otherwise, than that those madmen confessed him. And whereas our Saviour

(*Matt.* xii, 43) speaketh of an unclean spirit, that having gone out of a man, wandereth through dry places, seeking rest, and finding none, and returning into the same man, with seven other spirits worse than himself; it is manifestly a parable, alluding to a man, that after a little endeavour to quit his lusts, is vanquished by the strength of them; and becomes seven times worse than he was. So that I see nothing at all in the Scripture, that requireth a belief, that demoniacs were any other thing but madmen.

There is yet another fault in the discourses of some men; which may also be numbered amongst the sorts of madness; namely, that abuse of words, whereof I have spoken before in the fifth chapter, by the name of absurdity. And that is, when men speak such words, as put together, have in them no signification at all; but are fallen upon by some, through mis-understanding of the words they have received, and repeat by rote; by others from intention to deceive by obscurity. And this is incident to none but those, that converse in questions of matters incomprehensible, as the School-men; or in questions of abstruse philosophy. The common sort of men seldom speak insignificantly, and are therefore, by those other egregious persons counted idiots. But to be assured their words are without any thing correspondent to them in the mind, there would need some examples; which if any man require, let him take a School-man in his hands and see if he can translate any one chapter concerning any difficult point, as the Trinity; the Deity; the nature of Christ; transubstantia-tion; free-will, &c, into any of the modern tongues, so as to make the same intelligible; or into any tolerable Latin, such as they were acquainted withal, that lived when the Latin tongue was vulgar. What is the meaning of these words, *The first cause does not necessarily inflow any thing into the second, by force of the essential subordination of the second causes, by which it may help it to work*? They are the translation of the title of the sixth chapter of *Suarez'* first book, *Of the concourse, motion, and help of God.* When men write whole volumes of such stuff, are they not mad, or intend to make others so? And particularly, in the question of transubstantiation; where after certain words spoken; they that say, the white*ness*, round*ness*, magni*tude*, quali*ty*, corruptibili*ty*, all which are incorporeal, &c. go out of the wafer, into the body of our blessed Saviour, do they not make those *nesses*, *tudes*, and *ties*, to be so many spirits possessing his body? For by spirits, they mean always things, that being incorporeal, are nevertheless moveable from one place to another. So that this kind of absurdity, may rightly be numbered amongst the many sorts of madness; and all the time that guided by clear thoughts of their worldly lust, they forbear disputing, or writing thus, but lucid intervals. And thus much of the virtues and defects intellectual.

CHAPTER IX

Of the Several Subjects of Knowledge

THERE are of KNOWLEDGE two kinds; whereof one is *knowledge of fact*: the other *knowledge of the consequence of one affirmation to another*. The former is nothing else, but sense and memory, and is *absolute knowledge*; as when we see a fact doing, or remember it done: and this is the knowledge required in a witness. The latter is called *science*; and is *conditional*; as when we know, that, *if the figure shown be a circle, then any straight line through the centre shall divide it into two equal parts*. And this is the knowledge required in a philosopher; that is to say, of him that pretends to reasoning.

The register of *knowledge of fact* is called *history*. Whereof there be two sorts: one called *natural history*; which is the history of such facts, or effects of nature, as have no dependence on man's *will*; such as are the histories of *metals*, *plants*, *animals*, *regions*, and the like. The other, is *civil history*; which is the history of the voluntary actions of men in commonwealths.

The registers of science, are such *books* as contain the *demonstrations* of consequences of one affirmation, to another; and are commonly called *books of philosophy*; whereof the sorts are many, according to the diversity of the matter; and may be divided in such manner as I have divided them in the following table.

SCIENCE, that is, knowledge of consequences; which is called also **PHILOSOPHY.**

- Consequences from the accidents of bodies natural; which is called **NATURAL PHILOSOPHY.**
  - Consequences from the accidents common to all bodies natural; which are *quantity*, and *motion*
  - **PHYSICS** or consequences from *qualities.*
    - Consequences from the qualities of bodies *transient*, such as sometimes appear, sometimes vanish, *Meteorology.*
    - Consequences from the qualities of bodies *permanent*.
      - Consequences from the qualities of the *stars.*
      - Consequences of the qualities from *liquid* bodies, that fill the space between the stars; such as are the *air*, or substances ethereal.
      - Consequences from the qualities of *bodies terrestrial.*

- Consequences from the accidents of *politic* bodies; which is called **POLITICS,** and **CIVIL PHILOSOPHY.**
  - 1. Of consequences from the *institution* of **COMMONWEALTHS,** to the *rights*, and *duties* of the *body politic* or *sovereign*.
  - 2. Of consequences from the same, to the *duty* and *right* of the *subjects*.

Consequences from quantity, and motion *indeterminate*; which being the principles or first foundation of philosophy, is called *Philosophia Prima* — PHILOSOPHIA PRIMA.

Consequences from motion and quantity *determined.*
- Consequences from quantity, and motion determined.
  - By Figure — } *Mathematics* — GEOMETRY
  - By Number — } *Mathematics* — ARITHMETIC
- Consequences from the motion, and quantity of bodies in *special*
  - Consequences from the motion and quantity of the greater parts of the world, as the *earth and stars.* — *Cosmography* — ASTRONOMY, GEOGRAPHY
  - Consequences from the motions of special kinds, and figures of body. — *Mechanics.* Doctrine of *weight.* — *Science* of ENGINEERS, ARCHITECTURE, NAVIGATION

. . . . METEOROLOGY

Consequences from the *light* of the stars. Out of this, and the motion of the sun, is made the science of — SCIOGRAPHY

Consequences from the *influences* of the stars — ASTROLOGY

Consequences from the parts of the earth, that are *without sense.*
- Consequences from the qualities of *minerals*, as *stones, metals,* &c.
- Consequences from the qualities of *vegetables.*

Consequences from the qualities of *animals.*
- Consequences from the qualities of *animals in general.*
  - Consequences from *vision* — OPTICS
  - Consequences from *sounds* — MUSIC
  - Consequences from the rest of the *senses.*
- Consequences from the qualities of *men in special.*
  - Consequences from the *passions* of men — } ETHICS
  - Consequences from *speech.*
    - In *magnifying, vilifying,* &c. — } POETRY.
    - In *persuading,* — RHETORIC.
    - In *reasoning.* — LOGIC.
    - In *contracting,* — The *Science* of JUST and UNJUST.

CHAPTER X

Of Power, Worth, Dignity, Honour, and Worthiness

THE POWER *of a man*, to take it universally, is his present means; to obtain some future apparent good; and is either *original* or *instrumental*.

Natural power, is the eminence of the faculties of body, or mind: as extraordinary strength, form, prudence, arts, eloquence, liberality, nobility. *Instrumental* are those powers, which acquired by these, or by fortune, are means and instruments to acquire more: as riches, reputation, friends, and the secret working of God, which men call good luck. For the nature of power, is in this point, like to fame, increasing as it proceeds; or like the motion of heavy bodies, which the further they go, make still the more haste.

The greatest of human powers, is that which is compounded of the powers of most men, united by consent, in one person, natural, or civil, that has the use of all their powers depending on his will; such as is the power of a common-wealth: or depending on the wills of each particular; such as is the power of a faction or of divers factions leagued. Therefore to have servants, is power; to have friends, is power: for they are strengths united.

Also riches joined with liberality, is power; because it procureth friends, and servants: without liberality, not so; because in this case they defend not; but expose men to envy, as a prey.

Reputation of power, is power; because it draweth with it the adherence of those that need protection.

So is reputation of love of a man's country, called popularity, for the same reason.

Also, what quality soever maketh a man beloved, or feared of many; or the reputation of such quality, is power;

because it is a means to have the assistance, and service of many.

Good success is power; because it maketh reputation of wisdom, or good fortune; which makes men either fear him, or rely on him.

Affability of men already in power, is increase of power; because it gaineth love.

Reputation of prudence in the conduct of peace or war, is power; because to prudent men, we commit the government of ourselves, more willingly than to others.

Nobility is power, not in all places, but only in those commonwealths, where it has privileges: for in such privileges, consisteth their power.

Eloquence is power, because it is seeming prudence.

Form is power; because being a promise of good, it recommendeth men to the favour of women and strangers.

The sciences, are small power; because not eminent; and therefore, not acknowledged in any man; nor are at all, but in a few, and in them, but of a few things. For science is of that nature, as none can understand it to be, but such as in a good measure have attained it.

Arts of public use, as fortification, making of engines, and other instruments of war; because they confer to defence, and victory, are power: and though the true mother of them, be science, namely the mathematics; yet, because they are brought into the light, by the hand of the artificer, they be esteemed, the midwife passing with the vulgar for the mother, as his issue.

The *value*, or WORTH of a man, is as of all other things, his price; that is to say, so much as would be given for the use of his power: and therefore is not absolute; but a thing dependant on the need and judgment of another. An able conductor of soldiers, is of great price in time of war present, or imminent; but in peace not so. A learned and uncorrupt judge, is much worth in time of peace; but not so much in war. And as in other things, so in men, not the seller, but the buyer determines the price. For let a man, as most men do, rate themselves at the highest value they can; yet their true value is no more than it is esteemed by others.

The manifestation of the value we set on one another, is that which is commonly called honouring, and dishonouring. To value a man at a high rate, is to *honour* him; at a low rate, is to *dishonour* him. But high, and low, in this case, is to be understood by comparison to the rate that each man setteth on himself.

The public worth of a man, which is the value set on him by the commonwealth, is that which men commonly call DIGNITY. And this value of him by the commonwealth, is understood, by offices of command, judicature, public employment; or by names and titles, introduced for distinction of such value.

To pray to another, for aid of any kind, is *to* HONOUR; because a sign we have an opinion he has power to help; and the more difficult the aid is, the more is the honour.

To obey, is to honour, because no man obeys them, whom they think have no power to help, or hurt them. And consequently to disobey, is to *dishonour*.

To give great gifts to a man, is to honour him; because it is buying of protection, and acknowledging of power. To give little gifts, is to dishonour; because it is but alms, and signifies an opinion of the need of small helps.

To be sedulous in promoting another's good; also to flatter, is to honour; as a sign we seek his protection or aid. To neglect, is to dishonour.

To give way, or place to another, in any commodity, is to honour; being a confession of greater power. To arrogate, is to dishonour.

To show any sign of love, or fear of another, is to honour; for both to love, and to fear, is to value. To contemn, or less to love or fear, than he expects, is to dishonour; for it is undervaluing.

To praise, magnify, or call happy, is to honour; because nothing but goodness, power, and felicity is valued. To revile, mock, or pity, is to dishonour.

To speak to another with consideration, to appear before him with decency, and humility, is to honour him; as signs of fear to offend. To speak to him rashly, to do any thing before him obscenely, slovenly, impudently, is to dishonour.

To believe, to trust, to rely on another, is to honour him; sign of opinion of his virtue and power. To distrust, or not believe, is to dishonour.

To hearken to a man's counsel, or discourse of what kind soever is to honour; as a sign we think him wise, or eloquent, or witty. To sleep, or go forth, or talk the while, is to dishonour.

To do those things to another, which he takes for signs of honour, or which the law or custom makes so, is to honour; because in approving the honour done by others, he acknowledgeth the power which others acknowledge. To refuse to do them, is to dishonour.

To agree with in opinion, is to honour; as being a sign of approving his judgment, and wisdom. To dissent, is dishonour, and an upbraiding of error; and, if the dissent be in many things, of folly.

To imitate, is to honour; for it is vehemently to approve. To imitate one's enemy, is to dishonour.

To honour those another honours, is to honour him; as a sign of approbation of his judgment. To honour his enemies, is to dishonour him.

To employ in counsel, or in actions of difficulty, is to honour; as a sign of opinion of his wisdom, or other power. To deny employment in the same cases, to those that seek it, is to dishonour.

All these ways of honouring, are natural; and as well within as without commonwealths. But in commonwealths, where he, or they that have the supreme authority, can make whatsoever they please, to stand for signs of honour, there be other honours.

A sovereign doth honour a subject, with whatsoever title, or office, or employment, or action, that he himself will have taken for a sign of his will to honour him.

The king of Persia, honoured Mordecai, when he appointed he should be conducted through the streets in the king's garment, upon one of the king's horses, with a crown on his head, and a prince before him, proclaiming, *thus shall it be done to him that the king will honour*. And yet another king of Persia, or the same another time, to one that demanded for some great service, to wear one of the king's robes, gave him leave so to do; but with this addition, that he should wear it as the king's fool; and then it was dishonour. So that of civil honour, the fountain is in the person of the commonwealth, and dependeth on the will of the sovereign; and is therefore temporary, and called *civil honour*; such as magistracy, offices, titles; and in some places coats and scutcheons painted: and men honour such as have them, as having so many signs of favour in the commonwealth; which favour is power.

Honourable is whatsoever possession, action, or quality, is an argument and sign of power.

And therefore to be honoured, loved, or feared of many, is honourable; as arguments of power. To be honoured of few or none, *dishonourable*.

Dominion, and victory is honourable; because acquired by power; and servitude, for need, or fear, is dishonourable.

Good fortune, if lasting, honourable; as a sign of the favour of God. Ill fortune, and losses, dishonourable. Riches, are honourable for they are power. Poverty, dishonourable. Magnanimity, liberality, hope, courage, confidence, are honourable; for they proceed from the conscience of power. Pusillanimity, parsimony, fear, diffidence, are dishonourable.

Timely resolution, or determination of what a man is to do, is honourable; as being the contempt of small difficulties, and dangers. And irresolution, dishonourable; as a sign of too much valuing of little impediments, and little advantages: for when a man has weighed things as long as the time permits, and resolves not, the difference of weight is but little; and therefore if he resolve not, he overvalues little things, which is pusillanimity.

All actions, and speeches, that proceed, or seem to proceed, from much experience, science, discretion, or wit, are honourable; for all these are powers. Actions, or words that proceed from error, ignorance, or folly, dishonourable.

Gravity, as far forth as it seems to proceed from a mind employed on something else, is honourable; because employment is a sign of power. But if it seem to proceed from a purpose to appear grave, it is dishonourable. For the gravity of the former, is like the steadiness of a ship laden with merchandize; but of the latter, like the steadiness of a ship ballasted with sand, and other trash.

To be conspicuous, that is to say, to be known, for wealth, office, great actions, or any eminent good, is honourable; as a sign of the power for which he is conspicuous. On the contrary, obscurity, is dishonourable.

To be descended from conspicuous parents, is honourable; because they the more easily attain the aids, and friends of their ancestors. On the contrary, to be descended from obscure parentage, is dishonourable.

Actions proceeding from equity, joined with loss, are honourable; as signs of magnanimity: for magnanimity is a sign of power. On the contrary, craft, shifting, neglect of equity, is dishonourable.

Covetousness of great riches, and ambition of great honours, are honourable; as signs of power to obtain them. Covetousness, and ambition, of little gains, or preferments, is dishonourable.

Nor does it alter the case of honour, whether an action, so it be great and difficult, and consequently a sign of much power, be just or unjust: for honour consisteth only in the opinion of power. Therefore the ancient heathen did not think they dishonoured, but greatly honoured the Gods, when they introduced them in their poems, committing rapes, thefts, and other great, but unjust, or unclean acts: insomuch as nothing is so much celebrated in Jupiter, as his adulteries; nor in Mercury, as his frauds, and thefts: of whose praises, in a hymn of Homer, the greatest is this, that being born in the morning, he had invented music at noon, and before night, stolen away the cattle of Apollo, from his herdsmen.

Also amongst men, till there were constituted great commonwealths, it was thought no dishonour to be a pirate, or a highway thief; but rather a lawful trade, not only amongst the Greeks, but also amongst all other nations; as is manifest by the histories of ancient time. And at this day, in this part of the world, private duels are, and always will be honourable, though unlawful, till such time as there shall be honour ordained for them that refuse, and ignominy for them that make the challenge. For duels also are many times effects of courage; and the ground of courage is always strength or skill, which are power; though for the most part they be effects of rash speaking, and of the fear of dishonour, in one, or both the combatants; who engaged by rashness, are driven into the lists to avoid disgrace.

Scutcheons, and coats of arms hereditary, where they have any eminent privileges, are honourable; otherwise not: for their power consisteth either in such privileges, or in riches, or some such thing as is equally honoured in other men. This kind of honour, commonly called gentry, hath been derived from the ancient Germans. For there never was any such thing known, where the German customs were unknown. Nor is it now any where in use, where the Germans have not inhabited. The ancient Greek commanders, when they went to war, had their shields painted with such devices as they pleased; insomuch as an unpainted buckler was a sign of poverty, and of a common soldier; but they transmitted not the inheritance of them. The Romans transmitted the marks of their families: but they were the images, not the devices of their ancestors. Amongst the people of Asia, Africa, and America, there is not, nor was ever, any such thing. The Germans only had that custom; from whom it has been derived into England, France, Spain, and Italy, when in great numbers they either aided the Romans, or made their own conquests in these western parts of the world.

For Germany, being anciently, as all other countries, in their beginnings, divided amongst an infinite number of little lords or masters of families, that continually had wars one with another; those masters, or lords, principally to the end they might, when they were covered with arms, be known by their followers; and partly for ornament, both painted their armour, or their scutcheon, or coat, with the picture of some beast, or other thing; and also put some eminent and visible mark upon the crest of their helmets. And this ornament both of the arms, and crest, descended by inheritance to their children; to the eldest pure, and to the rest with some note of diversity, such as the old master, that is to say in Dutch, the *Here-alt* thought fit. But when many such families, joined together, made a greater monarchy, this duty of the Herealt, to distinguish scutcheons, was made a private office apart. And the issue of these lords, is the great and ancient gentry; which for the most part bear living creatures, noted for courage, and rapine; or castles, battlements, belts, weapons, bars, palisadoes, and other notes of war; nothing being then in honour, but virtue military. Afterwards, not only kings, but popular commonwealths, gave divers manners of scutcheons, to such as went forth to the war, or returned from it, for encouragement, or recompense to their service. All which, by an observing reader, may be found in such ancient histories, Greek and Latin, as make mention of the German nation and manners, in their times.

Titles of *honour*, such as are duke, count, marquis, and baron, are honourable; as signifying the value set upon them by the sovereign power of the commonwealth: which titles, were in old time titles of office, and command, derived some from the Romans, some from the Germans and French: dukes, in Latin *duces*, being generals in war: counts, *comites*, such as bear the general company out of friendship, and were left to govern and defend places conquered, and pacified: marquises, *marchiones*, were counts that governed the marches, or bounds of the empire. Which titles of duke, count, and marquis, came into the empire, about the time of Constantine the Great, from the customs of the German *militia*. But baron, seems to have been a title of the Gauls, and signifies a great man; such as were the king's, or prince's men, whom they employed in war about their persons; and seems to be derived from *vir*, to *ber*, and *bar*, that signified the same in the language of the Gauls, that *vir* in Latin; and thence to *bero*, and *baro*: so that such men were called *berones*, and after *barones*; and, in Spanish, *varones*. But he that would know more particularly the original of titles of honour, may find it, as I have done this, in Mr. Selden's most excellent treatise of that subject. In process of time these offices of honour, by occasion of trouble, and for reasons of good and peaceable government, were turned into mere titles; serving for the most part, to distinguish the precedence, place, and order of subjects in the commonwealth: and men were made dukes, counts, marquises, and barons of places, wherein they had neither possession, nor command: and other titles also, were devised to the same end.

WORTHINESS, is a thing different from the worth, or value of a man; and also from his merit, or desert, and consisteth in a particular power, or ability for that, whereof he is said to be worthy: which particular ability, is usually named FITNESS, or *aptitude*.

For he is worthiest to be a commander, to be a judge, or to have any other charge, that is best fitted, with the qualities required to the well discharging of it; and worthiest of riches, that has the qualities most requisite for the well using of them: any of which qualities being absent, one may nevertheless be a worthy man, and valuable for something else. Again, a man may be worthy of riches, office, and employment, that nevertheless, can plead no right to have it before another; and therefore cannot be said to merit or deserve it. For merit presupposeth a right, and that the thing deserved is due by promise: of which I shall say more hereafter, when I shall speak of contracts.

CHAPTER XI

Of the Difference of Manners

BY MANNERS, I mean not here, decency of behaviour; as how one should salute another, or how a man should wash his mouth, or pick his teeth before company, and such other points of the *small morals*; but those qualities of mankind, that concern their living together in peace, and unity. To which end we are to consider, that the felicity of this life, consisteth not in the repose of a mind satisfied. For there is no such *finis ultimus*, utmost aim, nor *summum bonum*, greatest good, as is spoken of in the books of the old moral philosophers. Nor can a man any more live, whose desires are at an end, than he, whose senses and imaginations are at a stand. Felicity is a continual progress of the desire, from one object to another; the attaining of the former, being still but the way to the latter. The cause whereof is, that the object of man's desire, is not to enjoy once only, and for one instant of time; but to assure for ever, the way of his future desire. And therefore the voluntary actions, and inclinations of all men, tend, not only to the procuring, but also to the assuring of a contented life; and differ only in the way: which ariseth partly from the diversity of passions, in divers men; and partly from the difference of the knowledge, or opinion each one has of the causes, which produce the effect desired.

So that in the first place, I put for a general inclination of all mankind, a perpetual and restless desire of power after power, that ceaseth only in death. And the cause of this, is not always that a man hopes for a more intensive delight, than he has already attained to; or that he cannot be content with a moderate power: but because he cannot assure the power and means to live well, which he hath present, without the acquisition of more. And from hence it is, that kings, whose power is greatest, turn their endeavours to the assuring it at home by laws, or abroad by wars: and when that is done, there succeedeth a new desire; in some, of fame from new conquest; in others, of ease and sensual pleasure; in others of admiration, or being flattered for excellence in some art, or other ability of the mind.

Competition of riches, honour, command, or other power, inclineth to contention, enmity, and war: because the way of one competitor, to the attaining of his desire is to kill, subdue, supplant, or repel the other. Particularly, competition of praise, inclineth to a reverence of antiquity. For men contend with the living, not with the dead; to these ascribing more than due, that they may obscure the glory of the other.

Desire of ease, and sensual delight, disposeth men to obey a common power: because by such desires, a man doth abandon the protection that might be hoped for from his own industry, and labour. Fear of death, and wounds, disposeth to the same; and for the same reason. On the contrary, needy men, and hardy, not contented with their present condition: as also, all men that are ambitious of military command are inclined to continue the causes of war; and to stir up trouble and sedition: for there is no honour military but by war; nor any such hope to mend an ill game, as by causing a new shuffle.

Desire of knowledge, and arts of peace, inclineth men to obey a common power: for such desire, containeth a desire of leisure; and consequently protection from some other power than their own.

Desire of praise, disposeth to laudable actions, such as please them whose judgment they value; for of those men whom we contemn, we contemn also the praises. Desire of fame after death does the same. And though after death, there be no sense of the praise given us on earth, as being joys, that are either swallowed up in the unspeakable joys of Heaven, or extinguished in the extreme torments of hell: yet is not such fame vain; because men have a present delight therein, from the foresight of it, and of the benefit that may redound thereby to their posterity: which though they now see not, yet they imagine; and anything that is pleasure to the sense, the same also is pleasure in the imagination.

To have received from one, to whom we think ourselves equal, greater benefits than there is hope to requite, disposeth to counterfeit love; but really secret hatred; and puts a man into the estate of a desperate debtor, that in declining the sight of his creditor, tacitly wishes him there, where he might never see him more. For benefits oblige; and obligation is thraldom; and unrequitable obligation perpetual thraldom; which is to one's equal, hateful. But to have received benefits from one, whom we acknowledge for superior, inclines to love; because the obligation is no new depression: and cheerful acceptation, which men call *gratitude*, is such an honour done to the obliger, as is taken generally for retribution. Also to receive benefits, though from an equal, or inferior, as long as there is hope of requital, disposeth to love: for in the intention of the receiver, the obligation is of aid and service mutual; from whence proceedeth an emulation of who shall exceed in benefiting; the most noble and profitable contention possible; wherein the victor is pleased with his victory, and the other revenged by confessing it.

To have done more hurt to a man, than he can, or is willing

to expiate, inclineth the doer to hate the sufferer. For he must expect revenge, or forgiveness; both which are hateful.

Fear of oppression, disposeth a man to anticipate, or to seek aid by society: for there is no other way by which a man can secure his life and liberty.

Men that distrust their own subtlety, are, in tumult and sedition, better disposed for victory, than they that suppose themselves wise, or crafty. For these love to consult, the other, fearing to be circumvented, to strike first. And in sedition, men being always in the precincts of battle, to hold together, and use all advantages of force, is a better stratagem, than any that can proceed from subtlety of wit.

Vain-glorious men, such as without being conscious to themselves of great sufficiency, delight in supposing themselves gallant men, are inclined only to ostentation; but not to attempt: because when danger or difficulty appears, they look for nothing but to have their insufficiency discovered.

Vain-glorious men, such as estimate their sufficiency by the flattery of other men, or the fortune of some precedent action, without assured ground of hope from the true knowledge of themselves, are inclined to rash engaging; and in the approach of danger, or difficulty, to retire if they can: because not seeing the way of safety, they will rather hazard their honour, which may be salved with an excuse; than their lives, for which no salve is sufficient.

Men that have a strong opinion of their own wisdom in matter of government, are disposed to ambition. Because without public employment in council or magistracy, the honour of their wisdom is lost. And therefore eloquent speakers are inclined to ambition; for eloquence seemeth wisdom, both to themselves and others.

Pusillanimity disposeth men to irresolution, and consequently to lose the occasions, and fittest opportunities of action. For after men have been in deliberation till the time of action approach, if it be not then manifest what is best to be done, it is a sign, the difference of motives, the one way and the other, are not great: therefore not to resolve then, is to lose the occasion by weighing of trifles; which is pusillanimity.

Frugality, though in poor men a virtue, maketh a man

unapt to achieve such actions, as require the strength of many men at once: for it weakeneth their endeavour, which is to be nourished and kept in vigour by reward.

Eloquence, with flattery, disposeth men to confide in them that have it; because the former is seeming wisdom, the latter seeming kindness. Add to them military reputation, and it disposeth men to adhere, and subject themselves to those men that have them. The two former having given them caution against danger from him; the latter gives them caution against danger from others.

Want of science, that is, ignorance of causes, disposeth, or rather constraineth a man to rely on the advice, and authority of others. For all men whom the truth concerns, if they rely not on their own, must rely on the opinion of some other, whom they think wiser than themselves, and see not why he should deceive them.

Ignorance of the signification of words, which is want of understanding, disposeth men to take on trust, not only the truth they know not; but also the errors; and which is more, the nonsense of them they trust: for neither error nor nonsense, can without a perfect understanding of words, be detected.

From the same it proceedeth, that men give different names, to one and the same thing, from the difference of their own passions: as they that approve a private opinion, call it opinion; but they that mislike it, heresy: and yet heresy signifies no more than private opinion; but has only a greater tincture of choler.

From the same also it proceedeth, that men cannot distinguish, without study and great understanding, between one action of many men, and many actions of one multitude; as for example, between one action of all the senators of Rome in killing Cataline, and the many actions of a number of senators in killing Caesar; and therefore are disposed to take for the action of the people, that which is a multitude of actions done by a multitude of men, led perhaps by the persuasion of one.

Ignorance of the causes, and original constitution of right, equity, law, and justice, disposeth a man to make custom and example the rule of his actions; in such manner, as to think that unjust which it hath been the custom to punish; and that just, of the impunity and approbation whereof they can produce an example, or, as the lawyers which only use this false measure of justice barbarously call it, a precedent; like little children, that have no other rule of good and evil manners, but the correction they receive from their parents and masters; save that children are constant to their rule, whereas, men are not so; because grown old, and stubborn, they appeal from custom to reason, and from reason to custom, as it serves their turn; receding from custom when their interest requires it, and setting themselves against reason, as oft as reason is against them: which is the cause, that the doctrine of right and wrong, is perpetually disputed, both by the pen and the sword: whereas the doctrine of lines, and figures, is not so; because men care not, in that subject, what be truth, as a thing that crosses no man's ambition, profit or lust. For I doubt not, but if it had been a thing contrary to any man's right of dominion, or to the interest of men that have dominion, *that the three angles of a triangle, should be equal to two angles of a square*; that doctrine should have been, if not disputed, yet by the burning of all books of geometry, suppressed, as far as he whom it concerned was able.

Ignorance of remote causes, disposeth men to attribute all events, to the causes immediate, and instrumental: for these are all the causes they perceive. And hence it comes to pass, that in all places, men that are grieved with payments to the public, discharge their anger upon the publicans, that is to say, farmers, collectors, and other officers of the public revenue; and adhere to such as find fault with the public government; and thereby, when they have engaged themselves beyond hope of justification, fall also upon the supreme authority, for fear of punishment, or shame of receiving pardon.

Ignorance of natural causes, disposeth a man to credulity, so as to believe many times impossibilities: for such know nothing to the contrary, but that they may be true; being unable to detect the impossibility. And credulity, because men like to be hearkened unto in company, disposeth them to lying: so that ignorance itself without malice, is able to make a man both to believe lies, and tell them; and sometimes also to invent them.

Anxiety for the future time, disposeth men to inquire into the causes of things: because the knowledge of them, maketh men the better able to order the present to their best advantage.

Curiosity, or love of the knowledge of causes, draws a man from the consideration of the effect, to seek the cause; and again, the cause of that cause; till of necessity he must come to this thought at last, that there is some cause, whereof there is no former cause, but is eternal; which is it men call God. So that it is impossible to make any profound inquiry into natural causes, without being inclined thereby to believe there is one God eternal; though they cannot have any idea of him in their mind, answerable to his nature. For as a man that is born blind, hearing men talk of warming themselves by the fire, and being brought to warm himself by the same, may easily conceive, and assure himself there is somewhat there, which men call *fire*, and is the cause of the heat he feels; but cannot imagine what it is like; nor have an idea of it in his mind, such as they have that see it: so also by the visible things in this world, and their admirable order, a man may conceive there is a cause of them, which men call God; and yet not have an idea, or image of him in his mind.

And they that make little, or no inquiry into the natural causes of things, yet from the fear that proceeds from the ignorance itself, of what it is that hath the power to do them much good or harm, are inclined to suppose, and feign unto themselves, several kinds of powers invisible; and to stand in awe of their own imaginations; and in time of distress to invoke them; as also in the time of an expected good success, to give them thanks; making the creatures of their own fancy, their gods. By which means it hath come to pass, that from the innumerable variety of fancy, men have created in the world innumerable sorts of gods. And this fear of things invisible, is the natural seed of that, which every one in himself calleth religion; and in them that worship, or fear that power otherwise than they do, superstition.

And this seed of religion, having been observed by many;

some of those that have observed it, have been inclined thereby to nourish, dress, and form it into laws; and to add to it of their own invention, any opinion of the causes of future events, by which they thought they should be best able to govern others, and make unto themselves the greatest use of their powers.

CHAPTER XII

Of Religion

SEEING there are no signs, nor fruit of *religion*, but in man only; there is no cause to doubt, but that the seed of *religion*, is also in man; and consisteth in some peculiar quality, or at least in some eminent degree thereof, not to be found in any other living creatures.

And first, it is peculiar to the nature of man, to be inquisitive into the causes of the events they see, some more, some less; but all men so much, as to be curious in the search of the causes of their own good and evil fortune.

Secondly, upon the sight of anything that hath a beginning, to think also it had a cause, which determined the same to begin, then when it did, rather than sooner or later.

Thirdly, whereas there is no other felicity of beasts, but the enjoying of their quotidian food, ease, and lusts; as having little or no foresight of the time to come, for want of observation, and memory of the order, consequence, and dependence of the things they see; man observeth how one event hath been produced by another; and remembereth in them antecedence and consequence; and when he cannot assure himself of the true causes of things, (for the causes of good and evil fortune for the most part are invisible), he supposes causes of them, either such as his own fancy suggesteth; or trusteth the authority of other men, such as he thinks to be his friends, and wiser than himeslf.

The two first, make anxiety. For being assured that there be causes of all things that have arrived hitherto, or shall arrive hereafter; it is impossible for a man, who continually endeavoureth to secure himself against the evil he fears, and procure the good he desireth, not to be in a perpetual solicitude of the time to come; so that every man, especially those that are over provident, are in a state like to that of Prometheus. For as Prometheus, which interpreted, is, *the prudent man*, was bound to the hill Caucasus, a place of large prospect, where, an eagle feeding on his liver, devoured in the day, as much as was repaired in the night: so that man, which looks too far before him, in the care of future time, hath his heart all the day long, gnawed on by fear of death, poverty, or other calamity; and has no repose, nor pause of his anxiety, but in sleep.

This perpetual fear, always accompanying mankind in the ignorance of causes, as it were in the dark, must needs have for object something. And therefore when there is nothing to be seen, there is nothing to accuse, either of their good, or evil fortune, but some *power*, or agent *invisible*: in which sense perhaps it was, that some of the old poets said, that the gods were at first created by human fear: which spoken of the gods, that is to say, of the many gods of the Gentiles, is very true. But the acknowledging of one God, eternal, infinite, and omnipotent, may more easily be derived, from the desire men have to know the causes of natural bodies, and their several virtues, and operations; than from the fear of what was to befall them in time to come. For he that from any effect he seeth come to pass, should reason to the next and immediate cause thereof, and from thence to the cause of that cause, and plunge himself profoundly in the pursuit of causes; shall at last come to this, that there must be, as even the heathen philosophers confessed, one first mover; that is, a first, and an eternal cause of all things; which is that which men mean by the name of God: and all this without thought of their fortune; the solicitude whereof, both inclines to fear, and hinders them from the search of the causes of other things; and thereby gives occasion of feigning of as many gods, as there be men that feign them.

And for the matter, or substance of the invisible agents, so fancied; they could not by natural cogitation, fall upon any other conceit, but that it was the same with that of the soul of man; and that the soul of man, was of the same substance, with that which appeareth in a dream, to one that sleepeth; or in a looking-glass, to one that is awake; which, men not knowing that such apparitions are nothing else but creatures of the fancy, think to be real, and external substances; and therefore call them ghosts; as the Latins called them *imagines*, and *umbrae*; and thought them spirits, that is, thin aerial bodies; and those invisible agents, which they feared, to be like them; save that they appear, and vanish when they please. But the opinion that such spirits were incorporeal, or immaterial, could never enter into the mind of any man by nature; because, though men may put together words of contradictory signification, as *spirit*, and *incorporeal*; yet they can never have the imagination of any thing answering to them: and therefore, men that by their own meditation, arrive to the acknowledgment of one infinite, omnipotent, and eternal God, chose rather to confess he is incomprehensible, and above their understanding, than to define his nature by *spirit incorporeal*, and then confess their definition to be unintelligible: or if they give him such a title, it is not *dogmatically*, with intention to make the divine nature understood; but *piously*, to honour him with attributes, of significations, as remote as they can from the grossness of bodies visible.

Then, for the way by which they think these invisible agents wrought their effects; that is to say, what immediate causes they used, in bringing things to pass, men that know not what it is that we call *causing*, that is, almost all men, have no other rule to guess by, but by observing, and remembering what they have seen to precede the like effect at some other time, or times before without seeing between the antecedent and subsequent event, any dependence or connexion at all: and therefore from the like things past, they expect the like things to come; and hope for good or evil luck, superstitiously, from things that have no part at all in the causing of it: as the Athenians did for their war at Lepanto, demand another Phormio; the Pompeian faction for their war in Africa, another Scipio; and others have done in divers other occasions since. In like manner they attribute their fortune to a stander by, to a lucky or unlucky place, to words spoken, especially if the name of God be amongst them; as charming and conjuring, the liturgy of witches; insomuch as to believe, they have power to turn a stone into bread, bread into a man, or any thing into any thing.

Thirdly, for the worship which naturally men exhibit to powers invisible, it can be no other, but such expressions of their reverence, as they would use towards men; gifts, petitions, thanks, submission of body, considerate addresses, sober behaviour, premeditated words, swearing, that is, assuring one another of their promises, by invoking them. Beyond that reason suggesteth nothing; but leaves them either to rest there; or for further ceremonies, to rely on those they believe to be wiser than themselves.

Lastly, concerning how these invisible powers declare to men the things which shall hereafter come to pass, especially concerning their good or evil fortune in general, or good or ill success in any particular undertaking, men are naturally at a stand; save that using to conjecture of the time to come, by the time past, they are very apt, not only to take casual things, after one or two encounters, for prognostics of the like encounter ever after, but also to believe the like prognostics from other men, of whom they have once conceived a good opinion.

And in these four things, opinion of ghosts, ignorance of second causes, devotion towards what men fear, and taking of things casual for prognostics, consisteth the natural seed of *religion*; which by reason of the different fancies, judgments, and passions of several men, hath grown up into ceremonies so different, that those which are used by one man, are for the most part ridiculous to another.

For these seeds have received culture from two sorts of men. One sort have been they, that have nourished, and ordered them, according to their own invention. The other have done it, by God's commandment, and direction: but both sorts have done it, with a purpose to make those men that relied on them, the more apt to obedience, laws, peace, charity, and civil society. So that the religion of the former sort, is a part of human politics; and teacheth part of the duty which earthly kings require of their subjects. And the religion of the latter sort is divine politics; and containeth precepts to those that have yielded themselves subjects in the kingdom of God. Of the former sort, were all the founders of commonwealths, and the lawgivers of the Gentiles: of the latter sort, were Abraham, Moses, and our blessed Saviour; by whom have been derived unto us the laws of the kingdom of God.

And for that part of religion, which consisteth in opinions concerning the nature of powers invisible, there is almost nothing that has a name, that has not been esteemed amongst the Gentiles, in one place or another, a god, or devil; or by their poets feigned to be inanimated, inhabited, or possessed by some spirit or other.

The unformed matter of the world, was a god, by the name of Chaos.

The heaven, the ocean, the planets, the fire, the earth, the winds, were so many gods.

Men, women, a bird, a crocodile, a calf, a dog, a snake, an onion, a leek, were deified. Besides that, they filled almost all places, with spirits called *demons*: the plains, with Pan, and Panises, or Satyrs; the woods, with Fawns, and Nymphs; the sea, with Tritons, and other Nymphs; every river, and fountain, with a ghost of his name, and with Nymphs; every house with its *Lares*, or familiars; every man with his *Genius*; hell with ghosts, and spiritual officers, as Charon, Cerberus, and the Furies; and in the night time, all places with *larvae*, *lemures*, ghosts of men deceased, and a whole kingdom of fairies and bugbears. They have also ascribed divinity, and built temples to mere accidents, and qualities; such as are time, night, day, peace, concord, love, contention, virtue, honour, health, rust, fever, and the like; which when they prayed for, or against, they prayed to, as if there were ghosts of those names hanging over their heads, and letting fall, or withholding that good, or evil, for, or against which they prayed. They invoked also their own wit, by the name of Muses; their own ignorance, by the name of Fortune; their own lusts by the name of Cupid; their own rage, by the name of Furies; their own privy members, by the name of Priapus;

and attributed their pollutions, to Incubi, and Succubae: insomuch as there was nothing, which a poet could introduce as a person in his poem, which they did not make either a *god*, or a *devil*.

The same authors of the religion of the Gentiles, observing the second ground for religion, which is men's ignorance of causes; and thereby their aptness to attribute their fortune to causes, on which there was no dependence at all apparent, took occasion to obtrude on their ignorance, instead of second causes, a kind of second and ministerial gods; ascribing the cause of fecundity, to Venus; the cause of arts, to Apollo; of subtlety and craft, to Mercury; of tempests and storms, to Æolus; and of other effects, to other gods; insomuch as there was amongst the heathen almost as great variety of gods, as of business.

And to the worship, which naturally men conceived fit to be used towards their gods, namely, oblations, prayers, thanks, and the rest formerly named; the same legislators of the Gentiles have added their images, both in picture, and sculpture; that the more ignorant sort, that is to say, the most part or generality of the people, thinking the gods for whose representation they were made, were really included, and as it were housed within them, might so much the more stand in fear of them: and endowed them with lands, and houses, and officers, and revenues, set apart from all other human uses; that is, consecrated, and made holy to those their idols; as caverns, groves, woods, mountains, and whole islands; and have attributed to them, not only the shapes, some of men, some of beasts, some of monsters; but also the faculties, and passions of men and beasts: as sense, speech, sex, lust, generation, and this not only by mixing one with another, to propagate the kind of gods; but also by mixing with men, and women, to beget mongrel gods, and but inmates of heaven, as Bacchus, Hercules, and others; besides anger, revenge, and other passions of living creatures, and the actions proceeding from them, as fraud, theft, adultery, sodomy, and any vice that may be taken for an effect of power, or a cause of pleasure; and all such vices, as amongst men are taken to be against law, rather than against honour.

Lastly, to the prognostics of time to come; which are naturally, but conjectures upon experience of time past; and supernaturally, divine revelation; the same authors of the religion of the Gentiles, partly upon pretended experience, partly upon pretended revelation, have added innumerable other superstitious ways of divination; and made men believe they should find their fortunes, sometimes in the ambiguous or senseless answers of the priests at Delphi, Delos, Ammon, and other famous oracles; which answers, were made ambiguous by design, to own the event both ways; or absurd, by the intoxicating vapour of the place, which is very frequent in sulphurous caverns: sometimes in the leaves of the Sybils; of whose prophecies, like those perhaps of Nostradamus (for the fragments now extant seem to be the invention of later times), there were some books in reputation in the time of the Roman republic: sometimes in the insignificant speeches of madmen, supposed to be possessed with a divine spirit, which possession they called enthusiasm; and these kinds of foretelling events, were accounted theomancy, or prophecy: sometimes in the aspect of the stars at their nativity; which was called horoscopy, and esteemed a part of judiciary astrology: sometimes in their own hopes and fears, called thumomancy, or presage: sometimes in the prediction of witches, that pretended conference with the dead; which is called necromancy, conjuring, and witchcraft; and is but juggling and confederate knavery: sometimes in the casual flight, or feeding of birds; called augury: sometimes in the entrails of a sacrificed beast; which was *aruspicina*: sometimes in dreams: sometimes in croaking of ravens, or chattering of birds: sometimes in the lineaments of the face; which was called metoposcopy; or by palmistry in the lines of the hand; in casual words, called *omina*: sometimes in monsters, or unusual accidents; as eclipses, comets, rare meteors, earthquakes, inundations, uncouth births, and the like, which they called *portenta*, and *ostenta*, because they thought them to portend, or foreshow some great calamity to come; sometimes, in mere lottery, as cross and pile; counting holes in a sieve; dipping of verses in Homer, and Virgil; and innumerable other such vain conceits. So easy are men to be drawn to believe any thing, from such men as have gotten credit with them; and can with gentleness, and dexterity, take hold of their fear, and ignorance.

And therefore the first founders, and legislators of commonwealths among the Gentiles, whose ends were only to keep the people in obedience, and peace, have in all places taken care; first, to imprint in their minds a belief, that those precepts which they gave concerning religion, might not be thought to proceed from their own device, but from the dictates of some god, or other spirit; or else that they themselves were of a higher nature than mere mortals, that their laws might the more easily be received: so Numa Pompilius pretended to receive the ceremonies he instituted amongst the Romans, from the nymph Egeria: and the first king and founder of the kingdom of Peru, pretended himself and his wife to be the children of the Sun; and Mahomet, to set up his new religion, pretended to have conferences with the Holy Ghost, in form of a dove. Secondly, they have had a care, to make it believed, that the same things were displeasing to the gods, which were forbidden by the laws. Thirdly, to prescribe ceremonies, supplications, sacrifices, and festivals, by which they were to believe, the anger of the gods might be appeased; and that ill success in war, great contagions of sickness, earthquakes, and each man's private misery, came from the anger of the gods, and their anger from the neglect of their worship, or the forgetting, or mistaking some point of the ceremonies required. And though amongst the ancient Romans, men were not forbidden to deny, that which in the poets is written of the pains, and pleasures after this life: which divers of great authority, and gravity in that state have in their harangues openly derided; yet that belief was always more cherished, than the contrary.

And by these, and such other institutions, they obtained in order to their end, which was the peace of the commonwealth, that the common people in their misfortunes, laying the fault on neglect, or error in their ceremonies, or on their own disobedience to the laws, were the less apt to mutiny against their governors; and being entertained with the pomp, and pastime of festivals, and public games, made in honour of the gods, needed nothing else but bread to keep them from discontent, murmuring, and commotion against the state. And therefore the Romans, that had conquered the greatest part of the then known world, made no scruple of tolerating any religion whatsoever in the city of Rome itself; unless it had something in it, that could not consist with their civil government; nor do we read, that any religion was there forbidden, but that of the Jews; who, being the peculiar kingdom of God, thought it unlawful to acknowledge subjection to any mortal king or state whatsoever. And thus you see how the religion of the Gentiles was a part of their policy.

But where God himself, by supernatural revelation, planted religion; there he also made to himself a peculiar kingdom: and gave laws, not only of behaviour towards himself, but also towards one another; and thereby in the kingdom of God, the policy, and laws civil, are a part of religion; and therefore the distinction of temporal, and spiritual domination, hath there no place. It is true, that God is king of all the earth: yet may he be king of a peculiar, and chosen nation. For there is no more incongruity therein, than that he that hath the general command of the whole army, should have withal a peculiar regiment, or company of his own. God is king of all the earth by his power: but of his chosen people, he is king by covenant. But to speak more largely of the kingdom of God, both by nature, and covenant, I have in the following discourse assigned another place (chapter xxxv).

From the propagation of religion, it is not hard to understand the causes of the resolution of the same into its first seeds, or principles; which are only an opinion of a deity, and powers invisible, and supernatural; that can never be so abolished out of human nature, but that new religions may again be made to spring out of them, by the culture of such men, as for such purpose are in reputation.

For seeing all formed religion, is founded at first, upon the faith which a multitude hath in some one person, whom they believe not only to be a wise man, and to labour to procure their happiness, but also to be a holy man, to whom God himself vouchsafeth to declare his will supernaturally; it followeth necessarily, when they that have the government of religion, shall come to have either the wisdom of those men, their sincerity, or their love suspected; or when they shall be unable to show any probable token of divine revelation; that the religion which they desire to uphold, must be suspected likewise; and, without the fear of the civil sword, contradicted and rejected.

That which taketh away the reputation of wisdom, in him that formeth a religion, or addeth to it when it is already formed, is the enjoining of a belief of contradictories: for both parts of a contradiction cannot possibly be true: and therefore to enjoin the belief of them, is an argument of ignorance; which detects the author in that; and discredits him in all things else he shall propound as from revelation supernatural: which revelation a man may indeed have of many things above, but of nothing against natural reason.

That which taketh away the reputation of sincerity, is the doing or saying of such things, as appear to be signs, that what they require other men to believe, is not believed by themselves; all which doings, or sayings are therefore called scandalous, because they be stumbling blocks, that make men to fall in the way of religion; as injustice, cruelty, profaneness, avarice, and luxury. For who can believe, that he that doth ordinarily such actions as proceed from any of these roots, believeth there is any such invisible power to be feared, as he affrighteth other men withal, for lesser faults?

That which taketh away the reputation of love, is the being detected of private ends: as when the belief they require of others, conduceth or seemeth to conduce to the acquiring of dominion, riches, dignity, or secure pleasure, to themselves only, or specially. For that which men reap benefit by to themselves, they are thought to do for their own sakes, and not for love of others.

Lastly, the testimony that men can render of divine calling, can be no other, than the operation of miracles; or true prophecy, which also is a miracle; or extraordinary felicity. And therefore, to those points of religion, which have been received from them that did such miracles; those that are added by such, as approve not their calling by some miracle, obtain no greater belief, than what the custom and laws of the places, in which they be educated, have wrought into them. For as in natural things, men of judgment require natural signs, and arguments; so in supernatural things, they require signs supernatural, which are miracles, before they consent inwardly, and from their hearts.

All which causes of the weakening of men's faith, do manifestly appear in the examples following. First, we have the example of the children of Israel; who when Moses, that had approved his calling to them by miracles, and by the happy conduct of them out of Egypt, was absent but forty days, revolted from the worship of the true God, recommended to them by him; and setting up (*Exod.* XXXIII, 1, 2) a golden calf for their god, relapsed into the idolatry of the Egyptians; from whom they had been so lately delivered. And again, after Moses, Aaron, Joshua, and that generation which had seen the great works of God in Israel, (*Judges* II, 11) were dead; another generation arose, and served Baal. So that miracles failing, faith also failed.

Again, when the sons of Samuel, (1 *Sam.* viii, 3) being constituted by their father judges in Bersabee, received bribes, and judged unjustly, the people of Israel refused any more to have God to be their king, in other manner than he was king of other people; and therefore cried out to Samuel, to chose them a king after the manner of the nations. So that justice failing, faith also failed: insomuch, as they deposed their God, from reigning over them.

And whereas in the planting of Christian religion, the oracles ceased in all parts of the Roman empire, and the number of Christians increased wonderfully every day, and in every place, by the preaching of the Apostles, and Evangelists; a great part of that success, may reasonably be attributed, to the contempt, into which the priests of the Gentiles of that time, had brought themselves, by their uncleanness, avarice, and juggling between princes. Also the religion of the church of Rome, was partly, for the same cause abolished in England, and many other parts of Christendom; insomuch, as the failing of virtue in the pastors, maketh faith fail in the people:

and partly from bringing of the philosophy, and doctrine of Aristotle into religion, by the Schoolmen; from whence there arose so many contradictions, and absurdities, as brought the clergy into a reputation both of ignorance, and of fraudulent intention; and inclined people to revolt from them, either against the will of their own princes, as in France and Holland; or with their will, as in England.

Lastly, amongst the points by the church of Rome declared necessary for salvation, there be so many, manifestly to the advantage of the Pope, and of his spiritual subjects, residing in the territories of other Christian princes, that were it not for the mutual emulation of those princes, they might without war, or trouble, exclude all foreign authority, as easily as it has been excluded in England. For who is there that does not see, to whose benefit it conduceth, to have it believed, that a king hath not his authority from Christ, unless a bishop crown him? That a king, if he be a priest, cannot marry? That whether a prince be born in lawful marriage, or not, must be judged by authority from Rome? That subjects may be freed from their allegiance, if by the court of Rome, the king be judged an heretic? That a king, as Chilperic of France, may be deposed by a pope, as Pope Zachary, for no cause; and his kingdom given to one of his subjects? That the clergy and regulars, in what country soever, shall be exempt from the jurisdiction of their king in cases criminal? Or who does not see, to whose profit redound the fees of private masses, and vales of purgatory; with other signs of private interest, enough to mortify the most lively faith, if, as I said, the civil magistrate, and custom did not more sustain it, than any opinion they have of the sanctity, wisdom, or probity of their teachers? So that I may attribute all the changes of religion in the world, to one and the same cause; and that is, unpleasing priests; and those not only amongst Catholics, but even in that church that hath presumed most of reformation.

CHAPTER XIII

Of the Natural Condition of Mankind as Concerning their Felicity, and Misery

NATURE hath made men so equal, in the faculties of the body, and mind; as that though there be found one man sometimes manifestly stronger in body, or of quicker mind than another; yet when all is reckoned together, the difference between man, and man, is not so considerable, as that one man can thereupon claim to himself any benefit, to which another may not pretend, as well as he. For as to the strength of body, the weakest has strength enough to kill the strongest, either by secret machination, or by confederacy with others, that are in the same danger with himself.

And as to the faculties of the mind, setting aside the arts grounded upon words, and especially that skill of proceeding upon general, and infallible rules, called science; which very few have, and but in few things; as being not a native faculty, born with us; nor attained, as prudence, while we look after somewhat else, I find yet a greater equality amongst men, than that of strength. For prudence, is but experience; which equal time, equally bestows on all men, in those things they equally apply themselves unto. That which may perhaps make such equality incredible, is but a vain conceit of one's own wisdom, which almost all men think they have in a greater degree, than the vulgar; that is, than all men but themselves, and a few others, whom by fame, or for concurring with themselves, they approve. For such is the nature of men, that howsoever they may acknowledge many others to be more witty, or more eloquent, or more learned; yet they will hardly believe there be many so wise as themselves; for they see their own wit at hand, and other men's at a distance. But this proveth rather that men are in that point equal, than unequal. For there is not ordinarily a greater sign of the equal distribution of any thing, than that every man is contented with his share.

From this equality of ability, ariseth equality of hope in
the attaining of our ends. And therefore if any two men desire
the same thing, which nevertheless they cannot both enjoy,
they become enemies; and in the way to their end, which is
principally their own conservation, and sometimes their
delectation only, endeavour to destroy, or subdue one
another. And from hence it comes to pass, that where an
invader hath no more to fear, than another man's single
power; if one plant, sow, build, or possess a convenient seat,
others may probably be expected to come prepared with forces
united, to dispossess, and deprive him, not only of the fruit
of his labour, but also of his life, or liberty. And the invader
again is in the like danger of another.

And from this diffidence of one another, there is no way
for any man to secure himself, so reasonable, as anticipation;
that is, by force, or wiles, to master the persons of all men
he can, so long, till he see no other power great enough to
endanger him: and this is no more than his own conservation
requireth, and is generally allowed. Also because there be
some, that taking pleasure in contemplating their own power
in the acts of conquest, which they pursue farther than their
security requires; if others, that otherwise would be glad to
be at ease within modest bounds, should not by invasion
increase their power, they would not be able, long time, by
standing only on their defence, to subsist. And by consequence, such augmentation of dominion over men being
necessary to a man's conservation, it ought to be allowed
him.

Again, men have no pleasure, but on the contrary a great
deal of grief, in keeping company, where there is no power
able to over-awe them all. For every man looketh that his
companion should value him, at the same rate he sets upon
himself: and upon all signs of contempt, or undervaluing,
naturally endeavours, as far as he dares, (which amongst them
that have no common power to keep them in quiet, is far
enough to make them destroy each other), to extort a greater
value from his contemners, by damage; and from others, by
the example.

So that in the nature of man, we find three principal causes of quarrel. First, competition; secondly, diffidence; thirdly, glory.

The first, maketh men invade for gain; the second, for safety; and the third, for reputation. The first use violence, to make themselves masters of other men's persons, wives, children, and cattle; the second, to defend them; the third, for trifles, as a word, a smile, a different opinion, and any other sign of undervalue, either direct in their persons, or by reflection in their kindred, their friends, their nation, their profession, or their name.

Hereby it is manifest, that during the time men live without a common power to keep them all in awe, they are in that condition which is called war; and such a war, as is of every man, against every man. For WAR, consisteth not in battle only, or the act of fighting; but in a tract of time, wherein the will to contend by battle is sufficiently known: and therefore the notion of *time*, is to be considered in the nature of war; as it is in the nature of weather. For as the nature of foul weather, lieth not in a shower or two of rain; but in an inclination thereto of many days together: so the nature of war, consisteth not in actual fighting; but in the known disposition thereto, during all the time there is no assurance to the contrary. All other time is PEACE.

Whatsoever therefore is consequent to a time of war, where every man is enemy to every man; the same is consequent to the time, wherein men live without other security, than what their own strength, and their own invention shall furnish them withal. In such condition, there is no place for industry; because the fruit thereof is uncertain: and consequently no culture of the earth; no navigation, nor use of the commodities that may be imported by sea; no commodious building; no instruments of moving, and removing, such things as require much force; no knowledge of the face of the earth; no account of time; no arts; no letters; no society; and which is worst of all, continual fear, and danger of violent death; and the life of man, solitary, poor, nasty, brutish, and short.

It may seem strange to some man, that has not well weighed these things; that nature should thus dissociate, and render men apt to invade, and destroy one another: and he may therefore, not trusting to this inference, made from the passions, desire perhaps to have the same confirmed by experience. Let him therefore consider with himself, when taking a journey, he arms himself, and seeks to go well accompanied; when going to sleep, he locks his doors; when even in his house he locks his chests; and this when he knows there be laws, and public officers, armed, to revenge all injuries shall be done him; what opinion he has of his fellow-subjects, when he rides armed; of his fellow citizens, when he locks his doors; and of his children, and servants, when he locks his chests. Does he not there as much accuse mankind by his actions, as I do by my words? But neither of us accuse man's nature in it. The desires, and other passions of man, are in themselves no sin. No more are the actions, that proceed from those passions, till they know a law that forbids them: which till laws be made they cannot know: nor can any law be made, till they have agreed upon the person that shall make it.

It may peradventure be thought, there was never such a time, nor condition of war as this; and I believe it was never generally so, over all the world: but there are many places, where they live so now. For the savage people in many places of America, except the government of small families, the concord whereof dependeth on natural lust, have no government at all; and live at this day in that brutish manner, as I said before. Howsoever, it may be perceived what manner of life there would be, where there were no common power to fear, by the manner of life, which men that have formerly lived under a peaceful government, use to degenerate into, in a civil war.

But though there had never been any time, wherein particular men were in a condition of war one against another; yet in all times, kings, and persons of sovereign authority, because of their independency, are in continual jealousies, and in the state and posture of gladiators; having their weapons pointing, and their eyes fixed on one another; that is, their forts, garrisons, and guns upon the frontiers of their kingdoms; and continual spies upon their neighbours; which is a posture of war. But because they uphold thereby, the industry of their subjects; there does not follow from it, that misery, which accompanies the liberty of particular men.

To this war of every man, against every man, this also is consequent; that nothing can be unjust. The notions of right and wrong, justice and injustice have there no place. Where there is no common power, there is no law: where no law, no injustice. Force, and fraud, are in war the two cardinal virtues. Justice, and injustice are none of the faculties neither of the body, nor mind. If they were, they might be in a man that were alone in the world, as well as his senses, and passions. They are qualities, that relate to men in society, not in solitude. It is consequent also to the same condition, that there be no propriety, no dominion, no *mine* and *thine* distinct; but only that to be every man's, that he can get; and for so long, as he can keep it. And thus much for the ill condition, which man by mere nature is actually placed in; though with a possibility to come out of it, consisting partly in the passions, partly in his reason.

The passions that incline men to peace, are fear of death; desire of such things as are necessary to commodious living; and a hope by their industry to obtain them. And reason suggesteth convenient articles of peace, upon which men may be drawn to agreement. These articles, are they, which otherwise are called the Laws of Nature: whereof I shall speak more particularly, in the two following chapters.

CHAPTER XIV

Of the First and Second Natural Laws, and of Contracts

THE RIGHT OF NATURE, which writers commonly call *jus naturale*, is the liberty each man hath, to use his own power, as he will himself, for the preservation of his own nature; that is to say, of his own life; and consequently, of doing any thing, which in his own judgment, and reason, he shall conceive to be the aptest means thereunto.

By LIBERTY, is understood, according to the proper signification of the word, the absence of external impediments: which impediments, may oft take away part of a man's power to do what he would; but cannot hinder him from using the power left him, according as his judgment, and reason shall dictate to him.

A LAW OF NATURE, *lex naturalis*, is a precept or general rule, found out by reason, by which a man is forbidden to do that, which is destructive of his life, or taketh away the means of preserving the same; and to omit that, by which he thinketh it may be best preserved. For though they that speak of this subject, use to confound *jus*, and *lex*, *right* and *law*: yet they ought to be distinguished; because RIGHT, consisteth in liberty to do, or to forbear; whereas LAW, determineth, and bindeth to one of them: so that law, and right, differ as much, as obligation, and liberty; which in one and the same matter are inconsistent.

And because the condition of man, as hath been declared in the precedent chapter, is a condition of war of every one against every one: in which case every one is governed by his own reason; and there is nothing he can make use of, that may not be a help unto him, in preserving his life against his enemies; it followeth, that in such a condition, every man has a right to every thing; even to one another's body. And therefore, as long as this natural right of every man to every thing endureth, there can be no security to any man, how strong or wise soever he be, of living out the time, which nature ordinarily alloweth men to live. and consequently it is a precept, or general rule of reason, *that every man, ought to endeavour peace, as far as he has hope of obtaining it; and when he cannot obtain it, that he may seek, and use, all helps, and advantages of war*. The first branch of which rule, containeth the first, and fundamental law of nature; which is, *to seek peace, and follow it*. The second, the sum of the right of nature; which is, *by all means we can, to defend ourselves*.

From this fundamental law of nature, by which men are commanded to endeavour peace, is derived this second law;

that a man be willing, when others are so too, as far-forth, as for peace, and defence of himself he shall think it necessary, to lay down this right to all things; and be contented with so much liberty against other men, as he would allow other men against himself. For as long as every man holdeth this right, of doing any thing he liketh; so long are all men in the condition of war. But if other men will not lay down their right, as well as he; then there is no reason for any one, to divest himself of his: for that were to expose himself to prey, which no man is bound to, rather than to dispose himself to peace. This is that law of the Gospel; *whatsoever you require that others should do to you, that do ye to them.* And that law of all men, *quod tibi fieri non vis, alteri ne feceris.*

To *lay down* a man's *right* to any thing, is to *divest* himself of the *liberty*, of hindering another of the benefit of his own right to the same. For he that renounceth, or passeth away his right, giveth not to any other man a right which he had not before; because there is nothing to which every man had not right by nature: but only standeth out of his way, that he may enjoy his own original right, without hindrance from him; not without hindrance from another. So that the effect which redoundeth to one man, by another man's defect of right, is but so much diminution of impediments to the use of his own right original.

Right is laid aside, either by simply renouncing it; or by transferring it to another. By *simply* RENOUNCING; when he cares not to whom the benefit thereof redoundeth. By TRANS-FERRING; when he intendeth the benefit thereof to some certain person, or persons. And when a man hath in either manner abandoned, or granted away his right; then he is said to be OBLIGED, or BOUND, not to hinder those, to whom such right is granted, or abandoned, from the benefit of it: and that he *ought*, and it is his DUTY, not to make void that voluntary act of his own: and that such hindrance is IN-JUSTICE, and INJURY, as being *sine jure*; the right being before renounced, or transferred. So that *injury*, or *injustice*, in the controversies of the world, is somewhat like to that, which in the disputations of scholars is called *absurdity*. For as it is there called an absurdity, to contradict what one maintained in the beginning: so in the world, it is called injustice, and injury, voluntarily to undo that, which from the beginning he had voluntarily done. The way by which a man either simply renounceth, or transferreth his right, is a declaration, or signification, by some voluntary and sufficient sign, or signs, that he doth so renounce, or transfer; or hath so renounced, or transferred the same, to him that accepteth it. And these signs are either words only, or actions only; or, as it happeneth most often, both words, and actions. And the same are the BONDS, by which men are bound, and obliged: bonds, that have their strength, not from their own nature, for nothing is more easily broken than a man's word, but from fear of some evil consequence upon that rupture.

Whensoever a man transferreth his right, or renounceth it; it is either in consideration of some right reciprocally transferred to himself; or for some other good he hopeth for thereby. For it is a voluntary act: and of the voluntary acts of every man, the object is some *good to himself*. And therefore there be some rights, which no man can be understood by any words, or other signs, to have abandoned, or transferred. As first a man cannot lay down the right of resisting them, that assault him by force, to take away his life; because he cannot be understood to aim thereby, at any good to himself. The same may be said of wounds, and chains, and imprisonment; both because there is no benefit consequent to such patience; as there is to the patience of suffering another to be wounded, or imprisoned: as also because a man cannot tell, when he seeth men proceed against him by violence, whether they intend his death or not. And lastly the motive, and end for which this renouncing, and transferring of right is introduced, is nothing else but the security of a man's person, in his life, and in the means of so preserving life, as not to be weary of it. And therefore if a man by words, or other signs, seem to despoil himself of the end, for which those signs were intended; he is not to be understood as if he meant it, or that it was his will; but that he was ignorant of how such words and actions were to be interpreted.

The mutual transferring of right, is that which men call CONTRACT.

There is difference between transferring of right to the

thing; and transferring, or tradition, that is delivery of the thing itself. For the thing may be delivered together with the translation of the right; as in buying and selling with ready-money; or exchange of goods, or lands: and it may be delivered some time after.

Again, one of the contractors, may deliver the thing contracted for on his part, and leave the other to perform his part at some determinate time after, and in the mean time be trusted; and then the contract on his part, is called PACT, or COVENANT: or both parts may contract now, to perform hereafter: in which cases, he that is to perform in time to come, being trusted, his performance is called *keeping of promise*, or faith; and the failing of performance, if it be voluntary, *violation of faith*.

When the transferring of right, is not mutual: but one of the parties transferreth, in hope to gain thereby friendship, or service from another, or from his friends; or in hope to gain the reputation of charity, or magnanimity; or to deliver his mind from the pain of compassion; or in hope of reward in heaven; this is not contract, but GIFT, FREEGIFT, GRACE: which words signify one and the same thing.

Signs of contract, are either *express*, or *by inference*. Express, are words spoken with understanding of what they signify: and such words are either of the time *present*, or *past*; as, *I give, I grant, I have given, I have granted, I will that this be yours*: or of the future; as, *I will give, I will grant*: which words of the future are called PROMISE.

Signs by inference, are sometimes the consequence of words; sometimes the consequence of silence; sometimes the consequence of actions; sometimes the consequence of forbearing an action: and generally a sign by inference, of any contract, is whatsoever sufficiently argues the will of the contractor.

Words alone, if they be of the time to come, and contain a bare promise, are an insufficient sign of a free-gift, and therefore not obligatory. For if they be of the time to come, as *tomorrow I will give*, they are a sign I have not given yet, and consequently that my right is not transferred, but remaineth till I transfer it by some other act. But if the words be of the time present, or past, as, *I have given*, or, *do give to be delivered tomorrow*, then is my tomorrow's right given away to day; and that by the virtue of the words, though there were no other argument of my will. And there is a great difference in the signification of these words, *volo hoc tuum esse cras*, and *cras dabo*; that is, between *I will that this be thine tomorrow*, and, *I will give it thee tomorrow*: for the word *I will*, in the former manner of speech, signifies an act of the will present; but in the latter, it signifies a promise of an act of the will to come: and therefore the former words, being of the present, transfer a future right; the latter, that be of the future, transfer nothing. But if there be other signs of the will to transfer a right, besides words; then, though the gift be free, yet may the right be understood to pass by words of the future: as if a man propound a prize to him that comes first to the end of a race, the gift is free; and though the words be of the future, yet the right passeth: for if he would not have his words so be understood, he should not have let them run.

In contracts, the right passeth, not only where the words are of the time present, or past, but also where they are of the future: because all contract is mutual translation, or change of right; and therefore he that promiseth only, because he hath already received the benefit for which he promiseth, is to be understood as if he intended the right should pass: for unless he had been content to have his words so understood, the other would not have performed his part first. And for that cause, in buying, and selling, and other acts of contract, a promise is equivalent to a covenant; and therefore obligatory.

He that performeth first in the case of a contract, is said to MERIT that which he is to receive by the performance of the other; and he hath it as *due*. Also when a prize is propounded to many, which is to be given to him only that winneth; or money is thrown amongst many, to be enjoyed by them that catch it; though this be a free gift; yet so to win, or so to catch, is to *merit*, and to have it as DUE. For the right is transferred in the propounding of the prize, and in throwing down the money; though it be not determined to whom, but by the event of the contention. But there is between these two sorts of merit, this difference, that in contract, I merit by virtue of my own power, and the contractor's need; but in this case of free gift, I am enabled to merit only by the benignity of the giver: in contract, I merit at the contractor's hand that he should depart with his right; in this case of gift, I merit not that the giver should part with his right; but that when he has parted with it, it should be mine, rather than another's. And this I think to be the meaning of that distinction of the Schools, between *meritum congrui*, and *meritum condigni*. For God Almighty, having promised Paradise to those men, hoodwinked with carnal desires, that can walk through this world according to the precepts, and limits prescribed by him; they say, he that shall so walk, shall merit Paradise *ex congruo*. But because no man can demand a right to it, by his own righteousness, or any other power in himself, but by the free grace of God only; they say, no man can merit Paradise *ex condigno*. This I say, I think is the meaning of that distinction; but because disputers do not agree upon the signification of their own terms of art, longer than it serves their turn; I will not affirm any thing of their meaning: only this I say; when a gift is given indefinitely, as a prize to be contended for, he that winneth meriteth, and may claim the prize as due.

If a covenant be made, wherein neither of the parties perform presently, but trust one another; in the condition of mere nature, which is a condition of war of every man against every man, upon any reasonable suspicion, it is void: but if there be a common power set over them both, with right and force sufficient to compel performance, it is not void. For he that performeth first, has no assurance the other will perform after; because the bonds of words are too weak to bridle men's ambition, avarice, anger, and other passions, without the fear of some coercive power; which in the condition of mere nature, where all men are equal, and judges of the justness of their own fears, cannot possibly be supposed. And therefore he which performeth first, does but betray himself to his enemy; contrary to the right, he can never abandon, of defending his life, and means of living.

But in a civil estate, where there is a power set up to constrain those that would otherwise violate their faith, that fear is no more reasonable; and for that cause, he which by the covenant is to perform first, is obliged so to do.

The cause of fear, which maketh such a covenant invalid, must be always something arising after the covenant made; as some new fact, or other sign of the will not to perform: else it cannot make the covenant void. For that which could not hinder a man from promising, ought not to be admitted as a hindrance of performing.

He that transferreth any right, transferreth the means of enjoying it, as far as lieth in his power. As he that selleth land, is understood to transfer the herbage, and whatsoever grows upon it: nor can he that sells a mill turn away the stream that drives it. And they that give to a man the right of government in sovereignty, are understood to give him the right of levying money to maintain soldiers; and of appointing magistrates for the administration of justice.

To make covenants with brute beasts, is impossible; because not understanding our speech, they understand not, nor accept of any translation of right; nor can translate any right to another: and without mutual acceptation, there is no covenant.

To make covenant with God, is impossible, but by mediation of such as God speaketh to, either by revelation supernatural, or by his lieutenants that govern under him, and in his name: for otherwise we know not whether our covenants be accepted, or not. And therefore they that vow anything contrary to any law of nature, vow in vain; as being a thing unjust to pay such vow. And if it be a thing commanded by the law of nature, it is not the vow, but the law that binds them.

The matter, or subject of a covenant, is always something that falleth under deliberation; for to covenant, is an act of the will; that is to say, an act, and the last act of deliberation; and is therefore always understood to be something to come; and which is judged possible for him that covenanteth, to perform.

And therefore, to promise that which is known to be impossible, is no covenant. But if that prove impossible afterwards, which before was thought possible, the covenant is valid, and bindeth, though not to the thing itself, yet to the value; or, if that also be impossible, to the unfeigned endeavour of performing as much as is possible: for to more no man can be obliged.

Men are freed of their covenants two ways; by performing; or by being forgiven. For performance, is the natural end of obligation; and forgiveness, the restitution of liberty; as being a retransferring of that right, in which the obligation consisted.

Covenants entered into by fear, in the condition of mere nature, are obligatory. For example, if I covenant to pay a ransom, or service for my life, to an enemy; I am bound by it: for it is a contract, wherein one receiveth the benefit of life; the other is to receive money, or service for it; and consequently, where no other law, as in the condition of mere nature, forbiddeth the performance, the covenant is valid. Therefore prisoners of war, if trusted with the payment of their ransom, are obliged to pay it: and if a weaker prince, make a disadvantageous peace with a stronger, for fear; he is bound to keep it; unless, as hath been said before, there ariseth some new, and just cause of fear, to renew the war. And even in commonwealths, if I be forced to redeem myself from a thief by promising him money, I am bound to pay it, till the civil law discharge me. For whatsoever I may lawfully do without obligation, the same I may lawfully covenant to do through fear: and what I lawfully covenant, I cannot lawfully break.

A former covenant, makes void a later. For a man that hath passed away his right to one man today, hath it not to pass tomorrow to another: and therefore the later promise passeth no right, but is null.

A covenant not to defend myself from force, by force, is always void. For, as I have showed before, no man can transfer, or lay down his right to save himself from death, wounds, and imprisonment, the avoiding whereof is the only end of laying down any right; and therefore the promise of not resisting force, in no covenant transferreth any right; nor is obliging. For though a man may covenant thus, *unless I do so, or so, kill me*; he cannot covenant thus, *unless I do so,*

or so, I will not resist you, when you come to kill me. For man by
nature chooseth the lesser evil, which is danger of death in
resisting; rather than the greater, which is certain and present
death in not resisting. And this is granted to be true by all
men, in that they lead criminals to execution, and prison,
with armed men, notwithstanding that such criminals have
consented to the law, by which they are condemned.

A covenant to accuse oneself, without assurance of pardon,
is likewise invalid. For in the condition of nature, where every
man is judge, there is no place for accusation: and in the civil
state, the accusation is followed with punishment; which being
force, a man is not obliged not to resist. The same is also true,
of the accusation of those, by whose condemnation a man falls
into misery; as of a father, wife, or benefactor. For the
testimony of such an accuser, if it be not willingly given, is
presumed to be corrupted by nature; and therefore not to be
received: and where a man's testimony is not to be credited,
he is not bound to give it. Also accusations upon torture, are
not to be reputed as testimonies. For torture is to be used but
as means of conjecture, and light, in the further examination,
and search of truth; and what is in that case confessed,
tendeth to the ease of him that is tortured; not to the inform-
ing of the torturers: and therefore ought not to have the credit
of a sufficient testimony: for whether he deliver himself by
true, or false accusation, he does it by the right of preserving
his own life.

The force of words, being, as I have formerly noted, too
weak to hold men to the performance of their covenants;
there are in man's nature, but two imaginable helps to
strengthen it. And those are either a fear of the consequence
of breaking their word; or a glory, or pride in appearing not
to need to break it. This latter is a generosity too rarely found
to be presumed on, especially in the pursuers of wealth,
command, or sensual pleasure; which are the greatest part of
mankind. The passion to be reckoned upon, is fear; whereof
there be two very general objects: one, the power of spirits
invisible; the other, the power of those men they shall therein
offend. Of these two, though the former be the greater power,
yet the fear of the latter is commonly the greater fear. The fear

of the former is in every man, his own religion: which hath place in the nature of man before civil society. The latter hath not so; at least not place enough, to keep men to their promises; because in the condition of mere nature, the inequality of power is not discerned, but by the event of battle. So that before the time of civil society, or in the interruption thereof by war, there is nothing can strengthen a covenant of peace agreed on, against the temptations of avarice, ambition, lust, or other strong desire, but the fear of that invisible power, which they every one worship as God; and fear as a revenger of their perfidy. All therefore that can be done between two men not subject to civil power, is to put one another to swear by the God he feareth: which *swearing*, or OATH, is a *form of speech, added to a promise; by which he that promiseth, signifieth, that unless he perform, he renounceth the mercy of his God, or calleth to him for vengeance on himself.* Such was the heathen form, *Let* Jupiter *kill me else, as I kill this beast.* So is our form, *I shall do thus, and thus, so help me God.* And this, with the rites and ceremonies, which every one useth in his own religion, that the fear of breaking faith might be the greater.

By this it appears, that an oath taken according to any other form, or rite, than his, that sweareth, is in vain; and no oath: and that there is no swearing by any thing which the swearer thinks not God. For though men have sometimes used to swear by their kings, for fear, or flattery; yet they would have it thereby understood, they attributed to them divine honour. And that swearing unnecessarily by God, is but prophaning of his name: and swearing by other things, as men do in common discourse, is not swearing, but an impious custom, gotten by too much vehemence of talking.

It appears also, that the oath adds nothing to the obligation. For a covenant, if lawful, binds in the sight of God, without the oath, as much as with it: if unlawful, bindeth not at all; though it be confirmed with an oath.

CHAPTER XV

Of Other Laws of Nature

FROM that law of nature, by which we are obliged to transfer to another, such rights, as being retained, hinder the peace of mankind, there followeth a third; which is this, *that men perform their covenants made*: without which, covenants are in vain, and but empty words; and the right of all men to all things remaining, we are still in the condition of war.

And in this law of nature, consisteth the fountain and original of JUSTICE. For where no covenant hath preceded, there hath no right been transferred, and every man has right to every thing; and consequently, no action can be unjust. But when a covenant is made, then to break it is *unjust*: and the definition of INJUSTICE, is no other than *the not performance of covenant*. And whatsoever is not unjust, is *just*.

But because covenants of mutual trust, where there is a fear of not performance on either part, as hath been said in the former chapter, are invalid; though the original of justice be the making of covenants; yet injustice actually there can be none, till the cause of such fear be taken away; which while men are in the natural condition of war, cannot be done. Therefore before the names of just, and unjust can have place, there must be some coercive power, to compel men equally to the performance of their covenants, by the terror of some punishment, greater than the benefit they expect by the breach of their covenant; and to make good that propriety, which by mutual contract men acquire, in recompense of the universal right they abandon: and such power there is none before the erection of a commonwealth. And this is also to be gathered out of the ordinary definition of justice in the Schools: for they say, that *justice is the constant will of giving to every man his own*. And therefore where there is no *own*, that is no propriety, there is no injustice; and where there is no coercive power erected, that is, where there is no commonwealth, there is no propriety; all men having right to all things: therefore where there is no commonwealth, there nothing is unjust. So that the nature of justice, consisteth in keeping of valid covenants: but the validity of covenants begins not but with the constitution of a civil power, sufficient to compel men to keep them: and then it is also that propriety begins.

The fool hath said in his heart, there is no such thing as justice; and sometimes also with his tongue; seriously alleging, that every man's conservation, and contentment, being committed to his own care, there could be no reason, why every man might not do what he thought conduced thereunto: and therefore also to make, or not make; keep, or not keep covenants, was not against reason, when it conduced to one's benefit. He does not therein deny, that there be covenants; and that they are sometimes broken, sometimes kept; and that such breach of them may be called injustice, and the observance of them justice: but he questioneth, whether injustice, taking away the fear of God, for the same fool hath said in his heart there is no God, may not sometimes stand with that reason, which dictateth to every man his own good; and particularly then, when it conduceth to such a benefit, as shall put a man in a condition, to neglect not only the dispraise, and revilings, but also the power of other men. The kingdom of God is gotten by violence: but what if it could be gotten by unjust violence? were it against reason so to get it, when it is impossible to receive hurt by it? and if it be not against reason, it is not against justice; or else justice is not to be approved for good. From such reasoning as this, successful wickedness hath obtained the name of virtue: and some that in all other things have disallowed the violation of faith; yet have allowed it, when it is for the getting of a kingdom. And the heathen that believed, that Saturn was deposed by his son Jupiter, believed nevertheless the same Jupiter to be the avenger of injustice: somewhat like to a piece of law in Coke's *Commentaries on Littleton*; where he says, if the right heir of the crown be attainted of treason; yet the crown shall descend to him, and *eo instante* the attainder be void: from which instances a man will be very prone to infer; that when the heir apparent of a kingdom, shall kill him that is in possession, though his father; you may call it injustice, or by what other name you will; yet it can never be against reason, seeing all the voluntary actions of men tend to the benefit of themselves; and those actions are most reasonable, that conduce most to their ends. This specious reasoning is nevertheless false.

For the question is not of promises mutual, where there is no security of performance on either side; as when there is no civil power erected over the parties promising; for such promises are no covenants: but either where one of the parties has performed already; or where there is a power to make him perform; there is the question whether it be against reason, that is, against the benefit of the other to perform, or not. And I say it is not against reason. For the manifestation whereof, we are to consider; first, that when a man doth a thing, which notwithstanding any thing can be foreseen, and reckoned on, tendeth to his own destruction, howsoever some accident which he could not expect, arriving may turn it to his benefit; yet such events do not make it reasonably or wisely done. Secondly, that in a condition of war, wherein every man to every man, for want of a common power to keep them all in awe, is an enemy, there is no man who can hope by his own strength, or wit, to defend himself from destruction, without the help of confederates; where every one expects the same defence by the confederation, that any one else does: and therefore he which declares he thinks it reason to deceive those that help him, can in reason expect no other means of safety, than what can be had from his own single power. He therefore that breaketh his covenant, and consequently declareth that he thinks he may with reason do so, cannot be received into any society, that unite themselves for peace and defence, but by the error of them that receive him; nor when he is received, be retained in it, without seeing the danger of their error; which errors a man cannot reasonably reckon upon as the means of his security: and therefore if he be left, or cast out of society, he perisheth; and if he live in society, it is by the errors of other men, which he could not foresee, nor reckon upon; and consequently against the reason of his preservation; and so, as all men that contribute not to his destruction, forbear him only out of ignorance of what is good for themselves.

As for the instance of gaining the secure and perpetual felicity of heaven, by any way; it is frivolous: there being but one way imaginable; and that is not breaking, but keeping of covenant.

And for the other instance of attaining sovereignty by rebellion; it is manifest, that though the event follow, yet because it cannot reasonably be expected, but rather the contrary; and because by gaining it so, others are taught to gain the same in like manner, the attempt thereof is against reason. Justice therefore, that is to say, keeping of covenant, is a rule of reason, by which we are forbidden to do anything destructive to our life; and consequently a law of nature.

There be some that proceed further; and will not have the law of nature, to be those rules which conduce to the preservation of man's life on earth; but to the attaining of an eternal felicity after death; to which they think the breach of covenant may conduce; and consequently be just and reasonable; such are they that think it a work of merit to kill, or depose, or rebel against, the sovereign power constituted over them by their own consent. But because there is no natural knowledge of man's estate after death; much less of the reward that is then to be given to breach of faith; but only a belief grounded upon other men's saying, that they know it supernaturally, or that they know those, that knew them, that knew others, that knew it supernaturally; breach of faith cannot be called a precept of reason, or nature.

Others, that allow for a law of nature, the keeping of faith, do nevertheless make exception of certain persons; as heretics, and such as use not to perform their covenant to others: and this also is against reason. For if any fault of a man, be sufficient to discharge our covenant made; the same ought in reason to have been sufficient to have hindered the making of it.

The names of just, and unjust, when they are attributed to men, signify one thing; and when they are attributed to actions, another. When they are attributed to men, they signify conformity, or inconformity of manners, to reason. But when they are attributed to actions, they signify the conformity, or inconformity to reason, not of manners, or manner of life, but of particular actions. A just man therefore, is he that taketh all the care he can, that his actions may be all just: and an unjust man, is he that neglecteth it. And such men are more often in our language styled by the names of righteous, and unrighteous; than just, and unjust; though the meaning be the same. Therefore a righteous man, does not lose that title, by one, or a few unjust actions, that proceed from sudden passion, or mistake of things, or persons: nor does an unrighteous man, lose his character, for such actions, as he does, or forbears to do, for fear: because his will is not framed by the justice, but by the apparent benefit of what he is to do. That which gives to human actions the relish of justice, is a certain nobleness or gallantness of courage, rarely found, by which a man scorns to be beholden for the contentment of his life, to fraud, or breach of promise. This justice of the manners, is that which is meant, where justice is called a virtue; and injustice a vice.

But the justice of actions denominates men, not just, but *guiltless*: and the injustice of the same, which is also called injury, gives them but the name of *guilty*.

Again, the injustice of manners, is the disposition, or aptitude to do injury; and is injustice before it proceed to act; and without supposing any individual person injured. But the injustice of an action, that is to say injury, supposeth an individual person injured; namely him, to whom the covenant was made: and therefore many times the injury is received by one man, when the damage redoundeth to another. As when the master commandeth his servant to give money to a stranger; if it be not done, the injury is done to the master, whom he had before covenanted to obey; but the damage redoundeth to the stranger, to whom he had no obligation; and therefore could not injure him. And so also in commonwealths, private men may remit to one another their debts; but not robberies or other violences, whereby they are endamaged; because the detaining of debt, is an injury to themselves; but robbery and violence, are injuries to the person of the commonwealth.

Whatsoever is done to a man, conformable to his own will signified to the doer, is no injury to him. For if he that doeth it, hath not passed away his original right to do what he please, by some antecedent covenant, there is no breach of covenant; and therefore no injury done him. And if he have; then his will to have it done being signified, is a release of that covenant: and so again there is no injury done him.

Justice of actions, is by writers divided into *commutative*, and *distributive*: and the former they say consisteth in proportion arithmetical; the latter in proportion geometrical. Commutative therefore, they place in the equality of value of the things contracted for; and distributive, in the distribution of equal benefit, to men of equal merit. As if it were injustice to sell dearer than we buy; or to give more to a man than he merits. The value of all things contracted for, is measured by the appetite of the contractors: and therefore the just value, is that which they be contented to give. And merit, besides that which is by covenant, where the performance on one part, meriteth the performance of the other part, and falls under justice commutative, not distributive, is not due by justice; but is rewarded of grace only. And therefore this distinction, in the sense wherein it useth to be expounded, is not right. To speak properly, commutative justice, is the justice, of a contractor; that is, a performance of covenant, in buying, and selling; hiring, and letting to hire; lending, and borrowing; exchanging, bartering, and other acts of contract.

And distributive justice, the justice of an arbitrator; that is to say, the act of defining what is just. Wherein, being trusted by them that make him arbitrator, if he perform his trust, he is said to distribute to every man his own: and this is indeed just distribution, and may be called, though improperly, distributive justice; but more properly equity; which also is a law of nature, as shall be shown in due place.

As justice dependeth on antecedent covenant; so does GRATITUDE depend on antecedent grace; that is to say, antecedent free gift: and is the fourth law of nature; which may be conceived in this form, *that a man which receiveth benefit from another of mere grace, endeavour that he which giveth it, have no reasonable cause to repent him of his good will.* For no man giveth, but with intention of good to himself; because gift is voluntary; and of all voluntary acts, the object is to every man his own good; of which if men see they shall be frustrated, there will be no beginning of benevolence, or trust; nor consequently of mutual help; nor of reconciliation of one man to another; and therefore they are to remain still in the condition of *war*; which is contrary to the first and fundamental law of nature, which commandeth men to *seek peace.* The breach of this law, is called *ingratitude*; and hath the same relation to grace, that injustice hath to obligation by covenant.

A fifth law of nature, is COMPLAISANCE; that is to say, *that every man strive to accommodate himself to the rest.* For the understanding whereof, we may consider, that there is in men's aptness to society, a diversity of nature, rising from their diversity of affections; not unlike to that we see in stones brought together for building of an edifice. For as that stone which by the asperity, and irregularity of figure, takes more room from others, than itself fills; and for the hardness, cannot be easily made plain, and thereby hindereth the building, is by the builders cast away as unprofitable, and troublesome: so also, a man that by asperity of nature, will strive to retain those things which to himself are superfluous, and to others necessary; and for the stubbornness of his passions, cannot be corrected, is to be left, or cast out of society, as cumbersome thereunto. For seeing every man, not only by right, but also by necessity of nature, is supposed to endeavour all he can, to obtain that which is necessary for his conservation; he that shall oppose himself against it, for things superfluous, is guilty of the war that thereupon is to follow; and therefore doth that, which is contrary to the fundamental law of nature, which commandeth *to seek peace.* The observers of this law, may be called SOCIABLE, the Latins call them *commodi*; the contrary, *stubborn, insociable, froward, intractable.*

A sixth law of nature, is this, *that upon caution of the future time, a man ought to pardon the offences past of them that repenting, desire it.* For PARDON, is nothing but granting of peace; which though granted to them that persevere in their hostility, be not peace, but fear; yet not granted to them that give caution of the future time, is sign of an aversion to peace; and therefore contrary to the law of nature.

A seventh is, *that in revenges,* that is, retribution of evil for evil, *men look not at the greatness of the evil past, but the greatness of the good to follow.* Whereby we are forbidden to inflict punishment with any other design, than for correction of the offender, or direction of others. For this law is consequent to the next before it, that commandeth pardon, upon security of the future time. Besides, revenge without respect to the example, and profit to come, is a triumph, or glorying in the hurt of another, tending to no end; for the end is always somewhat to come; and glorying to no end, is vain-glory, and contrary to reason, and to hurt without reason, tendeth to the introduction of war; which is against the law of nature; and is commonly styled by the name of *cruelty.*

And because all signs of hatred, or contempt, provoke to fight; insomuch as most men choose rather to hazard their life, than not to be revenged; we may in the eighth place, for a law of nature, set down this precept, *that no man by deed, word, countenance, or gesture, declare hatred, or contempt of another.* The breach of which law, is commonly called *contumely.*

The question who is the better man, has no place in the condition of mere nature; where, as has been shewn before, all men are equal. The inequality that now is, has been introduced by the laws civil. I know that Aristotle in the first book of his *Politics,* for a foundation of his doctrine, maketh men by nature, some more worthy to command, meaning the wiser sort, such as he thought himself to be for his philosophy; others to serve, meaning those that had strong bodies, but were not philosophers as he; as if master and servant were not introduced by consent of men, but by difference of wit: which is not only against reason; but also against experience. For there are very few so foolish, that had not rather govern themselves, than be governed by others: nor when the wise in their own conceit, contend by force, with them who distrust their own wisdom, do they always, or often, or almost at any time, get the victory. If nature therefore have made men equal, that equality is to be acknowledged: or if nature have made men unequal; yet because men that think themselves equal, will not enter into conditions of peace, but upon equal terms, such equality must be admitted. And therefore for the ninth law of nature, I put this, *that every man acknowledge another for his equal by nature*. The breach of this precept is *pride*.

On this law, dependeth another, *that at the entrance into conditions of peace, no man require to reserve to himself any right, which he is not content should be reserved to every one of the rest*. As it is necessary for all men that seek peace, to lay down certain rights of nature; that is to say, not to have liberty to do all they list: so is it necessary for man's life, to retain some; as right to govern their own bodies; enjoy air, water, motion, ways to go from place to place; and all things else, without which a man cannot live, or not live well. If in this case, at the making of peace, men require for themselves, that which they would not have to be granted to others, they do contrary to the precedent law, that commandeth the acknowledgment of natural equality, and therefore also against the law of nature. The observers of this law, are those we call *modest*, and the breakers *arrogant* men. The Greeks call the violation of this law πλεονεξια; that is, a desire of more than their share.

Also if *a man be trusted to judge between man and man*, it is a precept of the law of nature, *that he deal equally between them*. For without that, the controversies of men cannot be determined but by war. He therefore that is partial in judgment, doth what in him lies, to deter men from the use of judges, and arbitrators; and consequently, against the fundamental law of nature, is the cause of war.

The observance of this law, from the equal distribution to each man, of that which in reason belongeth to him, is called EQUITY, and, as I have said before, distributive justice: the violation, *acception of persons*, προσωποληψία.

And from this followeth another law, *that such things as cannot be divided, be enjoyed in common, if it can be; and if the quantity of the thing permit, without stint; otherwise proportionably to the number of them that have right*. For otherwise the distribution is unequal, and contrary to equity.

But some things there be, that can neither be divided, nor enjoyed in common. Then, the law of nature, which prescribeth equity, requireth, *that the entire right; or else, making the use alternate, the first possession, be determined by lot.* For equal distribution, is of the law of nature; and other means of equal distribution cannot be imagined.

Of *lots* there be two sorts, *arbitrary*, and *natural*. Arbitrary, is that which is agreed on by the competitors: natural, is either *primogeniture*, which the Greek calls κληρονομία, which signifies, *given by lot*; or *first seizure*.

And therefore those things which cannot be enjoyed in common, nor divided, ought to be adjudged to the first possessor; and in some cases to the first born, as acquired by lot.

It is also a law of nature, *that all men that mediate peace, be allowed safe conduct.* For the law that commandeth peace, as the *end*, commandeth intercession, as the *means*; and to intercession the means is safe conduct.

And because, though men be never so willing to observe these laws, there may nevertheless arise questions concerning a man's action; first, whether it were done, or not done; secondly, if done, whether against the law, or not against the law, the former whereof, is called a question *of fact*; the latter a question *of right*, therefore unless the parties to the question, covenant mutually to stand to the sentence of another, they are as far from peace as ever. This other to whose sentence they submit is called an ARBITRATOR. And therefore it is of the law of nature, *that they that are at controversy, submit their right to the judgment of an arbitrator.*

And seeing every man is presumed to do all things in order to his own benefit, no man is a fit arbitrator in his own cause; and if he were never so fit; yet equity allowing to each party equal benefit, if one be admitted to be judge, the other is to be admitted also; and so the controversy, that is, the cause of war, remains, against the law of nature.

For the same reason no man in any cause ought to be received for arbitrator, to whom greater profit, or honour, or pleasure apparently ariseth out of the victory of one party, than of the other: for he hath taken, though an unavoidable bribe, yet a bribe; and no man can be obliged to trust him. And thus also the controversy, and the condition of war remaineth, contrary to the law of nature.

And in a controversy of *fact*, the judge being to give no more credit to one, than to the other, if there be no other arguments, must give credit to a third; or to a third and fourth; or more: for else the question is undecided, and left to force, contrary to the law of nature.

These are the laws of nature, dictating peace, for a means of the conservation of men in multitudes; and which only concern the doctrine of civil society. There be other things tending to the destruction of particular men; as drunkenness, and all other parts of intemperance; which may therefore also be reckoned amongst those things which the law of nature hath forbidden; but are not necessary to be mentioned, nor are pertinent enough to this place.

And though this may seem too subtle a deduction of the laws of nature, to be taken notice of by all men; whereof the most part are too busy in getting food, and the rest too negligent to understand; yet to leave all men inexcusable, they have been contracted into one easy sum, intelligible even to the meanest capacity; and that is, *Do not that to another, which thou wouldest not have done to thyself*; which sheweth him, that he has no more to do in learning the laws of nature, but, when weighing the actions of other men with his own, they seem too heavy, to put them into the other part of the balance, and his own into their place, that his own passions, and self-love, may add nothing to the weight; and then there is none of these laws of nature that will not appear unto him very reasonable.

The laws of nature oblige *in foro interno*; that is to say, they bind to a desire they should take place: but *in foro externo*; that is, to the putting them in act, not always. For he that should be modest, and tractable, and perform all he promises, in such time, and place, where no man else should do so, should but make himself a prey to others, and procure his own certain ruin, contrary to the ground of all laws of nature, which tend to nature's preservation. And again, he that having sufficient security, that others shall observe the same laws towards him, observes them not himself, seeketh not peace, but war; and consequently the destruction of his nature by violence.

And whatsoever laws bind *in foro interno*, may be broken, not only by a fact contrary to the law, but also by a fact according to it, in case a man think it contrary. For though his action in this case, be according to the law; yet his purpose was against the law; which, where the obligation is *in foro interno*, is a breach.

The laws of nature are immutable and eternal; for injustice, ingratitude, arrogance, pride, iniquity, acception of persons, and the rest, can never be made lawful. For it can never be that war shall preserve life, and peace destroy it.

The same laws, because they oblige only to a desire, and endeavour, I mean an unfeigned and constant endeavour, are easy to be observed. For in that they require nothing but endeavour, he that endeavoureth their performance, fulfilleth them; and he that fulfilleth the law, is just.

And the science of them, is the true and only moral philosophy. For moral philosophy is nothing else but the science of what is *good*, and *evil*, in the conversation, and society of mankind. *Good*, and *evil*, are names that signify our appetites, and aversions; which in different tempers, customs, and doctrines of men, are different: and divers men, differ not only in their judgment, on the senses of what is pleasant, and unpleasant to the taste, smell, hearing, touch, and sight; but also of what is conformable, or disagreeable to reason, in the actions of common life. Nay, the same man, in divers times, differs from himself; and one time praiseth, that is, called good, what another time he dispraiseth, and calleth evil: from whence arise disputes, controversies, and at last war. And therefore so long as a man is in the condition of mere nature, which is a condition of war, as private appetite is the measure of good, and evil: and consequently all men agree on this, that peace is good, and therefore also the way, or means of peace, which, as I have shewed before, are *justice*, *gratitude*, *modesty*, *equity*, *mercy*, and the rest of the laws of nature, are good; that is to say; *moral virtues*; and their contrary *vices*, evil. Now the science of virtue and vice, is moral philosophy; and therefore the true doctrine of the laws of nature, is the true moral philosophy. But the writers of moral philosophy, though they acknowledge the same virtues and vices; yet not seeing wherein consisted their goodness; nor that they come to be praised, as the means of peaceable, sociable, and comfortable living, place them in a mediocrity of passions: as if not the cause, but the degree of daring, made fortitude; or not the cause, but the quantity of a gift, made liberality.

These dictates of reason, men used to call by the name of laws, but improperly: for they are but conclusions, or theorems concerning what conduceth to the conservation and defence of themselves; whereas law, properly, is the word of him, that by right hath command over others. But yet if we consider the same theorems, as delivered in the word of God, that by right commandeth all things; then are they properly called laws.

CHAPTER XVI

Of Persons, Authors and Things Personated

A PERSON, is he, *whose words or actions are considered, either as his own, or as representing the words or actions of another man, or of any other thing, to whom they are attributed, whether truly or by fiction.*

When they are considered as his own, then is he called a *natural person*: and when they are considered as representing the words and actions of another, then is he a *feigned* or *artificial person*.

The word person is Latin: instead whereof the Greeks have πρόσωπον, which signifies the *face*, as *persona* in Latin signifies the *disguise*, or *outward appearance* of a man, counterfeited on the stage; and sometimes more particularly that part of it, which disguiseth the face, as a mask or vizard: and from the stage, hath been translated to any representer of speech and action, as well in tribunals, as theatres. So that a *person*, is the same that an *actor* is, both on the stage and in common conversation; and to *personate*, is to *act*, or *represent* himself, or another; and he that acteth another, is said to bear his person, or act in his name; in which sense Cicero useth it where he says, *Unus sustineo tres personas; mei, adversarii, et judicis*: I bear three persons; my own, my adversary's, and the judge's; and is called in divers occasions, diversly; as a *representer*, or *representative*, a *lieutenant*, a *vicar*, an *attorney*, a *deputy*, a *procurator*, an *actor*, and the like.

Of persons artificial, some have their words and actions *owned* by those whom they represent. And then the person is the *actor*; and he that owneth his words and actions, is the AUTHOR: in which case the actor acteth by authority. For that which in speaking of goods and possessions, is called an *owner*, and in Latin *dominus*, in Greek κύριος speaking of actions, is called author. And as the right of possession, is called dominion; so the right of doing any action, is called AUTHORITY. So that by authority, is always understood a right of doing any act; and *done by authority*, done by commission, or licence from him whose right it is.

From hence it followeth, that when the actor maketh a covenant by authority, he bindeth thereby the author, no less than if he had made it himself; and no less subjecteth him to all the consequences of the same. And therefore all that hath been said formerly, (chapter XIV) of the nature of covenants between man and man in their natural capacity, is true also when they are made by their actors, representers, or procurators, that have authority from them, so far forth as is in their commission, but no further.

And therefore he that maketh a covenant with the actor, or representer, not knowing the authority he hath, doth it at his own peril. For no man is obliged by a covenant, whereof he is not author; nor consequently by a covenant made against, or beside the authority he gave.

When the actor doth anything against the law of nature by command of the author, if he be obliged by former covenant to obey him, not he, but the author breaketh the law of nature; for though the action be against the law of nature; yet it is not his: but contrarily, to refuse to do it, is against the law of nature, that forbiddeth breach of covenant.

And he that maketh a covenant with the author, by mediation of the actor, not knowing what authority he hath, but only takes his word: in case such authority be not made manifest unto him upon demand, is no longer obliged: for the covenant made with the author, is not valid, without his counter-assurance. But if he that so covenanteth, knew beforehand he was to expect no other assurance, than the actor's word; then is the covenant valid; because the actor in this case maketh himself the author. And therefore, as when the authority is evident, the covenant obligeth the author, not the actor; so when the authority is feigned, it obligeth the actor only; there being no author but himself.

There are few things, that are incapable of being represented by fiction. Inanimate things, as a church, an hospital, a bridge, may be personated by a rector, master, or overseer. But things inanimate, cannot be authors, nor therefore give authority to their actors: yet the actors may have authority to procure their maintenance, given them by those that are owners, or governors of those things. And therefore, such things cannot be personated, before there be some state of civil government.

Likewise children, fools, and madmen that have no use of reason, may be personated by guardians, or curators; but can be no authors, during that time, of any action done by them, longer than, when they shall recover the use of reason, they shall judge the same reasonable. Yet during the folly, he that hath right of governing them, may give authority to the guardian. But this again has no place but in a state civil, because before such estate, there is no dominion of persons.

An idol, or mere figment of the brain, may be personated; as were the gods of the heathen: which by such officers as the state appointed, were personated, and held possessions, and other goods, and rights, which men from time to time dedicated, and consecrated unto them. But idols cannot be authors: for an idol is nothing. The authority proceeded from the state: and therefore before introduction of civil government, the gods of the heathen could not be personated.

The true God may be personated. As he was; first, by Moses, who governed the Israelites, that were not his, but God's people, not in his own name with *hoc dicit Moses*; but in God's name, with *hoc dicit Dominus*. Secondly, by the Son of man, his own Son, our blessed Saviour Jesus Christ, that came to reduce the Jews, and induce all nations into the kingdom of his father; not as of himself, but as sent from his father. And thirdly, by the Holy Ghost, or Comforter, speaking, and working in the Apostles: which Holy Ghost, was a Comforter that came not of himself; but was sent, and proceeded from them both.

A multitude of men, are made *one* person, when they are by one man, or one person, represented; so that it be done with the consent of every one of that multitude in particular. For it is the *unity* of the representer, not the *unity* of the represented, that maketh the person *one*. And it is the representer that beareth the person, and but one person: and *unity*, cannot otherwise be understood in multitude.

And because the multitude naturally is not *one*, but *many*; they cannot be understood for one; but many authors, of every thing their representative saith, or doth in their name; every man giving their common representer, authority from himself in particular; and owning all the actions the representer doth, in case they give him authority without stint: otherwise, when they limit him in what, and how far he shall represent them, none of them owneth more than they gave him commission to act.

And if the representative consist of many men, the voice of the greater number, must be considered as the voice of them all. For if the lesser number pronounce, for example, in the affirmative, and the greater in the negative, there will be negatives more than enough to destroy the affirmatives; and thereby the excess of negatives, standing uncontradicted, are the only voice the representative hath.

And a representative of even number, especially when the number is not great, whereby the contradictory voices are oftentimes equal, is therefore oftentimes mute, and incapable of action. Yet in some cases contradictory voices equal in number, may determine a question; as in condemning, or absolving, equality of votes, even in that they condemn not, do absolve; but not on the contrary condemn, in that they absolve not. For when a cause is heard; not to condemn, is to absolve: but on the contrary, to say that not absolving, is condemning, is not true. The like it is in a deliberation of executing presently, or deferring till another time: for when the voices are equal, the not decreeing execution is a decree of dilation.

Or if the number be odd, as three, or more, men or assemblies; whereof every one has by a negative voice, authority to take away the effect of all the affirmative voices of the rest, this number is no representative; because by the diversity of opinions, and interests of men, it becomes oftentimes, and in cases of the greatest consequence, a mute person, and unapt, as for many things else, so for the government of a multitude, especially in time of war.

Of authors there be two sorts. The first simply so called; which I have before defined to be him, that owneth the action of another simply. The second is he, that owneth an action, or covenant of another conditionally; that is to say, he undertaketh to do it, if the other doth it not, at, or before a certain time. And these authors conditional, are generally called SURETIES, in Latin *fidejussores*, and *sponsores;* and particularly for debt, *praedes*; and for appearance before a judge, or magistrate, *vades*.

Part Two

OF COMMONWEALTH

CHAPTER XVII

Of the Causes, Generation, and Definition of a Commonwealth

THE final cause, end, or design of men, who naturally love liberty, and dominion over others, in the introduction of that restraint upon themselves, in which we see them live in commonwealths, is the foresight of their own preservation, and of a more contented life thereby; that is to say, of getting themselves out from that miserable condition of war, which is necessarily consequent, as hath been shown in chapter XIII, to the natural passions of men, when there is no visible power to keep them in awe, and tie them by fear of punishment to the performance of their covenants, and observation of those laws of nature set down in the fourteenth and fifteenth chapters.

For the laws of nature, as *justice*, *equity*, *modesty*, *mercy*, and, in sum, *doing to others, as we would be done to*, of themselves, without the terror of some power, to cause them to be observed, are contrary to our natural passions, that carry us to partiality, pride, revenge, and the like. And covenants, without the swords, are but words, and of no strength to secure a man at all. Therefore notwithstanding the laws of nature, which every one hath then kept, when he has the will to keep them, when he can do it safely, if there be no power erected, or not great enough for our security; every man will, and may lawfully rely on his own strength and art, for caution against all other men. And in all places, where men have lived by small families, to rob and spoil one another, has been a trade, and so far from being reputed against the law of nature, that the greater spoils they gained, the greater was their honour; and men observed no other laws therein, but the laws of honour; that is, to abstain from cruelty, leaving to men their lives, and instruments of husbandry. And as small families did then; so now do cities and kingdoms which are but greater families, for their own security, enlarge their dominions, upon all pretences of danger, and fear of invasion, or assistance that may be given to invaders, and endeavour as much as they can, to subdue, or weaken their neighbours, by open force, and secret arts, for want of other caution, justly; and are remembered for it in after ages with honour.

Nor is it the joining together of a small number of men, that gives them this security; because in small numbers, small additions on the one side or the other, make the advantage of strength so great, as is sufficient to carry the victory; and therefore gives encouragement to an invasion. The multitude sufficient to confide in for our security, is not determined by any certain number, but by comparison with the enemy we fear; and is then sufficient, when the odds of the enemy is not of so visible and conspicuous moment, to determine the event of war, as to move him to attempt.

And be there never so great a multitude; yet if their actions be directed according to their particular judgments, and particular appetites, they can expect thereby no defence, nor protection, neither against a common enemy, nor against the injuries of one another. For being distracted in opinions concerning the best use and application of their strength, they do not help but hinder one another; and reduce their strength by mutual opposition to nothing: whereby they are easily, not only subdued by a very few that agree together; but also when there is no common enemy, they make war upon each other, for their particular interests. For if we could suppose a great multitude of men to consent in the observation of justice, and other laws of nature, without a common power to keep them all in awe; we might as well suppose all mankind to do the same; and then there neither would be, nor need to be any civil government, or commonwealth at all; because there would be peace without subjection.

Nor is it enough for the security, which men desire should last all the time of their life, that they be governed, and directed by one judgment, for a limited time; as in one battle, or one war. For though they obtain a victory by their unanimous endeavour against a foreign enemy; yet afterwards when either they have no common enemy, or he that by one part is held for an enemy, is by another part held for a friend, they must needs by the difference of their interests dissolve, and fall again into a war amongst themselves.

It is true, that certain living creatures, as bees, and ants, live sociably one with another, which are therefore by Aristotle numbered amongst political creatures; and yet have no other direction, than their particular judgments and appetites; nor speech, whereby one of them can signify to another, what he thinks expedient for the common benefit: and therefore some man may perhaps desire to know, why mankind cannot do the same. To which I answer.

First, that men are continually in competition for honour and dignity, which these creatures are not; and consequently amongst men there ariseth on that ground, envy and hatred, and finally war; but amongst these not so.

Secondly, that amongst these creatures, the common good differeth not from the private; and being by nature inclined to their private, they procure thereby the common benefit. But man, whose joy consisteth in comparing himself with other men, can relish nothing but what is eminent.

Thirdly, that these creatures, having not, as man, the use of reason, do not see, nor think they see any fault, in the administration of their common business; whereas amongst men, there are very many, that think themselves wiser, and abler to govern the public, better than the rest; and these strive to reform and innovate, one this way, another that way; and thereby bring it into distraction and civil war.

Fourthly, that these creatures, though they have some use of voice, in making known to one another their desires, and other affections; yet they want that art of words, by which some men can represent to others, that which is good, in the likeness of evil; and evil, in the likeness of good; and augment, or diminish the apparent greatness of good and evil; discontenting men, and troubling their peace at their pleasure.

Fifthly, irrational creatures cannot distinguish between *injury*, and *damage*; and therefore as long as they be at ease, they are not offended with their fellows: whereas man is then most troublesome, when he is most at ease: for then it is that he loves to shew his wisdom, and control the actions of them that govern the commonwealth.

Lastly, the agreement of these creatures is natural; that of men, is by covenant only, which is artificial: and therefore it is no wonder if there be somewhat else required, besides covenant, to make their agreement constant and lasting; which is a common power, to keep them in awe, and to direct their actions to the common benefit.

The only way to erect such a common power, as may be able to defend them from the invasion of foreigners, and the injuries of one another, and thereby to secure them in such sort, as that by their own industry, and by the fruits of the earth, they may nourish themselves and live contentedly; is, to confer all their power and strength upon one man, or upon one assembly of men, that may reduce all their wills, by plurality of voices, unto one will: which is as much as to say, to appoint one man, or assembly of men, to bear their person; and every one to own, and acknowledge himself to be author of whatsoever he that so beareth their person, shall act, or cause to be acted, in those things which concern the common peace and safety; and therein to submit their wills, every one to his will, and their judgments, to his judgment. This is more than consent, or concord; it is a real unity of them all, in one and the same person, made by covenant of every man with every man, in such manner, as if every man should say to every man, *I authorize and give up my right of governing myself, to this man, or to this assembly of men, on this condition, that thou give up thy right to him, and authorize all his actions in like manner*. This done, the multitude so united in one person, is called a COMMONWEALTH, in Latin CIVITAS. This is the generation of the great LEVIATHAN, or rather, to speak more reverently, of that *mortal god*, to which we owe under the *immortal God*, our peace and defence. For by this authority, given him by every particular man in the commonwealth, he hath the use of so much power and strength conferred on him, that by terror thereof, he is enabled to perform the wills of them all, to peace at home, and mutual aid against their enemies abroad. And in him consisteth the essence of the commonwealth; which, to define it, is *one person, of whose acts a great multitude, by mutual covenants one with another, have made themselves every one the author, to the end he may use the strength and means of them all, as he shall think expedient, for their peace and common defence.*

And he that carrieth this person, is called SOVEREIGN, and said to have *sovereign power*; and every one besides, his SUBJECT.

The attaining to this sovereign power, is by two ways. One, by natural force; as when a man maketh his children, to submit themselves, and their children to his government, as being able to destroy them if they refuse; or by war subdueth his enemies to his will, giving them their lives on that condition. The other, is when men agree amongst themselves, to submit to some man, or assembly of men, voluntarily, on confidence to be protected by him against all others. This latter, may be called a political commonwealth, or commonwealth by *institution*; and the former, a commonwealth by *acquisition*. And first, I shall speak of a commonwealth by institution.

CHAPTER XVIII

Of the Rights of Sovereigns by Institution

A *commonwealth* is said to be *instituted*, when a *multitude* of men do agree, and *covenant, every one, with every one,* that to whatsoever *man*, or *assembly of men*, shall be given by the major part, the *right* to *present* the person of them all, that is to say, to be their *representative*; every one, as well he that *voted for it,* as he that *voted against it,* shall *authorize* all the actions and judgments, of that man, or assembly of men, in the same manner, as if they were his own, to the end, to live peaceably amongst themselves, and be protected against other men.

From this institution of a commonwealth are derived all the *rights*, and *faculties* of him, or them, on whom sovereign power is conferred by the consent of the people assembled.

First, because they covenant, it is to be understood, they are not obliged by former covenant to anything repugnant hereunto. And consequently they that have already instituted a commonwealth, being thereby bound by covenant, to own the actions, and judgments of one, cannot lawfully make a new covenant, amongst themselves, to be obedient to any other, in any thing whatsoever, without his permission. And therefore, they that are subjects to a monarch, cannot without his leave cast off monarchy, and return to the confusion of a disunited multitude; nor transfer their person from him that beareth it, to another man, or other assembly of men: for they are bound, every man to every man, to own, and be reputed author of all, that he that already is their sovereign, shall do, and judge fit to be done: so that any one man dissenting, all the rest should break their covenant made to that man, which is injustice: and they have also every man given the sovereignty to him that beareth their person; and therefore if they depose him, they take from him that which is his own, and so again it is injustice. Besides, if he that attempteth to depose his sovereign, be killed, or punished by him for such attempt, he is author of his own punishment, as being by the institution, author of all his sovereign shall do: and because it is injustice for a man to do anything, for which he may be punished by his own authority, he is also upon that title, unjust. And whereas some men have pretended for their disobedience to their sovereign, a new covenant, made, not with men, but with God; this also is unjust: for there is no covenant with God, but by mediation of somebody that representeth God's person; which none doth but God's lieutenant, who hath the sovereignty under God. But this pretence of covenant with God, is so evident a lie, even in the pretenders' own consciences, that it is not only an act of an unjust, but also of a vile, and unmanly disposition.

Secondly, because the right of bearing the person of them all, is given to him they make sovereign, by covenant only of one to another, and not of him to any of them; there can happen no breach of covenant on the part of the sovereign; and consequently none of his subjects, by any pretence of forfeiture, can be freed from his subjection. That he which is made sovereign maketh no covenant with his subjects beforehand, is manifest; because either he must make it with the whole multitude, as one party to the covenant; or he must make a several covenant with every man. With the whole, as one party, it is impossible; because as yet they are not one person: and if he make so many several covenants as there be men, those covenants after he hath the sovereignty are void; because what act soever can be pretended by any one of them for breach thereof, is the act both of himself, and of all the rest, because done in the person, and by the right of every one of them in particular. Besides, if any one, or more of them, pretend a breach of the covenant made by the sovereign at his institution; and others, or one other of his subjects, or himself alone, pretend there was no such breach, there is in this case, no judge to decide the controversy; it returns therefore to the sword again; and every man recovereth the right of protecting himself by his own strength, contrary to the design they had in the institution. It is therefore in vain to grant sovereignty by way of precedent covenant. The opinion that any monarch receiveth his power by covenant, that is to say, on condition, proceedeth from want of understanding this easy truth, that covenants being but words and breath, have no force to oblige, contain, constrain, or protect any man, but what it has from the public sword; that is, from the untied hands of that man, or assembly of men that hath the sovereignty, and whose actions are avouched by them all, and performed by the strength of them all, in him united. But when an assembly of men is made sovereign; then no man imagineth any such covenant to have passed in the institution; for no man is so dull as to say, for example, the people of Rome made a covenant with the Romans, to hold the sovereignty on such or such conditions; which not performed, the Romans might lawfully depose the Roman people. That men see not the reason to be alike in a monarchy, and in a popular government, proceedeth from the ambition of some, that are kinder to the government of an assembly, whereof they may hope to participate, than of monarchy, which they despair to enjoy.

Thirdly, because the major part hath by consenting voices declared a sovereign; he that dissented must now consent with the rest; that is, be contented to avow all the actions he shall do, or else justly be destroyed by the rest. For if he voluntarily entered into the congregation of them that were assembled, he sufficiently declared thereby his will, and therefore tacitly covenanted, to stand to what the major part should ordain: and therefore if he refuse to stand thereto, or make protestation against any of their decrees, he does contrary to his covenant, and therefore unjustly. And whether he be of the congregation, or not; and whether his consent be asked, or not, he must either submit to their decrees, or be left in the condition of war he was in before; wherein he might without injustice be destroyed by any man whatsoever.

Fourthly, because every subject is by this institution author of all the actions, and judgments of the sovereign instituted; it follows, that whatsoever he doth, it can be no injury to any of his subjects; nor ought he to be by any of them accused of injustice. For he that doth anything by authority from another, doth therein no injury to him by whose authority he acteth: but by this institution of a commonwealth, every particular man is author of all the sovereign doth: and consequently he that complaineth of injury from his sovereign, complaineth of that whereof he himself is author; and therefore ought not to accuse any man but himself; no nor himself of injury; because to do injury to one's self, is impossible. It is true that they that have sovereign power may commit iniquity; but no injustice, or injury in the proper signification.

Fifthly, and consequently to that which was said last, no man that hath sovereign power can justly be put to death, or otherwise in any manner by his subjects punished. For seeing every subject is author of the actions of his sovereign; he punisheth another for the actions committed by himself.

And because the end of this institution, is the peace and defence of them all; and whosoever has right to the end, has right to the means; it belongeth of right, to whatsoever man, or assembly that hath the sovereignty, to be judge both of the means of peace and defence, and also of the hindrances, and disturbances of the same; and to do whatsoever he shall think necessary to be done, both beforehand, for the preserving of peace and security, by prevention of discord at home, and hostility from abroad; and, when peace and security are lost, for the recovery of the same. And therefore,

Sixthly, it is annexed to the sovereignty, to be judge of what opinions and doctrines are averse, and what conducing to peace; and consequently, on what occasions, how far, and what men are to be trusted withal, in speaking to multitudes of people; and who shall examine the doctrines of all books before they be published. For the actions of men proceed from their opinions; and in the well-governing of opinions, consisteth the well-governing of men's actions, in order to their peace, and concord. And though in matter of doctrine, nothing ought to be regarded but the truth; yet this is not repugnant to regulating the same by peace. For doctrine repugnant to peace, can no more be true, than peace and concord can be against the law of nature. It is true, that in a commonwealth, where by the negligence, or unskilfulness of governors, and teachers, false doctrines are by time generally received; the contrary truths may be generally offensive. Yet the most sudden, and rough bursting in of a new truth, that can be, does never break the peace, but only sometimes awake the war. For those men that are so remissly governed, that they dare take up arms to defend, or introduce an opinion, are still in war; and their condition not peace but, only a cessation of arms for fear of one another; and they live, as it were, in the precincts of battle continually. It belongeth therefore to him that hath the sovereign power, to be judge, or constitute all judges of opinions and doctrines, as a thing necessary to peace; thereby to prevent discord and civil war.

Seventhly, is annexed to the sovereignty, the whole power of prescribing the rules, whereby every man may know, what goods he may enjoy, and what actions he may do, without being molested by any of his fellow-subjects; and this is it men call *propriety*. For before constitution of sovereign power, as hath already been shown, all men had right to all things; which necessarily causeth war: and therefore this propriety, being necessary to peace, and depending on sovereign power, is the act of that power, in order to the public peace. These rules of propriety, or *meum* and *tuum*, and of *good, evil, lawful,* and *unlawful* in the actions of subjects, are the civil laws; that is to say, the laws of each commonwealth in particular; though the name of civil law be now restrained to the ancient civil laws of the city of Rome; which being the head of a great part of the world, her laws at that time were in these parts the civil law.

Eighthly, is annexed to the sovereignty, the right of judicature; that is to say, of hearing and deciding all controversies, which may arise concerning law, either civil, or natural; or concerning fact. For without the decision of controversies, there is no protection of one subject, against the injuries of another; the laws concerning *meum* and *tuum* are in vain; and to every man remaineth, from the natural and necessary appetite of his own conservation, the right of protecting himself by his private strength, which is the condition of war, and contrary to the end for which every commonwealth is instituted.

Ninthly, is annexed to the sovereignty, the right of making war and peace with other nations, and commonwealths; that is to say, of judging when it is for the public good, and how great forces are to be assembled, armed, and paid for that end; and to levy money upon the subjects, to defray the expenses thereof. For the power by which the people are to be defended, consisteth in their armies; and the strength of an army, in the union of their strength under one command; which command the sovereign instituted, therefore hath; because the command of the *militia*, without other institution, maketh him that hath it sovereign. And therefore whosoever is made general of an army, he that hath the sovereign power is always generalissimo.

Tenthly, is annexed to the sovereignty, the choosing of all counsellors, ministers, magistrates, and officers, both in peace, and war. For seeing the sovereign is charged with the end, which is the common peace and defence, he is understood to have power to use such means, as he shall think most fit for his discharge.

Eleventhly, to the sovereign is committed the power of rewarding with riches, or honour, and of punishing with corporal or pecuniary punishment, or with ignominy, every subject according to the law he hath formerly made; or if there be no law made, according as he shall judge most to conduce to the encouraging of men to serve the commonwealth, or deterring of them from doing disservice to the same.

Lastly, considering what value men are naturally apt to set upon themselves; what respect they look for from others; and how little they value other men; from whence continually arise amongst them, emulation, quarrels, factions, and at last war, to the destroying of one another, and diminution of their strength against a common enemy; it is necessary that there be laws of honour, and a public rate of the worth of such men as have deserved, or are able to deserve well of the commonwealth; and that there be force in the hands of some or other, to put those laws in execution. But it hath already been shown, that not only the whole *militia*, or forces of the commonwealth; but also the judicature of all controversies, is annexed to the sovereignty. To the sovereign therefore it belongeth also to give titles of honour; and to appoint what order of place, and dignity, each man shall hold; and what signs of respect, in public or private meetings, they shall give to one another.

These are the rights, which make the essence of sovereignty; and which are the marks, whereby a man may discern in what man, or assembly of men, the sovereign power is placed, and resideth. For these are incommunicable, and inseparable. The power to coin money; to dispose of the estate and persons of infant heirs; to have præemption in markets; and all other statute prerogatives, may be transferred by the sovereign; and yet the power to protect his subjects be retained. But if he transfer the *militia*, he retains the judicature in vain, for want of execution of the laws: or if he grant away the power of raising money; the *militia* is in vain; or if he give away the government of doctrines, men will be frighted into rebellion with the fear of spirits. And so if we consider any one of the said rights, we shall presently see, that the holding of all the rest will produce no effect, in the conservation of peace and justice, the end for which all commonwealths are instituted. And this division is it, whereof it is said, *a kingdom divided in itself cannot stand*: for unless this division precede, division into opposite armies can never happen. If there had not first been an opinion received of the greatest part of England, that these powers were divided between the King, and the Lords, and the House of Commons, the people had never been divided and fallen into this civil war; first between those that disagreed in politics; and after between the dissenters about the liberty of religion; which have so instructed men in this point of sovereign right, that there be few now in England that do not see, that these rights are inseparable, and will be so generally acknowledged at the next return of peace; and so continue, till their miseries are forgotten; and no longer, except the vulgar be better taught than they have hitherto been.

And because they are essential and inseparable rights, it follows necessarily, that in whatsoever words any of them seem to be granted away, yet if the sovereign power itself be not in direct terms renounced, and the name of sovereign no more given by the grantees to him that grants them, the grant is void: for when he has granted all he can, if we grant back the sovereignty, all is restored, as inseparably annexed thereunto.

This great authority being indivisible, and inseparably annexed to the sovereignty, there is little ground for the opinion of them, that say of sovereign kings, though they be *singulis majores*, of greater power than every one of their subjects, yet they be *universis minores*, of less power than them all together. For if by *all together*, they mean not the collective body as one person, then *all together*, and *every one*, signify the same; and the speech is absurd. But if by *all together*, they understand them as one person, which person the sovereign bears, then the power of all together, is the same with the sovereign's power; and so again the speech is absurd: which absurdity they see well enough, when the sovereignty is in an assembly of the people; but in a monarch they see it not; and yet the power of sovereignty is the same in whomsoever it be placed.

And as the power, so also the honour of the sovereign, ought to be greater, than that of any, or all the subjects. For in the sovereignty is the fountain of honour. The dignities of lord, earl, duke, and prince are his creatures. As in the presence of the master, the servants are equal, and without any honour at all; so are the subjects, in the presence of the sovereign. And though they shine some more, some less, when they are out of his sight; yet in his presence, they shine no more than the stars in the presence of the sun.

But a man may here object, that the condition of subjects is very miserable; as being obnoxious to the lusts, and other irregular passions of him, or them that have so unlimited a power in their hands. And commonly they that live under a monarch, think it the fault of monarchy; and they that live under the government of democracy, or other sovereign assembly, attribute all the inconvenience to that form of commonwealth; whereas the power in all forms, if they be perfect enough to protect them, is the same: not considering that the state of man can never be without some incommodity or other; and that the greatest, that in any form of government can possibly happen to the people in general, is scarce sensible, in respect of the miseries, and horrible calamities, that accompany a civil war, or that dissolute condition of masterless men, without subjection to laws, and a coercive power to tie their hands from rapine and revenge: nor considering that the greatest pressure of sovereign governors, proceedeth not from any delight, or profit they can expect in the damage or weakening of their subjects, in whose vigour, consisteth their own strength and glory; but in the restiveness of themselves, that unwillingly contributing to their own defence, make it necessary for their governors to draw from them what they can in time of peace, that they may have means on any emergent occasion, or sudden need, to resist, or take advantage on their enemies. For all men are by nature provided of notable multiplying glasses, that is their passions and self-love, through which, every little payment appeareth a great grievance; but are destitute of those prospective glasses, namely moral and civil science, to see afar off the miseries that hang over them, and cannot without such payments be avoided.

CHAPTER XIX

Of the Several Kinds of Commonwealth by Institution, and of Succession to the Sovereign Power

THE difference of commonwealths, consisteth in the difference of the sovereign, or the person representative of all and every one of the multitude. And because the sovereignty is either in one man, or in an assembly of more than one; and into that assembly either every man hath right to enter, or not every one, but certain men distinguished from the rest; it is manifest, there can be but three kinds of commonwealth. For the representative must needs be one man, or more: and if more, then it is the assembly of all, or but of a part. When the representative is one man, then is the commonwealth a MONARCHY: when an assembly of all that will come together, then it is a DEMOCRACY, or popular commonwealth: when an assembly of a part only, then it is called an ARISTOCRACY. Other kind of commonwealth there can be none: for either one, or more, or all, must have the sovereign power, which I have shown to be indivisible, entire.

There be other names of government, in the histories, and books of policy; as *tyranny*, and *oligarchy*: but they are not the names of other forms of government, but of the same forms misliked. For they that are discontented under *monarchy*, call it *tyranny*; and they that are displeased with *aristocracy*, call it *oligarchy*: so also, they which find themselves grieved under a *democracy*, call it *anarchy*, which signifies want of government; and yet I think no man believes, that want of government, is any new kind of government: nor by the same reason ought they to believe, that the government is of one kind, when they like it, and another, when they mislike it, or are oppressed by the governors.

It is manifest, that men who are in absolute liberty, may, if they please, give authority to one man, to represent them every one; as well as give such authority to any assembly of men whatsoever; and consequently may subject themselves, if they think good, to a monarch, as absolutely, as to any other representative. Therefore, where there is already erected a sovereign power, there can be no other representative of the same people, but only to certain particular ends, by the sovereign limited. For that were to erect two sovereigns; and every man to have his person represented by two actors, that by opposing one another, must needs divide that power, which, if men will live in peace, is indivisible; and thereby reduce the multitude into the condition of war, contrary to the end for which all sovereignty is instituted. And therefore as it is absurd, to think that a sovereign assembly, inviting the people of their dominion, to send up their deputies, with power to make known their advice, or desires, should therefore hold such deputies, rather than themselves, for the absolute representatives of the people: so it is absurd also, to think the same in a monarchy. And I know not how this so manifest a truth, should of late be so little observed; that in a monarchy, he that had the sovereignty from a descent of six hundred years, was alone called sovereign, had the title of Majesty from every one of his subjects, and was unquestionably taken by them for their king, was notwithstanding never considered as their representative; the name without contradiction passing for the title of those men, which at his command were sent up by the people to carry their petitions, and give him, if he permitted it, their advice. Which may serve as an admonition, for those that are the true, and absolute representative of a people, to instruct men in the nature of that office, and to take heed how they admit of any other general representation upon any occasion whatsoever, if they mean to discharge the trust committed to them.

The difference between these three kinds of commonwealth, consisteth not in the difference of power; but in the difference of convenience, or aptitude to produce the peace, and security of the people; for which end they were instituted. And to compare monarchy with the other two, we may observe; first, that whosoever beareth the person of the people, or is one of that assembly that bears it, beareth also his own natural person. And though he be careful in his politic person to procure the common interest; yet he is more, or no less careful to procure the private good of himself, his family, kindred and friends; and for the most part, if the public interest chance to cross the private, he prefers the private: for the passions of men, are commonly more potent than their reason. From whence it follows, that where the public and private interest are most closely united, there is the public most advanced. Now in monarchy, the private interest is the same with the public. The riches, power, and honour of a monarch arise only from the riches, strength and reputation of his subjects. For no king can be rich, nor glorious, nor secure, whose subjects are either poor, or contemptible, or too weak through want or dissention, to maintain a war against their enemies: whereas in a democracy, or aristocracy, the public prosperity confers not so much to the private fortune of one that is corrupt, or ambitious, as doth many times a perfidious advice, a treacherous action, or a civil war.

Secondly, that a monarch receiveth counsel of whom, when, and where he pleaseth; and consequently may hear the opinion of men versed in the matter about which he deliberates, of what rank or quality soever, and as long before the time of action, and with as much secrecy, as he will. But when a sovereign assembly has need of counsel, none are admitted but such as have a right thereto from the beginning; which for the most part are of those who have been versed more in the acquisition of wealth than of knowledge; and are to give their advice in long discourses, which may, and do commonly excite men to action, but not govern them in it. For the *understanding* is by the flame of the passions, never enlightened, but dazzled. Nor is there any place, or time, wherein an assembly can receive counsel with secrecy, because of their own multitude.

Thirdly, that the resolutions of a monarch, are subject to

no other inconstancy, than that of human nature; but in assemblies, besides that of nature, there ariseth an inconstancy from the number. For the absence of a few, that would have the resolution once taken, continue firm, which may happen by security, negligence, or private impediments, or the diligent appearance of a few of the contrary opinion, undoes today, all that was concluded yesterday.

Fourthly, that a monarch cannot disagree with himself, out of envy, or interest; but an assembly may; and that to such a height, as may produce a civil war.

Fifthly, that in monarchy there is this inconvenience; that any subject, by the power of one man, for the enriching of a favourite or flatterer, may be deprived of all he possesseth; which I confess is a great and inevitable inconvenience. But the same may as well happen, where the sovereign power is in an assembly: for their power is the same; and they are as subject to evil counsel, and to be seduced by orators, as a monarch by flatterers; and becoming one another's flatterers, serve one another's covetousness and ambition by turns. And whereas the favourites of monarchs, are few, and they have none else to advance but their own kindred; the favourites of an assembly, are many; and the kindred much more numerous, than of any monarch. Besides, there is no favourite of a monarch, which cannot as well succour his friends, as hurt his enemies: but orators, that is to say, favourites of sovereign assemblies, though they have great power to hurt, have little to save. For to accuse, requires less eloquence, such is man's nature, than to excuse; and condemnation, than absolution more resembles justice.

Sixthly, that it is an inconvenience in monarchy, that the sovereignty may descend upon an infant, or one that cannot discern between good and evil: and consisteth in this, that the use of his power, must be in the hand of another man, or of some assembly of men, which are to govern by his right, and in his name; as curators, and protectors of his person, and authority. But to say there is inconvenience, in putting the use of the sovereign power, into the hand of a man, or an assembly of men; is to say that all government is more inconvenient, than confusion, and civil war. And therefore all the danger that can be pretended, must arise from the contention of those, that for an office of so great honour, and profit, may become competitors. To make it appear, that this inconvenience, proceedeth not from that form of government we call monarchy, we are to consider, that the precedent monarch hath appointed who shall have the tuition of his infant successor, either expressly by testament, or tacitly, by not controlling the custom in that case received: and then such inconvenience, if it happen, is to be attributed, not to the monarchy, but to the ambition, and injustice of the subjects; which in all kinds of government, where the people are not well instructed in their duty, and the rights of sovereignty, is the same. Or else the precedent monarch hath not at all taken order for such tuition; and then the law of nature hath provided this sufficient rule, that the tuition shall be in him, that hath by nature most interest in the preservation of the authority of the infant, and to whom least benefit can accrue by his death, or diminution. For seeing every man by nature seeketh his own benefit, and promotion; to put an infant into the power of those, that can promote themselves by his destruction, or damage, is not tuition, but treachery. So that sufficient provision being taken, against all just quarrel, about the government under a child, if any contention arise to the disturbance of the public peace, it is not to be attributed to the form of monarchy, but to the ambition of subjects, and ignorance of their duty. On the other side, there is no great commonwealth, the sovereignty whereof is in a great assembly, which is not, as to consultations of peace, and war, and making of laws, in the same condition, as if the government were in a child. For as a child wants the judgment to dissent from counsel given him, and is thereby necessitated to take the advice of them, or him, to whom he is committed: so an assembly wanteth the liberty, to dissent from the counsel of the major part, be it good, or bad. And as a child has need of a tutor, or protector, to preserve his person and authority: so also, in great commonwealths, the sovereign assembly, in all great dangers and troubles, have need of *custodes libertatis*; that is of dictators, or protectors of their authority; which are as much as temporary monarchs, to whom for a time, they may commit the entire exercise of their power; and have, at the end of that time, been oftener deprived thereof, than infant kings, by their protectors, regents, or any other tutors.

Though the kinds of sovereignty be, as I have now shown, but three; that is to say, monarchy, where one man has it; or democracy, where the general assembly of subjects hath it; or aristocracy, where it is in an assembly of certain persons nominated, or otherwise distinguished from the rest: yet he that shall consider the particular commonwealths that have been, and are in the world, will not perhaps easily reduce them to three, and may thereby be inclined to think there be other forms, arising from these mingled together. As for example, elective kingdoms; where kings have the sovereign power put into their hands for a time; or kingdoms, wherein the king hath a power limited: which governments, are nevertheless by most writers called monarchy. Likewise if a popular, or aristocratical commonwealth, subdue an enemy's country, and govern the same, by a president, procurator, or other magistrate; this may seem perhaps at first sight, to be a democratical, or aristocratical government. But it is not so. For elective kings, are not sovereigns, but ministers of the sovereign; nor limited kings, sovereigns, but ministers of them that have the sovereign power: nor are those provinces which are in subjection to a democracy, or aristocracy of another commonwealth, democratically or aristocratically governed, but monarchically.

And first, concerning an elective king, whose power is limited to his life, as it is in many places of Christendom at this day; or to certain years or months, as the dictator's power amongst the Romans; if he have right to appoint his successor, he is no more elective but hereditary. But if he have no power to elect his successor, then there is some other man, or assembly known, which after his decease may elect anew, or else the commonwealth dieth, and dissolveth with him, and returneth to the condition of war. If it be known who have the power to give the sovereignty after his death, it is known also that the sovereignty was in them before: for none have right to give that which they have not right to possess, and keep to themselves, if they think good. But if there be none that can give the sovereignty, after the decease of him that was first elected; then has he power, nay he is obliged by the law of nature, to provide, by establishing his successor, to keep those that had trusted him with the government, from relapsing into the miserable condition of civil war. And consequently he was, when elected, a sovereign absolute.

Secondly, that king whose power is limited, is not superior to him, or them that have the power to limit it; and he that is not superior, is not supreme; that is to say not sovereign. The sovereignty therefore was always in that assembly which had the right to limit him; and by consequence the government not monarchy, but either democracy, or aristocracy; as of old time in Sparta; where the kings had a privilege to lead their armies; but the sovereignty was in the Ephori.

Thirdly, whereas heretofore the Roman people governed the land of Judea, for example, by a president; yet was not Judea therefore a democracy; because they were not governed by any assembly, into the which, any of them, had the right to enter; nor an aristocracy; because they were not governed by any assembly, into which, any man could enter by their election: but they were governed by one person, which, though as to the people of Rome, was an assembly of the people, or democracy: yet as to the people of Judea, which had no right at all of participating in the government, was a monarch. For though where the people are governed by an assembly, chosen by themselves out of their own number, the government is called a democracy, or aristocracy; yet when they are governed by an assembly, not of their own choosing, it is a monarchy; not of *one* man, over another man; but of one people, over another people.

Of all these forms of government, the matter being mortal, so that not only monarchs, but also whole assemblies die, it is necessary for the conservation of the peace of men, that as there was order taken for an artificial man, so there be order also taken, for an artificial eternity of life; without which, men that are governed by an assembly, should return into the condition of war in every age; and they that are governed by one man, as soon as their governor dieth. This artificial eternity, is that which men call the right of *succession*.

There is no perfect form of government, where the disposing of the succession is not in the present sovereign. For if it be in any other particular man, or private assembly, it is in a person subject, and may be assumed by the sovereign at his pleasure; and consequently the right is in himself. And if it be in no particular man, but left to a new choice: then is the commonwealth dissolved; and the right is in him that can get it; contrary to the intention of them that did institute the commonwealth, for their perpetual, and not temporary security.

In a democracy, the whole assembly cannot fail, unless the multitude that are to be governed fail. And therefore questions of the right of succession, have in that form of government no place at all.

In an aristocracy, when any of the assembly dieth, the election of another into his room belongeth to the assembly, as the sovereign, to whom belongeth the choosing of all counsellors and officers. For that which the representative doth, as actor, every one of the subjects doth, as author. And though the sovereign assembly may give power to others, to elect new men, for supply of their court; yet it is still by their authority, that the election is made; and by the same it may, when the public shall require it, be recalled.

The greatest difficulty about the right of succession, is in monarchy: and the difficulty ariseth from this, that at first sight, it is not manifest who is to appoint the successor; nor many times, who it is whom he hath appointed. For in both these cases, there is required a more exact ratiocination, than every man is accustomed to use. As to the question, who shall appoint the successor, of a monarch that hath the sovereign authority; that is to say, who shall determine of the right of inheritance, (for elective kings and princes have not the sovereign power in propriety, but in use only), we are to consider, that either he that is in possession, has right to dispose of the succession, or else that right is again in the dissolved multitude. For the death of him that hath the sovereign power in propriety, leaves the multitude without any sovereign at all; that is, without any representative in whom they should be united, and be capable of doing any one action at all: and therefore they are incapable of election of any new monarch; every man having equal right to submit himself to such as he thinks best able to protect him; or if he can, protect himself by his own sword; which is a return to confusion, and to the condition of a war of every man against every man, contrary to the end for which monarchy had its first institution. Therefore it is manifest, that by the institution of monarchy, the disposing of the successor, is always left to the judgment and will of the present possessor.

And for the question, which may arise sometimes, who it is that the monarch in possession, hath designed to the succession and inheritance of his power; it is determined by his express words, and testament; or by other tacit signs sufficient.

By express words, or testament, when it is declared by him in his lifetime, *viva voce*, or by writing; as the first emperors of Rome declared who should be their heirs. For the word heir does not of itself imply the children, or nearest kindred of a man; but whomsoever a man shall any way declare, he would have to succeed him in his estate. If therefore a monarch declare expressly, that such a man shall be his heir, either by word or writing, then is that man immediately after the decease of his predecessor, invested in the right of being monarch.

But where testament, and express words are wanting, other natural signs of the will are to be followed: whereof the one is custom. And therefore where the custom is, that the next of kindred absolutely succeedeth, there also the next of kindred hath right to the succession; for that, if the will of him that was in possession had been otherwise, he might easily have declared the same in his life-time. And likewise where the custom is, that the next of the male kindred succeedeth, there also the right of succession is in the next of the kindred male, for the same reason. And so it is if the custom were to advance the female. For whatsoever custom a man may by a word control, and does not, it is a natural sign he would have that custom stand.

But where neither custom, nor testament hath preceded, there it is to be understood, first, that a monarch's will is, that the government remain monarchical; because he hath approved that government in himself. Secondly, that a child of his own, male, or female, be preferred before any other; because men are presumed to be more inclined by nature, to advance their own children, than the children of other men; and of their own, rather a male than a female; because men, are naturally fitter than women, for actions of labour and danger. Thirdly, where his own issue faileth, rather a brother than a stranger; and so still the nearer in blood, rather than the more remote; because it is always presumed that the nearer of kin, is the nearer in affection; and it is evident that a man receives always, by reflection, the most honour from the greatness of his nearest kindred.

But if it be lawful for a monarch to dispose of the succession by words of contract, or testament, men may perhaps object a great inconvenience: for he may sell, or give his right of governing to a stranger; which, because strangers, that is, men not used to live under the same government, nor speaking the same language, do commonly undervalue one another, may turn to the oppression of his subjects; which is indeed a great inconvenience: but it proceedeth not necessarily from the subjection to a stranger's government, but from the un-skilfulness of the governors, ignorant of the true rules of politics. And therefore the Romans when they had subdued many nations, to make their government digestible, were wont to take away that grievance, as much as they thought necessary, by giving sometimes to whole nations, and sometimes to principal men of every nation they conquered, not only the privileges, but also the name of Romans; and took many of them into the senate, and offices of charge, even in the Roman city. And this was it our most wise king, king James, aimed at, in endeavouring the union of his two realms of England and Scotland. Which if he could have obtained, had in all likelihood prevented the civil wars, which make both those kingdoms, at this present, miserable. It is not therefore any injury to the people, for a monarch to dispose of the succession by will; though by the fault of many princes, it hath been sometimes found inconvenient. Of the lawfulness of it, this also is an argument, that whatsoever inconvenience can arrive by giving a kingdom to a stranger, may arrive also by so marrying with strangers, as the right of succession may descend upon them: yet this by all men is accounted lawful.

CHAPTER XX

Of Dominion Paternal, and Despotical

A COMMONWEALTH *by acquisition*, is that, where the sovereign power is acquired by force; and it is acquired by force, when men singly, or many together by plurality of voices, for fear of death, or bonds, do authorize all the actions of that man, or assembly, that hath their lives and liberty in his power.

And this kind of dominion, or sovereignty, differeth from sovereignty by institution, only in this, that men who choose their sovereign, do it for fear of one another, and not of him whom they institute: but in this case, they subject themselves, to him they are afraid of. In both cases they do it for fear: which is to be noted by them, that hold all such covenants, as proceed from fear of death or violence, void: which if it were true, no man, in any kind of commonwealth, could be obliged to obedience. It is true, that in a commonwealth once instituted, or acquired, promises proceeding from fear of death or violence, are no covenants, nor obliging, when the thing promised is contrary to the laws; but the reason is not, because it was made upon fear, but because he that promiseth, hath no right in the thing promised. Also, when he may lawfully perform, and doth not, it is not the invalidity of the covenant, that absolveth him, but the sentence of the sovereign. Otherwise, whensoever a man lawfully promiseth, he unlawfully breaketh: but when the sovereign, who is the actor, acquitteth him, then he is acquitted by him that extorted the promise, as by the author of such absolution.

But the rights, and consequences of sovereignty, are the same in both. His power cannot, without his consent, be transferred to another: he cannot forfeit it: he cannot be accused by any of his subjects, of injury; he cannot be punished by them: he is judge of what is necessary for peace; and judge of doctrines: he is sole legislator; and supreme judge of controversies; and of the times and occasions of war, and peace: to him it belongeth to choose magistrates, counsellors, commanders, and all other officers, and ministers; and to determine of rewards, and punishments, honour, and order. The reasons whereof, are the same which are alleged in the precedent chapter, for the same rights, and consequences of sovereignty by institution.

Dominion is acquired two ways; by generation, and by conquest. The right of dominion by generation, is that, which the parent hath over his children; and is called PATERNAL. And is not so derived from the generation, as if therefore the parent had dominion over his child because he begat him; but from the child's consent, either express, or by other sufficient arguments declared. For as to the generation, God hath ordained to man a helper; and there be always two that are equally parents: the dominion therefore over the child, should belong equally to both; and he be equally subject to both, which is impossible; for no man can obey two masters. And whereas some have attributed the dominion to the man only, as being of the more excellent sex; they misreckon in it. For there is not always that difference of strength, or prudence between the man and the woman, as that the right can be determined without war. In commonwealths, this controversy is decided by the civil law; and for the most part, but not always, the sentence is in favour of the father; because for the most part commonwealths have been erected by the fathers, not by the mothers of families. But the question lieth now in the state of mere nature; where there are supposed no laws of matrimony; no laws for the education of children; but the law of nature, and the natural inclination of the sexes, one to another, and to their children. In this condition of mere nature, either the parents between themselves dispose of the dominion over the child by contract; or do not dispose thereof at all. If they dispose thereof, the right passeth according to the contract. We find in history that the Amazons contracted with the men of the neighbouring countries, to whom they had recourse for issue, that the issue male should be sent back, but the female remain with themselves: so that the dominion of the females was in the mother.

If there be no contract, the dominion is in the mother. For in the condition of mere nature, where there are no matrimonial laws, it cannot be known who is the father, unless it be declared by the mother: and therefore the right of dominion over the child dependeth on her will, and is consequently hers. Again, seeing the infant is first in the power of the mother, so as she may either nourish, or expose it; if she nourish it, it oweth its life to the mother; and is therefore obliged to obey her, rather than any other; and by consequence the dominion over it is hers. But if she expose it, and another find and nourish it, the dominion is in him that nourisheth it. For it ought to obey him by whom it is preserved; because preservation of life being the end, for which one man becomes subject to another, every man is supposed to promise obedience, to him, in whose power it is to save, or destroy him.

If the mother be the father's subject, the child, is in the father's power: and if the father be the mother's subject, as when a sovereign queen marrieth one of her subjects, the child is subject to the mother; because the father also is her subject.

If a man and woman, monarchs of two several kingdoms, have a child, and contract concerning who shall have the dominion of him, the right of the dominion passeth by the contract. If they contract not, the dominion followeth the dominion of the place of his residence. For the sovereign of each country hath dominion over all that reside therein.

He that hath the dominion over the child, hath dominion also over the children of the child; and over their children's children. For he that hath dominion over the person of a man, hath dominion over all that is his; without which, dominion were but a title, without the effect.

The right of succession to paternal dominion, proceedeth in the same manner, as doth the right of succession of monarchy; of which I have already sufficiently spoken in the precedent chapter.

Dominion acquired by conquest, or victory in war, is that which some writers call DESPOTICAL, from $\Delta\epsilon\alpha\pi\acute{o}\tau\eta s$, which signifieth a *lord*, or *master*; and is the dominion of the master over his servant. And this dominion is then acquired to the victor, when the vanquished to avoid the present stroke of death, covenanteth either in express words, or by other sufficient signs of the will, that so long as his life, and the liberty of his body is allowed him, the victor shall have the use thereof, at his pleasure. And after such covenant made, the vanquished is a SERVANT, and not before: for by the word *servant*, whether it be derived from *servire*, to serve, or from *servare*, to save, which I leave to grammarians to dispute, is not meant a captive, which is kept in prison, or bonds, till the owner of him that took him, or bought him of one that did, shall consider what to do with him: for such men, commonly called slaves, have no obligation at all; but may break their bonds, or the prison; and kill, or carry away captive their master, justly: but one, that being taken, hath corporal liberty allowed him; and upon promise not to run away, nor to do violence to his master, is trusted by him.

It is not therefore the victory, that giveth the right of dominion over the vanquished, but his own covenant. Nor is he obliged because he is conquered; that is to say, beaten, and taken, or put to flight; but because he cometh in, and submitteth to the victor; nor is the victor obliged by an enemy's rendering himself, without promise of life, to spare him for this his yielding to discretion; which obliges not the victor longer, than in his own discretion he shall think fit.

And that which men do, when they demand, as it is now called, *quarter*, which the Greeks called Ζωγρία, *taking alive*, is to evade the present fury of the victor, by submission, and to compound for their life, with ransom, or service: and therefore he that hath quarter, hath not his life given, but deferred till farther deliberation; for it is not a yielding on condition of life, but to discretion. And then only is his life in security, and his service due, when the victor hath trusted him with his corporal liberty. For slaves that work in prisons; or fetters, do it not of duty, but to avoid the cruelty of their task-masters.

The master of the servant, is master also of all he hath: and may exact the use thereof; that is to say, of his goods, of his labour, of his servants, and of his children, as often as he shall think fit. For he holdeth his life of his master, by the covenant of obedience; that is, of owning, and authorizing whatsoever the master shall do. And in case the master, if he refuse, kill him, or cast him into bonds, or otherwise punish him for his disobedience, he is himself the author of the same; and cannot accuse him of injury.

In sum, the rights and consequences of both *paternal* and *despotical* dominion, are the very same with those of a sovereign by institution; and for the same reasons: which reasons are set down in the precedent chapter. So that for a man that is monarch of divers nations, whereof he hath, in one the sovereignty by institution of the people assembled, and in another by conquest, that is by the submission of each particular, to avoid death or bonds; to demand of one nation more than of the other, from the title of conquest, as being a conquered nation, is an act of ignorance of the rights of sovereignty; for the sovereign is absolute over both alike; or else there is no sovereignty at all; and so every man may lawfully protect himself, if he can, with his own sword, which is the condition of war.

By this it appears; that a great family, if it be not part of some commonwealth, is of itself, as to the rights of sovereignty, a little monarchy: whether that family consist of a man and his children; or of a man and his servants; or of a man, and his children, and servants together: wherein the father or master is the sovereign. But yet a family is not properly a commonwealth; unless it be of that power by its own number, or by other opportunities, as not to be subdued without the hazard of war. For where a number of men are manifestly too weak to defend themselves united, every one may use his own reason in time of danger, to save his own life, either by flight, or by submission to the enemy, as he shall think best; in the same manner as a very small company of soldiers, surprised by an army, may cast down their arms, and demand quarter, or run away, rather than be put to the sword. And thus much shall suffice, concerning what I find by speculation, and deduction, of sovereign rights, from the nature, need, and designs of men, in erecting of commonwealths, and putting themselves under monarchs, or assemblies, entrusted with power enough for their protection.

Let us now consider what the Scripture teacheth in the same point. To Moses, the children of Israel say thus: *Speak thou to us, and we will hear thee*: *but let not God speak to us, lest we die*. (*Exod.* xx, 19.) This is absolute obedience to Moses. Concerning the right of kings, God himself by the mouth of Samuel, saith, (1 *Sam.* viii, 11, 12, &c.) *This shall be the right of the king you will have to reign over you. He shall take your sons, and set them to drive his chariots, and to be his horsemen, and to run before his chariots; and gather in his harvest; and to make his engines of war, and instruments of his chariots; and shall take your daughters to make perfumes, to be his cooks, and bakers. He shall take your fields, your vine-yards, and your olive-yards, and give them to his servants. He shall take the tithe of your corn and wine, and give it to the men of his chamber, and to his other servants. He shall take your man-servants, and your maid-servants, and the choice of your youth, and employ them in his business. He shall take the tithe of your flocks; and you shall be his servants.* This is absolute power, and summed up in the last words, *you shall be his servants*. Again, when the people heard what power their king was to have, yet they consented thereto, and say thus, (*verse* 10) *we will be as all other nations, and our king shall judge our causes, and go before us, to conduct our wars.* Here is confirmed the right that sovereigns have, both to the *militia*, and to all *judicature*; in which is contained as absolute power, as one man can possibly transfer to another. Again, the prayer of king Solomon to God, was this (1 *Kings* iii, 9): *Give to thy servant understanding, to judge thy people, and to discern between good and evil.* It belongeth therefore to the sovereign to be *judge*, and to prescribe the rules of *discerning good* and *evil*: which rules are laws; and therefore in him is the legislative power. Saul sought the life of David; yet when it was in his power to slay Saul, and his servants would have done it, David forbad them, saying, (1 *Sam.* xxiv, 6) *God forbid I should do such an act against my Lord, the anointed of God.* For obedience of servants St. Paul saith; (*Col.* iii, 22) *Servants obey your masters in all things*; and, (*Col.* iii. 20) *children obey your parents in all things.* There is simple obedience in those that are subject to paternal, or despotical dominion. Again, (*Matt.* xxiii, 2, 3) *The Scribes and Pharisees sit in Moses' chair, and therefore all that they shall bid you observe, that observe and do.* There again is simple obedience. And St. Paul, (*Titus* iii, 2) *Warn them that they subject themselves to princes, and to those that are in authority, and obey them.* This obedience is also simple. Lastly, our Saviour himself acknowledges, that men ought to pay such taxes as are by kings imposed, where he says, *give to Caesar that which is Caesar's*; and paid such taxes himself. And that the king's word, is sufficient to take anything from any subject, when there is need; and that the king is judge of that need: for he himself, as king of the Jews, commanded his disciples to take the ass, and ass's colt to carry him into Jerusalem, saying, (*Matt.* xxi, 2, 3) *Go into the village over against you, and you shall find a she ass tied, and her colt with her, untie them, and bring them to me. And if any man ask you, what you mean by it, say the Lord hath need of them: and they will let them go.* They will not ask whether his necessity be a sufficient title; nor whether he be judge of that necessity; but acquiesce in the will of the Lord.

To these places may be added also that of (*Genesis* iii, 5) *Ye shall be as gods, knowing good and evil.* And (*verse* 11) *Who told thee that thou wast naked? hast thou eaten of the tree, of which I commanded thee thou shouldest not eat?* For the cognizance or judicature of *good* and *evil*, being forbidden by the name of the fruit of the tree of knowledge, as a trial of Adam's obedience; the devil to inflame the ambition of the woman, to whom that fruit already seemed beautiful, told her that by tasting it, they should be as gods, knowing *good* and *evil.* Whereupon having both eaten, they did indeed take upon them God's office, which is judicature of good and evil; but acquired no new ability to distinguish between them aright. And whereas it is said, that having eaten, they saw they were naked; no man hath so interpreted that place, as if they had been formerly blind, and saw not their own skins: the meaning is plain, that it was then they first judged their nakedness, wherein it was God's will to create them, to be uncomely; and by being ashamed, did tacitly censure God himself. And thereupon God saith; *Hast thou eaten,* &c. as if he should say, doest thou that owest me obedience, take upon thee to judge of my commandments? Whereby it is clearly, though allegorically, signified, that the commands of them that have the right to command, are not by their subjects to be censured, nor disputed.

So that it appeareth plainly, to my understanding, both from reason, and Scripture, that the sovereign power, whether placed in one man, as in monarchy, or in one assembly of men, as in popular, and aristocratical commonwealths, is as great, as possibly men can be imagined to make it. And though of so unlimited a power, men may fancy many evil consequences, yet the consequences of the want of it, which is perpetual war of every man against his neighbour, are much worse. The condition of man in this life shall never be without inconveniences; but there happeneth in no commonwealth any great inconvenience, but what proceeds from the subject's disobedience, and breach of those covenants, from which the commonwealth hath its being. And whosoever thinking sovereign power too great, will seek to make it less, must subject himself, to the power, that can limit it; that is to say, to a greater.

The greatest objection is, that of the practice; when men ask, where, and when, such power has by subjects been acknowledged. But one may ask them again, when, or where has there been a kingdom long free from sedition and civil war. In those nations, whose commonwealths have been long-lived, and not been destroyed but by foreign war, the subjects never did dispute of the sovereign power. But howsoever, an argument from the practice of men, that have not sifted to the bottom, and with exact reason weighed the causes, and nature of commonwealths, and suffer daily those miseries, that proceed from the ignorance thereof, is invalid. For though in all places of the world, men should lay the foundation of their houses on the sand, it could not thence be inferred, that so it ought to be. The skill of making, and maintaining commonwealths, consisteth in certain rules, as doth arithmetic and geometry: not, as tennis-play, on practice only: which rules, neither poor men have the leisure, nor men that have had the leisure, have hitherto had the curiosity, or the method to find out.

CHAPTER XXI

Of the Liberty of Subjects

LIBERTY, or FREEDOM, signifieth, properly, the absence of opposition; by opposition, I mean external impediments of motion; and may be applied no less to irrational, and inanimate creatures, than to rational. For whatsoever is so tied, or environed, as it cannot move but within a certain space, which space is determined by the opposition of some external body, we say it hath not liberty to go further. And so of all living creatures, whilst they are imprisoned, or restrained, with walls, or chains; and of the water whilst it is kept in by banks, or vessels, that otherwise would spread itself into a larger space, we use to say, they are not at liberty, to move in such manner, as without those external impediments they would. But when the impediment of motion, is in the constitution of the thing itself, we use not to say; it wants the liberty; but the power to move; as when a stone lieth still, or a man is fastened to his bed by sickness.

And according to this proper, and generally received meaning of the word, a FREEMAN, *is he, that in those things, which by his strength and wit he is able to do, is not hindered to do what he has a will to.* But when the words *free*, and *liberty*, are applied to any thing but *bodies*, they are abused; for that which is not subject to motion, is not subject to impediment; and therefore, when it is said, for example, the way is free, no liberty of the way is signified, but of those that walk in it without stop. And when we say a gift is free, there is not meant any liberty of the gift, but of the giver, that was not bound by any law or covenant to give it. So when we *speak freely*, it is not the liberty of voice, or pronunciation, but of the man, whom no law hath obliged to speak otherwise than he did. Lastly, from the use of the word *free-will*, no liberty can be inferred of the will, desire, or inclination, but the liberty of the man; which consisteth in this, that he finds no stop, in doing what he has the will, desire, or inclination to do.

Fear and liberty are consistent; as when a man throweth his goods into the sea for *fear* the ship should sink, he doth it nevertheless very willingly, and may refuse to do it if he will: it is therefore the action of one that was *free*: so a man sometimes pays his debt, only for *fear* of imprisonment, which because nobody hindered him from detaining, was the action of a man at *liberty*. And generally all actions which men do in commonwealths, for *fear* of the law, are actions, which the doers had *liberty* to omit.

Liberty, and *necessity* are consistent: as in the water, that hath not only *liberty*, but a *necessity* of descending by the channel: so likewise in the actions which men voluntarily do: which, because they proceed from their will, proceed from *liberty*; and yet, because every act of man's will, and every desire, and inclination proceedeth from some cause, and that from another cause, in a continual chain, whose first link is in the hand of God the first of all causes, proceed from *necessity*. So that to him that could see the connexion of those causes, the *necessity* of all men's voluntary actions, would appear manifest. And therefore God, that seeth, and disposeth all things, seeth also that the *liberty* of man in doing what he will, is accompanied with the *necessity* of doing that which God will, and no more, nor less. For though men may do many things, which God does not command, nor is therefore author of them; yet they can have no passion, nor appetite to anything of which appetite God's will is not the cause. And did not his will assure the *necessity* of man's will, and consequently of all that on man's will dependeth, the *liberty* of men would be a contradiction, and impediment to the omnipotence and *liberty* of God. And this shall suffice, as to the matter in hand, of that natural *liberty*, which only is properly called *liberty*.

But as men, for the attaining of peace, and conservation of themselves thereby, have made an artificial man, which we call a commonwealth; so also have they made artificial chains, called *civil laws*, which they themselves, by mutual covenants, have fastened at one end, to the lips of that man, or assembly, to whom they have given the sovereign power; and at the other end to their own ears. These bonds, in their own nature but weak, may nevertheless be made to hold, by the danger, though not by the difficulty of breaking them.

In relation to these bonds only it is, that I am to speak now, of the *liberty* of *subjects*. For seeing there is no commonwealth in the world, wherein there be rules enough set down, for the regulating of all the actions, and words of men; as being a thing impossible: it followeth necessarily, that in all kinds of actions by the laws prætermitted, men have the liberty, of doing what their own reasons shall suggest, for the most profitable to themselves. For if we take liberty in the proper sense, for corporal liberty; that is to say, freedom from chains and prison; it were very absurd for men to clamour as they do, for the liberty they so manifestly enjoy. Again, if we take liberty, for an exemption from laws, it is no less absurd, for men to demand as they do, that liberty, by which all other men may be masters of their lives. And yet, as absurd as it is, this is it they demand; not knowing that the laws are of no power to protect them, without a sword in the hands of a man, or men, to cause those laws to be put in execution. The liberty of a subject, lieth therefore only in those things, which in regulating their actions, the sovereign hath prætermitted: such as is the liberty to buy, and sell, and otherwise contract with one another; to choose their own abode, their own diet, their own trade of life, and institute their children as they themselves think fit; and the like.

Nevertheless we are not to understand, that by such liberty, the sovereign power of life and death, is either abolished, or limited. For it has been already shown, that nothing the sovereign representative can do to a subject, on what pretence soever, can properly be called injustice, or injury; because every subject is author of every act the sovereign doth; so that he never wanteth right to anything, otherwise, than as he himself is the subject of God, and bound thereby to observe the laws of nature. And therefore it may, and doth often happen in commonwealths, that a subject may be put to death, by the command of the sovereign power; and yet neither do the other wrong: as when Jephtha caused his daughter to be sacrificed: in which, and the like cases, he that so dieth, had liberty to do the action, for which he is nevertheless, without injury put to death. And the same holdeth also in a sovereign prince, that putteth to death an innocent subject. For though the action be against the law of nature, as being contrary to equity, as was the killing of Uriah, by David; yet it was not an injury to Uriah, but to God. Not to Uriah, because the right to do what he pleased was given him by Uriah himself: and yet to God, because David was God's subject, and prohibited all iniquity by the law of nature: which distinction, David himself, when he repented the fact, evidently confirmed, saying, *To thee only have I sinned*. In the same manner, the people of Athens, when they banished the most potent of their commonwealth for ten years, thought they committed no injustice; and yet they never questioned what crime he had done; but what hurt he would do: nay they commanded the banishment of they knew not whom; and every citizen bringing his oystershell into the market place, written with the name of him he desired should be banished, without actually accusing him, sometimes banished an Aristides, for his reputation of justice; and sometimes a scurrilous jester, as Hyperbolus, to make a jest of it. And yet a man cannot say, the sovereign people of Athens wanted right to banish them; or an Athenian the liberty to jest, or to be just.

The liberty, whereof there is so frequent and honourable mention, in the histories, and philosophy of the ancient Greeks, and Romans, and in the writings, and discourse of those that from them have received all their learning in the politics, is not the liberty of particular men; but the liberty of the commonwealth: which is the same with that which every man then should have, if there were no civil laws, nor commonwealth at all. And the effects of it also be the same. For as amongst masterless men, there is perpetual war, of every man against his neighbour; no inheritance, to transmit to the son, nor to expect from the father; no propriety of goods, or lands; no security; but a full and absolute liberty in every particular man: so in states, and commonwealths not dependent on one another, every commonwealth, not every man, has an absolute liberty, to do what it shall judge, that is to say, what that man, or assembly that representeth it, shall judge most conducing to their benefit. But withal, they live in the condition of a perpetual war, and upon the confines of battle, with their frontiers armed, and cannons planted against their neighbours round about. The Athenians, and Romans were free; that is, free commonwealths: not that any particular men had the liberty to resist their own representative; but that their representative had the liberty to resist, or invade other people. There is written on the turrets of the city of Lucca in great characters at this day, the word LIBERTAS; yet no man can thence infer, that a particular man has more liberty, or immunity from the service of the commonwealth there, than in Constantinople. Whether a commonwealth be monarchical, or popular, the freedom is still the same.

But it is an easy thing, for men to be deceived, by the specious name of liberty; and for want of judgment to distinguish, mistake that for their private inheritance, and birthright, which is the right of the public only. And when the same error is confirmed by the authority of men in reputation for their writings on this subject, it is no wonder if it produce sedition, and change of government. In these western parts of the world, we are made to receive our opinions concerning the institution, and rights of commonwealths, from Aristotle, Cicero, and other men, Greeks and Romans, that living under popular states, derived those rights, not from the principles of nature, but transcribed them into their books, out of the practice of their own commonwealths, which were popular; as the grammarians describe the rules of language, out of the practice of the time; or the rules of poetry, out of the poems of Homer and Virgil. And because the Athenians were taught, to keep them from desire of changing their government, that they were freemen, and all that lived under monarchy were slaves; therefore Aristotle puts it down in his *Politics*, (*lib*. 6, *cap*. ii.) *In democracy*, LIBERTY *is to be supposed: for it is commonly held, that no man is* FREE *in any other government*. And as Aristotle; so Cicero, and other writers have grounded their civil doctrine, on the opinions of the Romans, who were taught to hate monarchy, at first, by them that having deposed their sovereign, shared amongst them the sovereignty of

Rome; and afterwards by their successors. And by reading of these Greek, and Latin authors, men from their childhood have gotten a habit, under a false show of liberty, of favouring tumults, and of licentious controlling the actions of their sovereigns, and again of controlling those controllers; with the effusion of so much blood, as I think I may truly say, there was never any thing so dearly bought, as these western parts have bought the learning of the Greek and Latin tongues.

To come now to the particulars of the true liberty of a subject; that is to say, what are the things, which though commanded by the sovereign, he may nevertheless, without injustice, refuse to do; we are to consider, what rights we pass away, when we make a commonwealth; or, which is all one, what liberty we deny ourselves, by owning all the actions, without exception, of the man, or assembly we make our sovereign. For in the act of our *submission*, consisteth both our *obligation*, and our *liberty*: which must therefore be inferred by arguments taken from thence; there being no obligation on any man, which ariseth not from some act of his own; for all men equally, are by nature free. And because such arguments, must either be drawn from the express words, *I authorize all his actions*, or from the intention of him that submitteth himself to his power, which intention is to be understood by the end for which he so submitteth; the obligation, and liberty of the subject, is to be derived, either from those words, or others equivalent; or else from the end of the institution of sovereignty, namely, the peace of the subjects within themselves, and their defence against a common enemy.

First therefore, seeing sovereignty by institution, is by covenant of every one to every one; and sovereignty by acquisition, by covenants of the vanquished to the victor, or child to the parent; it is manifest, that every subject has liberty in all those things, the right whereof cannot by covenant be transferred. I have shewn before in the 14th chapter, that covenants, not to defend a man's own body, are void. Therefore,

If the sovereign command a man, though justly condemned, to kill, wound, or maim himself; or not to resist those that assault him; or to abstain from the use of food, air, medicine, or any other thing, without which he cannot live; yet hath that man the liberty to disobey.

If a man be interrogated by the sovereign, or his authority, concerning a crime done by himself, he is not bound, without assurance of pardon, to confess it; because no man, as I have shown in the same chapter, can be obliged by covenant to accuse himself.

Again, the consent of a subject to sovereign power, is contained in these words, *I authorize, or take upon me, all his actions*; in which there is no restriction at all, of his own former natural liberty: for by allowing him to *kill me*, I am not bound to kill myself when he commands me. It is one thing to say, *kill me, or my fellow, if you please*; another thing to say, *I will kill myself, or my fellow*. It followeth therefore, that

No man is bound by the words themselves, either to kill himself, or any other man; and consequently, that the obligation a man may sometimes have, upon the command of the sovereign to execute any dangerous, or dishonourable office, dependeth not on the words of our submission; but on the intention, which is to be understood by the end thereof. When therefore our refusal to obey, frustrates the end for which the sovereignty was ordained; then there is no liberty to refuse: otherwise there is.

Upon this ground, a man that is commanded as a soldier to fight against the enemy, though his sovereign have right enough to punish his refusal with death, may nevertheless in many cases refuse, without injustice; as when he substituteth a sufficient soldier in his place: for in this case he deserteth not the service of the commonwealth. And there is allowance to be made for natural timorousness; not only to women, of whom no such dangerous duty is expected, but also to men of feminine courage. When armies fight, there is on one side, or both, a running away; yet when they do it not out of treachery, but fear, they are not esteemed to do it unjustly, but dishonourably. For the same reason, to avoid battle, is not injustice, but cowardice. But he that inrolleth himself a soldier, or taketh imprest money, taketh away the excuse of a timorous nature; and is obliged, not only to go to the battle, but also not to run from it, without his captain's leave. And when the defence of the commonwealth, requireth at once the help of all that are able to bear arms, every one is obliged; because otherwise the institution of the commonwealth, which they have not the purpose, or courage to preserve, was in vain.

To resist the sword of the commonwealth, in defence of another man, guilty, or innocent, no man hath liberty; because such liberty, takes away from the sovereign, the means of protecting us: and is therefore destructive of the very essence of government. But in case a great many men together, have already resisted the sovereign power unjustly, or committed some capital crime, for which every one of them expecteth death, whether have they not the liberty then to join together, and assist, and defend one another? Certainly they have: for they but defend their lives, which the guilty man may as well do, as the innocent. There was indeed injustice in the first breach of their duty; their bearing of arms subsequent to it, though it be to maintain what they have done, is no new unjust act. And if it be only to defend their persons, it is not unjust at all. But the offer of pardon taketh from them, to whom it is offered, the plea of self-defence, and maketh their perseverance in assisting, or defending the rest, unlawful.

As for other liberties, they depend on the silence of the law. In cases where the sovereign has prescribed no rule, there the subject hath the liberty to do, or forbear, according to his own discretion. And therefore such liberty is in some places more, and in some less; and in some times more, in other times less, according as they that have the sovereignty shall think most convenient. As for example, there was a time, when in England a man might enter into his own land and dispossess such as wrongfully possessed it, by force. But in aftertimes, that liberty of forcible entry, was taken away by a statute made, by the king, in parliament. And in some places of the world, men have the liberty of many wives: in other places, such liberty is not allowed.

If a subject have a controversy with his sovereign, of debt, or of right of possession of lands or goods, or concerning any service required at his hands, or concerning any penalty, corporal, or pecuniary, grounded on a precedent law; he hath the same liberty to sue for his right, as if it were against a subject; and before such judges, as are appointed by the sovereign. For seeing the sovereign demandeth by force of a former law, and not by virtue of his power; he declareth thereby, that he requireth no more, than shall appear to be due by that law. The suit therefore is not contrary to the will of the sovereign; and consequently the subject hath the liberty to demand the hearing of his cause; and sentence, according to that law. But if he demand, or take anything by pretence of his power; there lieth, in that case, no action of law; for all that is done by him in virtue of his power, is done by the authority of every subject, and consequently he that brings an action against the sovereign, brings it against himself.

If a monarch, or sovereign assembly, grant a liberty to all, or any of his subjects, which grant standing, he is disabled to provide for their safety, the grant is void; unless he directly renounce, or transfer the sovereignty to another. For in that he might openly, if it had been his will, and in plain terms, have renounced, or transferred it, and did not; it is to be understood it was not his will, but that the grant proceeded from ignorance of the repugnancy between such a liberty and the sovereign power; and therefore the sovereignty is still retained; and consequently all those powers, which are necessary to the exercising thereof; such as are the power of war, and peace, of judicature, of appointing officers, and councillors, of levying money, and the rest named in the 18th chapter.

The obligation of subjects to the sovereign, is understood to last as long, and no longer, than the power lasteth, by which he is able to protect them. For the right men have by nature to protect themselves, when none else can protect them, can by no covenant be relinquished. The sovereignty is the soul of the commonwealth; which once departed from the body, the members do no more receive their motion from it. The end of obedience is protection; which, wheresoever a man seeth it, either in his own, or in another's sword, nature applieth his obedience to it, and his endeavour to maintain it. And though sovereignty, in the intention of them that make it, be immortal; yet is it in its own nature, not only subject to violent death, by foreign war; but also through the ignorance, and passions of men, it hath in it, from the very institution, many seeds of a natural mortality, by intestine discord.

If a subject be taken prisoner in war; or his person, or his means of life be within the guards of the enemy, and hath his life and corporal liberty given him, on condition to be subject to the victor, he hath liberty to accept the condition; and having accepted it, is the subject of him that took him; because he had no other way to preserve himself. The case is the same, if he be detained on the same terms, in a foreign country. But if a man be held in prison, or bonds, or is not trusted with the liberty of his body; he cannot be understood to be bound by covenant to subjection; and therefore may, if he can, make his escape by any means whatsoever.

If a monarch shall relinquish the sovereignty, both for himself, and his heirs; his subjects return to the absolute liberty of nature; because, though nature may declare who are his sons, and who are the nearest of his kin; yet it dependeth on his own will, as hath been said in the precedent chapter, who shall be his heir. If therefore he will have no heir, there is no sovereignty, nor subjection. The case is the same, if he die without known kindred, and without declaration of his heir. For then there can no heir be known, and consequently no subjection be due.

If the sovereign banish his subject; during the banishment, he is not subject. But he that is sent on a message, or hath leave to travel, is still subject; but it is, by contract between sovereigns, not by virtue of the covenant of subjection. For whosoever entereth into another's dominion, is subject to all the laws thereof; unless he have a privilege by the amity of the sovereigns, or by special licence.

If a monarch subdued by war, render himself subject to the victor; his subjects are delivered from their former obligation, and become obliged to the victor. But if he be held prisoner, or have not the liberty of his own body; he is not understood to have given away the right of sovereignty:

and therefore his subjects are obliged to yield obedience to the magistrates formerly placed, governing not in their own name, but in his. For, his right remaining, the question is only of the administration; that is to say, of the magistrates and officers; which, if he have not means to name, he is supposed to approve those, which he himself had formerly appointed.

CHAPTER XXII

Of Systems Subject, Political, and Private

HAVING spoken of the generation, form, and power of a commonwealth, I am in order to speak next of the parts thereof. And first of systems, which resemble the similar parts, or muscles of a body natural. By SYSTEMS, I understand any numbers of men joined in one interest, or one business. Of which, some are *regular*, and some *irregular*. *Regular* are those, where one man, or assembly of men, is constituted representative of the whole number. All other are *irregular*.

Of regular, some are *absolute*, and *independent*, subject to none but their own representative: such are only commonwealths; of which I have spoken already in the five last precedent chapters. Others are dependent; that is to say, subordinate to some sovereign power, to which every one, as also their representative is *subject*.

Of systems subordinate, some are *political*, and some *private*. *Political*, otherwise called *bodies politic*, and *persons in law*, are those, which are made by authority from the sovereign power of the commonwealth. *Private*, are those, which are constituted by subjects amongst themselves, or by authority from a stranger. For no authority derived from foreign power, within the dominion of another, is public there, but private.

And of private systems, some are *lawful*; some *unlawful*. *Lawful*, are those which are allowed by the commonwealth: all other are *unlawful*. *Irregular* systems, are those which having no representative, consist only in concourse of people; which if not forbidden by the commonwealth, nor made on evil design, such as are conflux of people to markets, or shows, or any other harmless end, are lawful. But when the intention is evil, or (if the number be considerable), unknown, they are unlawful.

In bodies politic, the power of the representative is always limited: and that which prescribeth the limits thereof, is the power sovereign. For power unlimited, is absolute sovereignty. And the sovereign in every commonwealth, is the absolute representative of all the subjects; and therefore no other can be representative of any part of them, but so far forth, as he shall give leave. And to give leave to a body politic of subjects, to have an absolute representative to all intents and purposes, were to abandon the government of so much of the commonwealth, and to divide the dominion, contrary to their peace and defence; which the sovereign cannot be understood to do, by any grant, that does not plainly, and directly discharge them of their subjection. For consequences of words, are not the signs of his will, when other consequences are signs of the contrary: but rather signs of error, and misreckoning; to which all mankind is too prone.

The bounds of that power, which is given to the representative of a body politic, are to be taken notice of, from two things. One is their writ, or letters from the sovereign: the other is the law of the commonwealth.

For though in the institution or acquisition of a commonwealth, which is independent, there needs no writing, because the power of the representative has there no other bounds, but such as are set out by the unwritten law of nature: yet in subordinate bodies, there are such diversities of limitation necessary, concerning their businesses, times, and places, as can neither be remembered without letters, nor taken notice of, unless such letters be patent, that they may be read to them, and withal sealed, or testified, with the seals, or other permanent signs of the authority sovereign.

And because such limitation is not always easy, or perhaps possible to be described in writing; the ordinary laws, common to all subjects, must determine what the representative may lawfully do, in all cases, where the letters themselves are silent. And therefore,

In a body politic, if the representative be one man, whatsoever he does in the person of the body, which is not warranted in his letters, nor by the laws, is his own act, and not the act of the body, nor of any other member thereof besides himself: because further than his letters, or the laws limit, he representeth no man's person, but his own. But what he does according to these, is the act of every one: for of the act of the sovereign every one is author, because he is their representative unlimited; and the act of him that recedes not from the letters of the sovereign, is the act of the sovereign, and therefore every member of the body is author of it.

But if the representative be an assembly; whatsoever that assembly shall decree, not warranted by their letters, or the laws, is the act of the assembly, or body politic, and the act of every one by whose vote the decree was made; but not the act of any man that being present voted to the contrary; nor of any man absent, unless he voted it by procuration. It is the act of the assembly, because voted by the major part; and if it be a crime, the assembly may be punished, as far forth as it is capable, as by dissolution, or forfeiture of their letters (which is to such artificial, and fictitious bodies, capital) or, if the assembly have a common stock, wherein none of the innocent members have propriety, by pecuniary mulct. For from corporal penalties nature hath exempted all bodies politic. But they that gave not their vote, are therefore innocent, because the assembly cannot represent any man in things unwarranted by their letters, and consequently are not involved in their votes.

If the person of the body politic being in one man, borrow money of a stranger, that is, of one that is not of the same body, (for no letters need limit borrowing, seeing it is left to men's own inclinations to limit lending), the debt is the representative's. For if he should have authority from his letters, to make the members pay what he borroweth, he should have by consequence the sovereignty of them; and therefore the grant were either void, as proceeding from error, commonly incident to human nature, and an insufficient sign of the will of the granter; or if it be avowed by him, then is the representer sovereign, and falleth not under the present question, which is only of bodies subordinate. No member therefore is obliged to pay the debt so borrowed, but the representative himself: because he that lendeth it, being a stranger to the letters, and to the qualification of the body, understandeth those only for his debtors, that are engaged: and seeing the representer can engage himself, and none else, has him only for debtor; who must therefore pay him, out of the common stock, if there be any, or, if there be none, out of his own estate.

If he come into debt by contract, or mulct, the case is the same.

But when the representative is an assembly, and the debt to a stranger; all they, and only they are responsible for the debt, that gave their votes to the borrowing of it, or to the contract that made it due, or to the fact for which the mulct was imposed; because every one of those in voting did engage himself for the payment: for he that is author of the borrowing, is obliged to the payment, even of the whole debt; though when paid by any one, he be discharged.

But if the debt be to one of the assembly, the assembly only is obliged to the payment, out of their common stock, if they have any: for having liberty of vote, if he vote the money shall be borrowed, he votes it shall be paid; if he vote it shall not be borrowed, or be absent, yet because in lending, he voteth the borrowing, he contradicteth his former vote, and is obliged by the latter, and becomes both borrower and lender, and consequently cannot demand payment from any particular man, but from the common treasure only; which failing he hath no remedy, nor complaint, but against himself, that being privy to the acts of the assembly, and to their means to pay, and not being enforced, did nevertheless through his own folly lend his money.

It is manifest by this, that in bodies politic subordinate, and subject to a sovereign power, it is sometimes not only lawful, but expedient, for a particular man to make open protestation against the decrees of the representative assembly, and cause their dissent to be registered, or to take witness of it; because otherwise they may be obliged to pay debts contracted, and be responsible for crimes committed by other men. But in a sovereign assembly, that liberty is taken away, both because he that protesteth there, denies their sovereignty; and also because whatsoever is commanded by the sovereign power, is as to the subject, though not so always in the sight of God, justified by the command: for of such command every subject is the author.

The variety of bodies politic, is almost infinite: for they are not only distinguished by the several affairs, for which they are constituted, wherein there is an unspeakable diversity; but also by the times, places, and numbers, subject to many limitations. And as to their affairs, some are ordained for government; as first, the government of a province may be committed to an assembly of men, wherein all resolutions shall depend on the votes of the major part; and then this assembly is a body politic, and their power limited by commission. This word province signifies a charge, or care of business, which he whose business it is, committeth to another man, to be administered for, and under him; and therefore when in one commonwealth there be divers countries, that have their laws distinct one from another, or are far distant in place, the administration of the government being committed to divers persons, those countries where the sovereign is not resident, but governs by commission, are called provinces. But of the government of a province, by an assembly residing in the province itself, there be few examples. The Romans who had the sovereignty of many provinces; yet governed them always by presidents, and prætors; and not by assemblies, as they governed the city of Rome, and territories adjacent. In like manner, when there were colonies sent from England, to plant Virginia, and Sommer-islands; though the governments of them here, were committed to assemblies in London, yet did those assemblies never commit the government under them to any assembly there, but did to each plantation send one governor. For though every man, where he can be present by nature, desires to participate of government; yet where they cannot be present, they are by nature also inclined, to commit the government of their common interest rather to a monarchical, than a popular form of government: which is also evident in those men that have great private estates; who when they are unwilling to take the pains of administering the business that belongs to them, chuse rather to trust one servant, than an assembly either of their friends or servants. But howsoever it be in fact, yet we may suppose the government of a province, or colony committed to an assembly: and when it is, that which in this place I have to say, is this; that whatsoever debt is by that assembly contracted; or whatsoever unlawful act is decreed, is the act only of those that assented, and not of any that dissented, or were absent, for the reasons before alleged. Also that an assembly residing out of the bounds of that colony whereof they have the government, cannot execute any power over the persons, or goods of any of the colony, to seize on them for debt, or other duty, in any place without the colony itself, as having no jurisdiction, nor authority elsewhere, but are left to the remedy, which the law of the place alloweth them. And though the assembly have right, to impose a mulct upon any of their members, that shall break the laws they make; yet out of the colony itself, they have no right to execute the same. And that which is said here, of the rights of an assembly, for the government of a province, or a colony, is appliable also to an assembly for the government of a town, an university, or a college, or a church, or for any other government over the persons of men.

And generally, in all bodies politic, if any particular member conceive himself injured by the body itself, the cognizance of his cause belongeth to the sovereign, and those the sovereign hath ordained for judges in such causes, or shall ordain for that particular cause; and not to the body itself. For the whole body is in this case his fellow-subject, which in a sovereign assembly, is otherwise: for there, if the sovereign be not judge, though in his own cause, there can be no judge at all.

In a body politic, for the well ordering of foreign traffic, the most commodious representative is an assembly of all the members; that is to say, such a one, as every one that adventureth his money, may be present at all the deliberations, and resolutions of the body, if they will themselves. For proof whereof, we are to consider the end, for which men that are merchants, and may buy and sell, export, and import their merchandize, according to their own discretions, do nevertheless bind themselves up in one corporation. It is true, there be few merchants, that with the merchandize they buy at home, can freight a ship, to export it; or with that they buy abroad, to bring it home; and have therefore need to join together in one society; where every man may either participate of the gain, according to the proportion of his adventure; or take his own, and sell what he transports, or imports, at such prices as he thinks fit. But this is no body politic, there being no common representative to oblige them to any other law, than that which is common to all other subjects. The end of their incorporating, is to make their gain the greater; which is done two ways; by sole buying, and sole selling, both at home, and abroad. So that to grant to a company of merchants to be a corporation, or body politic, is to grant them a double monopoly, whereof one is to be sole buyers; another to be sole sellers. For when there is a company incorporate for any particular foreign country, they only export the commodities vendible in that country; which is sole buying at home, and sole selling abroad. For at home there is but one buyer, and abroad but one that selleth: both which is gainful to the merchant, because thereby they buy at home at lower, and sell abroad at higher rates: and abroad there is but one buyer of foreign merchandize, and but one that sells them at home; both which again are gainful to the adventurers.

Of this double monopoly one part is disadvantageous to the people at home, the other to foreigners. For at home by their sole exportation they set what price they please on the husbandry, and handy-works of the people; and by the sole importation, what price they please on all foreign commodities the people have need of; both which are ill for the people. On the contrary, by the sole selling of the native commodities abroad, and sole buying the foreign commodities upon the place, they raise the price of those, and abate the price of these, to the disadvantage of the foreigner: for where but one selleth, the merchandize is the dearer; and where but one buyeth, the cheaper. Such corporations therefore are no other than monopolies; though they would be very profitable for a commonwealth, if being bound up into one body in foreign markets they were at liberty at home, every man to buy, and sell at what price he could.

The end then of these bodies of merchants, being not a common benefit to the whole body, which have in this case no common stock, but what is deducted out of the particular adventures, for building, buying, victualling and manning of ships, but the particular gain of every adventurer, it is reason that every one be acquainted with the employment of his own; that is, that every one be of the assembly, that shall have the power to order the same; and be acquainted with their accounts. And therefore the representative of such a body must be an assembly, where every member of the body may be present at the consultations, if he will.

If a body politic of merchants, contract a debt to a stranger by the act of their representative assembly, every member is liable by himself for the whole. For a stranger can take no notice of their private laws, but considereth them as so many particular men, obliged every one to the whole payment, till payment made by one dischargeth all the rest: but if the debt be to one of the company, the creditor is debtor for the whole to himself, and cannot therefore demand his debt, but only from the common stock, if there be any.

If the commonwealth impose a tax upon the body, it is understood to be laid upon every member proportionably to his particular adventure in the company. For there is in this case no other common stock, but what is made of their particular adventures.

If a mulct be laid upon the body for some unlawful act, they only are liable by whose votes the act was decreed, or by whose assistance it was executed; for in none of the rest is there any other crime but being of the body; which if a crime, because the body was ordained by the authority of the commonwealth, is not his.

If one of the members be indebted to the body, he may be sued by the body; but his goods cannot be taken, nor his person imprisoned by the authority of the body; but only by authority of the commonwealth: for if they can do it by their own authority, they can by their own authority give judgment that the debt is due; which is as much as to be judge in their own cause.

Those bodies made for the government of men, or of traffic, be either perpetual, or for a time prescribed by writing. But there be bodies also whose times are limited, and that only by the nature of their business. For example, if a sovereign monarch, or a sovereign assembly, shall think fit to give command to the towns, and other several parts of their territory, to send to him their deputies, to inform him of the condition, and necessities of the subjects, or to advise with him for the making of good laws, or for any other cause, as with one person representing the whole country, such deputies, having a place and time of meeting assigned them, are there, and at that time, a body politic, representing every subject of that dominion; but it is only for such matters as shall be propounded unto them by that man, or assembly, that by the sovereign authority sent for them; and when it shall be declared that nothing more shall be propounded, nor debated by them, the body is dissolved. For if they were the absolute representatives of the people, then were it the sovereign assembly; and so there would be two sovereign assemblies, or two sovereigns, over the same people; which cannot consist with their peace. And therefore where there is once a sovereignty, there can be no absolute representation of the people, but by it. And for the limits of how far such a body shall represent the whole people, they are set forth in the writing by which they were sent for. For the people cannot choose their deputies to other intent, than is in the writing directed to them from their sovereign expressed.

Private bodies regular, and lawful, are those that are constituted without letters, or other written authority, saving the laws common to all other subjects. And because they be united in one person representative, they are held for regular; such as are all families, in which the father, or master ordereth the whole family. For he obligeth his children, and servants, as far as the law permitteth, though not further, because none of them are bound to obedience in those actions, which the law hath forbidden to be done. In all other actions, during the time they are under domestic government, they are subject to their fathers, and masters, as to their immediate sovereigns. For the father and master, being before the institution of commonwealth, absolute sovereigns in their own families, they lose afterwards no more of their authority, than the law of the commonwealth taketh from them.

Private bodies regular, but unlawful, are those that unite themselves into one person representative, without any public authority at all; such as are the corporations of beggars, thieves and gipsies, the better to order their trade of begging and stealing; and the corporations of men, that by authority from any foreign person, unite themselves in another's dominion, for the easier propagation of doctrines, and for making a party, against the power of the commonwealth.

Irregular systems, in their nature but leagues, or sometimes mere concourse of people, without union to any particular design, not by obligation of one to another, but proceeding only from a similitude of wills and inclinations, become lawful, or unlawful, according to the lawfulness, or unlawfulness of every particular man's design therein: and his design is to be understood by the occasion.

The leagues of subjects, because leagues are commonly made for mutual defence, are in a commonwealth, which is no more than a league of all the subjects together, for the most part unnecessary, and savour of unlawful design; and are for that cause unlawful, and go commonly by the name of factions, or conspiracies. For a league being a connexion of men by covenants, if there be no power given to any one man or assembly, as in the condition of mere nature, to compel them to performance, is so long only valid, as there ariseth no just cause of distrust: and therefore leagues between commonwealths, over whom there is no human power established, to keep them all in awe, are not only lawful, but also profitable for the time they last. But leagues of the subjects of one and the same commonwealth, where every one may obtain his right by means of the sovereign power, are unnecessary to the maintaining of peace and justice, and, in case the design of them be evil or unknown to the commonwealth, unlawful. For all uniting of strength by private men, is, if for evil intent, unjust; if for intent unknown, dangerous to the public, and unjustly concealed.

If the sovereign power be in a great assembly, and a number of men, part of the assembly, without authority, consult apart, to contrive the guidance of the rest; this is a faction, or conspiracy unlawful, as being a fraudulent seducing of the assembly for their particular interest. But if he, whose private interest is to be debated and judged in the assembly, make as many friends as he can; in him it is no injustice; because in this case he is no part of the assembly. And though he hire such friends with money, unless there be an express law against it, yet it is not injustice. For sometimes, as men's manners are, justice cannot be had without money; and every man may think his own cause just, till it be heard, and judged.

In all commonwealths, if private men entertain more servants, than the government of his estate, and lawful employment he has for them requires, it is faction, and unlawful. For having the protection of the commonwealth, he needeth not the defence of private force. And whereas in nations not thoroughly civilized, several numerous families have lived in continual hostility, and invaded one another with private force; yet it is evident enough, that they have done unjustly; or else they had no commonwealth.

And as factions for kindred, so also factions for government of religion, as of Papists, Protestants, &c. or of state, as patricians, and plebeians of old time in Rome, and of aristocraticals and democraticals of old time in Greece, are unjust, as being contrary to the peace and safety of the people, and a taking of the sword out of the hand of the sovereign.

Concourse of people is an irregular system, the lawfulness, or unlawfulness, whereof dependeth on the occasion, and on the number of them that are assembled. If the occasion be lawful, and manifest; the concourse is lawful; as the usual meeting of men at church, or at a public show, in usual numbers: for if the numbers be extraordinarily great, the occasion is not evident; and consequently he that cannot render a particular and good account of his being amongst them, is to be judged conscious of an unlawful, and tumultuous design. It may be lawful for a thousand men, to join to a petition to be delivered to a judge, or magistrate; yet if a thousand men come to present it, it is a tumultuous assembly; because there needs but one or two for that purpose. But in such cases as these, it is not a set number that makes the assembly unlawful, but such a number, as the present officers are not able to suppress, and bring to justice.

When an unusual number of men, assemble against a man whom they accuse; the assembly is an unlawful tumult; because they may deliver their accusation to the magistrate by a few, or by one man. Such was the case of St. Paul at Ephesus: where Demetrius and a great number of other men, brought two of Paul's companions before the magistrate, saying with one voice, *Great is Diana of the Ephesians*; which was their way of demanding justice against them for teaching the people such doctrine, as was against their religion, and trade. The occasion here, considering the laws of that people, was just; yet was their assembly judged unlawful, and the magistrate reprehended them for it in these words (*Acts* xix, 38–40.) *If Demetrius and the other workmen can accuse any man, of any thing, there be pleas, and deputies, let them accuse one another. And if you have any other thing to demand, your case may be judged in an assembly lawfully called. For we are in danger to be accused for this day's sedition; because there is no cause by which any man can render any reason of this concourse of people.* Where he calleth an assembly, whereof men can give no just account, a sedition, and such as they could not answer for. And this is all I shall say concerning *systems*, and assemblies of people, which may be compared, as I said, to the similar parts of man's body; such as be lawful, to the muscles; such as are unlawful, to wens, biles, and apostems, engendered by the unnatural conflux of evil humours.

CHAPTER XXIII

Of the Public Ministers of Sovereign Power

IN the last chapter I have spoken of the similar parts of a commonwealth: in this I shall speak of the parts organical, which are public ministers.

A PUBLIC MINISTER, is he, that by the sovereign, whether a monarch or an assembly, is employed in any affairs, with authority to represent in that employment, the person of the commonwealth. And whereas every man, or assembly that hath sovereignty, representeth two persons, or, as the more common phrase is, has two capacities, one natural, and another politic: as a monarch, hath the person not only of the commonwealth, but also of a man; and a sovereign assembly hath the person not only of the commonwealth, but also of the assembly: they that be servants to them in their natural capacity, are not public ministers; but those only that serve them in the administration of the public business. And therefore neither ushers, nor sergeants, nor other officers that wait on the assembly, for no other purpose, but for the commodity of the men assembled, in an aristocracy, or democracy; nor stewards, chamberlains, cofferers, or any other officers of the household of a monarch, are public ministers in a monarchy.

Of public ministers, some have charge committed to them of a general administration, either of the whole dominion, or of a part thereof. Of the whole, as to a protector, or regent, may be committed by the predecessor of an infant king, during his minority, the whole administration of his kingdom. In which case, every subject is so far obliged to obedience, as the ordinances he shall make, and the commands he shall give be in the king's name, and not inconsistent with his sovereign power. Of a part, or province; as when either a monarch, or a sovereign assembly, shall give the general charge thereof to a governor, lieutenant, præfect, or viceroy: and in this case also, every one of that province is obliged to all he shall do in the name of the sovereign, and that not incompatible with the sovereign's right. For such protectors, viceroys, and governors, have no other right, but what depends on the sovereign's will; and no commission that can be given them can be interpreted for a declaration of the will to transfer the sovereignty, without express and perspicuous words to that purpose. And this kind of public ministers resembleth the nerves, and tendons that move the several limbs of a body natural.

Others have special administration; that is to say, charges of some special business, either at home, or abroad: as at home, first, for the economy of a commonwealth, they that have authority concerning the *treasure*, as tributes, impositions, rents, fines, or whatsoever public revenue, to collect, receive issue, or take the accounts thereof, are public ministers: ministers, because they serve the person representative, and can do nothing against his command, nor without his authority: public, because they serve him in his political capacity.

Secondly, they that have authority concerning the *militia*; to have the custody of arms, forts, ports; to levy, pay, or conduct soldiers; or to provide for any necessary thing for the use of war, either by land or sea, are public ministers. But a soldier without command, though he fight for the common-wealth, does not therefore represent the person of it; because there is none to represent it to. For every one that hath command, represents it to them only whom he commandeth.

They also that have authority to teach, or to enable others to teach the people their duty to the sovereign power, and instruct them in the knowledge of what is just, and unjust, thereby to render them more apt to live in godliness, and in peace amongst themselves, and resist the public enemy, are public ministers: ministers, in that they do it not by their own authority, but by another's; and public, because they do it, or should do it, by no authority but that of the sovereign. The monarch, or the sovereign assembly only hath immediate authority from God, to teach and instruct the people; and no man but the sovereign, receiveth his power *Dei gratia* simply; that is to say, from the favour of none but God: all other, receive theirs from the favour and providence of God, and their sovereigns; as in a monarchy *Dei gratia et regis*; or *Dei providentia et voluntate regis*.

They also to whom jurisdiction is given, are public ministers. For in their seats of justice they represent the person of the sovereign; and their sentence, is his sentence: for, as hath been before declared, all judicature is essentially annexed to the sovereignty; and therefore all other judges are but ministers of him or them that have the sovereign power. And as controversies are of two sorts, namely of *fact*, and of *law*; so are judgments, some of fact, some of law: and consequently in the same controversy, there may be two judges, one of fact, another of law.

And in both these controversies, there may arise a controversy between the party judged, and the judge; which because they be both subjects to the sovereign, ought in equity to be judged by men agreed on by consent of both; for no man can be judge in his own cause. But the sovereign is already agreed on for judge by them both, and is therefore either to hear the cause, and determine it himself, or appoint for judge such as they shall both agree on. And this agreement is then understood to be made between them divers ways; as first, if the defendant be allowed to except against such of his judges, whose interest maketh him suspect them, (for as to the complainant, he hath already chosen his own judge), those which he excepteth not against, are judges he himself agrees on. Secondly, if he appeal to any other judge, he can appeal no further; for his appeal is his choice. Thirdly, if he appeal to the sovereign himself, and he by himself, or by delegates which the parties shall agree on, give sentence; that sentence is final: for the defendant is judged by his own judges, that is to say, by himself.

These properties of just and rational judicature considered, I cannot forbear to observe the excellent constitution of the courts of justice, established both for Common, and also for Public Pleas in England. By Common Pleas, I mean those, where both the complainant and defendant are subjects: and by public, which are also called Pleas of the Crown, those where the complainant is the sovereign. For whereas there were two orders of men, whereof one was Lords, the other Commons; the Lords had this privilege, to have for judges in all capital crimes, none but Lords; and of them, as many as would be present; which being ever acknowledged as a privilege of favour, their judges were none but such as they had themselves desired. And in all controversies, every subject, (as also in civil controversies the Lords), had for judges, men of the country where the matter in controversy lay; against which he might make his exceptions, till at last twelve men without exception being agreed on, they were judged by those twelve. So that having his own judges there could be nothing alleged by the party, why the sentence should not be final. These public persons, with authority from the sovereign power, either to instruct, or judge the people, are such members of the commonwealth, as may fitly be compared to the organs of voice in a body natural.

Public ministers are also all those, that have authority from the sovereign, to procure the execution of judgments given; to publish the sovereign's commands; to suppress tumults; to apprehend, and imprison malefactors; and other acts tending to the conservation of the peace. For every act they do by such authority, is the act of the commonwealth; and their service, answerable to that of the hands, in a body natural.

Public ministers abroad, are those that represent the person of their own sovereign, to foreign states. Such are ambassadors, messengers, agents, and heralds, sent by public authority, and on public business.

But such as are sent by authority only of some private party of a troubled state, though they be received, are neither public, nor private ministers of the commonwealth; because none of their actions have the commonwealth for author. Likewise, an ambassador sent from a prince, to congratulate, condole, or to assist at a solemnity; though the authority be public; yet because the business is private, and belonging to him in his natural capacity; is a private person. Also if a man be sent into another country, secretly to explore their counsels, and strength; though both the authority, and the business be public; yet because there is none to take notice of any person in him, but his own; he is but a private minister; but yet a minister of the commonwealth; and may be compared to an eye in the body natural. And those that are appointed to receive the petitions or other informations of the people, and are as it were the public ear, are public ministers, and represent their sovereign in that office.

Neither a councillor, nor a council of state, if we consider it with no authority of judicature or command, but only of giving advice to the sovereign when it is required, or of offering it when it is not required, is a public person. For the advice is addressed to the sovereign only, whose person cannot in his own presence, be represented to him, by another. But a body of councillors, are never without some other authority, either of judicature, or of immediate administration: as in a monarchy, they represent the monarch, in delivering his commands to the public ministers: in a democracy, the council, or senate propounds the result of their deliberations to the people, as a council; but when they appoint judges, or hear causes, or give audience to ambassadors, it is in the quality of a minister of the people: and in an aristocracy, the council of state is the sovereign assembly itself; and gives counsel to none but themselves.

CHAPTER XXIV

Of the Nutrition, and Procreation of a Commonwealth

THE NUTRITION of a commonwealth consisteth, in the *plenty*, and *distribution* of *materials* conducing to life: in *concoction*, or *preparation*; and, when concocted, in the *conveyance* of it, by convenient conduits, to the public use.

As for the plenty of matter, it is a thing limited by nature, to those commodities, which from the two breasts of our common mother, land and sea, God usually either freely giveth, or for labour selleth to mankind.

For the matter of this nutriment, consisting in animals,

vegetals, and minerals, God hath freely laid them before us, in or near to the face of the earth; so as there needeth no more but the labour, and industry of receiving them. Insomuch as plenty dependeth, next to God's favour, merely on the labour and industry of men.

This matter, commonly called commodities, is partly *native*, and partly *foreign*: *native*, that which is to be had within the territory of the commonwealth: *foreign*, that which is imported from without. And because there is no territory under the dominion of one commonwealth, except it be of very vast extent, that produceth all things needful for the maintenance, and motion of the whole body; and few that produce not some thing more than necessary; the superfluous commodities to be had within, become no more superfluous, but supply these wants at home, by importation of that which may be had abroad, either by exchange, or by just war, or by labour. For a man's labour also, is a commodity exchangeable for benefit, as well as any other thing: and there have been commonwealths that having no more territory, than hath served them for habitation, have nevertheless, not only maintained, but also encreased their power, partly by the labour of trading from one place to another, and partly by selling the manufactures whereof the materials were brought in from other places.

The distribution of the materials of this nourishment, is the constitution of *mine*, and *thine*, and *his*; that is to say, in one word *propriety*; and belongeth in all kinds of commonwealth to the sovereign power. For where there is no commonwealth, there is, as hath been already shown, a perpetual war of every man against his neighbour; and therefore every thing is his that getteth it, and keepeth it by force; which is neither *propriety*, nor *community*; but *uncertainty*. Which is so evident, that even Cicero, a passionate defender of liberty, in a public pleading, attributeth all propriety to the law civil. *Let the civil law*, saith he, *be once abandoned, or but negligently guarded, not to say oppressed, and there is nothing, that any man can be sure to receive from his ancestor, or leave to his children*. And again; *Take away the civil law, and no man knows what is his own, and what another man's*. Seeing therefore the introduction of *propriety* is an effect of commonwealth, which can do nothing but by the person that represents it, it is the act only of the sovereign; and consisteth in the laws, which none can make that have not the sovereign power. And this they well knew of old, who called that *Νόμος*, that is to say, *distribution*, which we call law; and defined justice, by *distributing* to every man *his own*.

In this distribution, the first law, is for division of the land itself: wherein the sovereign assigneth to every man a portion, according as he, and not according as any subject, or any number of them, shall judge agreeable to equity, and the common good. The children of Israel, were a commonwealth in the wilderness; but wanted the commodities of the earth, till they were masters of the Land of Promise; which afterward was divided amongst them, not by their own discretion, but by the discretion of Eleazar the Priest, and Joshua their General, who, when there were twelve tribes, making them thirteen by subdivision of the tribe of Joseph, made nevertheless but twelve portions of the land; and ordained for the tribe of Levi no land; but assigned them the tenth part of the whole fruits; which division was therefore arbitrary. And though a people coming into possession of a land by war, do not always exterminate the ancient inhabitants, as did the Jews, but leave to many, or most, or all of them their estates; yet it is manifest they hold them afterwards, as of the victor's distribution; as the people of England held all theirs of William the Conqueror.

From whence we may collect, that the propriety which a subject hath in his lands, consisteth in a right to exclude all other subjects from the use of them; and not to exclude their sovereign, be it an assembly, or a monarch. For seeing the sovereign, that is to say, the commonwealth, whose person he representeth, is understood to do nothing but in order to the common peace and security, this distribution of lands, is to be understood as done in order to the same: and consequently, whatsoever distribution he shall make in prejudice thereof, is contrary to the will of every subject, that committed his peace, and safety to his discretion, and conscience; and therefore by the will of every one of them, is to be reputed void. It is true, that a sovereign monarch, or the greater part of a sovereign assembly, may ordain the doing of many things in pursuit of their passions, contrary to their own consciences, which is a breach of trust, and of the law of nature; but this is not enough to authorize any subject, either to make war upon, or so much as to accuse of injustice, or any way to speak evil of their sovereign; because they have authorized all his actions, and in bestowing the sovereign power, made them their own. But in what cases the commands of sovereigns are contrary to equity, and the law of nature, is to be considered hereafter in another place.

In the distribution of land, the commonwealth itself, may be conceived to have a portion, and possess, and improve the same by their representative; and that such portion may be made sufficient, to sustain the whole expense to the common peace, and defence necessarily required. Which were very true, if there could be any representative conceived free from human passions, and infirmities. But the nature of men being as it is, the setting forth of public land, or of any certain revenue for the commonwealth, is in vain; and tendeth to the dissolution of government, and to the condition of mere nature, and war, as soon as ever the sovereign power falleth into the hands of a monarch, or of an assembly, that are either too negligent of money, or too hazardous in engaging the public stock into a long or costly war. Commonwealths can endure no diet: for seeing their expense is not limited by their own appetite, but by external accidents, and the appetites of their neighbours, the public riches cannot be limited by other limits, than those which the emergent occasions shall require. And whereas in England, there were by the Conqueror, divers lands reserved to his own use, besides forests and chases, either for his recreation, or preservation of woods, and divers services reserved on the land he gave his subjects; yet it seems they were not reserved for his maintenance in his public, but in his natural capacity. For he, and his successors did for all that, lay arbitrary taxes on all subjects' land, when they judged it necessary. Or if those public lands, and services, were ordained as a sufficient maintenance of the commonwealth, it was contrary to the scope of the institution; being, as it appeared by those ensuing taxes, insufficient, and, as it appears by the late small revenue of the crown, subject to alienation and diminution. It is therefore in vain, to assign a portion to the commonwealth; which may sell, or give it away; and does sell and give it away, when it is done by their representative.

As the distribution of lands at home; so also to assign in what places, and for what commodities, the subject shall traffic abroad, belongeth to the sovereign. For if it did belong to private persons to use their own discretion therein, some of them would be drawn for gain, both to furnish the enemy with means to hurt the commonwealth, and hurt it themselves, by importing such things, as pleasing men's appetites, be nevertheless noxious, or at least unprofitable to them. And therefore it belongeth to the commonwealth, that is, to the sovereign only, to approve, or disapprove both of the places, and matter of foreign traffic.

Further, seeing it is not enough to the sustentation of a commonwealth, that every man have a propriety in a portion of land, or in some few commodities, or a natural property in some useful art, and there is no art in the world, but is necessary either for the being, or well being almost of every particular man; it is necessary, that men distribute that which they can spare, and transfer their propriety therein, mutually one to another, by exchange, and mutual contract. And therefore it belongeth to the commonwealth, that is to say, to the sovereign, to appoint in what manner all kinds of contract between subjects, as buying, selling, exchanging, borrowing, lending, letting, and taking to hire, are to be made; and by what words and signs they shall be understood for valid. And for the matter, and distribution of the nourishment, to the several members of the commonwealth, thus much, considering the model of the whole work, is sufficient.

By concoction, I understand the reducing of all commodities, which are not presently consumed, but reserved for nourishment in time to come, to something of equal value, and withal so portable, as not to hinder the motion of men from place to place; to the end a man may have in what place soever, such nourishment as the place affordeth. And this is nothing else but gold, and silver, and money. For gold and silver, being, as it happens, almost in all countries of the world highly valued, is a commodious measure of the value of all things else between nations; and money, of what matter soever coined by the sovereign of a commonwealth, is a sufficient measure of the value of all things else, between the subjects of that commonwealth. By the means of which measures, all commodities, moveable and immoveable, are made to accompany a man to all places of his resort, within and without the place of his ordinary residence; and the same passeth from man to man, within the commonwealth; and goes round about, nourishing, as it passeth, every part thereof; in so much as this concoction, is as it were the sanguification of the commonwealth: for natural blood is in like manner made of the fruits of the earth; and circulating, nourisheth by the way every member of the body of man.

And because silver and gold have their value from the matter itself; they have first this privilege, that the value of them cannot be altered by the power of one, nor of a few commonwealths; as being a common measure of the commodities of all places. But base money, may easily be enhanced, or abased. Secondly, they have the privilege to make commonwealths move, and stretch out their arms, when need is, into foreign countries: and supply, not only private subjects that travel, but also whole armies with provision. But that coin, which is not considerable for the matter, but for the stamp of the place, being unable to endure change of air, hath its effect at home only; where also it is subject to the change of laws, and thereby to have the value diminished, to the prejudice many times of those that have it.

The conduits, and ways by which it is conveyed to the public use, are of two sorts: one, that conveyeth it to the public coffers; the other, that issueth the same out again for public payments. Of the first sort, are collectors, receivers, and treasurers; of the second, are the treasurers again, and the officers appointed for payment of several public or private ministers. And in this also, the artificial man maintains his resemblance with the natural; whose veins receiving the blood from the several parts of the body, carry it to the heart; where being made vital, the heart by the arteries sends it out again, to enliven, and enable for motion all the members of the same.

The procreation or children of a commonwealth, are those we call *plantations*, or *colonies*; which are numbers of men sent out from the commonwealth, under a conductor, or governor, to inhabit a foreign country, either formerly void of inhabitants, or made void then by war. And when a colony is settled, they are either a commonwealth of themselves, discharged of their subjection to their sovereign that sent them, as hath been done by many commonwealths, of ancient time, in which case the commonwealth from which they went, was called their metropolis or mother, and requires no more of them, than fathers require of the children, whom they emancipate and make free from their domestic government, which is honour, and friendship; or else they remain united to their metropolis, as were the colonies of the people of Rome; and then they are no commonwealths themselves, but provinces, and parts of the commonwealth that sent them. So that the right of colonies, saving honour and league with their metropolis, dependeth wholly on their licence or letters, by which their sovereign authorized them to plant.

CHAPTER XXV

Of Counsel

How fallacious it is to judge of the nature of things by the ordinary and inconstant use of words, appeareth in nothing more, than in the confusion of counsels, and commands, arising from the imperative manner of speaking in them both, and in many other occasions besides. For the words *do this*, are the words not only of him that commandeth; but also of him that giveth counsel; and of him that exhorteth; and yet there are but few, that see not that these are very different things, or that cannot distinguish between them, when they perceive who it is that speaketh, and to whom the speech is directed, and upon what occasion. But finding those phrases in men's writings, and being not able, or not willing to enter into a consideration of the circumstances, they mistake sometimes the precepts of counsellors, for the precepts of them that command; and sometimes the contrary; according as it best agreeth with the conclusions they would infer, or the actions they approve. To avoid which mistakes, and render to those terms of commanding, counselling and exhorting, their proper and distinct significations, I define them thus.

COMMAND is, where a man saith, *do this*, or *do not this*, without expecting other reason than the will of him that says it. From this it followeth manifestly, that he that commandeth, pretendeth thereby his own benefit: for the reason of his command is his own will only, and the proper object of every man's will, is some good to himself.

COUNSEL, is where a man saith, *do*, or *do not this*, and deduceth his reasons from the benefit that arriveth by it to him to whom he saith it. And from this it is evident, that he that giveth counsel, pretendeth only, whatsoever he intendeth, the good of him, to whom he giveth it.

Therefore between counsel and command, one great difference is, that command is directed to a man's own benefit; and counsel to the benefit of another man. And from this ariseth another difference, that a man may be obliged to do what he is commanded; as when he hath covenanted to obey: but he cannot be obliged to do as he is counselled, because the hurt of not following it, is his own; or if he should covenant to follow it, then is the counsel turned into the nature of a command. A third difference between them is, that no man can pretend a right to be of another man's counsel; because he is not to pretend benefit by it to himself: but to demand right to counsel another, argues a will to know his designs, or to gain some other good to himself: which, as I said before, is of every man's will the proper object.

This also is incident to the nature of counsel; that whatsoever it be, he that asketh it, cannot in equity accuse, or punish it: for to ask counsel of another, is to permit him to give such counsel as he shall think best; and consequently, he that giveth counsel to his sovereign, whether a monarch, or an assembly, when he asketh it, cannot in equity be punished for it, whether the same be conformable to the opinion of the most, or not, so it be to the proposition in debate. For if the sense of the assembly can be taken notice of, before the debate be ended, they should neither ask, nor take any further counsel; for the sense of the assembly, is the resolution of the debate, and end of all deliberation. And generally he that demandeth counsel, is author of it; and therefore cannot punish it; and what the sovereign cannot, no man else can. But if one subject giveth counsel to another, to do anything contrary to the laws, whether that counsel proceed from evil intention, or from ignorance only, it is punishable by the commonwealth; because ignorance of the law is no good excuse, where every man is bound to take notice of the laws to which he is subject.

EXHORTATION and DEHORTATION is counsel, accompanied with signs in him that giveth it, of vehement desire to have it followed: or to say it more briefly, *counsel vehemently pressed*. For he that exhorteth, doth not deduce the consequences of what he adviseth to be done, and tie himself therein to the rigour of true reasoning; but encourages him he counselleth to action: as he that dehorteth, deterreth him from it. And, therefore, they have in their speeches, a regard to the common passions and opinions of men, in deducing their reasons; and make use of similitudes, metaphors, examples, and other tools of oratory, to persuade their hearers of the utility, honour, or justice of following their advice.

From whence may be inferred, first, that exhortation and dehortation is directed to the good of him that giveth the counsel, not of him that asketh it, which is contrary to the duty of a counsellor; who, by the definition of counsel, ought to regard not his own benefit, but his whom he adviseth. And that he directeth his counsel to his own benefit, is manifest enough, by the long and vehement urging, or by the artificial giving thereof; which being not required of him, and consequently proceeding from his own occasions, is directed principally to his own benefit, and but accidentally to the good of him that is counselled, or not at all.

Secondly, that the use of exhortation and dehortation lieth only where a man is to speak to a multitude; because when the speech is addressed to one, he may interrupt him, and examine his reasons more rigorously than can be done in a multitude; which are too many to enter into dispute, and dialogue with him that speaketh indifferently to them all at once.

Thirdly, that they that exhort and dehort, where they are required to give counsel, are corrupt counsellors, and as it were bribed by their own interest. For though the counsel they give be never so good; yet he that gives it, is no more a good counsellor, than he that giveth a just sentence for a reward, is a just judge. But where a man may lawfully command, as a father in his family, or a leader in an army, his exhortations and dehortations, are not only lawful, but also necessary, and laudable. But then they are no more counsels, but commands; which when they are for execution of sour labour, sometimes necessity, and always humanity requireth to be sweetened in the delivery, by encouragement, and in the tune and phrase of counsel, rather than in harsher language of command.

Examples of the difference between command and counsel, we may take from the forms of speech that express them in Holy Scripture. *Have no other Gods but me; make to thyself no graven image; take not God's name in vain; sanctify the sabbath; honour they parents; kill not; steal not, &c.* are commands; because the reason for which we are to obey them, is drawn from the will of God our king, whom we are obliged to obey. But these words, *Sell all thou hast; give it to the poor; and follow me,* are counsel; because the reason for which we are to do so, is drawn from our own benefit: which is this, that we shall have *treasure in Heaven.* These words, *Go into the village over against you, and you shall find an ass tied, and her colt; loose her, and bring her to me,* are a command: for the reason of their fact is drawn from the will of their Master: but these words, *Repent and be baptized in the name of Jesus,* are counsel; because the reason why we should so do, tendeth not to any benefit of God Almighty, who shall still be king in what manner soever we rebel; but of ourselves, who have no other means of avoiding the punishment hanging over us for our sins.

As the difference of counsel from command, hath been now deduced from the nature of counsel, consisting in a deducing of the benefit, or hurt that may arise to him that is to be counselled, by the necessary or probable consequences of the action he propoundeth; so may also the differences between *apt* and *inept* counsellors be derived from the same. For experience, being but memory of the consequences of like actions formerly observed, and counsel but the speech whereby that experience is made known to another; the virtues, and defects of counsel, are the same with the virtues, and defects intellectual: and to the person of a commonwealth, his counsellors serve him in the place of memory, and mental discourse. But with this resemblance of the commonwealth, to a natural man, there is one dissimilitude joined, of great importance; which is, that a natural man receiveth his experience, from the natural objects of sense, which work upon him without passion, or interest of their own; whereas they that give counsel to the representative person of a commonwealth, may have, and have often their particular ends and passions, that render their counsels always suspected, and many times unfaithful. And therefore we may set down for the first condition of a good counsellor, *that his ends, and interests, be not inconsistent with the ends and interests of him he counselleth.*

Secondly, because the office of a counsellor, when an action comes into deliberation, is to make manifest the consequences of it, in such manner, as he that is counselled may be truly and evidently informed; he ought to propound his advice, in such form of speech, as may make the truth most evidently appear; that is to say, with as firm ratiocination, as significant and proper language, and as briefly, as the evidence will permit. And therefore *rash and unevident inferences*, such as are fetched only from examples, or authority of books, and are not arguments of what is good, or evil, but witnesses of fact, or of opinion; *obscure, confused, and ambiguous expressions, also all metaphorical speeches, tending to the stirring up of passion,* (because such reasoning, and such expressions, are useful only to deceive, or to lead him we counsel towards other ends than his own) *are repugnant to the office of a counsellor.*

Thirdly, because the ability of counselling proceedeth from experience, and long study; and no man is presumed to have experience in all those things that to the administration of a great commonwealth are necessary to be known, *no man is presumed to be a good counsellor, but in such business, as he hath not only been much versed in, but hath also much meditated on, and considered.* For seeing the business of a commonwealth is this, to preserve the people in peace at home, and defend them against foreign invasion, we shall find, it requires great knowledge of the disposition of mankind, of the rights of government, and of the nature of equity, law, justice, and honour, not to be attained without study: and of the strength, commodities, places, both of their own country, and their neighbours; as also of the inclinations, and designs of all nations that may any way annoy them. And this is not attained to, without much experience. Of which things, not only the whole sum, but every one of the particulars requires the age, and observation of a man in years, and of more than ordinary study. The wit required for counsel, as I have said before (chapter VIII) is judgment. And the differences of men in that point come from different education, of some to one kind of study or business, and of others to another. When for the doing of any thing, there be infallible rules, as in engines and edifices, the rules of geometry, all the experience of the world cannot equal his counsel, that has learnt, or found out the rule. And when there is no such rule, he that hath most experience in that particular kind of business, has therein the best judgment, and is the best counsellor.

Fourthly, to be able to give counsel to a commonwealth, in a business that hath reference to another commonwealth, *it is necessary to be acquainted with the intelligences, and letters* that come from thence, *and with all the records of treaties, and other transactions of state* between them; which none can do, but such as the representative shall think fit. By which we may see, that they who are not called to counsel, can have no good counsel in such cases to obtrude.

Fifthly, supposing the number of counsellors equal, a man is better counselled by hearing them apart, than in an assembly: and that for many causes. First, in hearing them apart, you have the advice of every man; but in an assembly many of them deliver their advice with *aye* or *no*, or with their hands, or feet, not moved by their own sense, but by the eloquence of another, or for fear of displeasing some that have spoken, or the whole assembly, by contradiction; or for fear of appearing duller in apprehension, than those that have applauded the contrary opinion. Secondly, in an assembly of many, there cannot choose but be some whose interests are contrary to that of the public; and these their interests make passionate, and passion eloquent, and eloquence draws others into the same advice. For the passions of men, which asunder are moderate, as the heat of one brand; in an assembly are like many brands, that inflame one another, especially when they blow one another with orations, to the setting of the commonwealth on fire, under pretence of counselling it. Thirdly, in hearing every man apart, one may examine, when there is need, the truth, or probability of his reasons, and of the grounds of the advice he gives, by frequent interruptions, and objections; which cannot be done in an assembly, where, in every difficult question, a man is rather astonished, and dazzled with the variety of discourse upon it, then informed of the course he ought to take. Besides, there cannot be an assembly of many, called together for advice, wherein there be not some, that have the ambition to be thought eloquent, and also learned in the politics; and give not their advice with care of the business propounded, but of the applause of their motley orations, made of the divers coloured threads or shreds of authors; which is an impertinence at least, that takes away the time of serious consultation, and in the secret way of counselling apart, is easily avoided. Fourthly, in deliberations that ought to be kept secret, whereof there be many occasions in public business, the counsels of many, and especially in assemblies, are dangerous; and therefore great assemblies are necessitated to commit such affairs to lesser numbers, and of such persons as are most versed, and in whose fidelity they have most confidence.

To conclude, who is there that so far approves the taking of counsel from a great assembly of counsellors, that wisheth for, or would accept of their pains, when there is a question of marrying his children, disposing of his lands, governing his household, or managing his private estate, especially if there be amongst them such as wish not his prosperity? A man that doth his business by the help of many and prudent counsellors, with every one consulting apart in his proper element, does it best, as he that useth able seconds at tennis play, placed in their proper stations. He does next best, that useth his own judgment only; as he that has no second at all. But he that is carried up and down to his business in a framed counsel, which cannot move but by the plurality of consenting opinions, the execution whereof is commonly, out of envy or interest, retarded by the part dissenting, does it worst of all, and like one that is carried to the ball, though by good players, yet in a wheel-barrow, or other frame, heavy of itself, and retarded also by the inconcurrent judgments, and endeavours of them that drive it; and so much the more, as they be more that set their hands to it; and most of all, when there is one, or more amongst them, that desire to have him lose. And though it be true, that many eyes see more than one; yet it is not to be understood of many counsellors; but then only, when the final resolution is in one man. Otherwise, because many eyes see the same thing in divers lines, and are apt to look asquint towards their private benefit; they that desire not to miss their mark, though they look about with two eyes, yet they never aim but with one; and therefore no great popular commonwealth was ever kept up, but either by a foreign enemy that united them; or by the reputation of some eminent man amongst them; or by the secret counsel of a few; or by the mutual fear of equal factions; and not by the open consultations of the assembly. And as for very little commonwealths, be they popular, or monarchical, there is no human wisdom can uphold them, longer than the jealousy lasteth of their potent neighbours.

CHAPTER XXVI

Of Civil Laws

BY CIVIL LAWS, I understand the laws, that men are therefore bound to observe, because they are members, not of this, or that commonwealth in particular, but of a commonwealth. For the knowledge of particular laws belongeth to them, that profess the study of the laws of their several countries; but the knowledge of civil law in general, to any man. The ancient law of Rome was called their *civil law*, from the word *civitas*, which signifies a commonwealth: and those countries, which having been under the Roman empire, and governed by that law, retain still such part thereof as they think fit, call that part the civil law, to distinguish it from the rest of their own civil laws. But that is not it I intend to speak of here; my design being not to show what is law here, and there; but what is law; as Plato, Aristotle, Cicero, and divers others have done, without taking upon them the profession of the study of the law.

And first it is manifest, that law in general, is not counsel, but command; nor a command of any man to any man; but only of him, whose command is addressed to one formerly obliged to obey him. And as for civil law, it addeth only the name of the person commanding, which is *persona civitatis*, the person of the commonwealth.

Which considered, I define civil law in this manner. CIVIL LAW, *is to every subject, those rules, which the commonwealth hath commanded him, by word, writing, or other sufficient sign of the will, to make use of, for the distinction of right, and wrong; that is to say, of what is contrary, and what is not contrary to the rule.*

In which definition, there is nothing that is not at first sight evident. For every man seeth, that some laws are addressed to all the subjects in general; some to particular provinces; some to particular vocations; and some to particular men; and are therefore laws, to every of those to whom the command is directed, and to none else. As also, that laws are the rules of just, and unjust; nothing being reputed unjust, that is not contrary to some law. Likewise, that none can make laws but the commonwealth; because our subjection is to the commonwealth only: and that commands, are to be signified by sufficient signs; because a man knows not otherwise how to obey them. And therefore, whatsoever can from this definition by necessary consequence be deduced, ought to be acknowledged for truth. Now I deduce from it this that followeth.

1. The legislator in all commonwealths, is only the sovereign, be he one man, as in a monarchy, or one assembly of men, as in a democracy, or aristocracy. For the legislator is he that maketh the law. And the commonwealth only prescribes, and commandeth the observation of those rules, which we call law: therefore the commonwealth is the legislator. But the commonwealth is no person, nor has capacity to do anything, but by the representative, that is, the sovereign; and therefore the sovereign is the sole legislator. For the same reason, none can abrogate a law made, but the sovereign; because a law is not abrogated, but by another law, that forbiddeth it to be put in execution.

2. The sovereign of a commonwealth, be it an assembly, or one man, is not subject to the civil laws. For having power to make, and repeal laws, he may when he pleaseth, free himself from that subjection, by repealing those laws that trouble him, and making of new; and consequently he was free before. For he is free, that can be free when he will: nor is it possible for any person to be bound to himself; because he that can bind, can release; and therefore he that is bound to himself only, is not bound.

3. When long use obtaineth the authority of a law, it is not the length of time that maketh the authority, but the will of the sovereign signified by his silence, for silence is sometimes an argument of consent; and it is no longer law, than the sovereign shall be silent therein. And therefore if the sovereign shall have a question of right grounded, not upon his present will, but upon the laws formerly made; the length of time shall bring no prejudice to his right; but the question shall be judged by equity. For many unjust actions, and unjust sentences, go uncontrolled a longer time than any man can remember. And our lawyers account no customs law, but such as are reasonable, and that evil customs are to be abolished. But the judgment of what is reasonable, and of what is to be abolished, belongeth to him that maketh the law, which is the sovereign assembly, or monarch.

4. The law of nature, and the civil law, contain each other, and are of equal extent. For the laws of nature, which consist in equity, justice, gratitude, and other moral virtues on these

depending, in the condition of mere nature, as I have said
before in the end of the fifteenth chapter, are not properly
laws, but qualities that dispose men to peace and obedience.
When a commonwealth is once settled, then are they actually
laws, and not before; as being then the commands of the
commonwealth; and therefore also civil laws: for it is the
sovereign power that obliges men to obey them. For in the
differences of private men, to declare, what is equity, what is
justice, and what is moral virtue, and to make them binding,
there is need of the ordinances of sovereign power, and
punishments to be ordained for such as shall break them;
which ordinances are therefore part of the civil law. The
law of nature therefore is a part of the civil law in all commonwealths of the world. Reciprocally also, the civil law is a
part of the dictates of nature. For justice, that is to say,
performance of covenant, and giving to every man his own,
is a dictate of the law of nature. But every subject in a commonwealth, hath covenanted to obey the civil law; either one
with another, as when they assemble to make a common
representative, or with the representative itself one by one,
when subdued by the sword they promise obedience, that they
may receive life; and therefore obedience to the civil law is
part also of the law of nature. Civil, and natural law are not
different kinds, but different parts of law; whereof one part
being written, is called civil, the other unwritten, natural.
But the right of nature, that is, the natural liberty of man, may
by the civil law be abridged, and restrained: nay, the end of
making laws, is no other, but such restraint; without the
which there cannot possibly be any peace. And law was
brought into the world for nothing else, but to limit the
natural liberty of particular men, in such manner, as they
might not hurt, but assist one another, and join together
against a common enemy.

5. If the sovereign of one commonwealth, subdue a people
that have lived under other written laws, and afterwards
govern them by the same laws, by which they were governed
before; yet those laws are the civil laws of the victor, and not
of the vanquished commonwealth. For the legislator is he,
not by whose authority the laws were first made, but by whose

authority they now continue to be laws. And therefore where there be divers provinces, within the dominion of a commonwealth, and in those provinces diversity of laws, which commonly are called the customs of each several province, we are not to understand that such customs have their force, only from length of time; but that they were anciently laws written, or otherwise made known, for the constitutions, and statutes of their sovereigns; and are now laws, not by virtue of the prescription of time, but by the constitutions of their present sovereigns. But if an unwritten law, in all the provinces of a dominion, shall be generally observed, and no iniquity appear in the use thereof; that law can be no other but a law of nature, equally obliging all mankind.

6. Seeing then all laws, written and unwritten, have their authority and force, from the will of the commonwealth; that is to say, from the will of the representative; which in a monarchy is the monarch, and in other commonwealths the sovereign assembly; a man may wonder from whence proceed such opinions, as are found in the books of lawyers of eminence in several commonwealths, directly, or by consequence making the legislative power depend on private men, or subordinate judges. As for example, *that the common law, hath no controller but the parliament*; which is true only where a parliament has the sovereign power, and cannot be assembled, nor dissolved, but by their own discretion. For if there be a right in any else to dissolve them, there is a right also to control them, and consequently to control their controllings. And if there be no such right, then the controller of laws is not *parliamentum*, but *rex in parliamento*. And where a parliament is sovereign, if it should assemble never so many, or so wise men, from the countries subject to them, for whatsoever cause; yet there is no man will believe, that such an assembly hath thereby acquired to themselves a legislative power. *Item*, that the two arms of a commonwealth, are *force and justice; the first whereof is in the king; the other deposited in the hands of the parliament*. As if a commonwealth could consist, where the force were in any hand, which justice had not the authority to command and govern.

7. That law can never be against reason, our lawyers are

agreed; and that not the letter, that is every construction of it, but that which is according to the intention of the legislator, is the law. And it is true: but the doubt is of whose reason it is, that shall be received for law. It is not meant of any private reason; for then there would be as much contradiction in the laws, as there is in the Schools; nor yet, as Sir Edward Coke makes it, an *artificial perfection of reason, gotten by long study, observation, and experience*, as his was. For it is possible long study may increase, and confirm erroneous sentences: and where men build on false grounds, the more they build, the greater is the ruin: and of those that study, and observe with equal time and diligence, the reasons and resolutions are, and must remain discordant: and therefore it is not that *juris prudentia*, or wisdom of subordinate judges; but the reason of this our artificial man the commonwealth, and his command, that maketh law: and the commonwealth being in their representative but one person, there cannot easily arise any contradiction in the laws; and when there doth, the same reason is able, by interpretation, or alteration, to take it away. In all courts of justice, the sovereign, which is the person of the commonwealth, is he that judgeth: the subordinate judge, ought to have regard to the reason, which moved his sovereign to make such law, that his sentence may be according thereunto; which then is his sovereign's sentence; otherwise it is his own, and an unjust one.

8. From this, that the law is a command, and a command consisteth in declaration, or manifestation of the will of him that commandeth, by voice, writing, or some other sufficient argument of the same, we may understand, that the command of the commonwealth is law only to those, that have means to take notice of it. Over natural fools, children, or madmen, there is no law, no more than over brute beasts; nor are they capable of the title of just, or unjust; because they had never power to make any covenant, or to understand the consequences thereof; and consequently never took upon them to authorize the actions of any sovereign, as they must do that make to themselves a commonwealth. And as those from whom nature or accident hath taken away the notice of all laws in general; so also every man, from whom any accident,

not proceeding from this own default, hath taken away the means to take notice of any particular law, is excused, if he observe it not: and to speak properly, that law is no law to him. It is therefore necessary, to consider in this place, what arguments, and signs be sufficient for the knowledge of what is the law; that is to say, what is the will of the sovereign, as well in monarchies, as in other forms of government.

And first, if it be a law that obliges all the subjects without exception, and is not written, nor otherwise published in such places as they may take notice thereof, it is a law of nature. For whatsoever men are to take knowledge of for law, not upon other men's words, but every one from his own reason, must be such as is agreeable to the reason of all men; which no law can be, but the law of nature. The laws of nature therefore need not any publishing, nor proclamation; as being contained in this one sentence, approved by all the world, *Do not that to another, which thou thinkest unreasonable to be done by another to thyself*.

Secondly, if it be a law that obliges only some condition of men, or one particular man, and be not written, nor published by word, then also it is a law of nature; and known by the same arguments, and signs, that distinguish those in such a condition, from other subjects. For whatsoever law is not written, or some way published by him that makes it law, can be known no way, but by the reason of him that is to obey it; and is therefore also a law not only civil, but natural. For example, if the sovereign employ a public minister, without written instructions what to do; he is obliged to take for instructions the dictates of reason; as if he make a judge, the judge is to take notice, that his sentence ought to be according to the reason of his sovereign, which being always understood to be equity, he is bound to it by the law of nature: or if an ambassador, he is, in all things not contained in his written instructions, to take for instruction that which reason dictates to be most conducing to his sovereign's interest; and so of all other ministers of the sovereignty, public and private. All which instructions of natural reason may be comprehended under one name of *fidelity*; which is a branch of natural justice.

The law of nature excepted, it belongeth to the essence of all other laws, to be made known, to every man that shall be obliged to obey them, either by word, or writing, or some other act, known to proceed from the sovereign authority. For the will of another cannot be understood, but by his own word, or act, or by conjecture taken from his scope and purpose; which in the person of the commonwealth, is to be supposed always consonant to equity and reason. And in ancient time, before letters were in common use, the laws were many times put into verse; that the rude people taking pleasure in singing, or reciting them, might the more easily retain them in memory. And for the same reason Solomon (*Prov.* vii, 3) adviseth a man, to bind the ten commandments upon his ten fingers. And for the law which Moses gave to the people of Israel at the renewing of the covenant (*Deut.* xi, 19), he biddeth them to teach it their children, by discoursing of it both at home, and upon the way; at going to bed, and at rising from bed; and to write it upon the posts, and doors of their houses, and (*Deut.* xxxi, 12) to assemble the people, man, woman, and child, to hear it read.

Nor is it enough the law be written, and published; but also that there be manifest signs, that it proceedeth from the will of the sovereign. For private men, when they have, or think they have force enough to secure their unjust designs, and convoy them safely to their ambitious ends, may publish for laws what they please, without, or against the legislative authority. There is therefore requisite, not only a declaration of the law, but also sufficient signs of the author and authority. The author, or legislator is supposed in every commonwealth to be evident, because he is the sovereign, who having been constituted by the consent of every one, is supposed by every one to be sufficiently known. And though the ignorance and security of men be such, for the most part, as that when the memory of the first constitution of their commonwealth is worn out, they do not consider, by whose power they used to be defended against their enemies, and to have their industry protected, and to be righted when injury is done them; yet because no man that considers, can make question of it, no excuse can be derived from the ignorance of where the sovereignty is placed. And it is a dictate of natural reason, and consequently an evident law of nature, that no man ought to weaken that power, the protection whereof he hath himself demanded, or wittingly received against others. Therefore of who is sovereign, no man, but by his own fault, (whatsoever evil men suggest,) can make any doubt. The difficulty consisteth in the evidence of the authority derived from him; the removing whereof, dependeth on the knowledge of the public registers, public counsels, public ministers, and public seals; by which all laws are sufficiently verified; verified, I say, not authorized: for the verification, is but the testimony and record, not the authority of the law; which consisteth in the command of the sovereign only.

If therefore a man have a question of injury, depending on the law of nature; that is to say, on common equity; the sentence of the judge, that by commission hath authority to take cognizance of such causes, is a sufficient verification of the law of nature in that individual case. For though the advice of one that professeth the study of the law, be useful for the avoiding of contention; yet it is but advice: it is the judge must tell men what is law, upon the hearing of the controversy.

But when the question is of injury, or crime, upon a written law; every man by recourse to the registers, by himself or others, may, if he will, be sufficiently informed, before he do such injury, or commit the crime, whether it be an injury, or not: nay he ought to do so: for when a man doubts whether the act he goeth about, be just, or unjust; and may inform himself, if he will; the doing is unlawful. In like manner, he that supposeth himself injured, in a case determined by the written law, which he may, by himself or others, see and consider; if he complain before he consults with the law, he does unjustly, and bewrayeth a disposition rather to vex other men, than to demand his own right.

If the question be of obedience to a public officer; to have seen his commission, with the public seal, and heard it read; or to have had the means to be informed of it, if a man would, is a sufficient verification of his authority. For every man is obliged to do his best endeavour, to inform himself of all written laws, that may concern his own future actions.

The legislator known; and the laws, either by writing, or by the light of nature, sufficiently published; there wanteth yet another very material circumstance to make them obligatory. For it is not the letter, but the intendment, or meaning, that is to say, the authentic interpretation of the law (which is the sense of the legislator), in which the nature of the law consisteth; and therefore the interpretation of all laws dependeth on the authority sovereign; and the interpreters can be none but those, which the sovereign, to whom only the subject oweth obedience, shall appoint. For else, by the craft of an interpreter, the law may be made to bear a sense, contrary to that of the sovereign: by which means the interpreter becomes the legislator.

All laws, written, and unwritten, have need of interpretation. The unwritten law of nature, though it be easy to such, as without partiality and passion, make use of their natural reason, and therefore leaves the violators whereof without excuse; yet considering there be very few, perhaps none, that in some cases are not blinded by self-love, or some other passion; it is now become of all laws the most obscure, and has consequently the greatest need of able interpreters. The written laws, if they be short, are easily misinterpreted, from the divers significations of a word, or two: if long, they be more obscure by the divers significations of many words: insomuch as no written law, delivered in few, or many words, can be well understood, without a perfect understanding of the final causes, for which the law was made; the knowledge of which final causes is in the legislator. To him therefore there cannot be any knot in the law, insoluble; either by finding out the ends, to undo it by; or else by making what ends he will, as Alexander did with his sword in the Gordian knot, by the legislative power; which no other interpreter can do.

The interpretation of the laws of nature, in a commonwealth, dependeth not on the books of moral philosophy. The authority of writers, without the authority of the commonwealth, maketh not their opinions law, be they never so true. That which I have written in this treatise, concerning the moral virtues, and of their necessity for the procuring, and maintaining peace, though it be evident truth, is not therefore presently law; but because in all commonwealths in the world, it is part of the civil law. For though it be naturally reasonable; yet it is by the sovereign power that it is law: otherwise, it were a great error, to call the laws of nature unwritten law; whereof we see so many volumes published, and in them so many contradictions of one another, and of themselves.

The interpretation of the law of nature, is the sentence of the judge constituted by the sovereign authority, to hear and determine such controversies, as depend thereon; and consisteth in the application of the law to the present case. For in the act of judicature, the judge doth no more but consider, whether the demand of the party, be consonant to natural reason, and equity; and the sentence he giveth, is therefore the interpretation of the law of nature; which interpretation is authentic; not because it is his private sentence; but because he giveth it by authority of the sovereign, whereby it becomes the sovereign's sentence; which is law for that time, to the parties pleading.

But because there is no judge subordinate, nor sovereign, but may err in a judgment of equity; if afterward in another like case he find it more consonant to equity to give a contrary sentence, he is obliged to do it. No man's error becomes his own law; nor obliges him to persist in it. Neither, for the same reason, becomes it a law to other judges, though sworn to follow it. For though a wrong sentence given by authority of the sovereign, if he know and allow it, in such laws as are mutable, be a constitution of a new law, in cases in which every little circumstance is the same; yet in laws immutable, such as are the laws of nature, they are no laws to the same or other judges, in the like cases for ever after. Princes succeed one another; and one judge passeth, another cometh; nay, heaven and earth shall pass; but not one tittle of the law of nature shall pass; for it is the eternal law of God. Therefore all the sentences of precedent judges that have ever been, cannot altogether make a law contrary to natural equity: nor any examples of former judges, can warrant an unreasonable sentence, or discharge the present judge of the trouble of studying what is equity, in the case he is to judge, from the principles of his own natural reason. For example sake, it is against the law of nature, *to punish the innocent*; and innocent is he that acquitteth himself judicially and is acknowledged for innocent by the judge. Put the case now, that a man is accused of a capital crime, and seeing the power and malice of some enemy, and the frequent corruption and partiality of judges, runneth away for fear of the event, and afterwards is taken, and brought to a legal trial, and maketh it sufficiently appear, he was not guilty of the crime, and being thereof acquitted, is nevertheless condemned to lose his goods; this is a manifest condemnation of the innocent. I say therefore, that there is no place in the world, where this can be an interpretation of a law of nature, or be made a law by the sentences of precedent judges, that had done the same. For he that judged it first, judged unjustly; and no injustice can be a pattern of judgment to succeeding judges. A written law may forbid innocent men to fly, and they may be punished for flying: but that flying for fear of injury, should be taken for presumption of guilt, after a man is already absolved of the crime judicially, is contrary to the nature of a presumption, which hath no place after judgment given. Yet this is set down by a great lawyer for the common law of England. *If a man*, saith he, *that is innocent, be accused of felony, and for fear flyeth for the same; albeit he judicially acquitteth himself of the felony; yet if it be found that he fled for the felony, he shall notwithstanding his innocency, forfeit all his goods, chattels, debts, and duties. For as to the forfeiture of them, the law will admit no proof against the presumption in law, grounded upon his flight.* Here you see, *an innocent man judicially acquitted, notwithstanding his innocency*, when no written law forbad him to fly, after his acquittal, *upon a presumption in law*, condemned to lose all the goods he hath. If the law ground upon his flight a presumption of the fact, which was capital, the sentence ought to have been capital: if the presumption were not of the fact, for what then ought he to lose his goods? This therefore is no law of England; nor is the condemnation grounded upon a presumption of law, but upon the presumption of the judges. It is also against law, to say that no proof shall be admitted against a presumption of law. For all judges, sovereign and subordinate, if they refuse to hear proof, refuse to do justice: for though the sentence be just, yet the judges that condemn without hearing the proofs offered, are unjust judges; and their presumption is but prejudice; which no man ought to bring with him to the seat of justice, whatsoever precedent judgments, or examples he shall pretend to follow. There be other things of this nature, wherein men's judgments have been perverted, by trusting to precedents: but this is enough to show, that though the sentence of the judge, be a law to the party pleading, yet it is no law to any judge, that shall succeed him in that office.

In like manner, when question is of the meaning of written laws, he is not the interpreter of them, that writeth a commentary upon them. For commentaries are commonly more subject to cavil, than the text; and therefore need other commentaries; and so there will be no end of such interpretation. And therefore unless there be an interpreter authorized by the sovereign, from which the subordinate judges are not to recede, the interpreter can be no other than the ordinary judges, in the same manner, as they are in cases of the unwritten law; and their sentences are to be taken by them that plead, for laws in that particular case; but not to bind other judges, in like cases to give like judgments. For a judge may err in the interpretation even of written laws; but no error of a subordinate judge, can change the law, which is the general sentence of the sovereign.

In written laws, men use to make a difference between the letter, and the sentence of the law: and when by the letter, is meant whatsoever can be gathered from the bare words, it is well distinguished. For the significations of almost all words, are either in themselves, or in the metaphorical use of them, ambiguous; and may be drawn in argument, to make many senses; but there is only one sense of the law. But if by the letter, be meant the literal sense, then the letter, and the sentence or intention of the law, is all one. For the literal sense is that, which the legislator intended, should by the letter of the law be signified. Now the intention of the legislator is always supposed to be equity: for it were a great contumely for a judge to think otherwise of the sovereign. He ought therefore, if the word of the law do not fully authorize a reasonable sentence, to supply it with the law of nature; or if the case be difficult, to respite judgment till he have received more ample authority. For example, a written law ordaineth, that he which is thrust out of his house by force, shall be restored by force: it happens that a man by negligence leaves his house empty, and returning is kept out by force, in which case there is no special law ordained. It is evident that this case is contained in the same law: for else there is no remedy for him at all; which is to be supposed against the intention of the legislator. Again, the word of the law commandeth to judge according to the evidence: a man is accused falsely of a fact, which the judge himself saw done by another, and not by him that is accused. In this case neither shall the letter of the law be followed to the condemnation of the innocent, nor shall the judge give sentence against the evidence of the witnesses; because the letter of the law is to the contrary: but procure of the sovereign that another be made judge, and himself witness. So that the incommodity that follows the bare words of a written law, may lead him to the intention of the law, whereby to interpret the same the better; though no incommodity can warrant a sentence against the law. For every judge of right, and wrong, is not judge of what is commodious, or incommodious to the commonwealth.

The abilities required in a good interpreter of the law, that is to say, in a good judge, are not the same with those of an advocate; namely the study of the laws. For a judge, as he ought to take notice of the fact, from none but the witnesses; so also he ought to take notice of the law from nothing but the statutes, and constitutions of the sovereign, alleged in the pleading, or declared to him by some that have authority from the sovereign power to declare them; and need not take care beforehand, what he shall judge; for it shall be given him what he shall say concerning the fact, by witnesses; and what he shall say in point of law, from those that shall in their pleadings show it, and by authority interpret it upon the place. The Lords of Parliament in England were judges, and most difficult causes have been heard and determined by them; yet few of them were much versed in the study of the laws, and fewer had made profession of them: and though they consulted with lawyers, that were appointed to be present there for that purpose; yet they alone had the authority of giving sentence. In like manner, in the ordinary trials of right, twelve men of the common people, are the judges, and give sentence, not only of the fact, but of the right; and pronounce simply for the complainant, or for the defendant; that is to say, are judges, not only of the fact, but also of the right: and in a question of crime, not only determine whether done, or not done; but also whether it be *murder, homicide, felony, assault*, and the like, which are determinations of law: but because they are not supposed to know the law of themselves, there is one that hath authority to inform them of it, in the particular case they are to judge of. But yet if they judge not according to that he tells them, they are not subject thereby to any penalty; unless it be made appear, that they did it against their consciences, or had been corrupted by reward.

The things that make a good judge, or good interpreter of the laws, are, first, *a right understanding* of that principal law of nature called *equity*; which depending not on the reading of other men's writings, but on the goodness of a man's own natural reason, and meditation, is presumed to be in those most, that have had most leisure, and had the most inclination to meditate thereon. Secondly, *contempt of unnecessary riches, and preferments*. Thirdly, *to be able in judgment to divest himself of all fear, anger, hatred, love, and compassion*. Fourthly, and lastly, *patience to hear; diligent attention in hearing; and memory to retain digest and apply what he hath heard*.

The difference and division of the laws, has been made in divers manners, according to the different methods, of those men that have written of them. For it is a thing that dependeth not on nature, but on the scope of the writer; and is subservient to every man's proper method. In the Institutions of Justinian, we find seven sorts of civil laws:

1. The *edicts, constitutions*, and *epistles of the prince*, that is, of the emperor; because the whole power of the people was in him. Like these, are the proclamations of the kings of England.

2. *The decrees of the whole people of Rome*, comprehending the

senate, when they were put to the question by the *senate*. These were laws, at first, by the virtue of the sovereign power residing in the people; and such of them as by the emperors were not abrogated, remained laws, by the authority imperial. For all laws that bind, are understood to be laws by his authority that has power to repeal them. Somewhat like to these laws, are the acts of parliament in England.

3. *The decrees of the common people*, excluding the senate, when they were put to the question by the *tribune* of the people. For such of them as were not abrogated by the emperors, remained laws by the authority imperial. Like to these, were the orders of the House of Commons in England.

4. *Senatus consulta*, the *orders of the senate*; because when the people of Rome grew so numerous, as it was inconvenient to assemble them; it was thought fit by the emperor, that men should consult the senate, instead of the people; and these have some resemblance with the acts of council.

5. *The edicts of prætors*, and in some cases of *ædiles*: such as are the chief justices in the courts of England.

6. *Responsa prudentum*; which were the sentences, and opinion of those lawyers, to whom the emperor gave authority to interpret the law, and to give answer to such as in matter of law demanded their advice; which answers, the judges in giving judgment were obliged by the constitutions of the emperor to observe: and should be like the reports of cases judged, if other judges be by the law of England bound to observe them. For the judges of the common law of England, are not properly judges, but *juris consulti*; of whom the judges, who are either the lords, or twelve men of the country, are in point of law to ask advice.

7. Also *unwritten customs*, which in their own nature are an imitation of law, by the tacit consent of the emperor, in case they be not contrary to the law of nature, are very laws.

Another division of laws, is into *natural* and *positive*. *Natural* are those which have been laws from all eternity; and are called not only *natural*, but also *moral* laws; consisting in the moral virtues, as justice, equity, and all habits of the mind that conduce to peace, and charity; of which I have already spoken in the fourteenth and fifteenth chapters.

Positive, are those which have not been from eternity; but have been made laws by the will of those that have had the sovereign power over others; and are either written, or made known to men, by some other argument of the will of their legislator.

Again, of positive laws some are *human*, some *divine*; and of human positive laws, some are *distributive*, some *penal*. *Distributive* are those that determine the rights of the subjects, declaring to every man what it is, by which he acquireth and holdeth a propriety in lands, or goods, and a right or liberty of action: and these speak to all the subjects. *Penal* are those, which declare, what penalty shall be inflicted on those that violate the law; and speak to the ministers and officers ordained for execution. For though every one ought to be informed of the punishments ordained beforehand for their transgression; nevertheless the command is not addressed to the delinquent, who cannot be supposed will faithfully punish himself, but to public ministers appointed to see the penalty executed. And these penal laws are for the most part written together with the laws distributive; and are sometimes called judgments. For all laws are general judgments, or sentences of the legislator; as also every particular judgment, is a law to him, whose case is judged.

Divine positive laws (for natural laws being eternal, and universal, are all divine), are those, which being the commandments of God, not from all eternity, nor universally addressed to all men, but only to a certain people, or to certain persons, are declared for such, by those whom God hath authorized to declare them. But this authority of man to declare what be these positive laws of God, how can it be known? God may command a man by a supernatural way, to deliver laws to other men. But because it is of the essence of law, that he who is to be obliged, be assured of the authority of him that declareth it, which we cannot naturally take notice to be from God, *how can a man without supernatural revelation be assured of the revelation received by the declarer?* and *how can he be bound to obey them?* For the first question, how a man can be assured of the revelation of another, without a revelation particularly to himself, it is evidently impossible. For though a man may be induced to believe such revelation, from the miracles they see him do, or from seeing the extraordinary sanctity of his life, or from seeing the extraordinary wisdom, or extraordinary felicity of his actions, all which are marks of God's extraordinary favour; yet they are not assured evidences of special revelation. Miracles are marvellous works: but that which is marvellous to one, may not be so to another. Sanctity may be feigned; and the visible felicities of this world, are most often the work of God by natural, and ordinary causes. And therefore no man can infallibly know by natural reason, that another has had a supernatural revelation of God's will; but only a belief; every one, as the signs thereof shall appear greater or lesser, a firmer or a weaker belief.

But for the second, how can he be bound to obey them; it is not so hard. For if the law declared, be not against the law of nature, which is undoubtedly God's law, and he undertake to obey it, he is bound by his own act; bound I say to obey it, but not bound to believe it: for men's belief, and interior cogitations, are not subject to the commands, but only to the operation of God, ordinary, or extraordinary. Faith of supernatural law, is not a fulfilling, but only an assenting to the same; and not a duty that we exhibit to God, but a gift which God freely giveth to whom he pleaseth; as also unbelief is not a breach of any of his laws; but a rejection of them all, except the laws natural. But this that I say, will be made yet clearer, by the examples and testimonies concerning this point in holy Scripture. The covenant God made with Abraham, in a supernatural manner, was thus, (*Gen.* xvii, 10) *This is the covenant which thou shalt observe between me and thee and thy seed after thee.* Abraham's seed had not this revelation, nor were yet in being; yet they are a party to the covenant, and bound to obey what Abraham should declare to them for God's law; which they could not be, but in virtue of the obedience they owed to their parents; who, if they be subject to no other earthly power, as here in the case of Abraham, have sovereign power over their children and servants. Again, where God saith to Abraham, *In thee shall all nations of the earth be blessed; for I know thou wilt command thy children, and thy house after thee to keep the way of the Lord, and to observe righteousness and judgment,*

it is manifest, the obedience of his family, who had no revelation, depended on their former obligation to obey their
sovereign. At Mount Sinai Moses only went up to God; the
people were forbidden to approach on pain of death; yet they
were bound to obey all that Moses declared to them for God's
law. Upon what ground, but on this submission of their own,
*Speak thou to us, and we will hear thee; but let not God speak to us,
lest we die?* By which two places it sufficiently appeareth, that
in a commonwealth, a subject that has no certain and assured
revelation particularly to himself concerning the will of God,
is to obey for such the command of the commonwealth: for
if men were at liberty, to take for God's commandments, their
own dreams and fancies, or the dreams and fancies of private
men; scarce two men would agree upon what is God's
commandment; and yet in respect of them, every man would
despise the commandments of the commonwealth. I conclude
therefore, that in all things not contrary to the moral law, that
is to say, to the law of nature, all subjects are bound to obey
that for divine law, which is declared to be so, by the laws of
the commonwealth. Which also is evident to any man's
reason; for whatsoever is not against the law of nature, may
be made law in the name of them that have the sovereign
power; and there is no reason men should be the less obliged
by it, when it is propounded in the name of God. Besides,
there is no place in the world where men are permitted to
pretend other commandments of God, than are declared for
such by the commonwealth. Christian states punish those
that revolt from the Christian religion, and all other states,
those that set up any religion by them forbidden. For in
whatsoever is not regulated by the commonwealth, it is
equity, which is the law of nature, and therefore an eternal
law of God, that every man equally enjoy his liberty.

There is also another distinction of laws, into *fundamental*
and *not fundamental*; but I could never see in any author, what
a fundamental law signifieth. Nevertheless one may very
reasonably distinguish laws in that manner.

For a fundamental law in every commonwealth is that,
which being taken away, the commonwealth faileth, and is
utterly dissolved; as a building whose foundation is destroyed.

And therefore a fundamental law is that, by which subjects are bound to uphold whatsoever power is given to the sovereign, whether a monarch, or a sovereign assembly, without which the commonwealth cannot stand; such as is the power of war and peace, of judicature, of election of officers, and of doing whatsoever he shall think necessary for the public good. Not fundamental is that, the abrogating whereof, draweth not with it the dissolution of the commonwealth; such as are the laws concerning controversies between subject and subject. Thus much of the division of laws.

I find the words *lex civilis*, and *jus civile*, that is to say *law* and *right civil*, promiscuously used for the same thing, even in the most learned authors; which nevertheless ought not to be so. For *right* is *liberty*, namely that liberty which the civil law leaves us: but *civil law* is an *obligation*, and takes from us the liberty which the law of nature gave us. Nature gave a right to every man to secure himself by his own strength, and to invade a suspected neighbour, by way of prevention: but the civil law takes away that liberty, in all cases where the protection of the law may be safely stayed for. Insomuch as *lex* and *jus*, are as different as *obligation* and *liberty*.

Likewise *laws* and *charters* are taken promiscuously for the same thing. Yet charters are donations of the sovereign; and not laws, but exemptions from law. The phrase of a law is, *jubeo, injungo, I command* and *enjoin*: the phrase of a charter is, *dedi, concessi, I have given, I have granted*: but what is given or granted, to a man, is not forced upon him, by a law. A law may be made to bind all the subjects of a commonwealth: a liberty, or charter is only to one man, or some one part of the people. For to say all the people of a commonwealth, have liberty in any case whatsoever, is to say, that in such case, there hath been no law made; or else having been made, is now abrogated.

CHAPTER XXVII

Of Crimes, Excuses, and Extenuations

A SIN, is not only a transgression of a law, but also any contempt of the legislator. For such contempt, is a breach of all his laws at once. And therefore may consist, not only in the *commission* of a fact, or in speaking of words by the laws forbidden, or in the *omission* of what the law commandeth, but also in the *intention*, or purpose to transgress. For the purpose to break the law, is some degree of contempt of him, to whom it belongeth to see it executed. To be delighted in the imagination only, of being possessed of another man's goods, servants, or wife, without any intention to take them from him by force or fraud, is no breach of the law, that saith, *Thou shalt not covet*: nor is the pleasure a man may have in imagining or dreaming of the death of him, from whose life he expecteth nothing but damage, and displeasure, a sin; but the resolving to put some act in execution, that tendeth thereto. For to be pleased in the fiction of that, which would please a man if it were real, is a passion so adherent to the nature both of man, and every other living creature, as to make it a sin, were to make sin of being a man. The consideration of this, has made me think them too severe, both to themselves, and others, that maintain, that the first motions of the mind, though checked with the fear of God, be sins. But I confess it is safer to err on that hand, than on the other.

A CRIME, is a sin, consisting in the committing, by deed or word, of that which the law forbiddeth, or the omission of what it hath commanded. So that every crime is a sin; but not every sin a crime. To intend to steal, or kill, is a sin, though it never appear in word, or fact: for God that seeth the thoughts of man, can lay it to his charge: but till it appear by something done, or said, by which the intention may be argued by a human judge, it hath not the name of crime: which distinction the Greeks observed, in the word ἁμάρτημα, and ἔγκλημα, or ἀιτία; whereof the former, which is translated *sin*, signifieth any swerving from the law whatsoever; but the two latter, which are translated *crime*, signify that sin only, whereof one man may accuse another. But of intentions, which never appear by any outward act, there is no place for human accusation. In like manner the Latins by *peccatum*, which is *sin*, signify all manner of deviation from the law; but by *crimen*, which word they derive from *cerno*, which signifies *to perceive*, they mean only such sins, as may be made appear before a judge; and therefore are not mere intentions.

From this relation of sin to the law, and of crime to the civil law, may be inferred, first, that where law ceaseth, sin ceaseth. But because the law of nature is eternal, violation of covenants, ingratitude, arrogance, and all facts contrary to any moral virtue, can never cease to be sin. Secondly, that the civil law ceasing, crimes cease: for there being no other law remaining, but that of nature, there is no place for accusation; every man being his own judge, and accused only by his own conscience, and cleared by the uprightness of his own intention. When therefore his intention is right, his fact is no sin: if otherwise, his fact is sin; but not crime. Thirdly, that when the sovereign power ceaseth, crime also ceaseth; for where there is no such power, there is no protection to be had from the law; and therefore every one may protect himself by his own power: for no man in the institution of sovereign power can be supposed to give away the right of preserving his own body; for the safety whereof all sovereignty was ordained. But this is to be understood only of those, that have not themselves contributed to the taking away of the power that protected them; for that was a crime from the beginning.

The source of every crime, is some defect of the understanding; or some error in reasoning; or some sudden force of the passions. Defect in the understanding, is *ignorance*; in reasoning, *erroneous opinion*. Again, ignorance is of three sorts; of the *law*, and of the *sovereign*, and of the *penalty*. Ignorance of the law of nature excuseth no man; because every man that hath attained to the use of reason, is supposed to know, he ought not to do to another, what he would not have done to himself. Therefore into what place soever a man shall come, if he do anything contrary to that law, it is a crime. If a man come from the Indies hither, and persuade men here to receive a new religion, or teach them anything that tendeth to disobedience of the laws of this country, though he be never so well persuaded of the truth of what he teacheth, he commits a crime, and may be justly punished for the same, not only because his doctrine is false, but also because he does that which he would not approve in another, namely, that coming from hence, he should endeavour to alter the religion there. But ignorance of the civil law, shall excuse a man in a strange country, till it be declared to him; because, till then no civil law is binding.

In the like manner, if the civil law of a man's own country, be not so sufficiently declared, as he may know it if he will; nor the action against the law of nature; the ignorance is a good excuse: in other cases ignorance of the civil law, excuseth not.

Ignorance of the sovereign power, in the place of a man's ordinary residence, excuseth him not; because he ought to take notice of the power, by which he hath been protected there.

Ignorance of the penalty, where the law is declared, excuseth no man: for in breaking the law, which without a fear of penalty to follow, were not a law, but vain words, he undergoeth the penalty, though he know not what it is; because, whosoever voluntarily doth any action, accepteth all the known consequences of it; but punishment is a known consequence of the violation of the laws, in every commonwealth; which punishment, if it be determined already by the law, he is subject to that; if not, then he is subject to arbitrary punishment. For it is reason, that he which does injury, without other limitation than that of his own will, should suffer punishment without other limitation, than that of his will whose law is thereby violated.

But when a penalty, is either annexed to the crime in the law itself, or hath been usually inflicted in the like cases; there the delinquent is excused from a greater penalty. For the punishment foreknown, if not great enough to deter men from the action, is an invitement to it: because when men compare the benefit of their injustice, with the harm of their punishment, by necessity of nature they chuse that which appeareth best for themselves: and therefore when they are punished more than the law had formerly determined, or more than others were punished for the same crime; it is the law that tempted, and deceiveth them.

No law, made after a fact done, can make it a crime: because if the fact be against the law of nature, the law was before the fact; and a positive law cannot be taken notice of, before it be made; and therefore cannot be obligatory. But when the law that forbiddeth a fact, is made before the fact be done; yet he that doth the fact, is liable to the penalty ordained after, in case no lesser penalty were made known before, neither by writing, nor by example, for the reason immediately before alleged.

From defect in reasoning, that is to say, from error, men are prone to violate the laws, three ways. First, by presumption of false principles: as when men, from having observed how in all places, and in all ages, unjust actions have been authorized, by the force, and victories of those who have committed them; and that potent men, breaking through the cobweb laws of their country, the weaker sort, and those that have failed in their enterprises, have been esteemed the only criminals; have thereupon taken for principles, and grounds of their reasoning, *that justice is but a vain word: that whatsoever a man can get by his own industry, and hazard, is his own: that the practice of all nations cannot be unjust: that examples of former times are good arguments of doing the like again*; and many more of that kind: which being granted, no act in itself can be a crime, but must be made so, not by the law, but by the success of them that commit it; and the same fact be virtuous, or vicious, as fortune pleaseth; so that what Marius makes a crime, Sylla shall make meritorious, and Caesar, the same laws standing, turn again into a crime, to the perpetual disturbance of the peace of the commonwealth.

Secondly, by false teachers, that either misinterpret the law of nature, making it thereby repugnant to the law civil; or by teaching for laws, such doctrines of their own, or traditions of former times, as are inconsistent with the duty of a subject.

Thirdly, by erroneous inferences from true principles;

which happens commonly to men that are hasty, and precipitate in concluding, and resolving what to do; such as are they, that have both a great opinion of their own understanding, and believe that things of this nature require not time and study, but only common experience, and a good natural wit; whereof no man thinks himself unprovided: whereas the knowledge, of right and wrong, which is no less difficult, there is no man will pretend to, without great and long study. And of those defects in reasoning, there is none that can excuse, though some of them may extenuate, a crime in any man, that pretendeth to the administration of his own private business; much less in them that undertake a public charge; because they pretend to the reason, upon the want whereof they would ground their excuse.

Of the passions that most frequently are the causes of crime, one, is vain glory, or a foolish overrating of their own worth; as if difference of worth, were an effect of their wit, or riches, or blood, or some other natural quality, not depending on the will of those that have the sovereign authority. From whence proceedeth a presumption that the punishments ordained by the laws, and extended generally to all subjects, ought not to be inflicted on them, with the same rigour they are inflicted on poor, obscure, and simple men, comprehended under the name of the *vulgar*.

Therefore it happeneth commonly, that such as value themselves by the greatness of their wealth, adventure on crimes, upon hope of escaping punishment, by corrupting public justice, or obtaining pardon by money, or other rewards.

And that such as have multitude of potent kindred; and popular men, that have gained reputation amongst the multitude, take courage to violate the laws, from a hope of oppressing the power, to whom it belongeth to put them in execution.

And that such as have a great, and false opinion of their own wisdom, take upon them to reprehend the actions, and call in question the authority of them that govern, and so to unsettle the laws with their public discourse, as that nothing shall be a crime, but what their own designs require should be so. It happeneth also to the same men, to be prone to all such crimes, as consist in craft, and in deceiving of their neighbours; because they think their designs are too subtle to be perceived. These I say are effects of a false presumption of their own wisdom. For of them that are the first movers in the disturbance of commonwealth, which can never happen without a civil war, very few are left alive long enough, to see their new designs established: so that the benefit of their crimes redoundeth to posterity, and such as would least have wished it: which argues they were not so wise, as they thought they were. And those that deceive upon hope of not being observed, do commonly deceive themselves, the darkness in which they believe they lie hidden, being nothing else but their own blindness; and are no wiser than children, that think all hid, by hiding their own eyes.

And generally all vain-glorious men, unless they be withal timorous, are subject to anger; as being more prone than others to interpret for contempt, the ordinary liberty of conversation: and there are few crimes that may not be produced by anger.

As for the passions, of hate, lust, ambition, and covetousness, what crimes they are apt to produce, is so obvious to every man's experience and understanding, as there needeth nothing to be said of them, saving that they are infirmities, so annexed to the nature, both of man, and all other living creatures, as that their effects cannot be hindered, but by extraordinary use of reason, or a constant severity in punishing them. For in those things men hate, they find a continual, and unavoidable molestation; whereby either a man's patience must be everlasting, or he must be eased by removing the power of that which molesteth him. The former is difficult; the latter is many times impossible, without some violation of the law. Ambition, and covetousness are passions also that are perpetually incumbent, and pressing; whereas reason is not perpetually present, to resist them: and therefore whensoever the hope of impunity appears, their effects proceed. And for lust, what it wants in the lasting, it hath in the vehemence, which sufficeth to weigh down the apprehension of all easy, or uncertain punishments.

Of all passions, that which inclineth men least to break the laws, is fear. Nay, excepting some generous natures, it is the only thing, when there is appearance of profit or pleasure by breaking the laws, that makes men keep them. And yet in many cases a crime may be committed through fear.

For not every fear justifies the action it produceth, but the fear only of corporeal hurt, which we call *bodily fear*, and from which a man cannot see how to be delivered, but by the action. A man is assaulted, fears present death, from which he sees not how to escape, but by wounding him that assaulteth him: if he wound him to death, this is no crime; because no man is supposed at the making of a commonwealth, to have abandoned the defence of his life, or limbs, where the law cannot arrive time enough to his assistance. But to kill a man, because from his actions, or his threatenings, I may argue he will kill me when he can, seeing I have time, and means to demand protection, from the sovereign power, is a crime. Again, a man receives words of disgrace or some little injuries, for which they that made the laws, had assigned no punishment, nor thought it worthy of a man that hath the use of reason, to take notice of, and is afraid, unless he revenge it, he shall fall into contempt, and consequently be obnoxious to the like injuries from others; and to avoid this, breaks the law, and protects himself for the future, by the terror of his private revenge. This is a crime: for the hurt is not corporeal, but phantastical, and, though in this corner of the world, made sensible by a custom not many years since begun, amongst young and vain men, so light, as a gallant man, and one that is assured of his own courage, cannot take notice of. Also a man may stand in fear of spirits, either through his own superstition, or through too much credit given to other men, that tell him of strange dreams and visions; and thereby be made believe they will hurt him, for doing, or omitting divers things, which nevertheless, to do, or omit, is contrary to the laws; and that which is so done, or omitted, is not to be excused by this fear; but is a crime. For, as I have shown before in the second chapter, dreams be naturally but the fancies remaining in sleep, after the impressions our senses had formerly received waking; and when men are by any accident unassured they have slept, seem to be real visions; and therefore he that presumes to break the law upon his own, or another's dream, or pretended vision, or upon other fancy of the power of invisible spirits, than is permitted by the commonwealth, leaveth the law of nature, which is a certain offence, and followeth the imagery of his own, or another private man's brain, which he can never know whether it signifieth any thing or nothing, nor whether he that tells his dream, say true, or lie; which if every private man should have leave to do, as they must by the law of nature, if any one have it, there could no law be made to hold, and so all commonwealth would be dissolved.

From these different sources of crimes, it appears already, that all crimes are not, as the Stoics of old time maintained, of the same ally. There is place, not only for EXCUSE, by which that which seemed a crime, is proved to be none at all; but also for EXTENUATION, by which the crime, that seemed great, is made less. For though all crimes do equally deserve the name of injustice, as all deviation from a straight line is equally crookedness, which the Stoics rightly observed: yet it does not follow that all crimes are equally unjust, no more than that all crooked lines are equally crooked; which the Stoics not observing, held it as great a crime, to kill a hen, against the law, as to kill one's father.

That which totally excuseth a fact, and takes away from it the nature of a crime, can be none but that, which at the same time, taketh away the obligation of the law. For the fact committed once against the law, if he that committed it be obliged to the law, can be no other than a crime.

The want of means to know the law, totally excuseth. For the law whereof a man has no means to inform himself, is not obligatory. But the want of diligence to inquire, shall not be considered as a want of means; nor shall any man, that pretendeth to reason enough for the government of his own affairs, be supposed to want means to know the laws of nature; because they are known by the reason he pretends to: only children, and madmen are excused from offences against the law natural.

Where a man is captive, or in the power of the enemy (and

he is then in the power of the enemy, when his person, or his means of living, is so), if it be without his own fault, the obligation of the law ceaseth; because he must obey the enemy, or die; and consequently such obedience is no crime: for no man is obliged, when the protection of the law faileth, not to protect himself, by the best means he can.

If a man, by the terror of present death, be compelled to do a fact against the law, he is totally excused; because no law can oblige a man to abandon his own preservation. And supposing such a law were obligatory; yet a man would reason thus, *If I do it not, I die presently; if I do it, I die afterwards; therefore by doing it, there is time of life gained;* nature therefore compels him to the fact.

When a man is destitute of food, or other thing necessary for his life, and cannot preserve himself any other way, but by some fact against the law; as if in a great famine he take the food by force, or stealth, which he cannot obtain for money nor charity; or in defence of his life, snatch away another man's sword; he is totally excused, for the reason next before alleged.

Again, facts done against the law by the authority of another, are by that authority excused against the author; because no man ought to accuse his own fact in another, that is but his instrument: but it is not excused against a third person thereby injured; because in the violation of the law, both the author and actor are criminals. From hence it followeth that when that man, or assembly, that hath the sovereign power, commandeth a man to do that which is contrary to a former law, the doing of it is totally excused: for he ought not to condemn it himself, because he is the author; and what cannot justly be condemned by the sovereign, cannot justly be punished by any other. Besides, when the sovereign commandeth anything to be done against his own former law, the command, as to that particular fact, is an abrogation of the law.

If that man, or assembly, that hath the sovereign power, disclaim any right essential to the sovereignty, whereby there accrueth to the subject, any liberty inconsistent with the sovereign power, that is to say, with the very being of a commonwealth, if the subject shall refuse to obey the command in anything contrary to the liberty granted, this is nevertheless a sin, and contrary to the duty of the subject: for he ought to take notice of what is inconsistent with the sovereignty, because it was erected by his own consent and for his own defence; and that such liberty as is inconsistent with it, was granted through ignorance of the evil consequence thereof. But if he not only disobey, but also resist a public minister in the execution of it, then it is a crime; because he might have been righted, without any breach of the peace, upon complaint.

The degrees of crime are taken on divers scales, and measured, first, by the malignity of the source, or cause; secondly, by the contagion of the example; thirdly, by the mischief of the effect; and fourthly, by the concurrence of times, places, and persons.

The same fact done against the law, if it proceed from presumption of strength, riches, or friends to resist those that are to execute the law, is a greater crime than if it proceed from hope of not being discovered, or of escape by flight: for presumption of impunity by force, is a root, from whence springeth, at all times, and upon all temptations, a contempt of all laws; whereas in the latter case, the apprehension of danger, that makes a man fly, renders him more obedient for the future. A crime which we know to be so, is greater than the same crime proceeding from a false persuasion that it is lawful; for he that committeth it against his own conscience, presumeth on his force, or other power, which encourages him to commit the same again: but he that doth it by error, after the error is shewn him, is conformable to the law.

He, whose error proceeds from the authority of a teacher, or an interpreter of the law publicly authorized, is not so faulty as he whose error proceedeth from a peremptory pursuit of his own principles and reasoning: for what is taught by one that teacheth by public authority, the commonwealth teacheth, and hath a resemblance of law, till the same authority controlleth it; and in all crimes that contain not in them a denial of the sovereign power, nor are against an evident law, excuseth totally: whereas he that groundeth his actions on his private judgment, ought, according to the rectitude, or error thereof, to stand or fall.

The same fact, if it have been constantly punished in other men, is a greater crime, than if there have been many precedent examples of impunity. For those examples are so many hopes of impunity, given by the sovereign himself: and because he which furnishes a man with such a hope and presumption of mercy, as encourageth him to offend, hath his part in the offence; he cannot reasonably charge the offender with the whole.

A crime arising from a sudden passion, is not so great, as when the same ariseth from long meditation: for in the former case there is a place for extenuation, in the common infirmity of human nature: but he that doth it with premeditation, has used circumspection, and cast his eye on the law, on the punishment, and on the consequence thereof to human society; all which, in committing the crime, he hath contemned and postposed to his own appetite. But there is no suddenness of passion sufficient for a total excuse: for all the time between the first knowing of the law, and the commission of the fact, shall be taken for a time of deliberation; because he ought by meditation of the law, to rectify the irregularity of his passions.

Where the law is publicly, and with assiduity, before all the people read and interpreted, a fact done against it, is a greater crime, than where men are left without such instruction, to enquire of it with difficulty, uncertainty, and interruption of their callings, and be informed by private men: for in this case, part of the fault is discharged upon common infirmity; but, in the former, there is apparent negligence, which is not without some contempt of the sovereign power.

Those facts which the law expressly condemneth, but the law-maker by other manifest signs of his will tacitly approveth, are less crimes, than the same facts, condemned both by the law and law-maker. For seeing the will of the law-maker is a law, there appear in this case two contradictory laws; which would totally excuse, if men were bound to take notice of the sovereign's approbation, by other arguments than are expressed by his command. But because there are punishments consequent, not only to the transgression of his law, but also to the observing of it, he is in part a cause of the transgression, and therefore cannot reasonably impute the whole crime to the delinquent. For example, the law condemneth duels; the punishment is made capital: on the contrary part, he that refuseth duel, is subject to contempt and scorn, without remedy; and sometimes by the sovereign himself thought unworthy to have any charge, or preferment in war. If thereupon he accept duel, considering all men lawfully endeavour to obtain the good opinion of them that have the sovereign power, he ought not in reason to be rigorously punished; seeing part of the fault may be discharged on the punisher: which I say, not as wishing liberty of private revenges, or any other kind of disobedience; but a care in governors, not to countenance anything obliquely, which directly they forbid. The examples of princes, to those that see them, are, and ever have been, more potent to govern their actions, than the laws themselves. And though it be our duty to do, not what they do, but what they say; yet will that duty never be performed, till it please God to give men an extraordinary, and supernatural grace to follow that precept.

Again, if we compare crimes by the mischief of their effects; first, the same fact, when it redounds to the damage of many, is greater, than when it redounds to the hurt of few. And therefore, when a fact hurteth, not only in the present, but also, by example, in the future, it is a greater crime, than if it hurt only in the present: for the former, is a fertile crime, and multiplies to the hurt of many; the latter is barren. To maintain doctrines contrary to the religion established in the commonwealth, is a greater fault, in an authorized preacher, than in a private person; so also is it, to live profanely, incontinently, or do any irreligious act whatsoever. Likewise in a professor of the law, to maintain any point, or do any act, that tendeth to the weakening of the sovereign power, is a greater crime, than in another man: also in a man that hath such reputation for wisdom, as that his counsels are followed, or his actions imitated by many, his fact against the law, is a greater crime, than the same fact in another: for such men not only commit crime, but teach it for law to all other men. And generally all crimes are the greater, by the scandal they give;

that is to say, by becoming stumbling-blocks to the weak, that look not so much upon the way they go in, as upon the light that other man carry before them.

Also facts of hostility against the present state of the commonwealth, are greater crimes, than the same acts done to private men: for the damage extends itself to all: such are the betraying of the strengths, or revealing of the secrets of the commonwealth to an enemy; also all attempts upon the representative of the commonwealth, be it a monarch, or an assembly; and all endeavours by word, or deed, to diminish the authority of the same, either in the present time, or in succession: which crimes the Latins understand by *crimina laesae majestatis*, and consist in design, or act, contrary to a fundamental law.

Likewise those crimes, which render judgments of no effect, are greater crimes, than injuries done to one, or a few persons; as to receive money to give false judgment, or testimony, is a greater crime, than otherwise to deceive a man of the like, or a greater sum; because not only he has wrong, that falls by such judgments; but all judgments are rendered useless, and occasion ministered to force, and private revenges.

Also robbery, and depeculation of the public treasure, or revenues, is a greater crime, than the robbing, or defrauding of a private man; because to rob the public, is to rob many at once.

Also the counterfeit usurpation of public ministry, the counterfeiting of public seals or public coin, than counterfeiting of a private man's person, or his seal; because the fraud thereof, extendeth to the damage of many.

Of facts against the law, done to private men, the greater crime, is that, where the damage in the common opinion of men, is most sensible. And therefore

To kill against the law, is a greater crime, than any other injury, life preserved.

And to kill with torment, greater, than simply to kill.

And mutilation of a limb, greater, than the spoiling a man of his goods.

And the spoiling a man of his goods, by terror of death, or wounds, than by clandestine surreption.

And by clandestine surreption, than by consent fraudulently obtained.

And the violation of chastity by force, greater, than by flattery.

And of a woman married, than of a woman not married.

For all these things are commonly so valued: though some men are more, and some less sensible of the same offence. But the law regardeth not the particular, but the general inclination of mankind.

And therefore the offence men take, from contumely, in words, or gesture, when they produce no other harm, than the present grief of him that is reproached, hath been neglected in the laws of the Greeks, Romans, and other both ancient and modern commonwealths; supposing the true cause of such grief to consist, not in the contumely, which takes no hold upon men conscious of their own virtue, but in the pusillanimity of him that is offended by it.

Also a crime against a private man, is much aggravated by the person, time, and place. For to kill one's parent, is a greater crime, than to kill another: for the parent ought to have the honour of a sovereign, though he surrendered his power to the civil law; because he had it originally by nature. And to rob a poor man, is a greater crime, than to rob a rich man; because it is to the poor a more sensible damage.

And a crime committed in the time or place appointed for devotion, is greater, than if committed at another time or place: for it proceeds from a greater contempt of the law.

Many other cases of aggravation, and extenuation might be added: but by these I have set down, it is obvious to every man, to take the altitude of any other crime proposed.

Lastly, because in almost all crimes there is an injury done, not only to some private men, but also to the commonwealth; the same crime, when the accusation is in the name of the commonwealth, is called public crime: and when in the name of a private man, a private crime; and the pleas according thereunto called public, *judicia publica*, Pleas of the Crown; or Private Pleas. As in an accusation of murder, if the accuser be a private man, the plea is a Private Plea; if the accuser be the sovereign, the plea is a Public Plea.

CHAPTER XXVIII

Of Punishments and Rewards

A PUNISHMENT, *is an evil inflicted by public authority, on him that hath done, or omitted that which is judged by the same authority to be a transgression of the law; to the end that the will of men may thereby the better be disposed to obedience.*

Before I infer any thing from this definition, there is a question to be answered, of much importance; which is, by what door the right or authority of punishing in any case, came in. For by that which has been said before, no man is supposed bound by covenant, not to resist violence; and consequently it cannot be intended, that he gave any right to another to lay violent hands upon his person. In the making of a commonwealth, every man giveth away the right of defending another; but not of defending himself. Also he obligeth himself, to assist him that hath the sovereignty, in the punishing of another; but of himself not. But to covenant to assist the sovereign, in doing hurt to another, unless he that so covenanteth have a right to do it himself, is not to give him a right to punish. It is manifest therefore that the right which the commonwealth, that is, he, or they that represent it, hath to punish, is not grounded on any concession, or gift of the subjects. But I have also showed formerly, that before the institution of commonwealth, every man had a right to every thing, and to do whatsoever he thought necessary to his own preservation; subduing, hurting, or killing any man in order thereunto. And this is the foundation of that right of punishing, which is exercised in every commonwealth. For the subjects did not give the sovereign that right; but only in laying down theirs, strengthened him to use his own, as he should think fit, for the preservation of them all: so that it was not given, but left to him, and to him only; and (excepting the limits set him by natural law) as entire, as in the condition of mere nature, and of war of every one against his neighbour.

From the definition of punishment, I infer, first, that neither private revenges, nor injuries of private men, can properly be styled punishment; because they proceed not from public authority.

Secondly, that to be neglected, and unpreferred by the public favour, is not a punishment; because no new evil is thereby on any man inflicted; he is only left in the estate he was in before.

Thirdly, that the evil inflicted by public authority, without precedent public condemnation, is not to be styled by the name of punishment; but of an hostile act; because the fact for which a man is punished, ought first to be judged by public authority, to be a transgression of the law.

Fourthly, that the evil inflicted by usurped power, and judges without authority from the sovereign is not punishment; but an act of hostility; because the acts of power usurped, have not for author, the person condemned; and therefore are not acts of public authority.

Fifthly, that all evil which is inflicted without intention, or possibility of disposing the delinquent, or, by his example, other men, to obey the laws, is not punishment; but an act of hostility: because without such an end, no hurt done is contained under that name.

Sixthly, whereas to certain actions, there be annexed by nature, divers hurtful consequences; as when a man in assaulting another, is himself slain, or wounded; or when he falleth into sickness by the doing of some unlawful act; such hurt, though in respect of God, who is the author of nature, it may be said to be inflicted, and therefore a punishment divine; yet it is not contained in the name of punishment in respect of men, because it is not inflicted by the authority of man.

Seventhly, if the harm inflicted be less than the benefit, or contentment that naturally followeth the crime committed, that harm is not within the definition; and is rather the price, or redemption, than the punishment of a crime: because it is of the nature of punishment, to have for end, the disposing of men to obey the law; which end, if it be less than the benefit of the transgression, it attaineth not, but worketh a contrary effect.

Eighthly, if a punishment be determined and prescribed in the law itself, and after the crime committed, there be a greater punishment inflicted, the excess is not punishment, but an act of hostility. For seeing the aim of punishment is not a revenge, but terror; and the terror of a great punishment unknown, is taken away by the declaration of a less, the unexpected addition is no part of the punishment. But where there is no punishment at all determined by the law, there whatsoever is inflicted, hath the nature of punishment. For he that goes about the violation of a law, wherein no penalty is determined, expecteth an indeterminate, that is to say, an arbitrary punishment.

Ninthly, harm inflicted for a fact done before there was a law that forbade it, is not punishment, but an act of hostility: for before the law, there is no transgression of the law: but punishment supposeth a fact judged, to have been a transgression of the law; therefore harm inflicted before the law made, is not punishment, but an act of hostility.

Tenthly, hurt inflicted on the representative of the commonwealth, is not punishment, but an act of hostility: because it is of the nature of punishment, to be inflicted by public authority, which is the authority only of the representative itself.

Lastly, harm inflicted upon one that is a declared enemy, falls not under the name of punishment: because seeing they were either never subject to the law, and therefore cannot transgress it; or having been subject to it, and professing to be no longer so, by consequence deny they can transgress it, all the harms that can be done them, must be taken as acts of hostility. But in declared hostility, all infliction of evil is lawful. From whence it followeth, that if a subject shall by fact, or word, wittingly, and deliberately deny the authority of the representative of the commonwealth (whatsoever penalty hath been formerly ordained for treason) he may lawfully be made to suffer whatsoever the representative will. For in denying subjection, he denies such punishment as by the law hath been ordained; and therefore suffers as an enemy of the commonwealth; that is, according to the will of the representative. For the punishments set down in the law, are to subjects, not to enemies: such as are they, that having been by their own acts subjects, deliberately revolting, deny the sovereign power.

The first, and most general distribution of punishments, is into *divine*, and *human*. Of the former I shall have occasion to speak, in a more convenient place hereafter.

Human, are those punishments that be inflicted by the commandment of man; and are either *corporal*, or *pecuniary*, or *ignominy*, or *imprisonment*, or *exile*, or mixed of these.

Corporal punishment is that, which is inflicted on the body directly, and according to the intention of him that inflicteth it: such as are stripes, or wounds, or deprivation of such pleasures of the body, as were before lawfully enjoyed.

And of these, some be *capital*, some *less* than *capital*. Capital, is the infliction of death; and that either simply, or with torment. Less than capital, are stripes, wounds, chains, and any other corporal pain, not in its own nature mortal. For if upon the infliction of a punishment death follow not in the intention of the inflictor, the punishment is not to be esteemed capital, though the harm prove mortal by an accident not to be foreseen; in which case death is not inflicted, but hastened.

Pecuniary punishment, is that which consisteth not only in the deprivation of a sum of money, but also of lands, or any other goods which are usually bought and sold for money. And in case the law, that ordaineth such a punishment, be made with design to gather money, from such as shall transgress the same, it is not properly a punishment, but the price of privilege and exemption from the law, which doth not absolutely forbid the fact, but only to those that are not able to pay the money: except where the law is natural, or part of religion; for in that case it is not an exemption from the law, but a transgression of it. As where a law exacteth a pecuniary mulct, of them that take the name of God in vain, the payment of the mulct, is not the price of a dispensation to swear, but the punishment of the transgression of a law indispensable. In like manner if the law impose a sum of money to be paid, to him that has been injured; this is but a satisfaction for the hurt done him; and extinguisheth the accusation of the party injured, not the crime of the offender.

Ignominy, is the infliction of such evil, as is made dishonourable; or the deprivation of such good, as is made honourable by the commonwealth. For there be some things honourable by nature; as the effects of courage, magnanimity, strength, wisdom, and other abilities of body and mind: others made honourable by the commonwealth; as badges, titles, offices, or any other singular mark of the sovereign's favour. The former, though they may fail by nature, or accident, cannot be taken away by a law; and therefore the loss of them is not punishment. But the latter, may be taken away by the public authority that made them honourable, and are properly punishments: such are degrading men condemned, of their badges, titles, and offices; or declaring them incapable of the like in time to come.

Imprisonment, is when a man is by public authority deprived of liberty; and may happen from two divers ends; whereof one is the safe custody of a man accused; the other is the inflicting of pain on a man condemned. The former is not punishment; because no man is supposed to be punished, before he be judicially heard, and declared guilty. And therefore whatsoever hurt a man is made to suffer by bonds, or restraint, before his cause be heard, over and above that which is necessary to assure his custody, is against the law of nature. But the latter is punishment, because evil, and inflicted by public authority, for somewhat that has by the same authority been judged a transgression of the law. Under this word imprisonment, I comprehend all restraint of motion, caused by an external obstacle, be it a house, which is called by the general name of a prison; or an island, as when men are said to be confined to it; or a place where men are set to work, as in old time men have been condemned to quarries, and in these times to galleys; or be it a chain, or any other such impediment.

Exile (banishment) is when a man is for a crime, condemned to depart out of the dominion of the commonwealth, or out of a certain part thereof: and during a prefixed time, or for ever, not to return into it: and seemeth not in its own nature, without other circumstances, to be a punishment; but rather an escape, or a public commandment to avoid punishment by flight. And Cicero says, there was never any such punishment ordained in the city of Rome; but calls it a refuge of men in danger. For if a man banished, be nevertheless permitted to enjoy his goods, and the revenue of his lands, the mere change of air is no punishment, nor does it tend to that benefit of the commonwealth, for which all punishments are ordained, that is to say, to the forming of men's wills to the observation of the law; but many times to the damage of the commonwealth. For a banished man, is a lawful enemy of the commonwealth that banished him; as being no more a member of the same. But if he be withal deprived of his lands, or goods, then the punishment lieth not in the exile, but is to be reckoned amongst punishments pecuniary.

All punishments of innocent subjects, be they great or little, are against the law of nature; for punishment is only for transgression of the law, and therefore there can be no punishment of the innocent. It is therefore a violation, first, of that law of nature, which forbiddeth all men, in their revenges, to look at anything but some future good: for there can arrive no good to the commonwealth, by punishing the innocent. Secondly, of that, which forbiddeth ingratitude: for seeing all sovereign power, is originally given by the consent of every one of the subjects, to the end they should as long as they are obedient, be protected thereby; the punishment of the innocent, is a rendering of evil for good. And thirdly, of the law that commandeth equity; that is to say, an equal distribution of justice; which in punishing the innocent is not observed.

But the infliction of what evil soever, on an innocent man, that is not a subject, if it be for the benefit of the commonwealth, and without violation of any former covenant, is no breach of the law of nature. For all men that are not subjects, are either enemies, or else they have ceased from being so by some precedent covenants. But against enemies, whom the commonwealth judgeth capable to do them hurt, it is lawful by the original right of nature to make war; wherein the sword judgeth not, nor doth the victor make distinction of nocent, and innocent, as to the time past nor has other respect of mercy, than as it conduceth to the good of his own people. And upon this ground it is, that also in subjects, who deliberately deny the authority of the commonwealth established, the vengeance is lawfully extended, not only to the fathers, but also to the third and fourth generation not yet in being, and consequently innocent of the fact, for which they are afflicted: because the nature of this offence, consisteth in the renouncing of subjection; which is a relapse into the condition of war, commonly called rebellion; and they that so offend, suffer not as subjects, but as enemies. For *rebellion*, is but war renewed.

REWARD, is either of *gift*, or by *contract*. When by contract, it is called *salary*, and *wages*; which is benefit due for service performed, or promised. When of gift, it is benefit proceeding from the *grace* of them that bestow it, to encourage, or enable men to do them service. And therefore when the sovereign of a commonwealth appointeth a salary to any public office, he that receiveth it, is bound in justice to perform his office; otherwise, he is bound only in honour, to acknowledgment, and an endeavour of requital. For though men have no lawful remedy, when they be commanded to quit their private business, to serve the public, without reward or salary; yet they are not bound thereto, by the law of nature, nor by the institution of the commonwealth, unless the service cannot otherwise be done; because it is supposed the sovereign may make use of all their means, insomuch as the most common soldier, may demand the wages of his warfare, as a debt.

The benefit which a sovereign bestoweth on a subject, for fear of some power and ability he hath to do hurt to the commonwealth, are not properly rewards; for they are not salaries; because there is in this case no contract supposed, every man being obliged already not to do the commonwealth disservice: nor are they graces; because they be extorted by fear, which ought not to be incident to the sovereign power: but are rather sacrifices, which the sovereign, considered in his natural person, and not in the person of the commonwealth, makes, for the appeasing the discontent of him he thinks more potent than himself; and encourage not to obedience, but on the contrary, to the continuance, and increasing of further extortion.

And whereas some salaries are certain, and proceed from the public treasure; and others uncertain, and casual, proceeding from the execution of the office for which the salary is ordained; the latter is in some cases hurtful to the commonwealth; as in the case of judicature. For where the benefit of the judges, and ministers of a court of justice ariseth from the multitude of causes that are brought to their cognizance, there must needs follow two inconveniences: one, is the nourishing of suits; for the more suits, the greater benefit: and another that depends on that, which is contention about jurisdiction; each court drawing to itself, as many causes as it can. But in offices of execution there are not those inconveniences; because their employment cannot be increased by any endeavour of their own. And thus much shall suffice for the nature of punishment and reward; which are, as it were, the nerves and tendons, that move the limbs and joints of a commonwealth.

Hitherto I have set forth the nature of man, whose pride and other passions have compelled him to submit himself to government: together with the great power of his governor, whom I compared to *Leviathan*, taking that comparison out of the two last verses of the one-and-fortieth of *Job*; where God having set forth the great power of *Leviathan*, calleth him king of the proud. *There is nothing*, saith he, *on earth, to be compared with him. He is made so as not to be afraid. He seeth every high thing below him; and is king of all the children of pride.* But because he is mortal, and subject to decay, as all other earthly creatures are; and because there is that in heaven, though not on earth, that he should stand in fear of, and whose laws he ought to obey; I shall in the next following chapters speak of his diseases, and the causes of his mortality; and of what laws of nature he is bound to obey.

CHAPTER XXIX

Of Those Things that Weaken, or Tend to the Dissolution of a Commonwealth

THOUGH nothing can be immortal, which mortals make; yet, if men had the use of reason they pretend to, their commonwealths might be secured, at least from perishing by internal diseases. For by the nature of their institution, they are designed to live, as long as mankind, or as the laws of nature, or as justice itself, which gives them life. Therefore when they come to be dissolved, not by external violence, but intestine disorder, the fault is not in men, as they are the *matter*; but as they are the *makers*, and orderers of them. For men, as they become at last weary of irregular jostling, and hewing one another, and desire with all their hearts, to conform themselves into one firm and lasting edifice: so for want, both of the art of making fit laws, to square their actions by, and also of humility, and patience, to suffer the rude and cumbersome points of their present greatness to be taken off, they cannot without the help of a very able architect, be compiled into any other than a crazy building, such as hardly lasting out their own time, must assuredly fall upon the heads of their posterity.

Amongst the *infirmities* therefore of a commonwealth, I will reckon in the first place, those that arise from an imperfect institution, and resemble the diseases of a natural body, which proceed from a defectuous procreation.

Of which, this is one, *that a man to obtain a kingdom, is sometimes content with less power, than to the peace, and defence of the commonwealth is necessarily required.* From whence it cometh to pass, that when the exercise of the power laid by, is for the public safety to be resumed, it hath the resemblance of an unjust act; which disposeth great numbers of men, when occasion is presented, to rebel; in the same manner as the bodies of children, gotten by diseased parents, are subject either to untimely death, or to purge the ill quality, derived from their vicious conception, by breaking out into biles and scabs. And when kings deny themselves some such necessary power, it is not always, though sometimes, out of ignorance of what is necessary to the office they undertake; but many times out of a hope to recover the same again at their pleasure. Wherein they reason not well; because such as will hold them to their promises, shall be maintained against them by foreign commonwealths; who in order to the good of their own subjects let slip few occasions to *weaken* the estate of their neighbours. So was Thomas Becket, archbishop of Canterbury, supported against Henry the Second, by the Pope; the subjection of ecclesiastics to the commonwealth, having been dispensed with by William the Conqueror at his reception, when he took an oath, not to infringe the liberty of the church. And so were the barons, whose power was by William Rufus, to have their help in transferring the succession from his elder brother to himself, increased to a degree inconsistent with the sovereign power, maintained in their rebellion against king John, by the French.

Nor does this happen in monarchy only. For whereas the style of the ancient Roman commonwealth, was, *the senate and people of Rome*; neither senate, nor people pretended to the whole power; which first caused the seditions, of Tiberius Gracchus, Caius Gracchus, Lucius Saturninus, and others; and afterwards the wars between the senate and the people, under Marius and Sylla; and again under Pompey and Caesar, to the extinction of their democracy, and the setting up of monarchy.

The people of Athens bound themselves but from one only action; which was, that no man on pain of death should propound the renewing of the war for the island of Salamis; and yet thereby, if Solon had not caused to be given out he was mad, and afterwards in gesture and habit of a madman, and in verse, propounded it to the people that flocked about him, they had had an enemy perpetually in readiness, even at the gates of their city; such damage, or shifts, are all commonwealths forced to, that have their power never so little limited.

In the second place, I observe the *diseases* of a commonwealth, that proceed from the poison of seditious doctrines, whereof one is, *That every private man is judge of good and evil actions*. This is true in the condition of mere nature, where there are no civil laws; and also under civil government, in such cases as are not determined by the law. But otherwise, it is manifest, that the measure of good and evil actions, is the civil law; and the judge the legislator, who is always representative of the commonwealth. From this false doctrine, men are disposed to debate with themselves, and dispute the commands of the commonwealth; and afterwards to obey, or disobey them, as in their private judgments they shall think fit; whereby the commonwealth is distracted and *weakened*.

Another doctrine repugnant to civil society, is, that *whatsoever a man does against his conscience, is sin*; and it dependeth on the presumption of making himself judge of good and evil. For a man's conscience, and his judgment is the same thing, and as the judgment, so also the conscience may be erroneous. Therefore, though he that is subject to no civil law, sinneth in all he does against his conscience, because he has no other rule to follow but his own reason; yet it is not so with him that lives in a commonwealth; because the law is the public conscience, by which he hath already undertaken to be guided. Otherwise in such diversity, as there is of private consciences, which are but private opinions, the commonwealth must needs be distracted, and no man dare to obey the sovereign power, further than it shall seem good in his own eyes.

It hath been also commonly taught, *that faith and sanctity, are not to be attained by study and reason, but by supernatural inspiration, or infusion*. Which granted, I see not why any man should render a reason of his faith; or why every Christian should not be also a prophet; or why any man should take the law of his country, rather than his own inspiration, for the rule of his action. And thus we fall again in the fault of taking upon us to judge of good and evil; or to make judges of it, such private men as pretend to be supernaturally inspired, to the dissolution of all civil government. Faith comes by hearing, and hearing by those accidents, which guide us into the presence of them that speak to us; which accidents are all contrived by God Almighty; and yet are not supernatural, but only, for the great number of them that concur to every effect, unobservable. Faith and sanctity, are indeed not very frequent; but yet they are not miracles, but brought to pass by education, discipline, correction, and other natural ways, by which God worketh them in his elect, at such times as he thinketh fit. And these three opinions, pernicious to peace and government, have in this part of the world, proceeded chiefly from the tongues, and pens of unlearned divines, who joining the words of Holy Scripture together, otherwise than is agreeable to reason, do what they can, to make men think, that sanctity and natural reason, cannot stand together.

A fourth opinion, repugnant to the nature of a commonwealth, is this, *that he that hath the sovereign power is subject to the civil laws.* It is true, that sovereigns are all subject to the laws of nature; because such laws be divine, and cannot by any man, or commonwealth be abrogated. But to those laws which the sovereign himself, that is, which the commonwealth maketh, he is not subject. For to be subject to laws, is to be subject to the commonwealth, that is to the sovereign representative, that is to himself; which is not subjection, but freedom from the laws. Which error, because it setteth the laws above the sovereign, setteth also a judge above him, and a power to punish him; which is to make a new sovereign; and again for the same reason a third, to punish the second; and so continually without end, to the confusion, and dissolution of the commonwealth.

A fifth doctrine, that tendeth to the dissolution of a commonwealth, is, *that every private man has an absolute propriety in his goods; such, as excludeth the right of the sovereign.* Every man has indeed a propriety that excludes the right of every other subject: and he has it only from the sovereign power; without the protection whereof, every other man should have equal right to the same. But if the right of the sovereign also be excluded, he cannot perform the office they have put him into; which is, to defend them both from foreign enemies, and from the injuries of one another; and consequently there is no longer a commonwealth.

And if the propriety of subjects, exclude not the right of the sovereign representative to their goods; much less to their offices of judicature, or execution, in which they represent the sovereign himself.

There is a sixth doctrine, plainly, and directly against the essence of a commonwealth; and it is this, *that the sovereign power may be divided.* For what is it to divide the power of a commonwealth, but to dissolve it; for powers divided mutually destroy each other. And for these doctrines, men are chiefly beholding to some of those, that making profession of the laws, endeavour to make them depend upon their own learning, and not upon the legislative power.

And as false doctrine, so also oftentimes the example of different government in a neighbouring nation, disposeth men to alteration of the form already settled. So the people of the Jews were stirred up to reject God, and to call upon the prophet Samuel, for a king after the manner of the nations: so also the lesser cities of Greece, were continually disturbed, with seditions of the aristocratical, and democratical factions; one part of almost every commonwealth, desiring to imitate the Lacedemonians; the other, the Athenians. And I doubt not, but many men have been contented to see the late troubles in England, out of an imitation of the Low Countries; supposing there needed no more to grow rich, than to change, as they had done, the form of their government. For the constitution of man's nature, is of itself subject to desire novelty. When therefore they are provoked to the same, by the neighbourhood also of those that have been enriched by it, it is almost impossible for them, not to be content with those that solicit them to change; and love the the first beginnings, though they be grieved with the continuance of disorder; like hot bloods, that having gotten the itch, tear themselves with their own nails, till they can endure the smart no longer.

And as to rebellion in particular against monarchy; one of the most frequent causes of it, is the reading of the books of policy, and histories of the ancient Greeks, and Romans; from which, young men, and all others that are unprovided of the antidote of solid reason, receiving a strong, and delightful impression, of the great exploits of war, achieved by the conductors of their armies, receive withal a pleasing idea, of all they have done besides; and imagine their great prosperity, not to have proceeded from the emulation of particular men, but from the virtue of their popular form of government: not considering the frequent seditions, and civil wars, produced by the imperfection of their policy. From the reading, I say, of such books, men have undertaken to kill their kings, because the Greek and Latin writers, in their books, and discourses of policy, make it lawful, and laudable, for any man so to do; provided, before he do it, he call him tyrant. For they say not *regicide*, that is, killing a king, but *tyrannicide*, that is, killing of a tyrant is lawful. From the same books, they that live under a monarch conceive an opinion, that the subjects in a popular commonwealth enjoy liberty; but that in a monarchy they are all slaves. I say, they that live under a monarchy conceive such an opinion; not they that live under a popular government: for they find no such matter. In sum, I cannot imagine, how anything can be more prejudicial to a monarchy, than the allowing of such books to be publicly read, without present applying such correctives of discreet masters, as are fit to take away their venom; which venom I will not doubt to compare to the biting of a mad dog, which is a disease the physicians call *hydrophobia*, or *fear of water*. For as he that is so bitten, has a continual torment of thirst, and yet abhorreth water; and is in such an estate, as if the poison endeavoured to convert him into a dog: so when a monarchy is once bitten to the quick, by those democratical writers, that continually snarl at that estate; it wanteth nothing more than a strong monarch, which nevertheless out of a certain *tyrannophobia*, or fear of being strongly governed, when they have him, they abhor.

As there have been doctors, that hold there be three souls in a man; so there be also that think there may be more souls, that is, more sovereigns, than one, in a commonwealth; and set up a *supremacy* against the *sovereignty*; *canons* against *laws*; and a *ghostly authority* against the *civil*; working on men's minds, with words and distinctions, that of themselves signify nothing, but bewray by their obscurity; that there walketh, as some think, invisibly another kingdom, as it were a kingdom of fairies, in the dark. Now seeing it is manifest, that the civil power, and the power of the commonwealth is the same thing; and that supremacy, and the power of making canons, and granting faculties, implieth a commonwealth; it followeth, that where one is sovereign, another supreme; where one can make laws, and another make canons; there must needs be two commonwealths, of one and the same subjects; which is a kingdom divided in itself, and cannot stand. For notwithstanding the insignificant distinction of *temporal*, and *ghostly*, they are still two kingdoms, and every subject is subject to two masters. For seeing the *ghostly* power challengeth the right to declare what is sin, it challengeth by consequence to declare what is law, sin being nothing but the transgression of the law; and again, the civil power challenging to declare what is law, every subject must obey two masters, who both will have their commands be observed as law; which is impossible. Or, if it be but one kingdom, either the *civil*, which is the power of the commonwealth, must be subordinate to the *ghostly*, and then there is no sovereignty but the *ghostly*; or the *ghostly* must be subordinate to the *temporal*, and then there is no *supremacy* but the *temporal*. When therefore these two powers oppose one another, the commonwealth cannot but be in great danger of civil war and dissolution. For the *civil* authority being more visible, and standing in the clearer light of natural reason, cannot choose but draw to it in all times a very considerable part of the people: and the *spiritual*, though it stand in the darkness of School distinctions, and hard words, yet because the fear of darkness and ghosts, is greater than other fears, cannot want a party sufficient to trouble, and sometimes to destroy a commonwealth. And this is a disease which not unfitly may be compared to the epilepsy, or falling sickness, which the Jews took to be one kind of possession by spirits, in the body natural. For as in this disease, there is an unnatural spirit, or wind in the head that obstructeth the roots of the nerves, and moving them violently, taketh away the motion which naturally they should have from the power of the soul in the brain, and thereby causeth violent, and irregular motions, which men call convulsions, in the parts; insomuch as he that is seized therewith, falleth down sometimes into the water, and sometimes into the fire, as a man deprived of his senses; so also in the body politic, when the spiritual power, moveth the members of a commonwealth, by the terror of punishments, and hope of rewards, which are the nerves of it, otherwise than by the civil power, which is the soul of the commonwealth, they ought to be moved; and by strange, and hard words suffocates their understanding, it must needs thereby distract the people, and either overwhelm the commonwealth with oppression, or cast it into the fire of a civil war.

Sometimes also in the merely civil government, there be more than one soul; as when the power of levying money, which is the nutritive faculty, has depended on a general assembly; the power of conduct and command, which is the motive faculty, on one man; and the power of making laws, which is the rational faculty, on the accidental consent, not only of those two, but also of a third; this endangereth the commonwealth, sometimes for want of consent to good laws: but most often for want of such nourishment, as is necessary to life, and motion. For although few perceive, that such government, is not government, but division of the commonwealth into three factions, and call it mixed monarchy; yet the truth is, that it is not one independent commonwealth, but three independent factions; nor one representative person, but three. In the kingdom of God, there may be three persons independent, without breach of unity in God that reigneth; but where men reign, that be subject to diversity of opinions, it cannot be so. And therefore if the king bear the person of the people, and the general assembly bear also the person of the people, and another assembly bear the person of a part of the people, they are not one person, nor one sovereign but three persons, and three sovereigns.

To what disease in the natural body of man, I may exactly compare this irregularity of a commonwealth, I know not. But I have seen a man, that had another man growing out of his side, with a head, arms, breast, and stomach, of his own: if he had had another man growing out of his other side, the comparison might then have been exact.

Hitherto I have named such diseases of a commonwealth, as are of the greatest, and most present danger. There be other not so great; which nevertheless are not unfit to be observed. As first, the difficulty of raising money, for the necessary uses of the commonwealth; especially in the approach of war. This difficulty ariseth from the opinion, that every subject hath a propriety in his lands and goods, exclusive of the sovereign's right to the use of the same. From whence it cometh to pass, that the sovereign power, which foreseeth the necessities and dangers of the commonwealth, finding the passage of money to the public treasury obstructed, by the tenacity of the people, whereas it ought to extend itself, to encounter, and prevent such dangers in their beginnings, contracteth itself as long as it can, and when it cannot longer, struggles with the people by stratagems of law, to obtain little sums, which not sufficing, he is fain at last violently to open the way for present supply, or perish; and being put often to these extremities, at last reduceth the people to their due temper; or else the commonwealth must perish. Insomuch as we may compare this distemper very aptly to an ague; wherein, the fleshy parts being congealed, or by venomous matter obstructed, the veins which by their natural course empty themselves into the heart, are not, as they ought to be, supplied from the arteries, whereby there succeedeth at first a cold contraction, and trembling of the limbs; and afterward a hot, and strong endeavour of the heart, to force a passage for the blood; and before it can do that, contenteth itself with the small refreshments of such things as cool for a time, till, if nature be strong enough, it break at last the contumacy of the parts obstructed, and dissipateth the venom into sweat; or, if nature be too weak, the patient dieth.

Again, there is sometimes in a commonwealth, a disease, which resembleth the pleurisy; and that is, when the treasure of the commonwealth, flowing out of its due course, is gathered together in too much abundance, in one, or a few private men, by monopolies, or by farms of the public revenues; in the same manner as the blood in a pleurisy, getting into the membrane of the breast, breedeth there an inflammation, accompanied with a fever, and painful stitches.

Also the popularity of a potent subject, unless the commonwealth have very good caution of his fidelity, is a dangerous disease; because the people, which should receive their motion from the authority of the sovereign, by the flattery and by the reputation of an ambitious man are drawn away from their obedience to the laws, to follow a man, of whose virtues, and designs they have no knowledge. And this is commonly of more danger in a popular government, than in a monarchy; because an army is of so great force, and multitude, as it may easily be made believe, they are the people. By this means it was, that Julius Caesar, who was set up by the people against the senate, having won to himself the affections of his army, made himself master both of senate and people. And this proceeding of popular, and ambitious men, is plain rebellion; and may be resembled to the effects of witchcraft.

Another infirmity of a commonwealth, is the immoderate greatness of a town, when it is able to furnish out of its own circuit, the number, and expense of a great army: as also the great number of corporations; which are as it were many lesser commonwealths in the bowels of a greater, like worms in the entrails of a natural man. To which may be added, the liberty of disputing against absolute power, by pretenders to political prudence; which though bred for the most part in the lees of the people, yet animated by false doctrines, are perpetually meddling with the fundamental laws, to the molestation of the commonwealth; like the little worms, which physicians call *ascariades*.

We may further add, the insatiable appetite, or βουλιμεα, of enlarging dominion; with the incurable *wounds* thereby many times received from the enemy; and the *wens*, of ununited conquests, which are many times a burthen, and with less danger lost, than kept; as also the *lethargy* of ease, and *consumption* of riot and vain expense.

Lastly, when in a war, foreign or intestine, the enemies get a final victory; so as, the forces of the commonwealth keeping the field no longer, there is no further protection of subjects in their loyalty; then is the commonwealth DISSOLVED, and every man at liberty to protect himself by such courses as his own discretion shall suggest unto him. For the sovereign is the public soul, giving life and motion to the commonwealth; which expiring, the members are governed by it no more, than the carcase of a man, by his departed, though immortal, soul. For though the right of a sovereign monarch cannot be extinguished by the act of another; yet the obligation of the members may. For he that wants protection, may seek it any where; and when he hath it, is obliged, without fraudulent pretence of having submitted himself out of fear, to protect his protection as long as he is able. But when the power of an assembly is once suppressed, the right of the same perisheth utterly; because the assembly itself is extinct; and consequently, there is no possibility for the sovereignty to re-enter.

CHAPTER XXX

Of the Office of the Sovereign Representative

THE OFFICE of the sovereign, be it a monarch or an assembly, consisteth in the end, for which he was trusted with the sovereign power, namely the procuration of *the safety of the people*; to which he is obliged by the law of nature, and to render an account thereof to God, the author of that law, and to none but him. But by safety here, is not meant a bare preservation, but also all other contentments of life, which every man by lawful industry, without danger, or hurt to the commonwealth, shall acquire to himself.

And this is intended should be done, not by care applied to individuals, further than their protection from injuries, when they shall complain; but by a general providence, contained in public instruction, both of doctrine, and example; and in the making and executing of good laws, to which individual persons may apply their own cases.

And because, if the essential rights of sovereignty, specified before in the eighteenth chapter, be taken away, the commonwealth is thereby dissolved, and every man returneth into the condition, and calamity of a war with every other man, which is the greatest evil that can happen in this life; it is the office of the sovereign, to maintain those rights entire; and consequently against his duty, first, to transfer to another, or to lay from himself any of them. For he that deserteth the means, deserteth the ends; and he deserteth the means, that being the sovereign, acknowledgeth himself subject to the civil laws; and renounceth the power of supreme judicature; or of making war, or peace by his own authority; or of judging of the necessities of the commonwealth; or of levying money and soldiers, when, and as much as in his own conscience he shall judge necessary; or of making officers, and ministers both of war and peace; or of appointing teachers, and examining what doctrines are conformable, or contrary to the defence, peace, and good of the people. Secondly, it is against his duty, to let the people be ignorant, or misinformed of the grounds, and reasons of those his essential rights; because thereby men are easy to be seduced, and drawn to resist him, when the commonwealth shall require their use and exercise.

And the grounds of these rights, have the rather need to be diligently, and truly taught; because they cannot be maintained by any civil law, or terror of legal punishment. For a civil law, that shall forbid rebellion, (and such is all resistance to the essential rights of the sovereignty), is not, as a civil law, any obligation, but by virtue only of the law of nature, that forbiddeth the violation of faith; which natural obligation, if men know not, they cannot know the right of any law the sovereign maketh. And for the punishment, they take it but for an act of hostility; which when they think they have strength enough, they will endeavour by acts of hostility, to avoid.

As I have heard some say, that justice is but a word, without substance; and that whatsoever a man can by force, or art, acquire to himself, not only in the condition of war, but also in a commonwealth, is his own, which I have already showed to be false: so there be also that maintain, that there are no grounds, nor principles of reason, to sustain those essential rights, which make sovereignty absolute. For if there were, they would have been found out in some place, or other; whereas we see, there has not hitherto been any commonwealth, where those rights have been acknowledged, or challenged. Wherein they argue as ill, as if the savage people of America, should deny there were any grounds, or principles of reason, so to build a house, as to last as long as the materials, because they never yet saw any so well built. Time, and industry, produce every day new knowledge. And as the art of well building is derived from principles of reason, observed by industrious men, that had long studied the nature of materials, and the divers effects of figure, and proportion, long after mankind began, though poorly, to build: so, long time after men have begun to constitute commonwealths, imperfect, and apt to relapse into disorder, there may principles of reason be found out, by industrious meditation, to make their constitution, excepting by external violence, everlasting. And such are those which I have in this discourse set forth: which whether they come not into the sight of those that have power to make use of them, or be neglected by them, or not, concerneth my particular interests, at this day, very little. But supposing that these of mine are not such principles of reason; yet I am sure they are principles from authority of Scripture; as I shall make it appear, when I shall come to speak of the kingdom of God, administered by Moses, over the Jews, his peculiar people by covenant.

But they say again, that though the principles be right, yet common people are not of capacity enough to be made to understand them. I should be glad, that the rich and potent subjects of a kingdom, or those that are accounted the most learned, were no less incapable than they. But all men know, that the obstructions to this kind of doctrine, proceed not so much from the difficulty of the matter, as from the interest of them that are to learn. Potent men, digest hardly any thing that setteth up a power to bridle their affections; and learned men, any thing that discovereth their errors, and thereby lesseneth their authority: whereas the common people's minds, unless they be tainted with dependance on the potent, or scribbled over with the opinions of their doctors, are like clean paper, fit to receive whatsoever by public authority shall be imprinted in them. Shall whole nations be brought to *acquiesce* in the great mysteries of the Christian religion, which are above reason, and millions of men be made believe, that the same body may be in innumerable places at one and the same time, which is against reason; and shall not men be able, by their teaching, and preaching, protected by the law, to make that received, which is so consonant to reason, that any un-prejudicated man, needs no more to learn it, than to hear it? I conclude therefore, that in the instruction of the people in the essential rights which are the natural and fundamental laws of sovereignty, there is no difficulty, whilst a sovereign has his power entire, but what proceeds from his own fault, or the fault of those whom he trusteth in the administration of the commonwealth; and consequently, it is his duty, to cause them so to be instructed, and not only his duty, but his benefit also, and security against the danger that may arrive to himself in his natural person from rebellion.

And, to descend to particulars, the people are to be taught, first, that they ought not to be in love with any form of government they see in their neighbour nations, more than with their own, nor, whatsoever present prosperity they behold in nations that are otherwise governed than they, to desire change. For the prosperity of a people ruled by an aristocratical, or democratical assembly, cometh not from aristocracy, nor from democracy, but from the obedience, and concord of the subjects: nor do the people flourish in a monarchy, because one man has the right to rule them, but because they obey him. Take away in any kind of state, the obedience, and consequently the concord of the people, and they shall not only not flourish, but in short time be dissolved. And they that go about by disobedience, to do no more than reform the commonwealth, shall find they do thereby destroy it; like the foolish daughters of Peleus, in the fable; which desiring to renew the youth of their decrepid father, did by the counsel of Medea, cut him in pieces, and boil him, together with strange herbs, but made not of him a new man. This desire of change, is like the breach of the first of God's commandments: for there God says, *Non habebis Deos alienos*; Thou shalt not have the Gods of other nations; and in another place concerning *kings*, that they are *Gods*.

Secondly, they are to be taught, that they ought not to be led with admiration of the virtue of any of their fellow-subjects, how high soever he stand, or how conspicuously soever he shine in the commonwealth; nor of any assembly, except the sovereign assembly, so as to defer to them any obedience, or honour, appropriate to the sovereign only, whom, in their particular stations, they represent; nor to receive any influence from them, but such as is conveyed by them from the sovereign authority. For that sovereign cannot be imagined to love his people as he ought, that is not jealous of them, but suffers them by the flattery of popular men, to be seduced from their loyalty, as they have often been, not only secretly, but openly, so as to proclaim marriage with them *in facie ecclesiae* by preachers, and by publishing the same in the open streets: which may fitly be compared to the violation of the second of the ten commandments.

Thirdly, in consequence to this, they ought to be informed, how great a fault it is, to speak evil of the sovereign representative, whether one man, or an assembly of men; or to argue and dispute his power; or any way to use his name irreverently, whereby he may be brought into contempt with his people, and their obedience, in which the safety of the commonwealth consisteth, slackened. Which doctrine the third commandment by resemblance pointeth to.

Fourthly, seeing people cannot be taught this, nor when it is taught, remember it, nor after one generation past, so much as know in whom the sovereign power is placed, without setting apart from their ordinary labour, some certain times, in which they may attend those that are appointed to instruct them; it is necessary that some such times be determined, wherein they may assemble together, and, after prayers and praises given to God, the sovereign of sovereigns, hear those their duties told them, and the positive laws, such as generally concern them all, read and expounded, and be put in mind of the authority that maketh them laws. To this end had the Jews every seventh day, a sabbath, in which the law was read and expounded; and in the solemnity whereof they were put in mind, that their king was God; that having created the world in six days, he rested the seventh day; and by their resting on it from their labour, that that God was their king, which redeemed them from their servile, and painful labour in Egypt, and gave them a time, after they had rejoiced in God, to take joy also in themselves, by lawful recreation. So that the first table of the commandments, is spent all in setting down the sum of God's absolute power; not only as God, but as king by pact, in peculiar, of the Jews; and may therefore give light, to those that have sovereign power conferred on them by the consent of men, to see what doctrine they ought to teach their subjects.

And because the first instruction of children, dependeth on

the care of their parents, it is necessary that they should be obedient to them, whilst they are under their tuition; and not only so, but that also afterwards, as gratitude requireth, they acknowledge the benefit of their education, by external signs of honour. To which end they are to be taught, that originally the father of every man was also his sovereign lord, with power over him of life and death; and that the fathers of families, when by instituting a commonwealth, they resigned that absolute power, yet it was never intended, they should lose the honour due unto them for their education. For to relinquish such right, was not necessary to the institution of sovereign power; nor would there be any reason, why any man should desire to have children, or take the care to nourish and instruct them, if they were afterwards to have no other benefit from them, than from other men. And this accordeth with the fifth commandment.

Again, every sovereign ought to cause justice to be taught, which, consisting in taking from no man what is his, is as much as to say, to cause men to be taught not to deprive their neighbours, by violence or fraud, of any thing which by the sovereign authority is theirs. Of things held in propriety, those that are dearest to a man are his own life, and limbs; and in the next degree, in most men, those that concern conjugal affection; and after them, riches and means of living. Therefore the people are to be taught, to abstain from violence to one another's person, by private revenges; from violation of conjugal honour; and from forcible rapine, and fraudulent surreption of one another's goods. For which purpose also it is necessary they be showed the evil consequences of false judgment, by corruption either of judges or witnesses, whereby the distinction of propriety is taken away, and justice becomes of no effect: all which things are intimated in the sixth, seventh, eighth, and ninth commandments.

Lastly, they are to be taught, that not only the unjust facts, but the designs and intentions to do them, though by accident hindered, are injustice; which consisteth in the pravity of the will, as well as in the irregularity of the act. And this is the intention of the tenth commandment, and the sum of the second table; which is reduced all to this one commandment of mutual charity, *thou shalt love thy neighbour as thyself*: as the sum of the first table is reduced to *the love of God*; whom they had then newly received as their king.

As for the means, and conduits, by which the people may receive this instruction, we are to search, by what means so many opinions, contrary to the peace of mankind, upon weak and false principles, have nevertheless been so deeply rooted in them. I mean those, which I have in the precedent chapter specified: as that men shall judge of what is lawful and unlawful, not by the law itself, but by their own consciences; that is to say, by their own private judgments: that subjects sin in obeying the commands of the commonwealth, unless they themselves have first judged them to be lawful: that their propriety in their riches is such, as to exclude the dominion, which the commonwealth hath over the same: that it is lawful for subjects to kill such, as they call tyrants: that the sovereign power may be divided, and the like; which come to be instilled into the people by this means. They whom necessity, or covetousness keepeth attent on their trades, and labour; and they, on the other side, whom superfluity, or sloth carrieth after their sensual pleasures; which two sorts of men take up the greatest part of mankind; being diverted from the deep meditation, which the learning of truth, not only in the matter of natural justice, but also of all other sciences necessarily requireth, receive the notions of their duty, chiefly from divines in the pulpit, and partly from such of their neighbours or familiar acquaintance, as having the faculty of discoursing readily, and plausibly, seem wiser and better learned in cases of law and conscience, than themselves. And the divines, and such others as make show of learning, derive their knowledge from the universities, and from the schools of law, or from books, which by men, eminent in those schools and universities, have been published. It is therefore manifest, that the instruction of the people, dependeth wholly, on the right teaching of youth in the universities. But are not, may some man say, the universities of England learned enough already to do that? or is it you, will undertake to teach the universities? Hard questions. Yet to the first, I doubt not to answer; that till towards the latter end of Henry the Eighth, the power of the Pope, was always upheld against the power of the commonwealth, principally by the universities; and that the doctrines maintained by so many preachers, against the sovereign power of the king, and by so many lawyers, and others, that had their education there, is a sufficient argument, that though the universities were not authors of those false doctrines, yet they knew not how to plant the true. For in such a contradiction of opinions, it is most certain, that they have not been sufficiently instructed; and it is no wonder if they yet retain a relish of that subtle liquor, wherewith they were first seasoned, against the civil authority. But to the latter question, it is not fit, nor needful for me to say either aye, or no: for any man that sees what I am doing, may easily perceive what I think.

The safety of the people, requireth further, from him, or them that have the sovereign power, that justice be equally administered to all degrees of people; that is, that as well the rich and mighty, as poor and obscure persons, may be righted of the injuries done them; so as the great, may have no greater hope of impunity, when they do violence, dishonour, or any injury to the meaner sort, than when one of these, does the like to one of them: for in this consisteth equity; to which, as being a precept of the law of nature, a sovereign is as much subject, as any of the meanest of his people. All breaches of the law, are offences against the commonwealth: but there be some, that are also against private persons. Those that concern the commonwealth only, may without breach of equity be pardoned; for every man may pardon what is done against himself, according to his own discretion. But an offence against a private man, cannot in equity be pardoned, without the consent of him that is injured; or reasonable satisfaction.

The inequality of subjects, proceedeth from the acts of sovereign power; and therefore has no more place in the presence of the sovereign, that is to say, in a court of justice, than the inequality between kings and their subjects, in the presence of the King of kings. The honour of great persons, is to be valued for their beneficence and the aids they give to men of inferior rank, or not at all. And the violences, oppressions, and injuries they do, are not extenuated, but aggravated by the greatness of their persons; because they have least need to commit them. The consequences of this partiality towards the great, proceed in this manner. Impunity maketh insolence; insolence, hatred; and hatred, an endeavour to pull down all oppressing and contumelious greatness, though with the ruin of the commonwealth.

To equal justice, apperteineth also the equal imposition of taxes; the equality whereof dependeth not on the equality of riches, but on the equality of the debt that every man oweth to the commonwealth for his defence. It is not enough, for a man to labour for the maintenance of his life; but also to fight, if need be, for the securing of his labour. They must either do as the Jews did after their return from captivity, in re-edifying the temple, build with one hand, and hold the sword in the other; or else they must hire others to fight for them. For the impositions, that are laid on the people by the sovereign power, are nothing else but the wages, due to them that hold the public sword, to defend private men in the exercise of their several trades, and callings. Seeing then the benefit that every one receiveth thereby, is the enjoyment of life, which is equally dear to poor and rich; the debt which a poor man oweth them that defend his life, is the same which a rich man oweth for the defence of his; saving that the rich, who have the service of the poor, may be debtors not only for their own persons but for many more. Which considered, the equality of imposition, consisteth rather in the equality of that which is consumed, than of the riches of the persons that consume the same. For what reason is there, that he which laboureth much, and sparing the fruits of his labour, con-sumeth little, should be more charged, than he that living idly, getteth little, and spendeth all he gets; seeing the one hath no more protection from the commonwealth, than the other? But when the impositions, are laid upon those things which men consume, every man payeth equally for what he useth: nor is the commonwealth defrauded by the luxurious waste of private men.

And whereas many men, by accident inevitable, become unable to maintain themselves by their labour; they ought not to be left to the charity of private persons; but to be provided for, as far forth as the necessities of nature require, by the laws of the commonwealth. For as it is uncharitableness in any man, to neglect the impotent; so it is in the sovereign of a commonwealth, to expose them to the hazard of such uncertain charity.

But for such as have strong bodies, the case is otherwise: they are to be forced to work; and to avoid the excuse of not finding employment, there ought to be such laws, as may encourage all manner of arts; as navigation, agriculture, fishing, and all manner of manufacture that requires labour. The multitude of poor, and yet strong people still increasing, they are to be transplanted into countries not sufficiently inhabited: where nevertheless, they are not to exterminate those they find there; but constrain them to inhabit closer together, and not to range a great deal of ground, to snatch what they find; but to court each little plot with art and labour, to give them their sustenance in due season. And when all the world is overcharged with inhabitants, then the last remedy of all is war; which provideth for every man, by victory, or death.

To the care of the sovereign, belongeth the making of good laws. But what is a good law? By a good law, I mean not a just law: for no law can be unjust. The law is made by the sovereign power, and all that is done by such power, is warranted, and owned by every one of the people; and that which every man will have so, no man can say is unjust. It is in the laws of a commonwealth, as in the laws of gaming: whatsoever the gamesters all agree on, is injustice to none of them. A good law is that, which is *needful*, for the *good of the people*, and withal *perspicuous*.

For the use of laws, which are but rules authorized, is not to bind the people from all voluntary actions; but to direct and keep them in such a motion, as not to hurt themselves by their own impetuous desires, rashness or indiscretion; as hedges are set, not to stop travellers, but to keep them in their way. And therefore a law that is not needful, having not the true end of a law, is not good. A law may be conceived to be good, when it is for the benefit of the sovereign; though it be not necessary for the people; but it is not so. For the good of the sovereign and people, cannot be separated. It is a weak sovereign, that has weak subjects; and a weak people, whose sovereign wanteth power to rule them at his will. Unnecessary laws are not good laws; but traps for money: which where the right of sovereign power is acknowledged, are superfluous; and where it is not acknowledged, insufficient to defend the people.

The perspicuity, consisteth not so much in the words of the law itself, as in a declaration of the causes, and motives for which it was made. That is it, that shows us the meaning of the legislator; and the meaning of the legislator known, the law is more easily understood by few, than many words. For all words, are subject to ambiguity; and therefore multiplication of words in the body of the law, is multiplication of ambiguity: besides it seems to imply, by too much diligence, that whosoever can evade the words, is without the compass of the law. And this is a cause of many unnecessary processes. For when I consider how short were the laws of ancient times; and how they grew by degrees still longer; methinks I see a contention between the penners, and pleaders of the law; the former seeking to circumscribe the latter; and the latter to evade their circumscriptions; and that the pleaders have got the victory. It belongeth therefore to the office of a legislator, (such as is in all commonwealths the supreme representative, be it one man, or an assembly), to make the reason perspicuous, why the law was made; and the body of the law itself, as short, but in as proper, and significant terms, as may be.

It belongeth also to the office of the sovereign, to make a right application of punishments, and rewards. And seeing the end of punishing is not revenge, and discharge of choler; but correction, either of the offender, or of others by his example; the severest punishments are to be inflicted for those crimes, that are of most danger to the public; such as are those which proceed from malice to the government established; those that spring from contempt of justice; those that provoke indignation in the multitude; and those, which unpunished, seem authorized, as when they are committed by sons, servants, or favourites of men in authority. For indignation carrieth men, not only against the actors, and authors of injustice; but against all power that is likely to protect them; as in the case of Tarquin; when for the insolent act of one of his sons, he was driven out of Rome, and the monarchy itself dissolved. But crimes of infirmity; such as are those which proceed from great provocation, from great fear, great need, or from ignorance whether the fact be a great crime, or not, there is place many times for lenity, without prejudice to the commonwealth; and lenity, when there is such place for it, is required by the law of nature. The punishment of the leaders and teachers in a commotion, not the poor seduced people, when they are punished, can profit the commonwealth by their example. To be severe to the people, is to punish that ignorance, which may in great part be imputed to the sovereign, whose fault it was, that they were no better instructed.

In like manner it belongeth to the office, and duty of the sovereign, to apply his rewards always so, as there may arise from them benefit to the commonwealth; wherein consisteth their use, and end; and is then done, when they that have well served the commonwealth, are with as little expense of the common treasure, as is possible, so well recompensed, as others thereby may be encouraged, both to serve the same as faithfully as they can, and to study the arts by which they may be enabled to do it better. To buy with money, or preferment, from a popular ambitious subject, to be quiet, and desist from making ill impressions in the minds of the people, has nothing of the nature of reward; (which is ordained not for disservice, but for service past;) nor a sign of gratitude, but of fear; nor does it tend to the benefit, but to the damage of the public. It is a contention with ambition, like that of Hercules with the monster Hydra, which having many heads, for every one that was vanquished, there grew up three. For in like manner, when the stubbornness of one popular man, is overcome with reward, there arise many more, by the example, that do the same mischief, in hope of like benefit: and as all sorts of manufacture, so also malice encreaseth by being vendible. And though sometimes a civil war, may be deferred by such ways as that, yet the danger grows still the greater, and the public ruin more assured. It is therefore against the duty of the sovereign, to whom the public safety is committed, to reward those that aspire to greatness by disturbing the peace of their country, and not rather to oppose the beginnings of such men, with a little danger, than after a long time with greater.

Another business of the sovereign, is to choose good counsellors; I mean such, whose advice he is to take in the government of the commonwealth. For this word counsel, *consilium*, corrupted from *considium*, is of a large signification, and comprehendeth all assemblies of men that sit together, not only to deliberate what is to be done hereafter, but also to judge of facts past, and of law for the present. I take it here in the first sense only: and in this sense, there is no choice of counsel, neither in a democracy, nor aristocracy; because the persons counselling are members of the person counselled. The choice of counsellors therefore is proper to monarchy; in which, the sovereign that endeavoureth not to make choice of those, that in every kind are the most able, dischargeth not his office as he ought to do. The most able counsellors, are they that have least hope of benefit by giving evil counsel, and most knowledge of those things that conduce to the peace, and defence of the commonwealth. It is a hard matter to know who expecteth benefit from public troubles but the signs that guide to a just suspicion, is the soothing of the people in their unreasonable, or irremediable grievances, by men whose estates are not sufficient to discharge their accustomed expenses, and may easily be observed by any one whom it concerns to know it. But to know, who has most knowledge of the public affairs, is yet harder; and they that know them, need them a great deal the less. For to know, who knows the rules almost of any art, is a great degree of the knowledge of the same art; because no man can be assured of the truth of another's rules, but he that is first taught to understand them. But the best signs of knowledge of any art, are, much conversing in it, and constant good effects of it. Good counsel comes not by lot, nor by inheritance; and therefore there is no more reason to expect good advice from the rich or noble, in matter of state, than in delineating the dimensions of a fortress; unless we shall think there needs no method in the study of the politics, as there does in the study of geometry, but only to be lookers on; which is not so. For the politics is the harder study of the two. Whereas in these parts of Europe, it hath been taken for a right of certain persons, to have place in the highest council of state by inheritance; it is derived from the conquests of the ancient Germans; wherein many absolute lords joining together to conquer other nations, would not enter into the confederacy, without such privileges, as might be marks of difference in time following, between their posterity, and the posterity of their subjects; which privileges being inconsistent with the sovereign power, by the favour of the sovereign, they may seem to keep; but contending for them as their right, they must needs by degrees let them go, and have at last no further honour, than adhereth naturally to their abilities.

And how able soever be the counsellors in any affair, the benefit of their counsel is greater, when they give every one his advice, and the reasons of it apart, than when they do it in an assembly, by way of orations; and when they have premeditated, than when they speak on the sudden; both because they have more time, to survey the consequences of action; and are less subject to be carried away to contradiction, through envy, emulation, or other passions arising from the difference of opinion.

The best counsel, in those things that concern not other nations, but only the ease and benefit the subjects may enjoy, by laws that look only inwards, is to be taken from the general informations, and complaints of the people of each province, who are best acquainted with their own wants, and ought therefore, when they demand nothing in derogation of the essential rights of sovereignty, to be diligently taken notice of. For without those essential rights, as I have often before said, the commonwealth cannot at all subsist.

A commander of an army in chief, if he be not popular, shall not be beloved nor feared as he ought to be by his army; and consequently, cannot perform that office with good success. He must therefore be industrious, valiant, affable, liberal and fortunate, that he may gain an opinion both of sufficiency, and of loving his soldiers. This is popularity, and breeds in the soldiers both desire, and courage, to recommend themselves to his favour; and protects the severity of the general in punishing, when need is, the mutinous, or negligent soldiers. But this love of soldiers, if caution be not given of the commander's fidelity, is a dangerous thing to sovereign power; especially when it is in the hands of an assembly not popular. It belongeth therefore to the safety of the people, both that they be good conductors, and faithful subjects, to whom the sovereign commits his armies.

But when the sovereign himself is popular; that is, reverenced and beloved of his people, there is no danger at all from the popularity of a subject. For soldiers are never so generally unjust, as to side with their captain though they love him, against their sovereign, when they love not only his person, but also his cause. And therefore those, who by violence have at any time suppressed the power of their lawful sovereign, before they could settle themselves in his place, have been always put to the trouble of contriving their titles to save the people from the shame of receiving them. To have a known right to sovereign power, is so popular a quality, as he that has it needs no more, for his own part, to turn the hearts of his subjects to him, but that they see him able absolutely to govern his own family: nor, on the part of his enemies, but a disbanding of their armies. For the greatest and most active part of mankind, has never hitherto been well contented with the present.

Concerning the offices of one sovereign to another, which are comprehended in that law, which is commonly called the *law of nations*, I need not say anything in this place; because the law of nations, and the law of nature, is the same thing. And every sovereign hath the same right, in procuring the safety of his people, that any particular man can have, in procuring the safety of his own body. And the same law, that dictateth to men that have no civil government, what they ought to do, and what to avoid in regard of one another, dictateth the same to commonwealths, that is, to the consciences of sovereign princes and sovereign assemblies; there being no court of natural justice, but in the conscience only; where not man, but God reigneth; whose laws, such of them as oblige all mankind, in respect of God, as he is the author of nature, are *natural*; and in respect of the same God, as he is King of kings, are *laws*. But of the kingdom of God, as King of kings, and as King also of a peculiar people, I shall speak in the rest of this discourse.

CHAPTER XXXI

Of the Kingdom of God by Nature

THAT the condition of mere nature, that is to say, of absolute liberty, such as is theirs, that neither are sovereigns, nor subjects, is anarchy, and the condition of war: that the precepts, by which men are guided to avoid that condition, are the laws of nature: that a commonwealth, without sovereign power, is but a word without substance, and cannot stand: that subjects owe to sovereigns, simple obedience, in all things wherein their obedience is not repugnant to the laws of God, I have sufficiently proved, in that which I have already written. There wants only, for the entire knowledge of civil duty, to know what are those laws of God. For without that, a man knows not, when he is commanded any thing by the civil power, whether it be contrary to the law of God, or not: and so, either by too much civil obedience, offends the Divine Majesty; or through fear of offending God, transgresses the commandments of the commonwealth. To avoid both these rocks, it is necessary to know what are the laws divine. And seeing the knowledge of all law, dependeth on the knowledge of the sovereign power, I shall say something in that which followeth, of the KINGDOM OF GOD.

God is king, let the earth rejoice, saith the psalmist. (xcvii, 1). And again, (*Psalm* xcix, 1) *God is king, though the nations be angry; and he that sitteth on the cherubim, though the earth be moved*. Whether men will or not, they must be subject always to the divine power. By denying the existence, or providence of God, men may shake off their ease, but not their yoke. But to call this power of God, which extendeth itself not only to man, but also to beasts, and plants, and bodies inanimate, by the name of kingdom, is but a metaphorical use of the word.

For he only is properly said to reign, that governs his subjects by his word, and by promise of rewards to those that obey it, and by threatening them with punishment that obey it not. Subjects therefore in the kingdom of God, are not bodies inanimate, nor creatures irrational; because they understand no precept as his: nor atheists, nor they that believe not that God has any care of the actions of mankind; because they acknowledge no word for his, nor have hope of his rewards or fear of his threatenings. They therefore that believe there is a God that governeth the world, and hath given precepts, and propounded rewards, and punishments to mankind, are God's subjects; all the rest, are to be understood as enemies.

To rule by words, requires that such words be manifestly made known; for else they are no laws: for to the nature of laws belongeth a sufficient, and clear promulgation, such as may take away the excuse of ignorance; which in the laws of men is but of one only kind, and that is, proclamation, or promulgation by the voice of man. But God declareth his laws three ways; by the dictates of *natural reason*, by *revelation*, and by the *voice* of some *man*, to whom by the operation of miracles, he procureth credit with the rest. From hence there ariseth a triple word of God, *rational, sensible*, and *prophetic*: to which correspondeth a triple hearing; *right reason, sense supernatural*, and *faith*. As for sense supernatural, which consisteth in revelation or inspiration, there have not been any universal laws so given, because God speaketh not in that manner but to particular persons, and to divers men divers things.

From the difference between the other two kinds of God's word, *rational*, and *prophetic*, there may be attributed to God, a twofold kingdom, *natural*, and *prophetic*: natural, wherein he governeth as many of mankind as acknowledge his providence, by the natural dictates of right reason; and prophetic, wherein having chosen but one peculiar nation, the Jews, for his subjects, he governed them, and none but them, not only by natural reason, but by positive laws, which he gave them by the mouths of his holy prophets. Of the natural kingdom of God I intend to speak in this chapter.

The right of nature, whereby God reigneth over men, and

punisheth those that break his laws, is to be derived, not from his creating them, as if he required obedience as of gratitude for his benefits; but from his *irresistible power*. I have formerly shown, how the sovereign right ariseth from pact: to show how the same right may arise from nature, requires no more, but to show in what case it is never taken away. Seeing all men by nature had right to all things, they had right every one to reign over all the rest. But because this right could not be obtained by force, it concerned the safety of every one, laying by that right, to set up men, with sovereign authority, by common consent, to rule and defend them: whereas if there had been any man of power irresistible, there had been no reason, why he should not by that power have ruled and defended both himself, and them, according to his own discretion. To those therefore whose power is irresistible, the dominion of all men adhereth naturally by their excellence of power; and consequently it is from that power, that the kingdom over men, and the right of afflicting men at his pleasure, belongeth naturally to God Almighty; not as Creator, and gracious; but as omnipotent. And though punishment be due for sin only, because by that word is understood affliction for sin; yet the right of afflicting, is not always derived from men's sin, but from God's power.

This question, *why evil men often prosper, and good men suffer adversity*, has been much disputed by the ancient, and is the same with this of ours, *by what right God dispenseth the prosperities and adversities of this life*; and is of that difficulty, as it hath shaken the faith, not only of the vulgar, but of philosophers, and which is more, of the Saints, concerning the Divine Providence. *How good*, saith David, (*Psalm* lxxiii, 1, 2, 3) *is the God of Israel to those that are upright in heart; and yet my feet were almost gone, my treadings had well-night slipt; for I was grieved at the wicked, when I saw the ungodly in such prosperity*. And Job, how earnestly does he expostulate with God, for the many afflictions he suffered, notwithstanding his righteousness? This question in the case of Job, is decided by God himself, not by arguments derived from Job's sin, but his own power. For whereas the friends of Job drew their arguments from his affliction to his sin, and he defended himself by the conscience of his innocence, God himself taketh up the matter, and having justified the affliction by arguments drawn from his power, such as this, (*Job* xxxviii, 4) *Where wast thou, when I laid the foundations of the earth*? and the like, both approved Job's innocence, and reproved the erroneous doctrine of his friends. Conformable to this doctrine is the sentence of our Saviour, concerning the man that was born blind, in these words, *Neither hath this man sinned, nor his fathers; but that the works of God might be made manifest in him.* And though it be said, *that death entered into the world by sin,* (by which is meant, that if Adam had never sinned, he had never died, that is, never suffered any separation of his soul from his body), it follows not thence, that God could not justly have afflicted him, though he had not sinned, as well as he afflicteth other living creatures, that cannot sin.

Having spoken of the right of God's sovereignty, as grounded only on nature; we are to consider next, what are the Divine laws, or dictates of natural reason; which laws concern either the natural duties of one man to another, or the honour naturally due to our Divine Sovereign. The first are the same laws of nature, of which I have spoken already in the fourteenth and fifteenth chapters of this treatise; namely, equity, justice, mercy, humility, and the rest of the moral virtues. It remaineth therefore that we consider, what precepts are dictated to men, by their natural reason only, without other word of God, touching the honour and worship of the Divine Majesty.

Honour consisteth in the inward thought, and opinion of the power, and goodness of another; and therefore to honour God, is to think as highly of his power and goodness, as is possible. And of that opinion, the external signs appearing in the words and actions of men, are called *worship*; which is one part of that which the Latins understand by the word *cultus*. For *cultus* signifieth properly, and constantly, that labour which a man bestows on anything, with a purpose to make benefit by it. Now those things whereof we make benefit, are either subject to us, and the profit they yield, followeth the labour we bestow upon them, as a natural effect; or they are not subject to us, but answer our labour, according to their own wills. In the first sense the labour bestowed on the earth, is called *culture*; and the education of children, a *culture* of their minds. In the second sense, where men's wills are to be wrought to our purpose, not by force, but by complaisance, it signifieth as much as courting, that is, a winning of favour by good offices; as by praises, by acknowledging their power, and by whatsoever is pleasing to them from whom we look for any benefit. And this is properly *worship*: in which sense *Publicola*, is understood for a worshipper of the people; and *cultus Dei*, for the worship of God.

From internal honour, consisting in the opinion of power and goodness, arise three passions; *love*, which hath reference to goodness; and *hope*, and *fear*, that relate to power: and three parts of external worship; *praise*, *magnifying*, and *blessing*: the subject of praise, being goodness; the subject of magnifying and blessing, being power, and the effect thereof felicity. Praise, and magnifying are signified both by words, and actions: by words, when we say a man is good, or great: by actions, when we thank him for his bounty, and obey his power. The opinion of the happiness of another, can only be expressed by words.

There be some signs of honour, both in attributes and actions, that be naturally so; as amongst attributes, *good*, *just*, *liberal*, and the like; and amongst actions, *prayers*, *thanks*, and *obedience*. Others are so by institution, or custom of men; and in some times and places are honourable; in others, dishonourable; in others, indifferent: such as are the gestures in salutation, prayer, and thanksgiving, in different times and places, differently used. The former is *natural*; the latter *arbitrary* worship.

And of arbitrary worship, there be two differences: for sometimes it is a *commanded*, sometimes *voluntary* worship: commanded, when it is such as he requireth, who is worshipped: free, when it is such as the worshipper thinks fit. When it is commanded, not the words, or gesture, but the obedience is the worship. But when free, the worship consists in the opinion of the beholders: for if to them the words, or actions by which we intend honour, seem ridiculous, and tending to contumely, they are no worship, because no signs of honour; and no signs of honour, because a sign is not a sign to him that giveth it, but to him to whom it is made, that is, to the spectator.

Again, there is a *public*, and a *private* worship. Public, is the worship that a commonwealth performeth, as one person. Private, is that which a private person exhibiteth. Public, in respect of the whole commonwealth, is free; but in respect of particular men, it is not so. Private, is in secret free; but in the sight of the multitude, it is never without some restraint, either from the laws, or from the opinion of men; which is contrary to the nature of liberty.

The end of worship amongst men, is power. For where a man seeth another worshipped, he supposeth him powerful, and is the readier to obey him; which makes his power greater. But God has no ends: the worship we do him, proceeds from our duty, and is directed according to our capacity, by those rules of honour, that reason dictateth to be done by the weak to the more potent men, in hope of benefit, for fear of damage, or in thankfulness for good already received from them.

That we may know what worship of God is taught us by the light of nature, I will begin with his attributes. Where, first, it is manifest, we ought to attribute to him *existence*. For no man can have the will to honour that, which he thinks not to have any being.

Secondly, that those philosophers, who said the world, or the soul of the world was God, spake unworthily of him; and denied his existence. For by God, is understood the cause of the world; and to say the world is God, is to say there is no cause of it, that is, no God.

Thirdly, to say the world was not created, but eternal, seeing that which is eternal has no cause, is to deny there is a God.

Fourthly, that they who attributing, as they think, ease to God, take from him the care of mankind; take from him his honour: for it takes away men's love, and fear of him; which is the root of honour.

Fifthly, in those things that signify greatness, and power; to say he is *finite*, is not to honour him: for it is not a sign of the will to honour God, to attribute to him less than we can; and finite, is less than we can; because to finite, it is easy to add more.

Therefore to attribute *figure* to him, is not honour; for all figure is finite:

Nor to say we conceive, and imagine, or have an *idea* of him, in our mind: for whatsoever we conceive is finite:

Nor to attribute to him *parts*, or *totality*; which are the attributes only of things finite:

Nor to say he is in this, or that *place*: for whatsoever is in place, is bounded, and finite:

Nor that he is *moved*, or *resteth*: for both these attributes ascribe to him place:

Nor that there be more Gods than one; because it implies them all finite: for there cannot be more than one infinite:

Nor to ascribe to him, (unless metaphorically, meaning not the passion but the effect) passions that partake of grief; as *repentance, anger, mercy*: or of want; as *appetite, hope, desire*; or of any passive faculty: for passion, is power limited by somewhat else.

And therefore when we ascribe to God a *will*, it is not to be understood, as that of man, for a *rational appetite*; but as the power, by which he effecteth everything.

Likewise when we attribute to him *sight*, and other acts of sense; as also *knowledge*, and *understanding*; which in us is nothing else, but a tumult of the mind, raised by external things that press the organical parts of man's body: for there is no such thing in God; and being things that depend on natural causes, cannot be attributed to him.

He that will attribute to God, nothing but what is warranted by natural reason, must either use such negative attributes, as *infinite, eternal, incomprehensible*; or superlatives, as *most high, most great*, and the like; or indefinite, as *good, just, holy, creator*; and in such sense, as if he meant not to declare what he is, (for that were to circumscribe him within the limits of our fancy,) but how much we admire him, and how ready we would be to obey him; which is a sign of humility, and of a will to honour him as much as we can. For there is but one name to signify our conception of his nature, and that is,

I AM: and but one name of his relation to us, and that is, *God*; in which is contained Father, King, and Lord.

Concerning the actions of divine worship, it is a most general precept of reason, that they be signs of the intention to honour God; such as are, first, *prayers*. For not the carvers when they made images, were thought to make them gods; but the people that *prayed* to them.

Secondly, *thanksgiving*; which differeth from prayer in divine worship, no otherwise, than that prayers precede, and thanks succeed the benefit; the end, both of the one and the other, being to acknowledge God, for author of all benefits, as well past, as future.

Thirdly, *gifts*, that is to say, *sacrifices* and *oblations*, if they be of the best, are signs of honour: for they are thanksgivings.

Fourthly, *not to swear by any but God*, is naturally a sign of honour: for it is a confession that God only knoweth the heart; and that no man's wit or strength can protect a man against God's vengeance on the perjured.

Fifthly, it is a part of rational worship, to speak considerately of God; for it argues a fear of him, and fear is a confession of his power. Hence followeth, that the name of God is not to be used rashly, and to no purpose; for that is as much, as in vain: and it is to no purpose, unless it be by way of oath, and by order of the commonwealth, to make judgments certain; or between commonwealths, to avoid war. And that disputing of God's nature is contrary to his honour: for it is supposed, that in this natural kingdom of God, there is no other way to know anything, but by natural reason, that is, from the principles of natural science; which are so far from teaching us any thing of God's nature, as they cannot teach us our own nature, nor the nature of the smallest creature living. And therefore, when men out of the principles of natural reason, dispute of the attributes of God, they but dishonour him: for in the attributes which we give to God, we are not to consider the signification of philosophical truth; but the signification of pious intention, to do him the greatest honour we are able. From the want of which consideration, have proceeded the volumes of disputation about the nature of God, that tend not to his honour, but to the honour of our own wits and learning; and are nothing else but inconsiderate and vain abuses of his sacred name.

Sixthly, in *prayers*, *thanksgivings*, *offerings*, and *sacrifices*, it is a dictate of natural reason, that they be every one in his kind the best, and most significant of honour. As for example, that prayers and thanksgiving, be made in words and phrases, not sudden, nor light, nor plebeian; but beautiful, and well composed. For else we do not God as much honour as we can. And therefore the heathens did absurdly, to worship images for gods; but their doing it in verse, and with music, both of voice and instruments, was reasonable. Also that the beasts they offered in sacrifice, and the gifts they offered, and their actions in worshipping, were full of submission, and commemorative of benefits received, was according to reason, as proceeding from an intention to honour him.

Seventhly, reason directeth not only to worship God in secret; but also, and especially, in public, and in the sight of men. For without that, that which in honour is most acceptable, the procuring others to honour him, is lost.

Lastly, obedience to his laws, that is, in this case to the laws of nature, is the greatest worship of all. For as obedience is more acceptable to God than sacrifice; so also to set light by his commandments, is the greatest of all contumelies. And these are the laws of that divine worship, which natural reason dictateth to private men.

But seeing a commonwealth is but one person, it ought also to exhibit to God but one worship; which then it doth, when it commandeth it to be exhibited by private men, publicly. And this is public worship; the property whereof, is to be *uniform*: for those actions that are done differently, by different men, cannot be said to be a public worship. And therefore, where many sorts of worship be allowed, proceeding from the different religions of private men, it cannot be said there is any public worship, nor that the commonwealth is of any religion at all.

And because words, and consequently the attributes of God, have their signification by agreement and constitution of men, those attributes are to be held significative of honour, that men intend shall so be; and whatsoever may be done by the wills of particular men, where there is no law but reason, may be done by the will of the commonwealth, by laws civil. And because a commonwealth hath no will, nor makes no laws, but those that are made by the will of him, or them that have the sovereign power; it followeth that those attributes which the sovereign ordaineth, in the worship of God, for signs of honour, ought to be taken and used for such, by private men in their public worship.

But because not all actions are signs by constitution, but some are naturally signs of honour, others of contumely; these latter, which are those that men are ashamed to do in the sight of them they reverence, cannot be made by human power a part of Divine worship; nor the former, such as are decent, modest, humble behaviour, ever be separated from it. But whereas there be an infinite number of actions and gestures of an indifferent nature; such of them as the commonwealth shall ordain to be publicly and universally in use, as signs of honour, and part of God's worship, are to be taken and used for such by the subjects. And that which is said in the Scripture, *It is better to obey God than man*, hath place in the kingdom of God by pact, and not by nature.

Having thus briefly spoken of the natural kingdom of God, and his natural laws, I will add only to this chapter a short declaration of his natural punishments. There is no action of man in this life, that is not the beginning of so long a chain of consequences, as no human providence is high enough, to give a man a prospect to the end. And in this chain, there are linked together both pleasing and unpleasing events; in such manner, as he that will do anything for his pleasure, must engage himself to suffer all the pains annexed to it; and these pains, are the natural punishments of those actions, which are the beginning of more harm than good. And hereby it comes to pass, that intemperance is naturally punished with diseases; rashness, with mischances; injustice, with the violence of enemies; pride, with ruin; cowardice, with oppression: negligent government of princes, with rebellion; and rebellion, with slaughter. For seeing punishments are consequent to the breach of laws; natural punishments must be naturally consequent to the breach of the laws of nature;

and therefore follow them as their natural, not arbitrary effects.

And thus far concerning the constitution, nature, and right of sovereigns, and concerning the duty of subjects, derived from the principles of natural reason. And now, considering how different this doctrine is, from the practice of the greatest part of the world, especially of these western parts, that have received their moral learning from Rome and Athens; and how much depth of moral philosophy is required, in them that have the administration of the sovereign power; I am at the point of believing this my labour, as useless, as the commonwealth of Plato. For he also is of opinion that it is impossible for the disorders of state, and change of governments by civil war, ever to be taken away, till sovereigns be philosophers. But when I consider again, that the science of natural justice, is the only science necessary for sovereigns and their principal ministers; and that they need not be charged with the sciences mathematical, as by Plato they are, farther than by good laws to encourage men to the study of them; and that neither Plato, nor any other philosopher hitherto, hath put into order, and sufficiently or probably proved all the theorems of moral doctrine, that men may learn thereby, both how to govern, and how to obey; I recover some hope, that one time or other, this writing of mine may fall into the hands of a sovereign, who will consider it himself, (for it is short, and I think clear,) without the help of any interested, or envious interpreter; and by the exercise of entire sovereignty, in protecting the public teaching of it, convert this truth of speculation, into the utility of practice.

Part Three

OF A
CHRISTIAN COMMONWEALTH

CHAPTER XXXII

Of the Principles of Christian Politics

I HAVE derived the rights of sovereign power, and the duty of subjects, hitherto from the principles of nature only: such as experience has found true, or consent concerning the use of words has made so; that is to say, from the nature of men, known to us by experience, and from definitions of such words as are essential to all political reasoning, universally agreed on. But in that I am next to handle, which is the nature and rights of a CHRISTIAN COMMONWEALTH, whereof there dependeth much upon supernatural revelations of the will of God; the ground of my discourse must be, not only the natural word of God, but also the prophetical.

Nevertheless, we are not to renounce our senses, and experience; nor, that which is the undoubted word of God, our natural reason. For they are the talents which he hath put into our hands to negotiate, till the coming again of our blessed Saviour; and therefore not to be folded up in the napkin of an implicit faith, but employed in the purchase of justice, peace, and true religion. For though there be many things in God's word above reason; that it is to say, which cannot by natural reason be either demonstrated, or confuted; yet there is nothing contrary to it; but when it seemeth so, the fault is either in our unskilful interpretation, or erroneous ratiocination.

Therefore, when anything therein written is too hard for our examination, we are bidden to captivate our understanding to the words; and not to labour in sifting out a philosophical truth by logic, of such mysteries as are not comprehensible, nor fall under any rule of natural science. For it is with the mysteries of our religion, as with wholesome pills for the sick; which swallowed whole, have the virtue to cure; but chewed, are for the most part cast up again without effect.

But by the captivity of our understanding, is not meant a submission of the intellectual faculty to the opinion of any other man; but of the will to obedience, where obedience is due. For sense, memory, understanding, reason, and opinion are not in our power to change; but always, and necessarily such, as the things we see, hear, and consider suggest unto us; and therefore are not effects of our will, but our will of them. We then captivate our understanding and reason, when we forbear contradiction; when we so speak, as by lawful authority we are commanded; and when we live accordingly; which, in sum, is trust and faith reposed in him that speaketh, though the mind be incapable of any notion at all from the words spoken.

When God speaketh to man, it must be either immediately; or by mediation of another man, to whom he had formerly spoken by himself immediately. How God speaketh to a man immediately, may be understood by those well enough, to whom he hath so spoken; but how the same should be understood by another, is hard, if not impossible to know. For if a man pretend to me, that God hath spoken to him supernaturally and immediately, and I make doubt of it, I cannot easily perceive what arguments he can produce, to oblige me to believe it. It is true, that if he be my sovereign, he may oblige me to obedience, so, as not by act or word to declare I believe him not; but not to think any otherwise than my reason persuades me. But if one that hath not such authority over me, should pretend the same, there is nothing that exacteth either belief, or obedience.

For to say that God hath spoken to him in the Holy Scripture, is not to say God hath spoken to him immediately, but by mediation of the prophets, or of the apostles, or of the church, in such manner as he speaks to all other Christian men. To say he hath spoken to him in a dream, is no more than to say he dreamed that God spake to him; which is not of force to win belief from any man, that knows dreams are for the most part natural, and may proceed from former thoughts; and such dreams as that, from self-conceit, and foolish arrogance, and false opinion of a man's own godliness, or other virtue by which he thinks he hath merited the favour of extraordinary revelation. To say he hath seen a vision, or heard a voice, is to say, that he hath dreamed between sleeping and waking: for in such manner a man doth many times naturally take his dream for a vision, as not having well observed his own slumbering. To say he speaks by supernatural inspiration, is to say he finds an ardent desire to speak, or some strong opinion of himself, for which he can allege no natural and sufficient reason. So that though God Almighty can speak to a man by dreams, visions, voice, and inspiration; yet he obliges no man to believe he hath so done to him that pretends it; who, being a man, may err, and, which is more, may lie.

How then can he, to whom God hath never revealed his will immediately, saving by the way of natural reason, know when he is to obey, or not to obey his word, delivered by him that says he is a prophet? Of four hundred prophets, of whom the king of Israel asked counsel, concerning the war he made against Ramoth Gilead, (1 *Kings* xxii) only Micaiah was a true one. The prophet that was sent to prophecy against the altar set up by Jeroboam, (1 *Kings* xiii) though a true prophet, and that by two miracles done in his presence, appears to be a prophet sent from God, was yet deceived by another old prophet, that persuaded him as from the mouth of God, to eat and drink with him. If one prophet deceive another, what certainty is there of knowing the will of God, by other way than that of reason? To which I answer out of the Holy Scripture, that there be two marks, by which together, not asunder, a true prophet is to be known. One is the doing of miracles; the other is the not teaching any other religion than that which is already established. Asunder, I say, neither of these is sufficient. *If a prophet rise amongst you, or a dreamer of dreams, and shall pretend the doing of a miracle, and the miracle come to pass; if he say, Let us follow strange Gods, which thou hast not known, thou shalt not hearken to him, &c. But that prophet and dreamer of dreams shall be put to death, because he hath spoken to you to revolt from the Lord your God.* (*Deut.* xiii, 1–5.) In which words two things are to be observed; first, that God will not have miracles alone serve for arguments, to approve the prophet's calling; but, as it is in the third verse, for an experiment of the constancy of our adherence to himself. For the works of the Egyptian sorcerers, though not so great as those of Moses, yet were great miracles. Secondly, that how great soever the miracle be, yet if it tend to stir up revolt against the king, or him that governeth by the king's authority, he that doth such miracle, is not to be considered otherwise than as sent to make trial of their allegiance. For these words, *revolt from the Lord your God*, are in this place equivalent to *revolt from your king*. For they had made God their king by pact at the foot of Mount Sinai; who rules them by Moses only; for he only spake with God, and from time to time declared God's commandments to the people. In like manner, after our Saviour Christ had made his disciples acknowledge him for the Messiah, (that is to say, for God's anointed, whom the nation of the Jews daily expected for their king, but refused when he came,) he omitted not to advertise them of the danger of miracles. *There shall arise,* saith he, *false Christs, and false prophets, and shall do great wonders and miracles, even to the seducing, if it were possible, of the very elect.* (*Matt.* xxiv, 24.) By which it appears, that false prophets may have the power of miracles; yet are we not to take their doctrine for God's word. St. Paul says farther to the Galatians, (*Gal.* i, 8) *that if himself, or an angel from heaven preach another gospel to them, than he had preached, let him be accursed.* That gospel was, that Christ was King; so that all preaching against the power of the king received, in consequence to these words, is by St. Paul accursed. For his speech is addressed to those, who by his preaching had already received Jesus for the Christ, that is to say, for King of the Jews.

And as miracles, without preaching that doctrine which God hath established; so preaching the true doctrine, without the doing of miracles, is an insufficient argument of immediate revelation. For if a man that teacheth not false doctrine, should pretend to be a prophet without showing any miracle, he is never the more to be regarded for his pretence, as is evident by *Deut.* xviii, v. 21, 22, *If thou say in thy heart, How shall we know that the word* (of the prophet) *is not that which the Lord hath spoken? when the prophet shall have spoken in the name of the Lord, that which shall not come to pass, that is the word which the Lord hath not spoken, but the prophet has spoken it out of the pride of his own heart, fear him not.* But a man may here again ask, when the prophet hath foretold a thing, how shall we know whether it will come to pass or not? For he may foretell it as a thing to arrive after a certain long time, longer than the time of man's life; or indefinitely, that it will come to pass one time or other: in which case this mark of a prophet is unuseful; and therefore the miracles that oblige us to believe a prophet, ought to be confirmed by an immediate, or a not long deferred event. So that it is manifest, that the teaching of the religion which God hath established, and the showing of a present miracle, joined together, were the only marks whereby the Scripture would have a true prophet, that is to say, immediate revelation, to be acknowledged; neither of them being singly sufficient to oblige any other man to regard what he saith.

Seeing therefore miracles now cease, we have no sign left, whereby to acknowledge the pretended revelations or inspirations of any private man; nor obligation to give ear to any doctrine, farther than it is conformable to the Holy Scriptures, which since the time of our Saviour, supply the place, and sufficiently recompense the want of all other prophecy; and from which, by wise and learned interpretation, and careful ratiocination, all rules and precepts necessary to the knowledge of our duty both to God and man, without enthusiasm or supernatural inspiration, may easily be deduced. And this Scripture is it, out of which I am to take the principles of my discourse, concerning the rights of those that are the supreme governors on earth of Christian commonwealths and of the duty of Christian subjects towards their sovereigns. And to that end, I shall speak in the next chapter, of the books, writers, scope and authority of the Bible.

CHAPTER XXXIII

Of the Number, Antiquity, Scope, Authority and Interpreters of the Books of Holy Scripture

BY the Books of HOLY SCRIPTURE, are understood those, which ought to be the *canon*, that is to say, the rules of Christian life.

And because all rules of life, which men are in conscience bound to observe, are laws; the question of the Scripture, is the question of what is law throughout all Christendom, both natural and civil. For though it be not determined in Scripture, what laws every Christian king shall constitute in his own dominions; yet it is determined what laws he shall not constitute. Seeing therefore I have already proved, that sovereigns in their own dominions are the sole legislators; those books only are canonical, that is, law, in every nation, which are established for such by the sovereign authority. It is true, that God is the sovereign of all sovereigns; and therefore, when he speaks to any subject, he ought to be obeyed, whatsoever any earthly potentate command to the contrary. But the question is not of obedience to God, but of *when* and *what* God hath said; which to subjects that have no supernatural revelation, cannot be known, but by that natural reason, which guideth them, for the obtaining of peace and justice, to obey the authority of their several commonwealths, that is to say, of their lawful sovereigns. According to this obligation, I can acknowledge no other books of the Old Testament, to be Holy Scripture, but those which have been commanded to be acknowledged for such, by the authority of the Church of England.

It is a question much disputed between the divers sects of Christian religion, *from whence the Scriptures derive their authority*; which question is also propounded sometimes in other terms, as, *how we know them to be the word of God*, or, *why we believe them to be so*: and the difficulty of resolving it, ariseth chiefly from the improperness of the words wherein the question itself is couched. For it is believed on all hands, that the first and original *author* of them is God; and consequently the question disputed, is not that. Again, it is manifest, that none can know they are God's word, (though all true Christians believe it,) but those to whom God himself hath revealed it supernaturally; and therefore the question is not rightly moved, of our *knowledge* of it. Lastly, when the question is propounded of our *belief*; because some are moved to believe for one, and others for other reasons; there can be rendered no one general answer for them all. The question truly stated is, *by what authority they are made law*.

As far as they differ not from the laws of nature, there is no doubt, but they are the law of God, and carry their authority with them, legible to all men that have the use of natural reason: but this is no other authority, than that of all other moral doctrine consonant to reason; the dictates whereof are laws, not *made*, but *eternal*.

If they be made law by God himself, they are of the nature of written law, which are laws to them only to whom God hath so sufficiently published them, as no man can excuse himself, by saying, he knew not they were his.

He therefore to whom God hath not supernaturally revealed that they are his, nor that those that published them, were sent by him, is not obliged to obey them, by any authority, but his, whose commands have already the force of laws; that is to say, by any other authority, than that of the commonwealth, residing in the sovereign, who only has the legislative power. Again, if it be not the legislative authority of the commonwealth, that giveth them the force of laws, it must be some other authority derived from God, either private, or public: if private, it obliges only him, to whom in particular God hath been pleased to reveal it. For if every man should be obliged, to take for God's law, what particular men, on pretence of private inspiration, or revelation, should obtrude upon him, in such a number of men, that out of pride and ignorance, take their own dreams, and extravagant fancies, and madness, for testimonies of God's spirit; or out of ambition, pretend to such divine testimonies, falsely, and contrary to their own consciences, it were impossible that any divine law should be acknowledged. If public, it is the authority of the *commonwealth*, or of the *church*. But the church, if it be one person, is the same thing with a commonwealth of Christians; called a *commonwealth*, because it consisteth of men united in one person, their sovereign; and a *church*, because it consisteth in Christian men, united in one Christian sovereign. But if the church be not one person, then it hath no authority at all: it can neither command, nor do any action at all; nor is capable of having any power, or right to anything: nor has any will, reason nor voice; for all these qualities are personal. Now if the whole number of Christians be not contained in one commonwealth, they are not one person; nor is there any universal church that hath any authority over them; and therefore the Scriptures are not made laws, by the universal church: or if it be one commonwealth, then all Christian monarchs and states are private persons, and subject to be judged, deposed, and punished by an universal sovereign of all Christendom. So that the question of the authority of the Scriptures, is reduced to this, *whether Christian kings, and the sovereign assemblies in Christian commonwealths, be absolute in their own territories, immediately under God; or subject to one vicar of Christ, constituted of the universal church; to be judged, condemned, deposed, and put to death, as he shall think expedient, or necessary for the common good.*

Which question cannot be resolved, without a more particular consideration of the Kingdom of God; from whence also, we are to judge of the authority of interpreting the Scripture. For, whosoever hath a lawful power over any writing, to make it law, hath the power also to approve, or disapprove the interpretation of the same.

CHAPTER XXXIX

Of the Signification in Scripture of the Word Church

THE word Church, (*Ecclesia*) signifieth in the books of Holy Scripture divers things. Sometimes, though not often, it is taken for *God's house*, that is to say, for a temple, wherein Christians assembled to perform holy duties, publicly, as (1 *Cor.* xiv, 34) *Let your women keep silence in the Churches*: but this is metaphorically put for the congregation there assembled; and hath been since used for the edifice itself, to distinguish between the temples of Christians and idolaters. The Temple of Jerusalem was *God's house*, and the house of prayer; and so is any edifice dedicated by Christians to the worship of Christ, *Christ's house*: and therefore the Greek fathers call it Κυριακὴ, the *Lord's house*: and thence in our language it came to be called *kyrke*, and *church*.

Church, when not taken for a house, signifieth the same that *ecclesia* signified in the Grecian commonwealth, that is to say, a congregation, or an assembly of citizens, called forth to hear the magistrate speak unto them; and which in the commonwealth of Rome was called *concio*: as he that spake was called *ecclesiastes*, and *concionator*. And when they were called forth by lawful authority, (*Acts* xix, 39) it was *Ecclesia legitima*, a *lawful Church*, ἔννομος ἐκκλησία. But when they were excited by tumultuous and seditious clamour, then it was a confused Church, ἐκκλησία συγκεχυμένη.

It is taken also sometimes for the men that have right to be of the congregation, though not actually assembled, that is to say, for the whole multitude of Christian men, how far soever they be dispersed: as (*Acts* viii, 3) where it is said, that *Saul made havoc of the Church*: and in this sense is Christ said to be the head of the Church. And sometimes for a certain part of Christians, as (*Col.* iv, 15) *Salute the Church that is in his house*. Sometimes also for the elect only; as (*Eph.* v, 27) *A glorious Church, without spot, or wrinkle, holy, and without blemish; which* is meant of the *Church triumphant*, or *Church to come*. Sometimes, for a congregation assembled of professors of Christianity, whether their profession be true or counterfeit; as it is understood, (*Matth.* xviii, 17) where it is said, *Tell it to the Church; and if he neglect to hear the Church, let him be to thee as a Gentile, or publican*.

And in this last sense only it is that the *Church* can be taken for one person; that is to say, that it can be said to have power to will, to pronounce, to command, to be obeyed, to make laws, or to do any other action whatsoever. For without authority from a lawful congregation, whatsoever act be done in a concourse of people, it is the particular act of every one of those that were present, and gave their aid to the performance of it; and not the act of them all in gross, as of one body; much less the act of them that were absent, or that being present, were not willing it should be done. According to this sense, I define a CHURCH to be, *a company of men professing Christian religion, united in the person of one sovereign, at whose command they ought to assemble, and without whose authority they ought not to assemble.* And because in all commonwealths, that assembly, which is without warrant from the civil sovereign, is unlawful; that Church also, which is assembled in any commonwealth that hath forbidden them to assemble, is an unlawful assembly.

It followeth also, that there is on earth, no such universal Church, as all Christians are bound to obey; because there is no power on earth, to which all other commonwealths are subject. There are Christians, in the dominions of several princes and states; but every one of them is subject to that commonwealth, whereof he is himself a member; and consequently, cannot be subject to the commands of any other person. And therefore a Church, such a one as is capable to command, to judge, absolve, condemn, or do any other act, is the same thing with a civil commonwealth, consisting of Christian men; and is called a *civil state*, for that the subjects of it are *men*: and a *Church*, for that the subjects thereof are *Christians. Temporal* and *spiritual* government, are but two words brought into the world, to make men see double, and mistake their *lawful sovereign*. It is true, that the bodies of the faithful, after the resurrection, shall be not only spiritual, but eternal; but in this life they are gross, and corruptible. There is therefore no other government in this life, neither of state, nor religion, but temporal; nor teaching of any doctrine, lawful to any subject, which the governor both of the state, and of the religion forbiddeth to be taught. And that governor must be one; or else there must needs follow faction and civil war in the commonwealth, between the *Church* and *State*; between *spiritualists* and *temporalists*; between the *sword of justice*, and the *shield of faith*: and, which is more, in every Christian man's own breast, between the *Christian*, and the *man*. The doctors of the Church, are called pastors; so also are civil sovereigns. But if pastors be not subordinate one to another, so as that there may be one chief pastor, men will be taught contrary doctrines; whereof both may be, and one must be false. Who that one chief pastor is, according to the law of nature, hath been already shown; namely, that it is the civil sovereign: and to whom the Scripture hath assigned that office, we shall see in the chapters following.

CHAPTER XL

Of the Rights of the Kingdom of God, in Abraham, Moses, the High-Priests, and the Kings of Judah

THE father of the faithful, and first in the kingdom of God by covenant, was Abraham. For with him was the covenant first made; wherein he obliged himself, and his seed after him, to acknowledge and obey the commands of God; not only such, as he could take notice of, (as moral laws,) by the light of nature; but also such, as God should in special manner deliver to him by dreams and visions. For as to the moral law, they were already obliged, and needed not have been contracted withal, by promise of the land of Canaan. Nor was there any contract, that could add to, or strengthen the obligation, by which both they, and all men else were bound naturally to obey God Almighty: and therefore the covenant which Abraham made with God, was to take for the commandment of God, that which in the name of God was commanded him in a dream, or vision; and to deliver it to his family, and cause them to observe the same.

In this contract of God with Abraham, we may observe three points of important consequence in the government of God's people. First, that at the making of this covenant, God spake only to Abraham; and therefore contracted not with any of his family, or seed, otherwise than as their wills, which make the essence of all covenants, were before the contract involved in the will of Abraham; who was therefore supposed to have had a lawful power, to make them perform all that he covenanted for them. According whereunto (*Gen.* xviii, 18, 19) God saith, *All the nations of the earth shall be blessed in him; for I know him that he will command his children and his household after him, and they shall keep the way of the Lord.* From whence may be concluded this first point, that they to whom God hath not spoken immediately, are to receive the positive commandments of God, from their sovereign; as the family and seed of Abraham did from Abraham their father, and Lord, and civil sovereign. And consequently in every commonwealth, they who have no supernatural revelation to the contrary, ought to obey the laws of their own sovereign, in the external acts and profession of religion. As for the inward *thought*, and *belief* of men, which human governors can take no notice of, (for God only knoweth the heart), they are not voluntary, nor the effects of the laws, but of the unrevealed will and of the power of God; and consequently fall not under obligation.

From whence proceedeth another point, that it was not unlawful for Abraham, when any of his subjects should pretend private vision or spirit, or other revelation from God, for the countenancing of any doctrine which Abraham should forbid, or when they followed or adhered to any such pretender, to punish them; and consequently that it is lawful now for the sovereign to punish any man that shall oppose his private spirit against the laws: for he hath the same place in the commonwealth, that Abraham had in his own family.

There ariseth also from the same, a third point; that as none but Abraham in his family, so none but the sovereign in a Christian commonwealth, can take notice what is, or what is not the word of God. For God spake only to Abraham; and it was he only, that was able to know what God said, and to interpret the same to his family: and therefore also, they that have the place of Abraham in a commonwealth, are the only interpreters of what God hath spoken.

The same covenant was renewed with Isaac; and afterwards with Jacob; but afterwards no more, till the Israelites were freed from the Egyptians, and arrived at the foot of Mount

Sinai: and then it was renewed by Moses, (as I have said before, chapter xxxv) in such manner, as they became from that time forward the peculiar kingdom of God; whose lieutenant was Moses, for his own time: and the succession to that office was settled upon Aaron, and his heirs after him, to be to God a sacerdotal kingdom for ever.

By this constitution, a kingdom is acquired to God. But seeing Moses had no authority to govern the Israelites, as a successor to the right of Abraham, because he could not claim it by inheritance; it appeareth not as yet, that the people were obliged to take him for God's lieutenant, longer than they believed that God spake unto him. And therefore his authority, notwithstanding the covenant they made with God, depended yet merely upon the opinion they had of his sanctity, and of the reality of his conferences with God, and the verity of his miracles; which opinion coming to change, they were no more obliged to take anything for the law of God, which he propounded to them in God's name. We are therefore to consider, what other ground there was, of their obligation to obey him. For it could not be the commandment of God that could oblige them; because God spake not to them immediately, but by the mediation of Moses himself: and our Saviour saith of himself, (*John* v, 31) *If I bear witness of myself, my witness is not true*; much less if Moses bear witness of himself, especially in a claim of kingly power over God's people, ought his testimony to be received. His authority therefore, as the authority of all other princes, must be grounded on the consent of the people, and their promise to obey him. And so it was: for *the people* (*Exod.* xx, 18, 19) *when they saw the thunderings, and the lightenings, and the noise of the trumpets, and the mountain smoking, removed, and stood afar off. And they said unto Moses, speak thou with us, and we will hear, but let not God speak with us lest we die.* Here was their promise of obedience; and by this it was they obliged themselves to obey whatsoever he should deliver unto them for the commandment of God.

CHAPTER XLI

Of the Office of Our Blessed Saviour

WE find in Holy Scripture three parts of the office of the Messiah: the first of a *Redeemer* or *Saviour*; the second of a *pastor, counsellor,* or *teacher,* that is, of a prophet sent from God to convert such as God hath elected to salvation: the third of a *king,* an *eternal king,* but under his Father, as Moses and the high-priests were in their several times. And to these three parts are correspondent three times. For our redemption he wrought at his first coming, by the sacrifice wherein he offered up himself for our sins upon the cross: our conversion he wrought partly then in his own person, and partly worketh now by his ministers, and will continue to work till his coming again. And after his coming again, shall begin that his glorious reign over his elect, which is to last eternally.

To the office of a Redeemer, that is, of one that payeth the ransom of sin, which ransom is death, it appertaineth, that he was sacrificed, and thereby bare upon his own head and carried away from us our iniquities, in such sort as God had required. Not that the death of one man, though without sin, can satisfy for the offences of all men, in the rigour of justice, but in the mercy of God, that ordained such sacrifices for sin, as he was pleased in his mercy to accept. In the old law (as we may read, *Levit.* xvi) the Lord required that there should, every year once, be made an atonement for the sins of all Israel, both priests and others; for the doing whereof, Aaron alone was to sacrifice for himself and the priests a young bullock; and for the rest of the people, he was to receive from them two young goats, of which he was to *sacrifice* one; but as for the other, which was the *scape-goat,* he was to lay his hands on the head thereof, and by a confession of the iniquities of the people, to lay them all on that head, and then by some opportune man, to cause the goat to be led into the wilderness, and there to *escape,* and carry away with him the iniquities of the people. As the sacrifice of the one goat was a sufficient, because an acceptable, price for the ransom of all Israel; so the death of the Messiah, is a sufficient price for the sins of all mankind, because there was no more required. Our Saviour Christ's sufferings seem to be here figured, as clearly as in the oblation of Isaac, or in any other type of him in the Old Testament. He was both the sacrificed goat, and the scape-goat; *he was oppressed, and he was afflicted* (*Isaiah* liii, 7); *he opened not his mouth: he is brought as a lamb to the slaughter, and as a sheep is dumb before the shearer, so he opened not his mouth*: here he is the *sacrificed goat*. *He hath borne our griefs* (verse 4), *and carried our sorrows*: and again, (verse 6), *the Lord hath laid upon him the iniquities of us all*: and so he is the *scape-goat*. *He was cut off from the land of the living* (ver. 8) *for the transgression of my people:* there again he is the *sacrificed goat*. And again, (verse 11) *he shall bear their sins*: he is the *scape goat*. Thus is the lamb of God equivalent to both those goats; sacrified, in that he died; and escaping, in his resurrection; being raised opportunely by his Father, and removed from the habitation of men in his ascension.

For as much therefore, as he that *redeemeth* hath no title to the *thing redeemed*, before *the redemption*, and ransom paid; and this ransom was the death of the Redeemer; it is manifest, that our Saviour, as man, was not king of those that he redeemed, before he suffered death; that is, during that time he conversed bodily on the earth. I say, he was not then king in present, by virtue of the pact, which the faithful make with him in baptism. Nevertheless, by the renewing of their pact with God in baptism, they were obliged to obey him for king, under his Father, whensoever he should be pleased to take the kingdom upon him. According whereunto, our Saviour himself expressly saith, (*John* xviii, 36) *My kingdom is not of this world*. Now seeing the Scripture maketh mention but of two worlds; this that is now, and shall remain unto the day of judgment, which is therefore also called the *last day*; and that which shall be after the day of judgment, when there shall be a new heaven, and a new earth: the kingdom of Christ is not to begin till the general resurrection. And that is it which our Saviour saith, (*Matth.* xvi, 27) *The Son of man shall come in the glory of his Father, with his angels; and then he shall reward every man according to his works.* To reward every man according to his works, is to execute the office of a king; and this is not to be till he come in the glory of his Father, with his angels. When our Saviour saith, (*Matth.* xxiii, 2, 3) *The Scribes and Pharisees sit in Moses' seat; all therefore whatsoever they bid you do, that observe and do;* he declared plainly, that he ascribed kingly power, for that time, not to himself, but to them. And so he doth also, where he saith (*Luke* xii, 14) *Who made me a judge or divider over you?* And (*John* xii, 47) *I came not to judge the world, but to save the world.* And yet our Saviour came into this world that he might be a king and a judge in the world to come: for he was the Messiah, that is, the Christ, that is, the anointed priest, and the sovereign prophet of God; that is to say, he was to have all the power that was in Moses the prophet, in the high-priests that succeeded Moses, and in the kings that succeeded the priests. And St. John says expressly (chapter v, verse 22) *the Father judgeth no man, but hath committed all judgment to the Son.* And this is not repugnant to that other place, *I came not to judge the world*: for this is spoken of the world present, the other of the world to come; as also where it is said, that at the second coming of Christ, (*Matth.* xix, 28) *Ye that have followed me in the regeneration, when the Son of Man shall sit in the throne of his glory, ye shall also sit on twelve thrones, judging the twelve tribes of Israel.*

If then Christ, whilst he was on earth, had no kingdom in this world, to what end was his first coming? It was to restore unto God, by a new covenant, the kingdom, which being his by the old covenant, had been cut off by the rebellion of the Israelites in the election of Saul. Which to do, he was to preach unto them, that he was the *Messiah*, that is, the king promised to them by the prophets; and to offer himself in sacrifice for the sins of them that should by faith submit themselves thereto; and in case the nation generally should refuse him, to call to his obedience such as should believe in him amongst the Gentiles. So that there are two parts of our Saviour's office during his abode upon the earth: one to proclaim himself the Christ; and another by teaching, and by working of miracles, to persuade and prepare men to live so, as to be worthy of the immortality believers were to enjoy, at such time as he should come in majesty to take possession of his Father's kingdom. And therefore it is, that the time of his preaching is often by himself called the *regeneration*; which is not properly a kingdom, and thereby a warrant to deny obedience to the magistrates that then were; for he commanded to obey those that sat then in Moses' chair, and to pay tribute to Caesar; but only an earnest of the kingdom of God that was to come, to those to whom God had given the grace to be his disciples, and to believe in him; for which cause the godly are said to be already in the *kingdom of grace*, as naturalized in that heavenly kingdom.

Hitherto, therefore, there is nothing done or taught by Christ, that tendeth to the diminution of the civil right of the Jews or of Caesar. For as touching the commonwealth which then was amongst the Jews, both they that bare rule amongst them, and they that were governed, did all expect the Messiah and kingdom of God; which they could not have done, if their laws had forbidden him, when he came, to manifest and declare himself. Seeing therefore he did nothing, but by preaching and miracles go about to prove himself to be that Messiah, he did therein nothing against their laws. The kingdom he claimed was to be in another world: he taught all men to obey in the meantime them that sat in Moses' seat: he allowed them to give Caesar his tribute, and refused to take upon himself to be a judge. How then could his words or actions be seditious, or tend to the overthrow of their then civil government? But God having determined his sacrifice for the reduction of his elect to their former covenanted obedience, for the means, whereby he would bring the same to effect, made use of their malice and ingratitude. Nor was it contrary to the laws of Caesar. For though Pilate himself, to gratify the Jews, delivered him to be crucified; yet before he did so, he pronounced openly, that he found no fault in him: and put for title of his condemnation, not as the Jews required, *that he pretended to be king*; but simply, *that he was king of the Jews*; and notwithstanding their clamour, refused to alter it; saying, *What I have written, I have written.*

As for the third part of his office, which was to be *king*,

I have already shown that his kingdom was not to begin till the resurrection. But then he shall be king, not only as God, in which sense he is king already, and ever shall be, of all the earth, in virtue of his omnipotence; but also peculiarly of his own elect, by virtue of the pact they make with him in their baptism.

CHAPTER XLII

Of Power Ecclesiastical

For the understanding of POWER ECCLESIASTICAL, what, and in whom it is, we are to distinguish the time from the ascension of our Saviour, into two parts; one before the conversion of kings, and men endued with sovereign civil power; the other after their conversion. For it was long after the ascension, before any king or civil sovereign embraced and publicly allowed the teaching of Christian religion.

And for the time between, it is manifest, that the *power ecclesiastical* was in the apostles; and after them in such as were by them ordained to preach the gospel, and to convert men to Christianity, and to direct them that were converted in the way of salvation; and after these, the power was delivered again to others by these ordained, and this was done by imposition of hands upon such as were ordained; by which was signified the giving of the Holy Spirit, or Spirit of God, to those whom they ordained ministers of God, to advance his kingdom. So that imposition of hands was nothing else but the seal of their commission to preach Christ, and teach his doctrine; and the giving of the Holy Ghost by that ceremony of imposition of hands, was an imitation of that which Moses did. For Moses used the same ceremony to his minister Joshua, as we read (*Deut.* xxxiv, 9) *And Joshua the son of Nun was full of the spirit of wisdom; for Moses had laid his hands upon him.* Our Saviour therefore, between his resurrection and ascension, gave his spirit to the apostles; first, by *breathing on them, and saying,* (*John* xx, 22) *Receive ye the Holy*

Spirit; and after his ascension (*Acts* ii, 2, 3) by sending down upon them *a mighty wind, and cloven tongues of fire*; and not by imposition of hands; as neither did God lay his hands on Moses: and his apostles afterward transmitted the same spirit by imposition of hands, as Moses did to Joshua. So that it is manifest hereby, in whom the power ecclesiastical continually remained, in those first times where there was not any Christian commonwealth; namely, in them that received the same from the apostles, by successive laying on of hands.

Here we have the person of God born now the third time. For as Moses, and the high-priests, were God's representative in the Old Testament; and our Saviour himself, as man, during his abode on earth: so the Holy Ghost, that is to say the apostles and their successors, in the office of preaching and teaching, that had received the holy Spirit, have represented him ever since. But a person, as I have shown before, (chapter XIII) is he that is represented, as often as he is represented; and therefore God, who has been represented, that is personated, thrice, may properly enough be said to be three persons; though neither the word *Person*, nor *Trinity*, be ascribed to him in the Bible. *St. John*, indeed (1 *Epist.* v, 7) saith, *There be three that bear witness in heaven, the Father, the Word, and the Holy Spirit; and these three are One*. But this disagreeth not, but accordeth fitly with three persons in the proper signification of persons; which is, that which is represented by another. For so God the Father, as represented by Moses, is one person; and as represented by his Son, another person; and as represented by the apostles, and by the doctors that taught by authority from them derived, is a third person; and yet every person here, is the person of one and the same God. But a man may here ask, what it was whereof these three bear witness. *St. John* therefore tells us (verse 11) that they bear witness, that *God hath given us eternal life in his Son*. Again, if it should be asked, wherein that testimony appeareth, the answer is easy; for he hath testified the same by the miracles he wrought, first by Moses; secondly, by his Son himself; and lastly by his apostles, that had received the Holy Spirit; all which in their times represented the person of God, and either prophecied or preached Jesus Christ. And as for the apostles, it was the character of the apostleship, in the twelve first and great apostles, to bear witness of his resurrection; as appeareth expressly (*Acts* i, 21, 22), where St. Peter, when a new apostle was to be chosen in the place of Judas Iscariot, useth these words, *Of these men which have companied with us all the time that the Lord Jesus went in and out amongst us, beginning at the baptism of John, unto that same day that he was taken up from us, must one be ordained to be a witness with us of his resurrection*: which words interpret the *bearing of witness*, mentioned by St. John. There is in the same place mentioned another Trinity of witnesses in earth. For (1 *John* v, 8) he saith, *there are three that bear witness in earth, the Spirit, and the water, and the blood, and these three agree in one*: that is to say, the graces of God's spirit, and the two sacraments, baptism, and the Lord's supper, which all agree in one testimony to assure the consciences of believers, of eternal life; of which testimony he saith (verse 10) *He that believeth on the Son of man hath the witness in himself*. In this Trinity on earth, the unity is not of the thing; for the spirit, the water, and the blood, are not the same substance, though they give the same testimony: but in the Trinity of heaven, the persons are the persons of one and the same God, though represented in three different times and occasions. To conclude, the doctrine of the Trinity, as far as can be gathered directly from the Scripture, is in substance this, that the God who is always one and the same, was the person represented by Moses; the person represented by his Son incarnate; and the person represented by the apostles. As represented by the apostles, the Holy Spirit, by which they spake, is God; as represented by his Son, that was God and man, the Son is that God; as represented by Moses and the high-priests, the Father, that is to say, the Father of our Lord Jesus Christ, is that God. From whence we may gather the reason why those names, *Father, Son*, and *Holy Spirit*, in the signification of the Godhead, are never used in the Old Testament: for they are persons, that is, they have their names from representing; which could not be, till divers men had represented God's person in ruling or in directing under him.

Thus we see how the power ecclesiastical was left by our Saviour to the apostles; and how they were, to the end they might the better exercise that power, endued with the Holy Spirit, which is therefore called sometimes in the New Testament *paracletus*, which signifieth an *assister*, or one called to for help, though it be commonly translated a *comforter*. Let us now consider the power itself, what it was, and over whom.

Cardinal Bellarmine, in his third general controversy, hath handled a great many questions concerning the ecclesiastical power of the pope of Rome; and begins with this, whether it ought to be monarchical, aristocratical, or democratical: all which sorts of power are sovereign and coercive. If now it should appear, that there is no coercive power left them by our Saviour, but only a power to proclaim the kingdom of Christ, and to persuade men to submit themselves thereunto; and by precepts and good counsel, to teach them that have submitted, what they are to do, that they may be received into the kingdom of God when it comes; and that the apostles, and other ministers of the Gospel, are our schoolmasters, and not our commanders, and their precepts not laws, but wholesome counsels: then were all that dispute in vain.

I have shown already, in the last chapter, that the kingdom of Christ is not of this world: therefore neither can his ministers, unless they be kings, require obedience in his name. For if the supreme king have not his regal power in this world; by what authority can obedience be required to his officers? *As my Father sent me,* so saith our Saviour, (*John* xx, 21) *I send you.* But our Saviour was sent to persuade the Jews to return to, and to invite the Gentiles to receive, the kingdom of his Father, and not to reign in majesty, no not as his Father's lieutenant, till the day of judgment.

The time between the ascension and the general resurrection, is called, not a reigning, but a regeneration; that is, a preparation of men for the second and glorious coming of Christ, at the day of judgment; as appeareth by the words of our Saviour, (*Matth.* xix, 28,) *You that have followed me in the regeneration, when the Son of Man shall sit in the throne of his glory, you shall also sit upon twelve thrones*; and of St. Paul (*Ephes.* vi, 15) *Having your feet shod with the preparation of the gospel of peace.*

And is compared by our Saviour, to fishing, that is, to winning men to obedience, not by coercion and punishing, but by persuasion: and therefore he said not to his apostles, he would make them so many Nimrods, *hunters of men; but fishers of men*. It is compared also to leaven, to sowing of seed, and to the multiplication of a grain of mustard-seed; by all which compulsion is excluded; and consequently there can in that time be no actual reigning. The work of Christ's ministers, is evangelization; that is, a proclamation of Christ, and a preparation for his second coming, as the evangelization of John the Baptist was a preparation to his first coming.

Again, the office of Christ's ministers in this world, is to make men believe and have faith in Christ; but faith hath no relation to, nor dependance at all upon compulsion or commandment; but only upon certainty or probability of arguments drawn from reason, or from something men believe already. Therefore the ministers of Christ in this world, have no power, by that title, to punish any man for not believing or for contradicting what they say; they have I say no power by that title of Christ's ministers, to punish such; but if they have sovereign civil power, by politic institution, then they may indeed lawfully punish any contradiction to their laws whatsoever: and St. Paul, of himself and other the then preachers of the gospel, saith in express words (2 *Cor.* i, 24), *We have no dominion over your faith, but are helpers of your joy.*

Another argument, that the ministers of Christ in this present world have no right of commanding, may be drawn from the lawful authority which Christ hath left to all princes, as well Christians as infidels. St. Paul saith (*Col.* iii, 20) *Children obey your parents in all things; for this is well pleasing to the Lord*: and (verse 22) *Servants, obey in all things your masters according to the flesh; not with eye-service, as men-pleasers, but in singleness of heart, as fearing the Lord*; this is spoken to them whose masters were infidels; and yet they are bidden to obey them *in all things*. And again, concerning obedience to princes (*Rom.* xiii, the first six verses), exhorting *to be subject to the higher powers*, he saith, *that all power is ordained of God*; and *that we ought to be subject to them, not only for fear of incurring their wrath, but also for conscience sake*. And *St. Peter* (1 Epistle ii,

13, 14, 15), *Submit yourselves to every ordinance of man, for the Lord's sake, whether it be to the king, as supreme; or unto governors, as to them that be sent by him for the punishment of evil doers, and for the praise of them that do well; for so is the will of God.* And again St. Paul (*Titus* iii, 1), *Put men in mind to be subject to principalities and powers, and to obey magistrates.* These princes and powers, whereof St. Peter and St. Paul here speak, were all infidels: much more therefore we are to observe those Christians, whom God hath ordained to have sovereign power over us. How then can we be obliged to obey any minister of Christ, if he should command us to do anything contrary to the command of the king, or other sovereign representant of the commonwealth whereof we are members, and by whom we look to be protected? It is therefore manifest, that Christ hath not left to his ministers in this world, unless they be also endued with civil authority, any authority to command other men.

But what, may some object, if a king, or a senate, or other sovereign person forbid us to believe in Christ? To this I answer, that such forbidding is of no effect; because belief and unbelief never follow men's commands. Faith is a gift of God, which man can neither give, nor take away by promise of rewards, or menaces of torture. And if it be further asked, what if we be commanded by our lawful prince to say with our tongue, we believe not; must we obey such command? Profession with the tongue is but an external thing, and no more than any other gesture whereby we signify our obedience; and wherein a Christian, holding firmly in his heart the faith of Christ, hath the same liberty which the prophet Elisha allowed to Naaman the Syrian. Naaman was converted in his heart to the God of Israel; for he saith (2 *Kings* v, 17, 18) *Thy servant will henceforth offer neither burnt offering nor sacrifice unto other gods, but unto the Lord. In this thing the Lord pardon thy servant, that when my master goeth into the house of Rimmon to worship there, and he leaneth on my hand, and I bow myself in the house of Rimmon: when I bow down myself in the house of Rimmon, the Lord pardon thy servant in this thing.* This the prophet approved, and bid him *Go in peace.* Here Naaman believed in his heart; but by bowing before the idol Rimmon, he denied the true God in effect, as much as if he had done it with his lips. But then what shall we answer to our Saviour's saying, (*Matth.* **x**, 33) *Whosoever denieth me before men, I will deny him before my Father which is in heaven*. This we may say, that whatsoever a subject, as Naaman was, is compelled to do in obedience to his sovereign, and doth it not in order to his own mind, but in order to the laws of his country, that action is not his, but his sovereign's; nor is it he that in this case denieth Christ before men, but his governor, and the law of his country. If any man shall accuse this doctrine, as repugnant to true and unfeigned Christianity; I ask him, in case there should be a subject in any Christian commonwealth, that should be inwardly in his heart of the Mahomedan religion, whether if his sovereign command him to be present at the divine service of the Christian church, and that on pain of death, he think that Mahomedan obliged in conscience to suffer death for that cause, rather than obey that command of his lawful prince. If he say, he ought rather to suffer death, then he authorizeth all private men to disobey their princes in maintenance of their religion, true or false: if he say, he ought to be obedient, then he alloweth to himself that which he denieth to another, contrary to the words of our Saviour, (*Luke* vi, 31) *Whatsoever you would that men should do unto you, that do ye unto them*; and contrary to the law of nature, which is the indubitable everlasting law of God, *Do not to another, that which thou wouldest not he should do unto thee*.

But what then shall we say of all those martyrs we read of in the history of the Church, that they have needlessly cast away their lives? For answer hereunto, we are to distinguish the persons that have been for that cause put to death: whereof some have received a calling to preach, and profess the kingdom of Christ openly; others have had no such calling, nor more has been required of them than their own faith. The former sort, if they have been put to death, for bearing witness to this point, that Jesus Christ is risen from the dead, were true martyrs; for a *martyr* is, (to give the true definition of the word) a witness of the resurrection of Jesus the Messiah; which none can be but those that conversed with him on earth, and saw him after he was risen: for a witness must have seen what he testifieth, or else his testimony is not good. And that none but such can properly be called martyrs of Christ, is manifest out of the words of St. Peter, (*Acts* i, 21, 22) *Wherefore of these men which have companied with us all the time that the Lord Jesus went in and out amongst us, beginning from the baptism of John unto that same day he was taken up from us, must one be ordained to be a martyr* (that is a witness) *with us of his resurrection*: where we may observe, that he which is to be a witness of the truth of the resurrection of Christ, that is to say, of the truth of this fundamental article of Christian religion, that Jesus was the Christ, must be some disciple that conversed with him, and saw him before and after his resurrection; and consequently must be one of his original disciples: whereas they which were not so, can witness no more but that their antecessors said it, and are therefore but witnesses of other men's testimony; and are but second martyrs, or martyrs of Christ's witnesses.

He, that to maintain every doctrine which he himself draweth out of the history of our Saviours' life, and of the Acts or Epistles of the apostles, or which he believeth upon the authority of a private man, will oppose the laws and authority of the civil state, is very far from being a martyr of Christ, or a martyr of his martyrs. It is one article only, which to die for, meriteth so honourable a name; and that article is this, that *Jesus is the Christ*; that is to say, He that hath redeemed us, and shall come again to give us salvation, and eternal life in his glorious kingdom. To die for every tenet that serveth the ambition or profit of the clergy, is not required; nor is it the death of the witness, but the testimony itself that makes the martyr: for the word signifieth nothing else, but the man that beareth witness, whether he be put to death for his testimony, or not.

Also he that is not sent to preach this fundamental article, but taketh it upon him of his private authority, though he be a witness, and consequently a martyr, either primary of Christ, or secondary of his apostles, disciples, or their successors; yet is he not obliged to suffer death for that cause; because being not called thereto, it is not required at his hands; nor ought he to complain, if he loseth the reward he expecteth from those that never set him on work. None therefore can be a martyr, neither of the first nor second degree, that have not a warrant to preach Christ come in the flesh; that is to say, none, but such as are sent to the conversion of infidels. For no man is a witness to him that already believeth, and therefore needs no witness; but to them that deny, or doubt, or have not heard it. Christ sent his apostles, and his seventy disciples, with authority to preach; he sent not all that believed. And he sent them to unbelievers; *I send you*, saith he, (*Matth.* x, 16) *as sheep amongst wolves*; not as sheep to other sheep.

Lastly, the points of their commission, as they are expressly set down in the gospel, contain, none of them, any authority over the congregation.

We have first (*Matth.* x, 6, 7,) that the twelve apostles were sent *to the lost sheep of the house of Israel*, and commanded to preach *that the kingdom of God was at hand*. Now preaching, in the original, is that act, which a crier, herald, or other officer useth to do publicly in proclaiming of a king. But a crier hath not right to command any man. And (*Luke* x, 2) the seventy disciples are sent out as *Labourers, not as Lords of the harvest*: and are bidden (verse 9) to say, *The kingdom of God is come nigh unto you*; and by kingdom here is meant, not the kingdom of grace, but the kingdom of glory; for they are bidden (verse 11, 12) to denounce it to those cities which shall not receive them, as a threatening *that it shall be more tolerable in that day for Sodom, than for such a city*. And (*Matth.* xx, 28) our Saviour telleth his disciples, that sought priority of place, their office was to minister, *even as the son of man came, not to be ministered unto, but to minister*. Preachers therefore have not magisterial, but ministerial power: *Be not called masters*, saith our Saviour, (*Matth.* xxiii, 10) *for one is your master, even Christ*.

Another point of their commission, is, to *Teach all nations*; as it is in *St. Matth.* xxviii, 19, or as in *St. Mark* xvi, 15; *Go into all the world, and preach the gospel to every creature*. Teaching therefore, and preaching, is the same thing. For they that proclaim the coming of a king, must withal make known by what right he cometh, if they mean men shall submit themselves unto him: as St. Paul did to the Jews of Thessalonica, when (*Acts* xvii, 2, 3) *three Sabbath days he reasoned with them out of the Scriptures, opening, and alleging that Christ must needs have suffered, and risen again from the dead, and that this Jesus is Christ.* But to teach out of the Old Testament that Jesus was Christ, that is to say, king, and risen from the dead, is not to say that men are bound, after they believe it, to obey those that tell them so, against the laws and commands of their sovereigns; but that they shall do wisely, to expect the coming of Christ hereafter, in patience and faith, with obedience to their present magistrates.

Another point of their commission, is to *baptize, in the name of the Father, and of the Son, and of the Holy Ghost.* What is baptism? Dipping into water. But what is it to dip a man into the water in the name of anything? The meaning of these words of baptism is this. He that is baptized, is dipped or washed, as a sign of becoming a new man, and a loyal subject to that God, whose person was represented in old time by Moses, and the high-priests, when he reigned over the Jews; and to Jesus Christ his Son, God and Man, that hath redeemed us, and shall in his human nature represent his Father's person in his eternal kingdom after the resurrection; and to acknowledge the doctrine of the apostles, who, assisted by the spirit of the Father and of the Son, were left for guides to bring us into that kingdom, to be the only and assured way thereunto. This being our promise in baptism; and the authority of earthly sovereigns being not to be put down till the day of judgment; for that is expressly affirmed by St. Paul (1 *Cor.* xv, 22, 23, 24) where he saith, *As in Adam all die, so in Christ all shall be made alive. But every man in his own order, Christ the first fruits, afterward they that are Christ's at his coming; then cometh the end, when he shall have delivered up the kingdom to God, even the Father, when he shall have put down all rule, and all authority and power*: it is manifest, that we do not in baptism constitute over us another authority, by which our external actions are to be governed in this life; but promise to take the doctrine of the apostles for our direction in the way to life eternal.

The power of *remission and retention of sins,* called also the power of *loosing* and *binding,* and sometimes the *keys of the kingdom of heaven,* is a consequence of the authority to baptize, or refuse to baptize. For baptism is the sacrament of allegiance of them that are to be received into the kingdom of God; that is to say, into eternal life; that is to say, to remission of sin: for as eternal life was lost by the committing, so it is recovered by the remitting of men's sins. The end of baptism is remission of sins: and therefore St. Peter, when they that were converted by his sermon on the day of Pentecost, asked what they were to do, advised them (*Acts* , ii, 38) to *repent, and be baptized in the name of Jesus, for the remission of sins.* And therefore, seeing to baptize is to declare the reception of men into God's kingdom; and to refuse to baptize is to declare their exclusion; it followeth, that the power to declare them cast out, or retained in it, was given to the same apostles, and their substitutes and successors. And therefore after our Saviour had breathed upon them, saying (*John* xx, 22) *Receive the Holy Ghost,* he addeth in the next verse, *Whosesoever sins ye remit, they are remitted unto them; and whosesoever sins ye retain, they are retained.* By which words, is not granted an authority to forgive or retain sins, simply and absolutely, as God forgiveth or retaineth them, who knoweth the heart of man, and truth of his penitence and conversion; but conditionally, to the penitent: and this forgiveness, or absolution, in case the absolved have but a feigned repentance, is thereby, without other act, or sentence of the absolved, made void, and hath no effect at all to salvation, but on the contrary to the aggravation of his sin. Therefore the apostles, and their successors, are to follow but the outward marks of repentance; which appearing, they have no authority to deny absolution; and if they appear not, they have no authority to absolve. The same also is to be observed in baptism: for to a converted Jew, or Gentile, the apostles had not the power to deny baptism; nor to grant it to the unpenitent. But seeing no man is able to discern the truth of another man's repentance, further than by external marks, taken from his words and actions, which are subject to hypocrisy; another question will arise, who it is that is constituted judge of those marks? And this question is decided by our Saviour himself; *If thy brother,* saith he, (*Matth.* xviii, 15, 16, 17) *shall trespass against thee, go and tell him his fault, between thee and him alone; if he shall hear thee, thou hast gained thy brother. But if he will not hear thee, then take with thee one or two more. And if he shall neglect to hear them, tell it unto the Church; but if he neglect to hear the Church, let him be unto thee as an heathen man and a publican.* By which it is manifest, that the judgment concerning the truth of repentance, belonged not to any one man, but to the Church, that is, to the assembly of the faithful, or to them that have authority to be their representant. But besides the judgment, there is necessary also the pronouncing of sentence. And this belonged always to the apostle, or some pastor of the Church, as prolocutor; and of this our Saviour speaketh in the 18th verse, *Whatsoever ye shall bind on earth, shall be bound in heaven; and whatsoever ye shall loose on earth, shall be loosed in heaven.* And conformable hereunto was the practise of St. Paul (1 *Cor.* v, 3, 4, 5), where he saith, *For I verily, as absent in body, but present in spirit, have determined already, as though I were present, concerning him that hath so done this deed; in the name of our Lord Jesus Christ, when ye are gathered together, and my spirit, with the power of our Lord Jesus Christ, to deliver such a one to Satan;* that is to say, to cast him out of the Church, as a man whose sins are not forgiven. Paul here pronounceth the sentence; but the assembly was first to hear the cause, for St. Paul was absent, and by consequence to condemn him. But in the same chapter (verses 11, 12) the judgment in such a case is more expressly attributed to the assembly: *But now I have written unto you not to keep company, if any man that is called a brother be a fornicator, &c. with such a one, no not to eat. For what have I to do to judge them that are without? Do not ye judge them that are within?* The sentence therefore by which a man was put out of the Church, was pronounced by the apostle, or pastor; but the judgment concerning the merit of the cause, was in the Church; that is to say, as the times were before the conversion of kings, and men that had sovereign authority in the commonwealth, the assembly of the Christians dwelling in the same city: as in Corinth, in the assembly of the Christians of Corinth.

This part of the power of the keys, by which men were thrust out from the kingdom of God, is that which is called *excommunication*; and to *excommunicate*, is in the original, ἀποσυνάγωγον ποιεῖν, to cast out of the synagogue; that is, out of the place of divine service; a word drawn from the custom of the Jews, to cast out of their synagogues such as they thought, in manners or doctrine, contagious, as lepers were by the law of Moses separated from the congregation of Israel, till such time as they should be by the priest pronounced clean.

The use and effect of excommunication, whilst it was not yet strengthened with the civil power, was no more than that they, who were not excommunicate, were to avoid the company of them that were. It was not enough to repute them as heathen, that never had been Christians; for with such they might eat and drink; which with excommunicate persons they might not do; as appeareth by the words of St. Paul, (1 *Cor.* v, 9, 10, &c.) where he telleth them, he had formerly forbidden them to *company with fornicators*; but, because that could not be without going out of the world, he restraineth it to such fornicators, and otherwise vicious persons, as were of the brethren; *with such a one*, he saith, they ought not to keep company, *no not to eat*. And this is no more than our Saviour saith (*Matth.* xviii, 17), *Let him be to thee as a heathen, and as a publican.* For publicans, which signifieth farmers and receivers of the revenue of the commonwealth, were so hated and detested by the Jews that were to pay it, as that *publican* and *sinner* were taken amongst them for the same thing: insomuch, as when our Saviour accepted the invitation of Zacchaeus a publican; though it were to convert him, yet it was objected to him as a crime. And therefore, when our Saviour to *heathen* added *publican*, he did forbid them to eat with a man excommunicate.

As for keeping them out of their synagogues, or places of assembly, they had no power to do it, but that of the owner of the place, whether he were Christian, or heathen. And because all places are by right in the dominion of the commonwealth; as well he that was excommunicated, as he that never was baptized, might enter into them by commission from the civil magistrate; as Paul before his conversion entered into their synagogues at Damascus, (*Acts* ix, 2) to apprehend Christians, men and women, and to carry them bound to Jerusalem, by commission from the high-priest.

By which it appears, that upon a Christian, that should

become an apostate, in a place where the civil power did persecute, or not assist the Church, the effect of excommunication had nothing in it, neither of damage in this world, nor of terror: not of terror, because of their unbelief; nor of damage, because they are returned thereby into the favour of the world; and in the world to come were to be in no worse estate, than they which never had believed. The damage redounded rather to the Church, by provocation of them they cast out, to a freer execution of their malice.

Excommunication therefore had its effect only upon those, that believed that Jesus Christ was to come again in glory, to reign over and to judge both the quick and the dead, and should therefore refuse entrance into his kingdom to those whose sins were retained, that is, to those that were excommunicated by the Church. And thence it is, that St. Paul calleth excommunication, a delivery of the excommunicate person to Satan. For without the kingdom of Christ, all other kingdoms, after judgment, are comprehended in the kingdom of Satan. This is it that the faithful stood in fear of, as long as they stood excommunicate, that is to say, in an estate wherein their sins were not forgiven. Whereby we may understand, that excommunication, in the time that Christian religion was not authorized by the civil power, was used only for a correction of manners, not of errors in opinion: for it is a punishment, whereof none could be sensible but such as believed, and expected the coming again of our Saviour to judge the world; and they who so believed, needed no other opinion, but only uprightness of life, to be saved.

There lieth excommunication for injustice; as (*Matth*. xviii), If thy brother offend thee, tell it him privately; then with witnesses; lastly, tell the Church; and then if he obey not, *Let him be to thee as an heathen man and a publican*. And there lieth excommunication for a scandalous life, as (1 *Cor*. v, 11) *If any man that is called a brother, be a fornicator, or covetous, or an idolater, or a drunkard, or an extortioner, with such a one ye are not to eat*. But to excommunicate a man that held this foundation, that *Jesus was the Christ*, for difference of opinion in other points, by which that foundation was not destroyed, there appeareth no authority in the Scripture, nor example in the apostles. There is indeed in St. Paul (*Titus* iii, 10) a text that seemeth to be to the contrary; *A man that is an heretic, after the first and second admonition, reject.* For an *heretic*, is he, that being a member of the Church, teacheth nevertheless some private opinion, which the Church has forbidden: and such a one, St. Paul adviseth Titus, after the first and second admonition, to *reject.* But to *reject*, in this place, is not to *ex-communicate* the man; but to *give over admonishing him, to let him alone, to set by disputing with him*, as one that is to be convinced only by himself. The same apostle saith (2 *Tim.* ii, 23) *Foolish and unlearned questions avoid*: the word *avoid* in this place, and *reject* in the former, is the same in the original, παραιτον: but foolish questions may be set by without excommunication. And again, (*Titus* iii, 9) *Avoid foolish questions*, where the original περιῖστασο (*set them by*) is equivalent to the former word *reject*. There is no other place that can so much as colourably be drawn, to countenance the casting out of the Church faithful men, such as believed the foundation, only for a singular superstructure of their own, proceeding perhaps from a good and pious conscience. But on the contrary, all such places as command avoiding such disputes, are written for a lesson to pastors, such as Timothy and Titus were, not to make new articles of faith, by determining every small controversy, which oblige men to a needless burthen of conscience, or provoke them to break the union of the Church. Which lesson the apostles themselves observed well. St. Peter and St. Paul, though their controversy were great, as we may read in *Gal.* ii, 11, yet they did not cast one another out of the Church. Nevertheless, during the apostles' times, there were other pastors that observed it not; as Diotrephes (3 *John*, 9, &c.) who cast out of the Church such as St. John himself thought fit to be received into it, out of a pride he took in preeminence. So early it was, that vain glory and ambition had found entrance into the Church of Christ.

That a man be liable to excommunication, there be many conditions requisite; as first, that he be a member of some commonalty, that is to say, of some lawful assembly, that is to say, of some Christian Church, that hath power to judge of the cause for which he is to be excommunicated. For where there is no community, there can be no excommunication; nor where there is no power to judge, can there be any power to give sentence.

From hence it followeth, that one Church cannot be excommunicated by another: for either they have equal power to excommunicate each other, in which case excommunication is not discipline, nor an act of authority, but schism, and dissolution of charity; or one is so subordinate to the other, as that they both have but one voice; and then they be but one Church; and the part excommunicated is no more a Church, but a dissolute number of individual persons.

And because the sentence of excommunication, importeth an advice, not to keep company nor so much as to eat with him that is excommunicate, if a sovereign prince or assembly be excommunicate, the sentence is of no effect. For all subjects are bound to be in the company and presence of their own sovereign, when he requireth it, by the law of nature; nor can they lawfully either expel him from any place of his own dominion, whether profane or holy; nor go out of his dominion without his leave; much less, if he call them to that honour, refuse to eat with him. And as to other princes and states, because they are not parts of one and the same congregation, they need not any other sentence to keep them from keeping company with the state excommunicate: for the very institution uniteth many men into one community, so it dissociateth one community from another: so that excommunication is not needful for keeping kings and states asunder; nor has any further effect than is in the nature of policy itself, unless it be to instigate princes to war upon one another.

Nor is the excommunication of a Christian subject, that obeyeth the laws of his own sovereign, whether Christian or heathen, of any effect. For if he believe that *Jesus is the Christ, he hath the Spirit of God* (1 *John* v, 1): *and God dwelleth in him, and he in God* (1 *John* iv, 15.) But he that hath the spirit of God; he that dwelleth in God; he in whom God dwelleth, can receive no harm by the excommunication of men. Therefore, he that believeth Jesus to be the Christ, is free from all the dangers threatened to persons excommunicate. He that believeth it not, is no Christian. Therefore a true and unfeigned Christian is not liable to excommunication: nor he also that is a professed Christian, till his hypocrisy appear in his manners, that is, till his behaviour be contrary to the law of his sovereign, which is the rule of manners, and which Christ and his apostles have commanded us to be subject to. For the Church cannot judge of manners but by external actions, which actions can never be unlawful, but when they are against the law of the commonwealth.

If a man's father, or mother, or master, be excommunicate, yet are not the children forbidden to keep them company, nor to eat with them: for that were, for the most part, to oblige them not to eat at all, for want of means to get food: and to authorize them to disobey their parents and masters, contrary to the precept of the apostles.

In sum, the power of excommunication cannot be extended further than to the end for which the apostles and pastors of the Church have their commission from our Saviour; which is not to rule by command and co-action, but by teaching and direction of men in the way of salvation in the world to come. And as a master in any science may abandon his scholar, when he obstinately neglecteth the practise of his rules; but not accuse him of injustice, because he was never bound to obey him: so a teacher of Christian doctrine may abandon his disciples that obstinately continue in an unchristian life; but he cannot say, they do him wrong, because they are not obliged to obey him. For to a teacher that shall so complain, may be applied the answer of God to Samuel in the like place, (1 *Sam.* viii, 7) *They have not rejected thee, but me.* Excommunication therefore, when it wanteth the assistance of the civil power, as it doth, when a Christian state or prince is excommunicate by a foreign authority, is without effect; and consequently ought to be without terror. The name of *Fulmen excommunicationis,* that is, *the thunderbolt of excommunication,* proceeded from an imagination of the Bishop of Rome, which first used it, that he was king of kings, as the heathen made Jupiter king of the gods, and assigned him, in their poems, and pictures, a thunderbolt, wherewith to subdue and punish the giants, that should dare to deny his power. Which imagination was grounded on two errors; one, that the kingdom of

Christ is of this world, contrary to our Saviour's own words, (*John* xviii, 36) *My kingdom is not of this world*; the other, that he is Christ's vicar, not only over his own subjects, but over all the Christians of the world; whereof there is no ground in Scripture, and the contrary shall be proved in its due place.

St. Paul coming to Thessalonica, where was a Synagogue of the Jews, (*Acts*, xvii, 2, 3) *as his manner was, went in unto them, and three Sabbath days reasoned with them out of the Scriptures, opening and alleging, that Christ must needs have suffered and risen again from the dead; and that this Jesus whom he preached was the Christ*. The Scriptures here mentioned were the Scriptures of the Jews, that is, the Old Testament. The men, to whom he was to prove that Jesus was the Christ and risen again from the dead, were also Jews, and did believe already that, they were the word of God. Hereupon (as it is in verse 4) some of them believed, and (as it is in verse 5) some believed not. What was the reason, when they all believed the Scripture, that they did not all believe alike; but that some approved, others disapproved the interpretation of St. Paul that cited them; and every one interpreted them to himself? It was this; St. Paul came to them without any legal commission, and in the manner of one that would not command, but persuade; which he must needs do, either by miracles, as Moses did to the Israelites in Egypt, that they might see his authority in God's works; or by reasoning from the already received Scripture, that they might see the truth of his doctrine in God's word. But whosoever persuadeth by reasoning from principles written, maketh him to whom he speaketh judge, both of the meaning of those principles, and also of the force of his inferences upon them. If these Jews of Thessalonica were not, who else was the judge of what St. Paul alleged out of Scripture? If St. Paul, what needed he to quote any places to prove his doctrine? It had been enough to have said, I find it so in Scripture, that is to say, in your laws, of which I am interpreter, as sent by Christ. The interpreter therefore of the Scripture, to whose interpretation the Jews of Thessalonica were bound to stand, could be none: every one might believe, or not believe, according as the allegation seemed to himself to be agreeable, or not agreeable to the meaning of the places alleged. And generally in all cases of the world, he that pretendeth any proof, maketh judge of his proof him to whom he addresseth his speech. And as to the case of the Jews in particular, they were bound by express words (*Deut.* xvii) to receive the determination of all hard questions, from the priests and judges of Israel for the time being. But this is to be understood of the Jews that were yet unconverted.

For the conversion of the Gentiles, there was no use of alleging the Scriptures, which they believed not. The apostles therefore laboured by reason to confute their idolatry; and that done, to persuade them to the faith of Christ, by their testimony of his life and resurrection. So that there could not yet be any controversy concerning the authority to interpret Scripture; seeing no man was obliged during his infidelity, to follow any man's interpretation of any Scripture, except his sovereign's interpretation of the laws of his country.

Let us now consider the conversion itself, and see what there was therein that could be cause of such an obligation. Men were converted to no other thing than to the belief of that which the apostles preached: and the apostles preached nothing, but that Jesus was the Christ, that is to say, the king that was to save them, and reign over them eternally in the world to come; and consequently that he was not dead, but risen again from the dead, and gone up into heaven, and should come again one day to judge the world, (which also should rise again to be judged,) and reward every man according to his works. None of them preached that himself, or any other apostle, was such an interpreter of the Scripture, as all that became Christians, ought to take their interpretation for law. For to interpret the laws, is part of the administration of a present kingdom; which the apostles had not. They prayed then, and all other pastors ever since, *let thy kingdom come*; and exhorted their converts to obey their then ethnic princes. The New Testament was not yet published in one body. Every of the evangelists was interpreter of his own gospel; and every apostle of his own epistle; and of the Old Testament our Saviour himself saith to the Jews (*John* v, 39) *Search the Scriptures; for in them ye think to have eternal life, and they are they that testify of me.* If he had not meant they should interpret them, he would not have bidden them take thence the proof of his being the Christ: he would either have interpreted them himself, or referred them to the interpretation of the priests.

When a difficulty arose, the apostles and elders of the Church assembled themselves together, and determined what should be preached and taught, and how they should interpret the Scriptures to the people; but took not from the people the liberty to read and interpret them to themselves. The apostles sent divers letters to the Churches, and other writings for their instruction; which had been in vain, if they had not allowed them to interpret, that is, to consider the meaning of them. And as it was in the apostles' time, it must be till such time as there should be pastors, that could authorize an interpreter, whose interpretation should generally be stood to: but that could not be till kings were pastors, or pastors kings.

There be two senses, wherein a writing may be said to be *canonical*; for *canon*, signifieth a *rule*; and a rule is a precept, by which a man is guided and directed in any action whatsoever. Such precepts, though given by a teacher to his disciple, or a counsellor to his friend, without power to compel him to observe them, are nevertheless canons; because they are rules. But when they are given by one, whom he that receiveth them is bound to obey, then are those canons, not only rules, but laws. The question therefore here, is of the power to make the Scriptures, which are the rules of Christian faith, laws.

That part of the Scripture, which was first law, was the Ten Commandments, written in two tables of stone, and delivered by God himself to Moses; and by Moses made known to the people. Before that time there was no written law of God, who as yet having not chosen any people to be his peculiar kingdom, had given no law to men, but the law of nature, that is to say, the precepts of natural reason, written in every man's own heart. Of these two tables, the first containeth the law of sovereignty; 1. That they should not obey, nor honour the gods of other nations, in these words, *Non habebis deos alienos coram me*, that is, *thou shalt not have for gods, the gods that other nations worship, but only me:* whereby they were forbidden to obey, or honour, as their king and governor, any other God, than him that spake unto them then by Moses, and afterwards by the high-priest. 2. That they *should not make any image to represent him;* that is to say, they were not to choose to themselves, neither in heaven, nor in earth, any representative of their own fancying, but obey Moses and Aaron, whom he had appointed to that office. 3. That *they should not take the name of God in vain;* that is, they should not speak rashly of their king, nor dispute his right, nor the commissions of Moses and Aaron, his lieutenants. 4. That *they should every seventh day abstain from their ordinary labour,* and employ that time in doing him public honour. The second table containeth the duty of one man towards another, as *to honour parents; not to kill; not to commit adultery; not to steal; not to corrupt judgment by false witness;* and finally, *not so much as to design in their heart the doing of any injury one to another.* The question now is, who it was that gave to these written tables the obligatory force of laws. There is no doubt but they were made laws by God himself: but because a law obliges not, nor is law to any, but to them that acknowledge it to be the act of the sovereign; how could the people of Israel, that were forbidden to approach the mountain to hear what God said to Moses, be obliged to obedience to all those laws which Moses propounded to them? Some of them were indeed the laws of nature, as all the second table; and therefore to be acknowledged for God's laws; not to the Israelites alone, but to all people: but of those that were peculiar to the Israelites, as those of the first table, the question remains; saving that they had obliged themselves, presently after the propounding of them, to obey Moses, in these words (*Exod.* xx, 19), *Speak thou to us, and we will hear thee; but let not God speak to us, lest we die.* It was therefore only Moses then, and after him the high-priest, whom, by Moses, God declared should administer this his peculiar kingdom, that had on earth the power to make this short Scripture of the Decalogue to be law in the commonwealth of Israel. But Moses, and Aaron, and the succeeding high-priests, were the civil sovereigns. Therefore hitherto, the canonizing or making the Scripture law, belonged to the civil sovereign.

The judicial law, that is to say, the laws that God prescribed to the magistrates of Israel for the rule of their administration of justice, and of the sentences or judgments they should pronounce in pleas between man and man; and the Levitical law, that is to say, the rule that God prescribed touching the rites and ceremonies of the priests and Levites, were all delivered to them by Moses only; and therefore also became laws, by virtue of the same promise of obedience to Moses. Whether these laws were then written, or not written, but dictated to the people by Moses, after his being forty days with God in the Mount, by word of mouth, is not expressed in the text; but they were all positive laws, and equivalent to holy Scripture, and made canonical by Moses the civil sovereign.

After the Israelites were come into the plains of Moab over against Jericho, and ready to enter into the land of promise, Moses to the former laws added divers others; which therefore are called *Deuteronomy*; that is, *second laws*. And are, (as it is written *Deut.* xxix, 1) *the words of a covenant which the Lord commanded Moses to make with the children of Israel, besides the covenant which he made with them in Horeb.* For having explained those former laws, in the beginning of the book of *Deuteronomy*, he addeth others, that begin at the xiith chapter, and continue to the end of the xxvith of the same book. This law (*Deut.* xxvii, 3) they were commanded to write upon great stones plastered over, at their passing over Jordan: this law also was written by Moses himself in a book, and delivered into the hands of the *priests, and to the elders of Israel* (*Deut.* xxxi, 9), and commanded (verse 26) *to be put in the side of the ark*; for in the ark itself was nothing but the *ten commandments*. This was the law, which Moses (*Deut.* xvii, 18) commanded the kings of Israel should keep a copy of: and this is the law, which having been long time lost, was found again in the temple in the time of Josiah, and by his authority received for the law of God. But both Moses at the writing, and Josiah at the recovery thereof, had both of them the civil sovereignty. Hitherto therefore the power of making Scripture canonical, was in the civil sovereign.

Besides this book of the law, there was no other book, from the time of Moses till after the Captivity, received amongst the Jews for the law of God. For the prophets, except a few, lived in the time of the Captivity itself; and the rest lived but a little before it; and were so far from having their prophecies generally received for laws, as that their persons were persecuted, partly by false prophets, and partly by the kings which were seduced by them. And this book itself, which was confirmed by Josiah for the law of God, and with it all the history of the works of God, was lost in the captivity and sack of the city of Jerusalem, as appears by that of 2 *Esdras*, xiv, 21, *thy law is burnt; therefore no men knoweth the things that are done of thee, or the works that shall begin.* And before the captivity, between the time when the law was lost, (which is not mentioned in the Scripture, but may probably be thought to be the time of Rehoboam, when (1 *Kings* xiv, 26) Shishak, king of Egypt, took the spoil of the temple), and the time of Josiah when it was found again, they had no written word of God, but ruled according to their own discretion, or by the direction of such as each of them esteemed prophets.

From hence we may infer, that the Scriptures of the Old Testament, which we have at this day, were not canonical nor a law unto the Jews, till the renovation of their covenant with God at their return from the captivity, and restoration of their commonwealth under Esdras. But from that time forward they were accounted the law of the Jews, and for such translated into Greek by seventy elders of Judea, and put into the library of Ptolemy at Alexandria, and approved for the word of God. Now seeing Esdras was the high-priest, and the high-priest was their civil sovereign, it is manifest that the Scriptures were never made laws, but by the sovereign civil power.

By the writings of the fathers that lived in the time before that the Christian religion was received, and authorized by Constantine the emperor, we may find, that the books we now have of the New Testament were held by the Christians of that time, except a few, (in respect of whose paucity the rest were called the Catholic Church, and others heretics), for the dictates of the Holy Ghost, and consequently for the canon or rule of faith: such was the reverence and opinion they had of their teachers; as generally the reverence, that the disciples bear to their first masters in all manner of doctrine they receive from them, is not small. Therefore there is no doubt, but when

St. Paul wrote to the Churches he had converted; or any other apostle or disciple of Christ, to those which had then embraced Christ; they received those their writings for the true Christian doctrine. But in that time, when not the power and authority of the teacher, but the faith of the hearer, caused them to receive it, it was not the apostles that made their own writings canonical, but every convert made them so to himself.

But the question here, is not what any Christian made a law or canon to himself, which he might again reject by the same right he received it; but what was so made a canon to them, as without injustice they could not do anything contrary thereunto. That the New Testament should in this sense be canonical, that is to say a law, in any place where the law of the commonwealth had not made it so, is contrary to the nature of a law. For a law, as has been already shown, is the commandment of that man or assembly, to whom we have given sovereign authority to make such rules for the direction of our actions as he shall think fit, and to punish us when we do any thing contrary to the same. When therefore any other man shall offer unto us any other rules, which the sovereign ruler *hath not prescribed, they are but counsel and advice*; which, whether good or bad, he that is counselled, may without injustice refuse to observe; and when contrary to the laws already established, without injustice cannot observe, how good soever he conceiveth it to be. I say, he cannot in this case observe the same in his actions, nor in his discourse with other men; though he may without blame believe his private teachers, and wish he had the liberty to practise their advice, and that it were publicly received for law. For internal faith is in its own nature invisible, and consequently exempted from all human jurisdiction: whereas the words and actions that proceed from it, as breaches of our civil obedience, are injustice both before God and man. Seeing then our Saviour hath denied his kingdom to be in this world, seeing he had said, he came not to judge, but to save the world, he hath not subjected us to other laws than those of the commonwealth; that is, the Jews to the law of Moses, which he saith (*Matth.* v, 17) he came not to destroy, but to fulfil; and other nations to the laws of their several sovereigns, and all men to the laws of nature; the observing whereof, both he himself, and his apostles, have in their teaching recommended to us, as a necessary condition of being admitted by him in the last day into his eternal kingdom, wherein shall be protection, and life everlasting. Seeing then our Saviour, and his apostles, left not new laws to oblige us in this world, but new doctrine to prepare us for the next; the books of the New Testament, which contain that doctrine, until obedience to them was commanded by them that God had given power to on earth to be legislators, were not obligatory canons, that is, laws, but only good and safe advice, for the direction of sinners in the way to salvation, which every man might take and refuse at his own peril, without injustice.

Again, our Saviour Christ's commission to his apostles and disciples, was to proclaim his kingdom, not present, but to come; and to teach all nations, and to baptize them that should believe; and to enter into the houses of them that should receive them, and where they were not received, to shake off the dust of their feet against them; but not to call for fire from heaven to destroy them, nor to compel them to obedience by the sword. In all which there is nothing of power, but of persuasion. He sent them out as sheep unto wolves, not as kings to their subjects. They had not in commission to make laws; but to obey, and teach obedience to laws made; and consequently they could not make their writings obligatory canons, without the help of the sovereign civil power. And therefore the Scripture of the New Testament is their only law, where the lawful civil power hath made it so. And there also the king, or sovereign, maketh it a law to himself; by which he subjecteth himself, not to the doctor or apostle that converted him, but to God himself and his Son Jesus Christ, as immediately as did the apostles themselves.

That which may seem to give the New Testament, in respect of those that have embraced Christian doctrine, the force of laws, in the times and places of persecution, is the decrees they made amongst themselves in their synod. For we read (*Acts* xv, 28) the style of the council of the apostles, the elders, and the whole Church, in this manner; *It seemed good to the Holy*

Ghost, and to us, to lay upon you no greater burthen than these necessary things, &c.; which is a style that signifieth a power to lay a burthen on them that had received their doctrine. Now *to lay a burthen on another,* seemeth the same as *to oblige;* and therefore the acts of that council were laws to the then Christians. Nevertheless, they were no more laws than are these other precepts, *Repent; be baptized; keep the command-ments; believe the gospel; come unto me; sell all that thou hast; give it to the poor;* and, *follow me;* which are not commands, but invitations, and callings of men to Christianity, like that of *Isaiah* lv, 1; *Ho, every man that thirsteth, come ye to the waters, come, and buy wine and milk without money.* For first, the apostles' power was no other than that of our Saviour, to invite men to embrace the kingdom of God; which they themselves acknowledged for a kingdom, not present, but to come; and they that have no kingdom, can make no laws. And secondly, if their acts of council were laws, they could not without sin be disobeyed. But we read not any where, that they who received not the doctrine of Christ, did therein sin; but that they died in their sins; that is, that their sins against the laws to which they owed obedience, were not pardoned. And those laws were the laws of nature, and the civil laws of the state, whereto every Christian man had by pact submitted himself. And therefore by the burthen, which the apostles might lay on such as they had converted, are not to be understood laws, but conditions proposed to those that sought salvation; which they might accept or refuse at their own peril, without a new sin, though not without the hazard of being condemned and excluded out of the kingdom of God for their sins past. And therefore of infidels, St. John saith not, the wrath of God shall *come* upon them, but (*John* iii, 36) *the wrath of God remaineth upon them*; and not that they shall be condemned, but that (*John* iii, 18) *they are condemned already.* Nor can it be conceived that the benefit of faith *is remission of sins,* unless we conceive withal, that the damage of infidelity *is the retention of the same sins.*

But to what end is it, may some man ask, that the apostles, and other pastors of the Church after their time, should meet together to agree upon what doctrine should be taught, both for faith and manners, if no man were obliged to observe their decrees? To this may be answered, that the apostles and elders of that council were obliged even by their entrance into it, to teach the doctrine therein concluded and decreed to be taught, so far forth, as no precedent law, to which they were obliged to yield obedience, was to the contrary; but not that all other Christians should be obliged to observe what they taught. For though they might deliberate what each of them should teach; yet they could not deliberate what others should do, unless their assembly had had a legislative power; which none could have but civil sovereigns. For though God be the sovereign of all the world, we are not bound to take for his law whatsoever is propounded by every man in his name; nor anything contrary to the civil law, which God hath expressly commanded us to obey.

Seeing then the acts of council of the apostles, were then no laws, but counsels; much less are laws the acts of any other doctors or council since, if assembled without the authority of the civil sovereign. And consequently, the Books of the New Testament, though most perfect rules of Christian doctrine, could not be made laws by any other authority than that of kings or sovereign assemblies.

The first council, that made the Scriptures we now have canon, is not extant: for that collection of the canons of the apostles, attributed to Clemens, the first bishop of Rome after St. Peter, is subject to question. For though the canonical books be there reckoned up: yet these words, *sint vobis omnibus clericis et laicis libri venerandi, etc.* contain a distinction of clergy and laity, that was not in use so near St. Peter's time. The first council for settling the canonical Scripture, that is extant, is that of Laodicea, (*Can.* lix) which forbids the reading of other books than those in the churches: which is a mandate that is not addressed to every Christian, but to those only that had authority to read any thing publicly in the church; that is, to ecclesiastics only.

Of ecclesiastical officers in the time of the apostles, some were magisterial, some ministerial. Magisterial were the offices of the preaching of the gospel of the kingdom of God to infidels; of administering the sacraments, and divine service; and of teaching the rules of faith and manners to those that were converted. Ministerial was the office of deacons, that is, of them that were appointed to the administration of the secular necessities of the church, at such time as they lived upon a common stock of money, raised out of the voluntary contributions of the faithful.

Amongst the officers magisterial, the first and principal were the apostles; whereof there were at first but twelve; and these were chosen and constituted by our Saviour himself; and their office was not only to preach, teach, and baptize, but also to be martyrs, witnesses of our Saviour's resurrection. This testimony was the specifical and essential mark, whereby the apostleship was distinguished from other magistracy ecclesiastical; as being necessary for an apostle, either to have seen our Saviour after his resurrection, or to have conversed with him before, and seen his works, and other arguments of his divinity; whereby they might be taken for sufficient witnesses. And therefore at the election of a new apostle in the place of Judas Iscariot, St. Peter saith (*Acts* i, 21, 22) *Of these men that have companied with us, all the time that the Lord Jesus went in and out amongst us, beginning from the baptism of John unto that same day that he was taken up from us,* must *one be ordained to be a witness with us of his resurrection*: whereby this word *must*, is implied a necessary property of an apostle, to have companied with the first and prime apostles, in the time that our Saviour manifested himself in the flesh.

The first apostle, of those which were not constituted by Christ in the time he was upon the earth, was Matthias, chosen in this manner. There were assembled together in Jerusalem about one hundred and twenty Christians (*Acts* i, 15). These (verse 23) appointed two, Joseph the Just and Matthias, and caused lots to be drawn; *and* (verse 26) *the lot fell on Matthias, and he was numbered with the apostles*. So that here we see the ordination of this apostle was the act of the congregation, and not of St. Peter nor of the eleven, otherwise than as members of the assembly.

After him there was never any other apostle ordained, but Paul and Barnabas; which was done as we read (*Acts* xiii, 1, 2, 3) in this manner. *There were in the Church that was at*

Antioch, certain prophets and teachers; as Barnabas, and Simeon that was called Niger, and Lucius by Cyrene, and Manaen; which had been brought up with Herod the Tetrarch, and Saul. As they ministered unto the Lord, and fasted, the Holy Ghost said, Separate me Barnabas and Saul for the work whereunto I have called them. And when they had fasted and prayed, and laid their hands on them, they sent them away.

By which it is manifest, that though they were called by the Holy Ghost, their calling was declared unto them and their mission authorized by the particular Church of Antioch. And that this their calling was to the apostleship, is apparent by that, that they are both called (*Acts* xiv, 14) apostles: and that it was by virtue of this act of the Church of Antioch, that they were apostles, St. Paul declareth plainly (*Rom.* i, 1), in that he useth the word, which the Holy Ghost used at his calling: for he styleth himself, *An apostle separated unto the gospel of God;* alluding to the words of the Holy Ghost, *Separate me Barnabas and Saul, &c.* But seeing the work of an apostle, was to be a witness of the resurrection of Christ, a man may here ask, how St. Paul, that conversed not with our Saviour before his passion, could know he was risen? To which is easily answered that our Saviour himself appeared to him in the way to Damascus, from heaven, after his ascension; *and chose him for a vessel to bear his name before the Gentiles, and kings, and children of Israel:* and consequently, having seen the Lord after his passion, he was a competent witness of his resurrection. And as for Barnabas, he was a disciple before the passion. It is therefore evident that Paul and Barnabas were apostles; and yet chosen and authorized, not by the first apostles alone, but by the Church of Antioch; as Matthias was chosen and authorized by the Church of Jerusalem.

Bishop, a word formed in our language out of the Greek Επισκοπος, signifieth an overseer or superintendent of any business, and particularly a pastor or shepherd; and thence by metaphor was taken, not only amongst the Jews that were originally shepherds, but also amongst the heathen, to signify the office of a king, or any other rule or guide of people, whether he ruled by laws or doctrine. And so the apostles were the first Christian bishops, instituted by Christ himself: in which sense the apostleship of Judas is called (*Acts* i, 20) *his bishopric*. And afterwards, when there were constituted elders in the Christian Churches, with charge to guide Christ's flock by their doctrine and advice; these elders were also called bishops. Timothy was an elder, (which word *elder*, in the New Testament, is a name of office, as well as of age); yet he was also a bishop. And bishops were then content with the title of elders. Nay St. John himself, the apostle beloved of our Lord, beginneth his second Epistle with these words, *The elder to the elect lady*. By which it is evident, that *bishop, pastor, elder, doctor*, that is to say, *teacher*, were but so many divers names of the same office in the time of the apostles; for there was then no government by coercion, but only by doctrine and persuading. The kingdom of God was yet to come, in a new world: so that there could be no authority to compel in any Church, till the commonwealth had embraced the Christian faith: and consequently no diversity of authority, though there were diversity of employments.

Besides these magisterial employments in the Church, namely, apostles, bishops, elders, pastors, and doctors, whose calling was to proclaim Christ to the Jews and infidels, and to direct and to teach those that believed, we read in the New Testament of no other. For by the names of *evangelists* and *prophets*, is not signified any office, but several gifts, by which several men were profitable to the Church: as evangelists, by writing the life and acts of our Saviour, such as were St. Matthew and St. John apostles, and St. Mark and St. Luke disciples, and whosoever else wrote of that subject, (as St. Thomas, and St. Barnabas are said to have done; though the Church have not received the books that have gone under their names): and as prophets, by the gift of interpreting the Old Testament, and sometimes by declaring their special revelations to the Church. For neither these gifts, nor the gifts of languages, nor the gift of casting out devils, nor of curing other diseases, nor any thing else, did make an officer in the Church, save only the due calling and election to the charge of teaching.

As the apostles, Matthias, Paul, and Barnabas, were not made by our Saviour himself, but were elected by the Church,

that is, by the assembly of Christians; namely, Matthias by the
Church of Jerusalem, and Paul and Barnabas by the Church
of Antioch; so were also the *presbyters* and *pastors* in other
cities, elected by the Churches of those cities. For proof
whereof let us consider, first, how St. Paul proceeded in the
ordination of presbyters, in the cities where he had converted
men to the Christian faith, immediately after he and Barnabas
had received their apostleship. We read (*Acts* xiv, 23) that
they ordained elders in every Church; which at first sight may be
taken for an argument, that they themselves chose, and gave
them their authority: but if we consider the original text, it
will be manifest that they were authorized and chosen by the
assembly of the Christians of each city. For the words there
are, χειροτονήσαντες αντοις πρεσβυτέρους κατ᾽ ἐκκλησίαν
that is, *when they had ordained them elders by the holding up of hands
in every congregation*. Now it is well enough known, that in all
those cities the manner of choosing magistrates and officers,
was by plurality of suffrages; and, because the ordinary way of
distinguishing the affirmative votes from the negatives, was
by holding up of hands, to ordain an officer in any of the cities,
was no more but to bring the people together, to elect them by
plurality of votes, whether it were by plurality of elevated
hands, or by plurality of voices, or plurality of balls, or beans,
or small stones, of which every man cast in one, into a vessel
marked for the affirmative or negative; for divers cities had
divers customs in that point. It was therefore the assembly
that elected their own elders: the apostles were only presidents
of the assembly, to call them together for such election, and
to pronounce them elected, and to give them the benediction
which now is called consecration. And for this cause, they that
were presidents of the assemblies, as in the absence of the
apostles the elders were, were called προεστῶτες, and in Latin
antistites; which words signify the principal person of the
assembly, whose office was to number the votes, and to declare
thereby who was chosen; and where the votes were equal, to
decide the matter in question, by adding his own; which is the
office of a president in council. And, because all the Churches
had their presbyters ordained in the same manner, where the
words is *constitute*, (as *Titus* i, 5) ἵνα καταστησῃς κατα πόλιν

πρεσβυτέρους, *For this cause left I thee in Crete, that thou shouldest constitute elders in every city*, we are to understand the same thing, namely, that he should call the faithful together, and ordain them presbyters by plurality of suffrages. It had been a strange thing, if in a town, where men perhaps had never seen any magistrate otherwise chosen, than by an assembly, those of the town becoming Christians should so much as have thought on any other way of election of their teachers and guides, that is to say, of their presbyters, (otherwise called bishops) than this of plurality of suffrages, intimated by St. Paul (*Acts* xiv, 23) in the word χειροτονήσαντες. Nor was there ever any choosing of bishops, before the emperors found it necessary to regulate them, in order to the keeping of the peace amongst them, but by the assemblies of the Christians in every several town.

The same is also confirmed by the continual practice, even to this day, in the election of the bishops of Rome. For if the bishop of any place had the right of choosing another, to the succession of the pastoral office, in any city, at such times as he went from thence to plant the same in another place; much more had he had the right to appoint his successors in that place, in which he last resided and died: and we find not that ever any bishop of Rome appointed his successor. For they were a long time chosen by the people, as we may see by the sedition raised about the election between *Damasus* and *Ursicinus*; which Ammianus Marcellinus saith was so great, that *Juventius* the præfect, unable to keep the peace between them, was forced to go out of the city; and that there were above an hundred men found dead upon that occasion in the church itself. And though they afterwards were chosen, first, by the whole clergy of Rome, and afterwards by the cardinals; yet never any was appointed to the succession by his predecessor. If therefore they pretended no right to appoint their own successors, I think I may reasonably conclude they had no right to appoint the successors of other bishops, without receiving some new power; which none could take from the Church to bestow on them, but such as had a lawful authority, not only to teach, but to command the Church; which none could do, but the civil sovereign.

The word *minister*, in the original Διάκονος, signifieth one that voluntarily doth the business of another man; and differeth from a servant only in this, that servants are obliged by their condition, to do what is commanded them; whereas ministers are obliged only by their undertaking, and bound therefore to no more than that they have undertaken: so that both they that teach the word of God, and they that administer the secular affairs of the Church, are both ministers, but they are ministers of different persons. For the pastors of the Church, called (*Acts* vi, 4) *the ministers of the word*, are ministers of Christ, whose word it is: but the ministry of a deacon, which is called (verse 2 of the same chapter) *serving of tables*, is a service done to the Church or congregation: so that neither any one man, nor the whole church, could ever of their pastor say, he was their minister: but of a deacon, whether the charge he undertook were to serve tables, or distribute maintenance to the Christians, when they lived in each city on a common stock or upon collections, as in the first times, or to take a care of the house of prayer, or of the revenue, or other worldly business of the Church, the whole congregation might properly call him their minister.

For their employment, as deacons, was to serve the congregation; though upon occasion they omitted not to preach the gospel, and maintain the doctrine of Christ, every one according to his gifts, as St. Stephen did; and both to preach and baptize, as Philip did. For that Philip, which (*Acts* viii, 5) preached the gospel at Samaria, and (verse 38) baptized the Eunuch, was Philip the deacon, not Philip the apostle. For it is manifest (verse 1) that when Philip preached in Samaria, the apostles were at Jerusalem, and (verse 14) *when they heard that Samaria had received the word of God, sent Peter and John to them*; by imposition of whose hands, they that were baptized (verse 15), received, which before by the baptism of Philip they had not received, the Holy Ghost. For it was necessary for the conferring of the Holy Ghost, that their baptism should be administered or confirmed by a minister of the word, not by a minister of the Church. And therefore to confirm the baptism of those that Philip the deacon had baptized, the apostles sent out of their own number from Jerusalem to Samaria, Peter and John; who conferred on them that before were but baptized, those graces that were signs of the Holy Spirit, which at that time did accompany all true believers; which what they were may be understood by that which St. Mark saith (chapter xvi, 17), *these signs follow them that believe in my name; they shall cast out devils; they shall speak with new tongues; they shall take up serpents; and if they drink any deadly thing, it shall not hurt them; they shall lay hands on the sick, and they shall recover.* This to do, was it that Philip could not give; but the apostles could, and, as appears by this place, effectually did to every man that truly believed and was by a minister of Christ himself baptized: which power either Christ's ministers in this age cannot confer or else there are very few true believers, or Christ hath very few ministers.

That the first deacons were chosen, not by the apostles, but by a congregation of the disciples, that is, of Christian men of all sorts, is manifest out of *Acts* vi, where we read that the *Twelve*, after the number of disciples was multiplied, called them together, and having told them, that it was not fit that the apostles should leave the word of God and serve tables, said unto them, (verse 3) *Brethren, look you out among you seven men of honest report, full of the Holy Ghost and of wisdom, whom we may appoint over this business.* Here it is manifest, that though the apostles declared them elected; yet the congregation chose them; which also (verse 5) is more expressly said, where it is written, that *the saying pleased the whole multitude, and they chose seven, &c.*

Under the Old Testament, the tribe of Levi were only capable of the priesthood, and other inferior offices of the Church. The land was divided amongst the other tribes, Levi excepted, which, by the subdivision of the tribe of Joseph into Ephraim and Manasseh, were still twelve. To the tribe of Levi were assigned certain cities for their habitation, with the suburbs for their cattle: but for their portion, they were to have the tenth of the fruits of the land of their brethren. Again, the priests for their maintenance had the tenth of that tenth, together with part of the oblations and sacrifices. For God had said to Aaron (*Numb.* xviii, 20) *Thou shalt have no inheritance in their land; neither shalt thou have any part amongst them; I am thy part and thine inheritance amongst the children of Israel.* For God being then king, and having constituted the tribe of Levi to be his public ministers, he allowed them for their maintenance the public revenue, that is to say, the part that God had reserved to himself; which were tithes and offerings: and that is it which is meant, where God saith, *I am thine inheritance.* And therefore to the Levites might not unfitly be attributed the name of *clergy*, from κλῆρος, which signifieth lot or inheritance; not that they were heirs of the kingdom of God, more than other; but that God's inheritance was their maintenance. Now, seeing in this time God himself was their king, and Moses, Aaron, and the succeeding high-priests, were his lieutenants; it is manifest, that the right of tithes and offerings was constituted by the civil power.

After their rejection of God in the demanding of a king, they enjoyed still the same revenue; but the right thereof was derived from that, that the kings did never take it from them: for the public revenue was at the disposing of him that was the public person; and that, till the Captivity, was the king. And again, after the return from the Captivity, they paid their tithes as before to the priest. Hitherto therefore Church livings were determined by the civil sovereign.

Of the maintenance of our Saviour and his apostles, we read only they had a purse, which was carried by Judas Iscariot; and that of the apostles, such as were fishermen did sometimes use their trade; and that when our Saviour sent the twelve apostles to preach, he forbad them (*Matth.* x, 9, 10): *to carry gold, and silver, and brass in their purses, for that the workman is worthy of his hire.* By which it is probable, their ordinary maintenance was not unsuitable to their employment; for their employment was (verse 8) *freely to give, because they had freely received*; and their maintenance was the *free gift* of those that believed the good tiding they carried about of the coming of the Messiah their Saviour. To which we may add, that which was contributed out of gratitude by such as our Saviour had healed of diseases; of which are mentioned (*Luke* viii, 2, 3) *Certain women which had been healed of evil spirits and infirmities; Mary Magdalen, out of whom went seven devils; and Joanna the wife of Chuza, Herod's steward, and Susanna, and many others, which ministered unto him of their substance.*

After our Saviour's ascension, the Christians of every city lived in common (*Acts* iv, 34, 35) upon the money which was made of the sale of their lands and possessions, and laid down at the feet of the apostles, of good will, not of duty; for, *whilst the land remained,* saith St. Peter to Ananias (*Acts* v, 4), *was it not thine? and after it was sold, was it not in thy power?* which sheweth he needed not have saved his land nor his money by lying, as not being bound to contribute any thing at all, unless he had pleased. And as in the time of the apostles, so also all the time downward, till after Constantine the Great, we shall find that the maintenance of the bishops and pastors of the Christian Church was nothing but the voluntary contribution of them that had embraced their doctrine. There was yet no mention of tithes: but such was in the time of Constantine and his sons the affection of Christians to their pastors, as Ammianus Marcellinus saith, describing the sedition of Damasus and Ursicinus about the bishopric, that it was worth their contention, in that the bishops of those times, by the liberality of their flock, and especially of matrons, lived splendidly, were carried in coaches, and were sumptuous in their fare and apparel.

But here may some ask, whether the pastors were then bound to live upon voluntary contribution, as upon alms; *For who,* saith St. Paul (1 *Cor.* ix, 7) *goeth to war at his own charges? or who feedeth a flock, and eateth not of the milk of the flock?* And again, (verse 13) *Do ye not know that they which minister about holy things, live of the things of the temple; and they which wait at the altar, partake with the altar;* that is to say, have part of that which is offered at the altar for their maintenance? And then he concludeth, (verse 14) *Even so hath the Lord appointed, that they which preach the gospel should live of the gospel.* From which place may be inferred indeed, that the pastors of the Church ought to be maintained by their flocks; but not that the pastors were to determine, either the quantity, or the kind of their own allowance, and be, as it were, their own carvers. Their allowance must needs therefore be determined, either by the gratitude and liberality of every particular man of their flock, or by the whole congregation. By the whole congregation it could not be, because their acts were then no laws; therefore the maintenance of pastors before emperors and civil sovereigns had made laws to settle it, was nothing but benevolence. They that served at the altar lived on what was offered. So may the pastors also take what is offered them by their flock; but not exact what is not offered. In what court should they sue for it, who had no tribunals? Or, if they had arbitrators amongst themselves, who should execute their judgments, when they had no power to arm their officers? It remaineth, therefore, that there could be no certain maintenance assigned to any pastors of the Church, but by the whole congregation; and then only, when their decrees should have the force, not only of *canons*, but also of *laws;* which laws could not be made, but by emperors, kings, or other civil sovereigns. The right of tithes in Moses' law, could not be applied to the then ministers of the gospel; because Moses and the high-priests were the civil sovereigns of the people under God, whose kingdom amongst the Jews was present; whereas the kingdom of God by Christ is yet to come.

Hitherto hath been shewn what the pastors of the Church are; what are the points of their commission, as that they were to preach, to teach, to baptize, to be presidents in their several congregations; what is ecclesiastical censure, viz. excommunication, that is to say, in those places where Christianity was forbidden by the civil laws, a putting of themselves out of the company of the excommunicate, and where Christianity was by the civil law commanded, a putting the excommunicate out of the congregations of Christians; who elected the pastors and ministers of the Church, that it was the congregation; who consecrated and blessed them, that it was the pastor; what was their due revenue, that it was none but their own possessions, and their own labour, and the voluntary contributions of devout and grateful Christians. We are to consider now, what office in the Church those persons have, who being civil sovereigns, have embraced also the Christian faith.

And first, we are to remember, that the right of judging what doctrines are fit for peace, and to be taught the subjects, is in all commonwealths inseparably annexed, as hath been already proved (chapter XVIII), to the sovereign power civil, whether it be in one man, or in one assembly of men. For it is evident to the meanest capacity, that men's actions are derived from the opinions they have of the good or evil, which from those actions redound unto themselves; and consequently, men that are once possessed of an opinion, that their obedience to the sovereign power will be more hurtful to them than their disobedience, will disobey the laws, and thereby overthrow the commonwealth, and introduce confusion and civil war; for the avoiding whereof, all civil government was ordained. And therefore in all commonwealths of the heathen, the sovereigns have had the name of pastors of the people, because there was no subject that could lawfully teach the people, but by their permission and authority.

This right of the heathen kings cannot be thought taken from them by their conversion to the faith of Christ; who never ordained that kings, for believing in him, should be deposed, that is, subjected to any but himself, or, which is all one, be deprived of the power necessary for the conservation of peace amongst their subjects, and for their defence against foreign enemies. And therefore Christian kings are still the supreme pastors of their people, and have power to ordain what pastors they please, to teach the Church, that is, to teach the people committed to their charge.

Again, let the right of choosing them be, as before the conversion of kings, in the Church; for so it was in the time of the apostles themselves, as hath been shown already in this chapter; even so also the right will be in the civil sovereign, Christian. For in that he is a Christian, he allows the teaching; and in that he is the sovereign, which is as much as to say, the Church by representation, the teachers he elects are elected by the Church. And when an assembly of Christians choose their pastor in a Christian commonwealth, it is the sovereign that electeth him, because it is done by his authority; in the same manner, as when a town choose their mayor, it is the act of him that hath the sovereign power: for every act done, is the act of him, without whose consent it is invalid. And therefore whatsoever examples may be drawn out of history, concerning the election of pastors by the people, or by the clergy, there are no arguments against the right of any civil sovereign, because they that elected them did it by his authority.

Seeing then in every Christian commonwealth, the civil sovereign is the supreme pastor, to whose charge the whole flock of his subjects is committed, and consequently that it is by his authority that all other pastors are made, and have power to teach, and perform all other pastoral offices; it followeth also, that it is from the civil sovereign that all other pastors derive their right of teaching, preaching, and other functions pertaining to that office, and that they are but his ministers; in the same manner as the magistrates of towns, judges in courts of justice, and commanders of armies, are all but ministers of him that is the magistrate of the whole commonwealth, judge of all causes, and commander of the whole militia, which is always the civil sovereign. And the reason hereof, is not because they that teach, but because they that are to learn, are his subjects. For let it be supposed, that a Christian king commit the authority of ordaining pastors in his dominions to another king, as divers Christian kings allow that power to the Pope; he doth not thereby constitute a pastor over himself, nor a sovereign pastor over his people; for that were to deprive himself of the civil power; which, depending on the opinion men have of their duty to him and the fear they have of punishment in another world, would depend also on the skill and loyalty of doctors, who are no less subject, not only to ambition, but also to ignorance, than any other sort of men. So that where a stranger hath authority to appoint teachers, it is given him by the sovereign in whose dominions he teacheth. Christian doctors are our school-masters to Christianity; but kings are fathers of families, and may receive schoolmasters for their subjects from the recommendation of a stranger, but not from the command; especially when the ill teaching them shall redound to the great and manifest profit of him that recommends them: nor can they be obliged to retain them, longer than it is for the public good; the care of which they stand so long charged withal, as they retain any other essential right of the sovereignty.

If a man therefore should ask a pastor, in the execution of his office, as the chief-priests and elders of the people (*Matth.* xxi, 23) asked our Saviour, *By what authority doest thou these things, and who gave thee this authority?* he can make no other just answer, but that he doth it by the authority of the commonwealth, given him by the king, or assembly that representeth it. All pastors, except the supreme, execute their charges in the right, that is by the authority of the civil sovereign, that is, *jure civili.* But the king, and every other sovereign, executeth his office of supreme pastor by immediate authority from God, that is to say, in *God's right* or *jure divino.* And therefore none but kings can put into their titles a mark of their submission to God only, *Dei gratiâ rex, &c.* Bishops ought to say in the beginning of their mandates, *By the favour of the King's Majesty, bishop of such a diocese:* or as civil ministers, *in His Majesty's name.* For in saying, *Divina providentia,* which is the same with *Dei gratiâ,* though disguised, they deny to have received their authority from the civil state: and slily slip off the collar of their civil subjection, contrary to the unity and defence of the commonwealth.

From this consolidation of the right politic and ecclesiastic in Christian sovereigns, it is evident, they have all manner of power over their subjects, that can be given to man, for the government of men's external actions, both in policy and religion; and may make such laws as themselves shall judge fittest, for the government of their own subjects, both as they are the commonwealth, and as they are the Church; for both State and Church are the same men.

If they please, therefore, they may, as many Christian kings now do, commit the government of their subjects in matters of religion to the Pope; but then the Pope is in that point subordinate to them, and exerciseth that charge in another's dominion *jure civili,* in the right of the civil sovereign; not *jure divino,* in God's right; and may therefore be discharged of that office, when the sovereign, for the good of his subjects, shall think it necessary. They may also, if they please, commit the care of religion to one supreme pastor, or to an assembly of pastors; and give them what power over the Church, or one over another, they think most convenient; and what titles of honour, as of archbishops, bishops, priests, or presbyters, they will; and make such laws for their maintenance, either by tithes or otherwise, as they please, so they do it out of a sincere conscience, of which God only is the judge. It is the civil sovereign that is to appoint judges and interpreters of the canonical Scriptures; for it is he that maketh them laws. It is he also that giveth strength to excommunications; which but for such laws and punishments, as may humble obstinate libertines, and reduce them to union with the rest of the Church, would be contemned. In sum, he hath the supreme power in all causes, as well ecclesiastical as civil, as far as concerneth actions and words, for those only are known and may be accused; and of that which cannot be accused, there is no judge at all but God, that knoweth the heart. And these rights are incident to all sovereigns, whether monarchs or assemblies: for they that are the representants of a Christian people, are representants of the Church: for a Church, and a commonwealth of Christian people, are the same thing.

CHAPTER XLIII

Of What is Necessary for a Man's Reception into the Kingdom of Heaven

THE most frequent pretext of sedition, and civil war, in Christian commonwealths, hath a long time proceeded from a difficulty, not yet sufficiently resolved, of obeying at once both God and man, then when their commandments are one contrary to the other. It is manifest enough, that when a man receiveth two contrary commands, and knows that one of them is God's, he ought to obey that, and not the other, though it be the command even of his lawful sovereign (whether a monarch, or a sovereign assembly), or the command of his father. The difficulty therefore consisteth in this, that men, when they are commanded in the name of God, know not in divers cases, whether the command be from God, or whether l e that commandeth do but abuse God's name for some private ends of his own. For as there were in the Church of the Jews, many false prophets, that sought reputation with the people, by feigned dreams and visions; so there have been in all times in the Church of Christ, false teachers, that seek reputation with the people, by fantastical and false doctrines; and by such reputation, (as is the nature of ambition), to govern them for their private benefit.

But this difficulty of obeying both God and the civil sovereign on earth, to those that can distinguish between what is *necessary*, and what is not *necessary for the reception into the kingdom of God*, is of no moment. For if the command of the civil sovereign be such, as that it may be obeyed without the forfeiture of life eternal; not to obey it is unjust; and the precept of the apostle takes place: *Servants obey your masters in all things;* and *Children obey your parents in all things;* and the precept of our Saviour, *The Scribes and Pharisees sit in Moses' chair; all therefore they shall say, that observe and do.* But if the command be such as cannot be obeyed, without being damned to eternal death; then it were madness to obey it, and the council of our Saviour takes place, (*Matth.* x, 28), *Fear not those that kill the body, but cannot kill the soul.* All men therefore that would avoid, both the punishments that are to be in this world inflicted, for disobedience to their earthly sovereign, and those that shall be inflicted in the world to come, for disobedience to God, have need be taught to distinguish well between what is, and what is not necessary to eternal salvation.

All that is NECESSARY *to salvation*, is contained in two virtues, *faith in Christ*, and *obedience to laws*. The latter of these if it were perfect, were enough to us. But because we are all guilty of disobedience to God's law, not only originally in Adam, but also actually by our own transgressions, there is required at our hands now, not only *obedience* for the rest of our time, but also a *remission of sins* for the time past; which remission is the reward of our faith in Christ. That nothing else is necessarily required to salvation, is manifest from this, that the kingdom of heaven is shut to none but to sinners; that is to say, to the disobedient, or transgressors of the law; nor to them, in case they repent, and believe all the articles of Christian faith necessary to salvation.

The obedience required at our hands by God, that accepteth in all our actions the will for the deed, is a serious endeavour to obey him; and is called also by all such names as signify that endeavour. And therefore obedience is sometimes called by the names of *charity* and *love*, because they imply a will to obey; and our Saviour himself maketh our love to God, and to one another, a fulfilling of the whole law: and sometimes by the name of *righteousness*; for righteousness is but the will to give to every one his own; that is to say, the will to obey the laws: and sometimes by the name of *repentance*; because to repent, implieth a turning away from sin, which is the same with the return of the will to obedience. Whosoever therefore unfeignedly desireth to fulfil the commandments of God, or repenteth him truly of his transgressions, or that loveth God with all his heart, and his neighbour as himself, hath all the obedience necessary to his reception into the kingdom of God. For if God should require perfect innocence, there could no flesh be saved.

But what commandments are those that God hath given us? Are all those laws which were given to the Jews by the hand of Moses, the commandments of God? If they be, why are not Christians taught to obey them? If they be not, what others are so, besides the law of nature? For our Saviour Christ hath not given us new laws, but counsel to observe those we are subject to; that is to say, the laws of nature, and the laws of our several sovereigns: nor did he make any new law to the Jews in his sermon on the Mount, but only expounded the law of Moses, to which they were subject before. The laws of God therefore are none but the laws of nature, whereof the principal is, that we should not violate our faith, that is, a commandment to obey our civil sovereigns, which we constituted over us by mutual pact one with another. And this law of God, that commandeth obedience to the law civil commandeth by consequence obedience to all the precepts of the Bible; which, as I have proved in the precedent chapter, is there only law, where the civil sovereign hath made it so; and in other places, but counsel; which a man at his own peril may without injustice refuse to obey.

Knowing now what is the obedience necessary to salvation,

and to whom it is due; we are to consider next concerning faith, whom, and why we believe; and what are the articles, or points necessary to be believed by them that shall be saved. And first, for the person whom we believe, because it is impossible to believe any person, before we know what he saith, it is necessary he be one that we have heard speak. The person, therefore, whom Abraham, Isaac, Jacob, Moses, and the prophets, believed, was God himself, that spake unto them supernaturally: and the person, whom the apostles and disciples that conversed with Christ believed, was our Saviour himself. But of them, to whom neither God the father, nor our Saviour, ever spake, it cannot be said that the person whom they believed, was God. They believed the apostles, and after them the pastors and doctors of the Church, that recommended to their faith the history of the Old and New Testament: so that the faith of Christians ever since our Saviour's time, hath had for foundation, first, the reputation of their pastors, and afterwards, the authority of those that made the Old and New Testament to be received for the rule of faith; which none could do but Christian sovereigns; who are therefore the supreme pastors, and the only persons whom Christians now hear speak from God; except such as God speaketh to in these days supernaturally. But because there be many false prophets *gone out into the world*, other men are to examine such spirits, as St. John adviseth us, (1st Epistle iv, 1) *whether they be of God, or not*. And therefore, seeing the examination of doctrines belongeth to the supreme pastor, the person, which all they that have no special revelation are to believe, is, in every commonwealth, the supreme pastor, that is to say, the civil sovereign.

The causes why men believe any Christian doctrine, are various. For faith is the gift of God: and he worketh it in each several man, by such ways as it seemeth good unto himself. The most ordinary immediate cause of our belief, concerning any point of Christian faith, is, that we believe the Bible to be the word of God. But why we believe the Bible to be the word of God, is much disputed, as all questions must needs be, that are not well stated. For they make not the question to be, *why we believe it*, but, *how we know it*; as if *believing* and *knowing* were all one. And thence while one side ground their know-ledge upon the infallibility of the Church, and the other side, on the testimony of the private spirit, neither side concludeth what it pretends. For how shall a man know the infallibility of the Church, but by knowing first the infallibility of the Scrip-ture? Or how shall a man know his own private spirit to be other than a belief, grounded upon the authority and argu-ments of his teachers, or upon the presumption of his own gifts? Besides, there is nothing in the Scripture, from which can be inferred the infallibility of the Church; much less, of any particular Church; and least of all, the infallibility of any particular man.

It is manifest therefore, that Christian men do not know, but only believe the Scripture to be the word of God; and that the means of making them believe, which God is pleased to afford men ordinarily, is according to the way of nature, that is to say, from their teachers. It is the doctrine of St. Paul concerning Christian faith in general (*Rom.* x, 17), *Faith cometh by hearing*, that is, by hearing our lawful pastors. He saith also, (verses 14, 15, of the same chapter), *How shall they believe in him of whom they have not heard? and how shall they hear without a preacher? and how shall they preach, except they be sent?* Whereby it is evident, that the ordinary cause of believing that the Scriptures are the word of God, is the same with the cause of the believing of all other articles of our faith, namely, the hearing of those that are by the law allowed and appointed to teach us, as our parents in their houses, and our pastors in the churches. Which also is made more manifest by experience. For what other cause can there be assigned, why in Christian commonwealths all men either believe, or at least profess the Scripture to be the word of God, and in other commonwealths scarce any; but that in Christian commonwealths they are taught from their infancy; and in other places they are taught otherwise?

But if teaching be the cause of faith, why do not all believe? It is certain therefore that faith is the gift of God, and he giveth it to whom he will. Nevertheless, because to them to whom he giveth it, he giveth it by the means of teachers, the immediate cause of faith is hearing. In a school, where many are taught, and some profit, others profit not, the cause of learning in them that profit, is the master; yet it cannot be thence inferred, that learning is not the gift of God. All good things proceed from God; yet cannot all that have them, say they are inspired; for that implies a gift supernatural, and the immediate hand of God; which he that pretends to, pretends to be a prophet, and is subject to the examination of the Church.

But whether men *know*, or *believe*, or *grant* the Scriptures to be the word of God; if out of such places of them, as are without obscurity, I shall show what articles of faith are necessary, and only necessary for salvation, those men must needs *know*, *believe*, or *grant* the same.

The *unum necessarium*, only article of faith, which the Scripture maketh simply necessary to salvation, is this, that JESUS IS THE CHRIST. By the name of *Christ* is understood the king, which God had before promised by the prophets of the Old Testament, to send into the world, to reign (over the Jews, and over such of other nations as should believe in him), under himself eternally; and to give them that eternal life, which was lost by the sin of Adam. Which when I have proved out of Scripture, I will further show when, and in what sense, some other articles may be also called *necessary*.

For proof that the belief of this article, *Jesus is the Christ*, is all the faith required to salvation, my first argument shall be from the scope of the Evangelists; which was by the description of the life of our Saviour, to establish that one article, *Jesus is the Christ*. The sum of St. Matthew's Gospel is this, that Jesus was of the stock of David, born of a Virgin; which are the marks of the true Christ: that the Magi came to worship him as King of the Jews: that Herod for the same cause sought to kill him: that John the Baptist proclaimed him: that he preached by himself and his apostles that he was that king: that he taught the law, not as a scribe, but as a man of authority: that he cured diseases by his word only, and did many other miracles, which were foretold the Christ should do: that he was saluted king when he entered into Jerusalem: that he forewarned them to beware of all others that should pretend to be Christ: that he was taken, accused, and put to death, for saying he was king: that the cause his condemnation written on the cross was, JESUS OF NAZARETH, THE KING OF THE JEWS. All which tend to no other end than this, that men should believe that *Jesus is the Christ*. Such therefore was the scope of St. Matthew's Gospel. But the scope of all the evangelists, as may appear by reading them, was the same. Therefore the scope of the whole Gospel was the establishing of that only article. And St. John expressly makes it his conclusion, (*John* xx, 31), *These things are written, that you may know that Jesus is the Christ, the Son of the living God.*

My second argument is taken from the subjects of the sermons of the apostles, both whilst our Saviour lived on earth, and after his ascension. The apostles, in our Saviour's time, were sent, (*Luke* ix, 2) *to preach the kingdom of God.* For neither there, nor, *Matth.* x, 7, giveth he any commission to them other than this, *As ye go, preach, saying, the kingdom of heaven is at hand*; that is, that Jesus the *Messiah*, the *Christ*, the *King* which was to come. That their preaching also after his ascension was the same, is manifest out of *Acts* xvii, 6, 7, *They drew*, saith St. Luke, *Jason and certain brethren unto the rulers of the city, crying, these that have turned the world upside down are come hither also, whom Jason hath received: and these all do contrary to the decrees of Caesar, saying, that there is another king, one Jesus.* And out of the 2nd and 3rd verses of the same chapter where it is said, that St. Paul, *as his manner was, went in unto them; and three sabbath days reasoned with them out of the Scriptures; opening and alleging, that Christ must needs have suffered, and risen again from the dead, and that this Jesus, whom he preached, is Christ.*

The third argument is from those places of Scripture, by which all the faith required to salvation is declared to be easy. For if an inward assent of the mind to all the doctrines concerning Christian faith now taught, whereof the greatest part are disputed, were necessary to salvation, there would be nothing in the world so hard as to be a Christian. The thief upon the cross, though repenting, could not have been saved for saying, *Lord remember me when thou comest into thy kingdom*; by which he testified no belief of any other article, but this, that *Jesus was the king*. Nor could it be said (as it is, *Matth.* xi, 30), that *Christ's yoke is easy, and his burthen light*: nor that

little children believe in him, as it is *Matth.* xviii, 6. Nor could St.
Paul have said, (1 *Cor.* i, 21), *It pleased God by the foolishness of
preaching, to save them that believe.* Nor could St. Paul himself
have been saved, much less have been so great a doctor of the
Church so suddenly, that never perhaps thought of transubstantiation nor purgatory, nor many other articles now
obtruded.

The fourth argument is taken from places express, and such
as receive no controversy of interpretation; as first, *John* v, 39;
*Search the Scriptures; for in them ye think ye have eternal life; and
they are they that testify of me.* Our Saviour here speaketh of the
Scriptures only of the Old Testament; for the Jews at that
time could not search the Scriptures of the New Testament,
which were not written. But the Old Testament hath nothing
of Christ, but the marks by which men might know him when
he came; as that he should descend from David; be born at
Bethlehem, and of a Virgin; do great miracles, and the like.
Therefore to believe that this Jesus was He, was sufficient to
eternal life: but more than sufficient is not necessary; and
consequently no other article is required. Again, (*John* xi, 26)
Whosoever liveth and believeth in me, shall not die eternally. Therefore to believe in Christ, is faith sufficient to eternal life; and
consequently no more faith than that is necessary. But to
believe in Jesus, and to believe that Jesus is the Christ, is all
one, as appeareth in the verses immediately following. For
when our Saviour (verse 26) had said to Martha, *Believest
thou this?* she answereth (verse 27), *Yea, Lord, I believe that thou
art the Christ, the Son of God, which should come into the world.*
Therefore this article alone is faith sufficient to life eternal;
and more than sufficient is not necessary. Thirdly, *John* xx, 31:
*These things are written that ye might believe, that Jesus is the Christ,
the Son of God, and that believing ye might have life through his name.*
There, to believe that *Jesus is the Christ*, is faith sufficient to
the obtaining of life; and therefore no other article is necessary. Fourthly, 1 *John* iv, 2: *Every spirit that confesseth that Jesus
Christ is come in the flesh, is of God.* And 1 *John* v, 1: *Whosoever
believeth that Jesus is the Christ, is born of God.* And verse 5,
*Who is he that overcometh the world, but he that believeth that Jesus
is the Son of God?* Fifthly, *Acts* viii, 36, 37: *See,* saith the Eunuch,

here is water, what doth hinder me to be baptized? And Philip said, if thou believest with all thy heart, thou mayst. And he answered and said, I believe that Jesus Christ is the Son of God. Therefore this article believed, *Jesus is the Christ*, is sufficient to baptism, that is to say, to our reception into the kingdom of God, and by consequence, only necessary. And generally in all places where our Saviour saith to any man, *Thy faith hath saved thee*, the cause he saith it, is some confession, which directly, or by consequence, implieth a belief, that *Jesus is the Christ*.

The last argument is from the places, where this article is made the foundation of faith: for he that holdeth the foundation, shall be saved. Which places are first, *Matth.* xxiv, 23, 24: *If any man shall say unto you, Lo here is Christ, or there, believe it not; for there shall arise false Christs, and false prophets, and shall shew great signs and wonders, &c.* Here we see this article, *Jesus is the Christ*, must be held, though he that shall teach the contrary should do great miracles. The second place is, *Gal.* i, 8: *Though we, or an angel from heaven, preach any other gospel unto you, than that we have preached unto you, let him be accursed.* But the gospel which Paul, and the other apostles, preached, was only this article, that *Jesus is the Christ:* therefore for the belief of this article, we are to reject the authority of an angel from heaven; much more of any mortal man, if he teach the contrary. This is therefore the fundamental article of Christian faith. A third place is, 1 *John,* iv, 1, 2: *Beloved, believe not every spirit: hereby ye shall know the Spirit of God; every spirit that confesseth that Jesus Christ is come in the flesh, is of God.* By which it is evident, that this article, is the measure and rule, by which to estimate and examine all other articles; and is therefore only fundamental. A fourth is *Matth.* xvi, 16, 18, where after St. Peter had professed this article, saying to our Saviour, *Thou art Christ the Son of the living God*, our Saviour answered, *Thou art Peter, and upon this rock I will build my Church*; from whence I infer, that this article is that, on which all other doctrines of the Church are built, as on their foundation. A fifth is 1 *Cor.* iii, 11, 12, &c. *Other foundation can no man lay, than that which is laid, Jesus is the Christ. Now if any man build upon this foundation, gold, silver, precious stones, wood, hay, stubble; every man's work shall be made manifest; for the day shall declare it, because it shall be revealed by fire, and the fire shall try every man's work of what sort it is. If any man's work abide, which he hath built thereupon, he shall receive a reward. If any man's work shall be burnt, he shall suffer loss; but he himself shall be saved, yet so as by fire.* Which words, being partly plain and easy to understand, and partly allegorical and difficult; out of that which is plain, may be inferred, that pastors that teach this foundation, that *Jesus is the Christ,* though they draw from it false consequences, which all men are sometimes subject to, they may nevertheless be saved; much more that they may be saved, who being no pastors, but hearers, believe that which is by their lawful pastors taught them. Therefore the belief of this article is sufficient; and by consequence, there is no other article of faith necessarily required to salvation.

Now for the part which is allegorical, as *that the fire shall try every man's work,* and that *they shall be saved, but so as by fire,* or *through fire,* (for the original is διὰ πυρὸς,) it maketh nothing against this conclusion which I have drawn from the other words, that are plain. Nevertheless, because upon this place there hath been an argument taken, to prove the fire of purgatory, I will also here offer you my conjecture concerning the meaning of this trial of doctrines, and saving of men as by fire. The apostle here seemeth to allude to the words of the prophet *Zechariah,* (xiii, 8, 9), who speaking of the restoration of the kingdom of God, saith thus; *Two parts therein shall be cut off, and die, but the third shall be left therein; and I will bring the third part through the fire, and will refine them as silver is refined, and will try them as gold is tried; they shall call on the name of the Lord, and I will hear them.* The day of judgment is the day of the restoration of the kingdom of God; and at that day it is, that St. Peter tells us (2 *Peter* iii, 7, 10, 12) shall be the conflagration of the world, wherein the wicked shall perish; but the remnant which God will save, shall pass through that fire unhurt, and be therein, (as silver and gold are refined by the fire from their dross,) tried, and refined from their idolatry, and be made to call upon the name of the true God. Alluding whereto, St. Paul here saith, that *the day,* that is the day of judgment, the great day of our Saviour's coming to restore the kingdom of God in Israel, shall try every man's doctrine, by judging which are gold, silver, precious stones, wood, hay, stubble; and then they that have built false consequences on the true foundation, shall see their doctrines condemned; nevertheless they themselves shall be saved, and pass unhurt through this universal fire, and live eternally, to call upon the name of the true and only God. In which sense there is nothing that accordeth not with the rest of Holy Scripture, or any glimpse of the fire of purgatory.

But a man may here ask, whether it be not as necessary to salvation, to believe, that God is omnipotent; Creator of the world; that Jesus Christ is risen; and that all men else shall rise again from the dead at the last day; as to believe that *Jesus is the Christ*. To which I answer, they are; and so are many more articles: but they are such, as are contained in this one, and may be deduced from it, with more or less difficulty. For who is there that does not see, that they who believe Jesus to be the Son of the God of Israel, and that the Israelites had for God the Omnipotent Creator of all things, do therein also believe, that God is the Omnipotent Creator of all things? Or how can a man believe, that Jesus is the king that shall reign eternally, unless he believe him also risen again from the dead? For a dead man cannot exercise the office of a king. In sum, he that holdeth this foundation, *Jesus is the Christ*, holdeth expressly all that he seeth rightly deduced from it, and implicitly all that is consequent thereunto, though he have not skill enough to discern the consequence. And therefore it holdeth still good, that the belief of this one article is sufficient faith to obtain remission of sins to the *Penitent*, and consequently to bring them into the kingdom of heaven.

Now that I have shown, that all the obedience required to salvation, consisteth in the will to obey the law of God, that is to say, in repentance; and all the faith required to the same is comprehended in the belief of this article, *Jesus is the Christ*; I will further allege those places of the Gospel, that prove, that all that is necessary to salvation is contained in both these joined together. The men to whom St. Peter preached on the day of Pentecost, next after the ascension of our Saviour, asked him, and the rest of the apostles, saying, (*Acts* ii, 37), *Men and brethren, what shall we do?* To whom St. Peter answered (in the next verse) *Repent, and be baptized every one of you, for the remission of sins, and ye shall receive the gift of the Holy Ghost.* Therefore repentance, and baptism, that is, believing that *Jesus is the Christ*, is all that is necessary to salvation. Again, our Saviour being asked by a certain ruler (*Luke* xviii, 18), *What shall I do to inherit eternal life?* answered, (verse 20) *Thou knowest the commandments, do not commit adultery, do not kill, do not steal, do not bear false witness, honour thy father and thy mother.* Which when he said he had observed, our Saviour added, (verse 22) *Sell all thou hast, give it to the poor, and come and follow me*: which was as much as to say, rely on me that am the king. Therefore to fulfil the law, and to believe that Jesus is the king, is all that is required to bring a man to eternal life. Thirdly, St. Paul saith (*Rom*. i, 17), *The just shall live by faith*; not every one, but the *just*; therefore *faith* and *justice* (that is, the *will to be just*, or *repentance*) are all that is necessary to life eternal. And (*Mark* i, 15) our Saviour preached, saying, *The time is fulfilled, and the kingdom of God is at hand, repent and believe the evangile*, that is, the good news that the Christ was come. Therefore, to repent, and to believe that Jesus is the Christ, is all that is required to salvation.

Seeing then it is necessary that faith and obedience, implied in the word repentance, do both concur to our salvation; the question by which of the two we are justified, is impertinently disputed. Nevertheless, it will not be impertinent, to make manifest in what manner each of them contributes thereunto; and in what sense it is said, that we are to be justified by the one, and by the other. And first, if by righteousness be understood the justice of the works themselves, there is no man that can be saved; for there is none that hath not transgressed the law of God. And therefore when we are said to be justified by works, it is to be understood of the will, which God doth always accept for the work itself, as well in good, as in evil men. And in this sense only it is, that a man is called *just*, or *unjust*; and that his justice justifies him, that is, gives him the title, in God's acceptation, of *just*; and renders him capable of *living by his faith*, which before he was not. So that justice justifies in that sense, in which to *justify*, is the same as that to *denominate a man just*; and not in the signification of discharging the law; whereby the punishment of his sins should be unjust.

But a man is then also said to be justified, when his plea, though in itself insufficient, is accepted; as when we plead our will, our endeavour to fulfil the law, and repent us of our failings, and God accepteth it for the performance itself. And because God accepteth not the will for the deed, but only in the faithful; it is therefore faith that makes good our plea; and in this sense it is, that faith only justifies. So that *faith* and *obedience* are both necessary to salvation; yet in several senses each of them is said to justify.

Having thus shown what is necessary to salvation; it is not hard to reconcile our obedience to God, with our obedience to the civil sovereign; who is either Christian, or infidel. If he be a Christian, he alloweth the belief of this article, that *Jesus is the Christ*; and of all the articles that are contained in, or are by evident consequence deduced from it: which is all the faith necessary to salvation. And because he is a sovereign, he requireth obedience to all his own, that is, to all the civil laws; in which also are contained all the laws of nature, that is all the laws of God: for besides the laws of nature, and the laws of the Church, which are part of the civil law, (for the Church that can make laws is the commonwealth), there be no other laws divine. Whosoever therefore obeyeth his Christian sovereign, is not thereby hindered, neither from believing, nor from obeying God. But suppose that a Christian king should from this foundation *Jesus is the Christ*, draw some false consequences, that is to say, make some superstructions of hay or stubble, and command the teaching of the same; yet seeing St. Paul says he shall be saved; much more shall he be saved, that teacheth them by his command; and much more yet, he that teaches not, but only believes his lawful teacher. And in case a subject be forbidden by the civil sovereign to profess some of those his opinions, upon what just ground can he disobey? Christian kings may err in deducing a consequence, but who shall judge? Shall a private man judge, when the question is of his own obedience? Or shall any man judge but he that is appointed thereto by the Church, that is, by the civil sovereign that representeth it? Or if the pope, or an apostle judge, may he not err in deducing of a consequence?

Did not one of the two, St. Peter or St. Paul, err in a super-structure, when St. Paul withstood St. Peter to his face? There can therefore be no contradiction between the laws of God, and the laws of a Christian commonwealth.

And when the civil sovereign is an infidel, every one of his own subjects that resisteth him, sinneth against the laws of God, (for such are the laws of nature), and rejecteth the counsel of the apostles, that admonisheth all Christians to obey their princes, and all children and servants to obey their parents and masters in all things. And for their *faith*, it is internal, and invisible; they have the license that Naaman had, and need not put themselves into danger for it. But if they do, they ought to expect their reward in heaven, and not complain of their lawful sovereign; much less make war upon him. For he that is not glad of any just occasion of martyrdom, has not the faith he professeth, but pretends it only, to set some colour upon his own contumacy. But what infidel king is so unreasonable, as knowing he has a subject, that waiteth for the second coming of Christ, after the present world shall be burnt, and intendeth then to obey him, (which is the intent of believing that Jesus is the Christ,) and in the mean time thinketh himself bound to obey the laws of that infidel king, (which all Christians are obliged in conscience to do), to put to death or to persecute such a subject?

And thus much shall suffice, concerning the kingdom of God, and policy ecclesiastical. Wherein I pretend not to advance any position of my own, but only to show what are the consequences that seem to me deducible from the principles of Christian politics, (which are the holy Scriptures,) in confirmation of the power of civil sovereigns, and the duty of their subjects. And in the allegation of Scripture, I have endeavoured to avoid such texts as are of obscure or controverted interpretation; and to allege none, but in such sense as is most plain, and agreeable to the harmony and scope of the whole Bible; which was written for the re-establishment of the kingdom of God in Christ. For it is not the bare words, but the scope of the writer, that giveth the true light, by which any writing is to be interpreted; and they that insist upon single texts, without considering the main design, can derive nothing from them clearly; but rather by casting atoms of Scripture, as dust before men's eyes, make every thing more obscure than it is; an ordinary artifice of those that seek not the truth, but their own advantage.

I am my soul,
my body is the vessel for my
   soul.
If I am away, my spirit
      remains.
when I am gone, there is
still the remembrance of my
spirit and its carrier.

keep thyself clean and bright,
for I am the window upon from
which I view the world.

BIBLIOGRAPHY

SIR WILLIAM MOLESWORTH brought out his edition of *The English Works of Thomas Hobbes*, in eleven volumes, in 1830, and his edition of the *Opera Latina*, in five volumes, in 1845. The text of *Leviathan* is taken from the third volume of *The English Works*; we have included the whole of the first two Parts and sections of the third, and have entirely omitted the fourth Part. Other works of Hobbes interesting to the social and political theorist are *De Cive*, which Hobbes himself translated into English under the title of *Philosophical Rudiments Concerning Government and Society* (Vol. II of *The English Works*), *Human Nature*, *De Corpore Politico*, *Of Liberty and Necessity* (Vol. III of *The English Works*), *A Dialogue between a Philosopher and a Student of The Common Laws of England*, and *Behemoth*, Hobbes's accounts of events in England between 1640 and 1660 (Vol. VI of *The English Works*).

G. C. Robertson's *Hobbes* (London, 1886); J. Laird's *Hobbes* (London, 1934); J. H. Warrender's *The Political Philosophy of Hobbes* (Oxford, 1957); R. Peter's *Hobbes* (Pelican, 1956), and Michael Oakeshott's *Introduction* to the Blackwell edition of *Leviathan* (1946) are among the best English studies of Hobbes's political thought.

lassitude.
famous
knavery.
confute.
farther / further.
indued.
rating : P68

CHRONOLOGICAL TABLE

1588. April 5th. Hobbes is born.

1602. He goes to Magdalen Hall at Oxford.

1608. He becomes tutor to the younger son of Wm. Cavendish, Earl of Devonshire.

1628. His translation of Thucydides published.

1629. Second visit to the Continent, when he discovers and 'falls in love' with geometry.

1634-7. Third visit to the Continent, where he is converted to 'materialism'. Friendship with Gassendi.

1636. Visit to Galileo.

1640. His first political treatise, the *Elements of Law*, circulates in MS.

1641. Flight to the Continent, where he spends the next ten years.

1642. First edition of *De Cive*.

1646. Hobbes appointed tutor in mathematics to the future Charles II.

1647. Second enlarged edition of *De Cive*.

1650. *The Elements of Law* published in two separated parts under the titles of *Human Nature* and *De Corpore Politico*.

1651. *Leviathan* published. Hobbes returns to England.

1655. *De Corpore* published.

1657. *De Homine* published.

1679. Dec. 4th. Hobbes dies.

1681. *A Dialogue between a Philosopher and a Student of the Common Laws of England* (completed in 1666) published.

1682. *Behemoth* (completed in 1668) published.

CONTENTS OF THE CHAPTERS

The Third Part – Of a Christian Commonwealth

* Part of this chapter is omitted.

N.B. – This edition omits the whole of Part Four of *Leviathan* and a large part of Part Three; it excludes whatever, in the editor's opinion, adds little or nothing to Hobbes's philosophy of man and government.

INDEX

Aaron, 333, 334, 358, 371

Abdera, 107

Abraham: God's covenant with, 260; sovereign right of, 331–2

absolute power, lack of, 285–6

absolute sovereignty, objections to, 296–8

absurdity, 28, 83, 110; causes of, 84–5; like to injury or injustice, 147; privilege of, 84

action, voluntary, 22. *See also* passions

actions, justice of, 160

actor, defined, 169

Acts of Apostles, 225, 329, 339, 340, 345, 346, 348, 350, 355, 362, 365–6, 367–71, 373, 384, 386, 389

Adam: disobedience of, 202; and language, 73–4

addition, reasoning a form of, 16, 81–2

administration, ministers for, 226–7

admiration, 93

affliction, not always due to sin, 312–13

Amazons, 197

ambassadors, 229–30

ambition, 92; cause of, 125

anarchy, 53–4; name for misliked democracy, 186

anger, 91

Antioch, Church of, 366, 368

aphorisms, 84

apostates, and excommunication, 351

apostles: appointed by Christ, 365; appointed by congregation, 365, 367; ecclesiastical power in, 338–40, 346–57, 362; sermons of, 384

apparitions, unnatural, 66–7

appetite or desire, 22–5, 88–9

arbitration, sixteenth law of nature, 165

architecture, 113

aristocracy; compared with monarchy, 188; defined, 186, 191, 192; right of succession, 193

Aristotle, 9, 62, 140, 163, 208

arithmetic, 113

arms, coats of, 120–1

army, choice of commanders, 308–9

arrogance, tenth law of nature against, 164

assembly, 217

astrology, 113

astronomy, 113

authors: defined, 169; inanimate things not, 170; two sorts, 172

aversions, 22, 23, 88–9

Baal, 139

Babel, Tower of, 74

Bacon, Francis, 3

baptism, 370–1; apostles and, 347

Barnabas, St., 365–6, 368

beasts, covenant impossible with, 152

Becket, Thomas, 286

beginnings, curiosity as to, 129

belief, 99–100

Bellarmine, Cardinal, 341

benevolence, 92

Bentham, Jeremy, 14, 15, 43

bishops, 366–7; of Rome, 369

blushing, 94

Bodin, Jean, 7, 47

bribery, 275

Brutus, Marcus, 66

Burke, Edmund, 7, 9, 14

cabals, unlawful, 223

Cadmus, 73

capital punishment, 280

casual things, taken for prognostics, 132

causes, desire to know, 129

causes, second, ignorance of, 131

charity, 92; mutual, 301; public, 304

399

Fontana Philosophy Classics

This series of texts and anthologies, with substantial introductions, was originated by G. J. Warnock and is being continued under the editorship of A. M. Quinton.

Leviathan
Thomas Hobbes   *Edited by* John Plamenatz

An Essay Concerning Human Understanding
John Locke   *Edited by* A. D. Woozley

The Principles of Human Knowledge and
Three Dialogues Between Hylas and Philonous
George Berkeley   *Edited by* G. J. Warnock

A Treatise of Human Nature
David Hume **Book I**   *Edited by* D. G. C. Macnabb

In preparation: **Books II and III**   *Edited by* P. S. Árdal

Hume on Religion
Edited by Richard Wollheim

Utilitarianism
Edited by Mary Warnock

Fontana Philosophy Classics

George Berkeley
The Principles of Human Knowledge
Three Dialogues Between Hylas and Philonous

Edited with an introduction by Geoffrey Warnock

The writings of George Berkeley (1685-1753) offer, in a style of admirable clarity and concision, a striking variety of philosophical accomplishments. He formulated for the first time the classical critique of the so-called Representational Theory of sense-perception: he made a robust defence of 'common sense' against its sceptical critics; and at the same time he worked out his own strange and fascinating 'immaterialist' doctrine, motivated largely by the desire to defend a theistic world-view against what he took to be the dangerous and unfounded pretensions of the physical sciences. In the history of philosophy he is a figure of permanent importance and inexhaustible interest.

Fontana Philosophy Classics

John Stuart Mill
Utilitarianism
On Liberty
Essay on Bentham

Edited with an introduction by Mary Warnock

Utilitarianism was not only a major school of philosophical thought, but a powerful reforming influence on government and legislation in the nineteenth century and after. The father of the school, Jeremy Bentham, was a most effective exponent of Utilitarian ideas particularly in the fields of politics and law; but his disciple John Stuart Mill gave, partly by way of criticism of Bentham, the most subtle and comprehensive statement of Utilitarian thought, which, particularly in moral philosophy, is still vigorously alive. Mill's position as set out in *Utilitarianism*, though often violently attacked, has never been refuted.